A Supreme Court Unlike Any Other

A Supreme Court Unlike Any Other

The Deepening Divide Between the Justices and the People

KEVIN J. MCMAHON

The University of Chicago Press
Chicago and London

The University of Chicago Press, Chicago 60637
The University of Chicago Press, Ltd., London
© 2024 by The University of Chicago
Published 2024
Printed in the United States of America

33 32 31 30 29 28 27 26 25 24   1 2 3 4 5

ISBN-13: 978-0-226-83106-0 (cloth)
ISBN-13: 978-0-226-83108-4 (paper)
ISBN-13: 978-0-226-83107-7 (e-book)
DOI: https://doi.org/10.7208/chicago/9780226831077.001.0001

Library of Congress Cataloging-in-Publication Data

Names: McMahon, Kevin J., author.
Title: A Supreme Court unlike any other : the deepening divide between the justices
    and the people / Kevin J. McMahon.
Description: Chicago ; London : The University of Chicago Press, 2024. |
    Includes bibliographical references and index.
Identifiers: LCCN 2023027042 | ISBN 9780226831060 (cloth) |
    ISBN 9780226831084 (paperback) | ISBN 9780226831077 (ebook)
Subjects: LCSH: United States. Supreme Court. | Judges—Selection and appointment—
    United States. | Judges—Selection and appointment—Political aspects—United
    States. | United States—Politics and government—21st century. | United States—
    Politics and government—20th century.
Classification: LCC KF8742 .M363 2024 | DDC347.73/2634—dc23/eng/20230616
LC record available at https://lccn.loc.gov/2023027042

♾ This paper meets the requirements of ANSI/NISO Z39.48-1992 (Permanence of Paper).

For Pamela

Contents

Figures and Tables

Figures

Tables

Democracy in Court? Presidents and Justices

If I had ever thought of writing a three-volume series when I first began my work on the presidency and the Supreme Court, I had forgotten about it long ago. But then a string of events described below convinced me to write this book. It is the third volume in my work on this subject. The titles of the first two are *Reconsidering Roosevelt on Race: How the Presidency Paved the Road to Brown* (University of Chicago Press, 2004) and *Nixon's Court: His Challenge to Judicial Liberalism and Its Political Consequences* (University of Chicago Press, 2011).

Together, the three books explore and analyze nearly a century of presidential efforts to shape the High Court. In doing so, they consider the political and doctrinal consequences of presidential policies toward the judiciary, and (in this volume) how the political construction of the Court affects its democratic legitimacy. Together, I title the three books *Democracy in Court? Presidents and Justices*—an early title I chose for my dissertation and then abandoned at some point in that long process. It is a title designed to tell—to signal my exploration of how democratically elected politicians, particularly presidents, attempt (often successfully) to move the Supreme Court in a desired ideological direction while simultaneously advancing their electoral interests and managing their governing coalition.

In each of the books, I have attempted to add to the story, and to highlight aspects of the presidential-judicial relationship that had previously been ignored or underexamined in the scholarship. Although this book began in roughly the same place, with a consideration of the political construction of the Rehnquist and Roberts Courts, it is quite a bit different from the first two. Unlike my earlier work, in which I argued that both Franklin D. Roosevelt and Richard Nixon had an unmistakable imprint on the Court, I began this work at a historic moment in which presidential effectiveness appeared more limited. Indeed, most commentators had concluded that the Republican presidents Ronald Reagan, George H. W. Bush, George W. Bush, and Donald J. Trump hadn't yet delivered the doctrinal product they promised. The path to the construction of deeply conservative constitutional doctrine was instead pockmarked with failure. I wanted to understand why. Doing so required me to consider the Court's construction during increasingly polarized times. And in undertaking that exploration, I became far more intrigued about the current Court's democratic legitimacy given the unsteady political foundation supporting it.

While I never expected to write a three-volume series, I kept getting invited (as often happens in academia) to participate in conferences and contribute chapters or articles on the subject I had researched and written most about: the presidency and the Supreme Court. One of those invitations came from Christopher Schmidt at Chicago Kent Law School. The symposium to which he invited me, titled "The Supreme Court and American Politics," fit perfectly with my interests, so I agreed to write a piece for it. I figured it would be a one-off. I would develop an idea I had in that article and then return to a larger, much different (and still unfinished) project. But then events refocused my attention back to that symposium piece. The law review issue happened to be released just after Justice Anthony Kennedy retired from the bench and President Donald Trump nominated Brett Kavanaugh as his replacement. Some of the arguments in the piece received widespread attention and were picked up by several columnists. In the course of being interviewed by various news outlets about that work, I began thinking about expanding on the ideas there. A few weeks later, I had a conversation with my mentor, Shep Melnick. At some point, we began speaking about my law review article, and he said something like: "Maybe you should use that idea as the basis of the third book in your trilogy." That word—"trilogy"—struck me and stayed with me. And soon thereafter, it all came together.

Reconsidering Roosevelt on Race had essentially ended with the Court's decision on *Brown* in 1954. *Nixon's Court* picked up the story soon after that, with Richard Nixon's efforts to take advantage of the electoral unmooring after that decision—what would become his "southern strategy." But that book essentially ended in the 1970s. There more was to tell. And this book seeks to tell it. As I mentioned above, I have tried to fill in different pieces of the puzzle in each work, and to tackle questions for which scholars had yet to provide fully developed answers. This book focuses far more on the selection process than did the first two, and far less on the work of presidential administrations—most significantly the Justice Department—in shaping the contours of constitutional law. Somewhat ironically, while focusing on the present, it covers a much larger swath of history to outline the three historical shifts I spotlight. This book also builds on the first two, leaning on them to help reveal the historically unprecedented nature of constitutional politics today. At the same time, each book stands alone. While they fit together chronologically, they can be read independently of each other.

I began writing this book in earnest in the fall of 2018, but I draw on work published several years before that time. With a project that takes so long to complete, there are many individuals to thank. Paul Collins, Tom Keck, and Michael Paris were willing to workshop a large portion of the manuscript in the middle of the pandemic. What had been planned as a day-long event on Trinity College's beautiful campus became a long conversation over Zoom. Their comments led me to make essential revisions and provided significant guidance as I worked toward completing the manuscript. Others offered a kind ear as I recounted the arguments I make in these pages, read individual chapters of the manuscript (often as conference papers), or provided support for the project in some other way. Those individuals include Vanessa Baird, Don Beachler, Sonia Cardenas, Stefanie Chambers, Jeff Dudas, Mary Dudas, Sean Fitzpatrick, Renny Fulco, Howard Gillman, Mark Graber, Lisa Holmes, Ken Kersch, Chris Kirkey, Steven Lichtman, Jennifer Lucas, Lida Maxwell, Shep Melnick, Garrison Nelson, Julie Novkov, Patrick O'Brien, Gerry Rosenberg, Todd Ryan, Bruce Sandys, Steve Skowronek, Anna Terwiel, Mary Beth White, Keith Whittington, Abby Fisher Williamson, David Yalof, Mauri Ziff, and Josh Zoffer. Pamela Hagg read the entire manuscript and provided extraordinary direction as I sought to tighten my arguments and refine my writing so that the book might appeal to a broader audience. I thank Evan Young for his work copyediting the manuscript and Derek Gottlieb for producing the index.

I have the privilege of being in a department of teacher-scholars, and several of my colleagues read some of my work or listened to my arguments. Their names appear in the list above. All of my colleagues provided excellent examples of how to shine in the classroom and with their scholarship. Lea Bain, Maxwell Christian, Garrett Kirk, Sean McAloon, and Bryce Schuler, five Trinity students, collected data on state legislative elections for me that support part of my analysis in chapter 13. Trinity's Dave Tatem provided his expertise in helping me create the Demers cartograms in that same chapter.

When COVID-19 arrived on our doorsteps and everyone was shuttered inside their homes, I had the great benefit of frequent get-togethers with four friends—Matt Asensio, Kevin Hughes, Robbie Low, and Will Scurr. For well over a year, no matter the temperature or the amount of precipitation, we would gather near a fire to share stories and experiences as well as our hopes for the time when COVID-19 wasn't part of the conversation. I thank them for their friendship during that time of isolation and Zoom meetings.

My editor for the first two books in this series was John Tryneski, who was invaluable to the publication of those works. John retired from the University of Chicago Press in 2016, and soon thereafter I began having conversations with the new political science and law editor at Chicago, Chuck Meyers, about this book. Chuck helped guide the project in its infancy. But before I was able to finish it, he retired from that position. I must admit I was a bit concerned when Chuck relayed his retirement news to me. I would need to convince another editor of the value of this project—a project that had already taken too long to complete. But Sara Doskow put all my worries to rest. She has been a wonderful editor, pushing me to clarify my arguments and sharpen my analysis. Without her direction and support, this would be a much lesser book.

Acknowledgments typically end with words about those closest to the author, and I continue that tradition here. Until his death in 2021, my dad was always there, ready to share a story and a smile. Until her death in 2023, my mom was there to record it all, displaying the power of an extraordinary memory. My siblings Tom and Mary and my extended family have provided me great encouragement with my book projects over the years. My son Brooks was a just young boy when I dedicated *Nixon's Court* to him. Today, he is a fine young man who would make any father extremely proud. My wife, Pamela, has been with me every step of the way. Each day I am *overwhelmed* by her—by her compassion, creativity, and dedication to excel in anything she tries. This book is for her.

1

The Supreme Court's Democracy Gap
and the Erosion of Legitimacy

The whole theory of democracy, my dear fellow, is that the majority rules, that is the whole theory of it.

ASSOCIATE JUSTICE ANTONIN SCALIA
Rome, Italy, June 13, 1996[1]

Click. That's all it took. When the US Supreme Court announced its decision in the most anticipated case of the twenty-first century, none of the justices read portions of their opinions from the bench, as they had in years past. There were no declaratory statements from the author of the Court's majority opinion; no angry words spoken in dissent. With pandemic protocols still in place, there was just a click, to post the decision online. And in a flash, a constitutional right that had been in the law books for nearly fifty years—the right of women to end an unwanted pregnancy—was gone. Even though a draft of the opinion had leaked weeks earlier, many were still surprised, and outraged. Others rejoiced—victory had finally come for them after many years of effort. *Roe v. Wade*, a decision detested in conservative circles, was no longer the law.[2]

But more Americans were left wondering if the Court truly represented their interests, given that a clear majority had hoped the justices would uphold *Roe*, not decimate it.[3] Many believed the Court had become too politicized, with the justices behaving as mere politicians clad in robes.[4] Working behind the cloak of the Court's red velvet drapes in its white marble palace atop Capitol Hill, these supposed wizards of the law, detractors alleged, were simply fulfilling the wishes of the presidents who had appointed them and the senators who had confirmed them. Finally, some questioned how five individuals, unknown to most, unelected and with lifetime tenure, could make such a disruptive, law-altering and life-altering decision in a nation that celebrates its commitment to democracy—that pledges to abide by the principles that the people decide and the majority rules.

This is a book about what I call the Supreme Court's "democracy gap"—the distance between the Court and the electoral processes that endow it with democratic legitimacy. It is about how we ended up with the Court we currently have, so distinct from those of the past; it is about three major shifts that have transformed the Court over time; and finally, it is about what can be done to narrow this democracy gap. It is not a critique of the current Court's conservatism. It is a critique of the construction of a Court that happens to be conservative, one that has used its institutional authority to aggressively advance its ideological agenda. A liberal Court built in the same fashion that acted in the same fashion would be equally inconsistent with the nation's democratic traditions. And its legitimacy would be similarly uncertain.

More than sixty years ago, two political scientists, one a democratic theorist and the other a Supreme Court scholar, wrote separately about the Court's place in American democracy. At the time, others were ringing alarm bells about the power of unelected justices who serve for life, but Robert Dahl and Robert McCloskey argued that over the course of the nation's history there was usually little distance between the Court and the democratically elected governing regime. For McCloskey, this narrow divide meant that the Court had rarely "lagged far behind nor forged far ahead of America."[5] So, he concluded, the perception of the Court as an anti-majoritarian institution, in conflict with the nation's democratic principles, was largely inaccurate.

But a lot has changed in six decades. And I argue that those changes have widened and deepened the Court's democracy gap, eroding its legitimacy.[6] This is largely the result of two historical shifts. A third shift has worked to counter these developments, but not to a degree sufficient to prevent the construction of a historically distinct Supreme Court, unlike any other in American history.

The first shift (part I) concerns the politics of choosing and confirming justices. In the past, presidents who had the opportunity to shape Supreme Courts for a generation led dominant political regimes that were supported by grand electoral coalitions. Consider Franklin D. Roosevelt's Democratic Party. Together, FDR and Harry Truman won five straight presidential elections—only Thomas Jefferson's Democratic-Republican Party and Abraham Lincoln's Republican Party won more. Less than a year before making his first appointment to the Court in the summer of 1937, Roosevelt won all but two of the nation's forty-eight states and more than 60 percent of the vote.

But with today's fractured politics, these dominant regimes are absent. Presidents who once won in landslides have been replaced by ones who win narrowly or who aren't the choice of the majority of voters. And in contrast to the late 1950s, when Dahl and McCloskey reached their conclusions about the affinity between the Court's decisions and the will of the political majority, the popular vote and Electoral College results are often not aligned. The Democratic Party's nominee has won the popular vote in seven of the past eight presidential elections, but Republican presidents have appointed six of the nine sitting justices.

Not only are dominant political regimes and electoral routs no longer the norm; the Senate's role in approving justices is increasingly hollow and little more than theatrical. In earlier times of political polarization, this was not the case. Instead, the Senate played a powerful role in determining who sat on the Court. For example, despite a string of usually overwhelming victories at the polls, more often than not the Republican presidents of the late 1960s through the early 1990s had to compromise when filling a Court vacancy to secure confirmation in a Senate controlled by Democrats. Today, however, the Senate is a bit player, the overseer of a confirmation sideshow.[7] With the filibuster gone, dissent is dismissed by the majority if a president of the same party selects a nominee considered ideological kin. Consequently, the current conservative majority has been largely constructed during a period of *weak* Republican performance in presidential elections. The Court's five most conservative members—the five who joined the *Dobbs* decision—are "numerical minority justices." This is my term for justices who won confirmation with a Senate majority, but with the support of senators who represented a numerical minority of voters. A Court comprising numerical minority justices is both new historically and troubling for democratic legitimacy. And this development is at the very heart of progressive concerns about the Court today. Liberals fear that this conservative majority will continue to defy the majoritarian traditions of the Court highlighted by Dahl and McCloskey, and constitutionally decapitate decades-old rulings still supported by a majority of Americans, as it did in upsetting *Roe* in *Dobbs*.

The second shift (part II) that has widened the democracy gap concerns who is being selected for the Court, and why. The makeup of the current Court diverges in distinctive and noteworthy ways from those of the past. Today, the justices emerge from a "supreme elite," representing a small sliver—more like a tiny speck—of America that is closed off to the vast majority. Presidents, particularly those on the Right, must choose from this spectacularly shallow pool of candidates deemed eligible by groups like the Federalist Society. Presidents intent on choosing from outside this supreme elite have been strongly cautioned against or successfully prevented from doing so. This change happened in large part because of great efforts by movement conservatives to redefine "quality" and prevent the "ideological drift" of a Republican-appointed justice to the left. Democratic presidents have had far fewer opportunities to fill vacancies in the last half century. Nevertheless, they have pursued a similar course, choosing from a liberal supreme elite, albeit with a keener focus on confirmation success and ethnic, gender, and racial diversity.

In the past, elected presidents played a more central role in the selection of nominees, often choosing individuals who had risen to prominence as members of their administration or as key allies in Congress. They also chose candidates with notably more eclectic and heterogeneous backgrounds and educational resumes; indeed, many justices who distinguished themselves on past Courts—who became legends of the law—would likely never make it through the confirmation process, or even be nominated, in the current checklist-driven age of a cookie-cutter Court. Appointing presidents often knew these nominees well and expected them to advance the governing regime's principles once on the Court. Today, presidents maintain distance. They often meet the nominees they appoint to a lifetime position just briefly before doing so. And unlike justices of the past, these nominees have usually spent far more time in the federal judiciary than in the elected branches of government. They are conditioned in the judiciary—imbued with the values celebrated by the federal courts and insulated from the vagaries and endearing values of democracy. Finally, unlike those of the past, justices of today have never sought elective office. They haven't needed to. They attained power through the appointment process, based on perceptions of their ideological commitments, a new definition of "quality," and as a result of their Washington connections, often initially forged in the halls of the Harvard or Yale law schools and then fortified during a clerkship at the Court.

The third and final shift (part III) relevant to the Court and democratic legitimacy concerns the greater attention the Court has received in recent campaigns, particularly at the senatorial and presidential levels. This has a lot to do with how choosers and confirmers win elective office today. In contrast to past elections, where the Court usually attracted little notice, in recent campaign seasons it has been a centerpiece of America's democratic politics,[8] helping to raise the politicization of the Court to unprecedented levels. It has become commonplace for presidential and senatorial candidates to all but assure voters that if elected they will deliver a Court to their ideological liking, or assist in doing so. Perhaps they have promised an unattainable ideal, but they still rally voters to the polls in pursuit of that ideal. While I consider the possibility that the Court's increasing isolation from democratic forces (as detailed in parts I and II) eliminates any electorally earned legitimacy, I conclude the opposite: namely, that by putting the Court issue before the voters, these ultimate choosers and confirmers enhance the democratic legitimacy of ideologically allied justices and their doctrinal commitments. The only questions are by how much, and whether Court-themed electoral success sufficiently offsets the countervailing forces that have widened the democracy gap.

The expectation at this writing in late 2023 is that an enduring conservative Court majority will advance its agenda in the face of liberal resistance and frustration, and I end this book with a section on what's next for constitutional politics. I begin by showing just how limited the options are for progressives to institute democratically inspired change under existing law. First, the reality is that presidents and senates of the next decade will have few—if any—opportunities to alter the composition of the Court because the justices are serving for much longer than they once did. Indeed, Clarence Thomas, who turned seventy-five a few months before the 2023 term and is the Court's oldest member, once declared his intention to obliterate the record of the longest-serving justice, held by William O. Douglas at thirty-six years, seven months, one week, and one day. Said Thomas: "The liberals made my life miserable for 43 years, and I'm going to make their lives miserable for 43 years."[9] Taking Justice Thomas's words at face value and assuming no justice dies or retires before the end of those forty-three years, we will not see another Court vacancy until 2034. Of course, that may not happen. Words spoken many years ago are not written in stone, and death can come suddenly. But if this scenario holds, then that would mean if someone new captures the White House in 2024 and serves two full terms, that president will not have an opportunity to alter the high bench organically—something that has never occurred in the nation's history.[10] In fact, only one elected president who served a full four-year term did not have a chance to name a justice to the high bench.[11] If they have few opportunities to alter the Court's makeup, progressives would have just as much difficulty trying to cast aside the Court's decisions through the constitutional amendment process, one that especially stifles any change *they* might propose, for reasons I outline in chapter 13.

In the book's final chapter, I analyze two prominent reform proposals for reducing the Court's democracy gap and potentially enhancing its legitimacy. The first would expand the size of the Court to counter today's conservative imbalance with more progressive justices. The second would reduce the length of time justices may sit on the high bench and provide each president who serves a full term two vacancies to fill, thereby transforming a replacement system defined by the randomness of death and the strategic timing of retirements into one governed by routine turnover instead. Finally, I consider a third option: doing nothing to the Court itself and waiting to see if the conservative doctrinal path the six Republican-appointed justices have begun to trailblaze produces a progressive backlash that will both tame the Court and reshape America's electoral politics.

This book explores the political construction of the Court in an increasingly polarized age. Focusing less on the justices' doctrinal product than many other works, I argue that the Court today is more distant from American democracy than the one Dahl and McCloskey observed sixty years ago. What this will mean for the Court is uncertain. Even greater isolation from the democratically elected branches of government is one clear possibility; the continuing loss of democratic legitimacy is certainly another; and a Court that "stray[s further] from the mainstreams of American life" is a third.[12] The combination of the three may produce a constitutional crisis unseen in our nation's history, further broadening the chasm between the Court and the country, challenging the historical reverence Americans have held for the highest tribunal in the land, and perhaps unleashing a revolt against the authority of the justices. In short, we may very well be encountering uncharted constitutional territory with consequences for the whole of American politics.

PART I

Constructing a Historically Distinct Court:
How the Conservative Quest for Judicial Success
Isolated the Justices from Majoritarian Democracy

Numerical Minority Justices as a
Conservative Majority

On April 7, 2017, something extraordinary took place on the floor of the United States Senate—something that had never happened before. Neil Gorsuch was confirmed to be the next justice on the nation's highest tribunal. That in itself was not unusual. Typically, every handful of years the Senate votes on a nominee for the Court. But this confirmation was different. Gorsuch had been appointed by a president who had failed to win the popular vote, and he was confirmed with the support of a majority of senators who had won fewer—indeed far fewer—votes in their most recent election than their colleagues in opposition. Never before had a "minority president"—elected by a numerical minority of voters—named a "numerical minority justice" to the Court.[1] Eighteen months later it happened again, when the Senate confirmed Brett Kavanaugh as the second Donald Trump–appointed justice. Two years after that, it occurred a third time with the confirmation of Amy Coney Barrett. There are now a majority of Supreme Court justices—Clarence Thomas, Samuel Alito, Gorsuch, Kavanaugh, and Barrett—who fit the description of a numerical minority justice. And they are the five most conservative justices on the high bench.[2]

As I noted in chapter 1, "numerical minority justice" is my term for a nominee who won confirmation with a Senate majority, but with the support of senators who represented a numerical minority of voters. Gorsuch, for example, was supported by a majority of senators—fifty-one Republicans and three Democrats. But the number of votes won by those fifty-four senators in their most recent election totaled 54,556,602. The forty-five senators who opposed Gorsuch, all Democrats, earned 76,506,169 votes in their most recent election—a nearly 22-million-vote difference.[3] In percentage terms, that's 58 to 42 (table 2.1).[4]

TABLE 2.1. The Five Numerical Minority Justices

President	President's Popular Vote	Nominee	Year of Nomination	Senate Vote	Popular Vote of Senators Supporting	Popular Vote of Senators Opposing	Percentage Difference
George H. W. Bush	53.37%	Clarence Thomas	1991	52–48	41,372,437 47.27%	46,149,882 52.73%	–5.46%
George W. Bush	50.73%	Samuel Alito	2005	58–42	59,183,521 49.22%	61,064,342 50.78%	–1.56%
Donald Trump	45.93%	Neil Gorsuch	2017	54–45	54,557,602 41.63%	76,506,169 58.37%	–16.75%
Donald Trump	45.93%	Brett Kavanaugh	2018	50–48	54,102,052 40.76%	78,623,957 59.24%	–18.48%
Donald Trump	45.93%	Amy Coney Barrett	2020	52–48	58,164,408 45.69%	69,130,873 54.31%	–8.61%

The confirmation vote for Brett Kavanaugh was even more stark. The fifty senators supporting his nomination—all but one of them Republican—garnered 54,102,052 votes in their most recent election, while the forty-eight senators opposing him—all Democrats—won 78,623,597 votes: a more than 24.5-million-vote difference, 59 to 41 percent.

The Amy Coney Barrett vote was much closer by comparison, but still striking. The fifty-two senators supporting her collected 58,164,408 votes in their most recent election; the forty-eight opposing her won 69,130,873—an 8.5 percent difference.

Clarence Thomas was the first justice confirmed by a group of senators who had garnered fewer votes in their most recent election than those who opposed him. Nominated in 1991 by President George Bush,[5] Thomas initially provoked controversy because he was perceived as a strident conservative and because he was selected to replace the Court's most liberal member, the legendary Thurgood Marshall. Controversy over his nomination grew when Anita Hill, one of his former aides, accused him of sexual harassment in the workplace, and those allegations shifted some votes to the opposition.[6] While Thomas meets the definition of a numerical minority justice, his nomination was a bit different from the three Trump justices: namely, he was appointed by a president who, unlike Trump, had won the White House with a decisive victory.[7]

The second numerical minority justice was Samuel Alito, nominated by President George W. Bush in late 2005. Bush had initially captured the presidency with fewer popular votes than his Democratic opponent, but there were no vacancies in his first term and so he did not make an appointment to the Court as a minority president. After narrowly winning reelection—this time capturing the popular vote as well—he named Alito to replace Justice Sandra Day O'Connor.[8] Like Thomas, then, Alito was not appointed by a minority president.

None of the Court's other members are numerical minority justices. The only other Republican-appointed justice, John Roberts, won Senate confirmation by a fairly comfortable margin (78–22). Today he is the most ideologically moderate of the Republican-appointed justices. The Senate confirmed Democratic President Barack Obama's two selections, Sonia Sotomayor and Elena Kagan, by relatively slim margins: sixty-eight to thirty-one and sixty-three to thirty-seven, respectively. But neither of them comes close to fitting the description of a numerical minority justice. The most recent Democrat-appointed justice, Ketanji Brown Jackson, was confirmed in a much closer vote, fifty-three to forty-seven. But the difference in the popular vote between the supporting and opposing senators was still significant. Those supporting her—fifty Democrats and three Republicans—captured nearly 85 million votes in their most recent elections, while those opposing her—all Republicans—received just 62.5 million. That's a difference of nearly twenty-two-and-a-half million votes, or 15.2 percent.

Notably, the term "numerical minority justice" is not based on a normative critique of the conservativism of these five justices. Rather, it is purely descriptive. It simply describes the discrepancy between the number of votes collected by those senators supporting the confirmation of these justices and the number collected by those senators opposing them. As I suggested in chapter 1, ideologically liberal justices confirmed under the same terms would raise similar questions about the Court majority's democratic legitimacy. Additionally, as I discuss in part III, I do not argue that these justices are devoid of any democratic legitimacy. The question is how much their status as numerical minority justices reduces that legitimacy.

Significantly, by historical standards, these five justices are quite young. The oldest, Clarence Thomas, turned seventy-five a few months before the beginning of the Court's 2023 term. He is ten years younger than Stephen Breyer, who retired in 2022 just short of his eighty-fourth birthday. And Thomas has pledged on at least one occasion to serve until 2034.[9]

So, if this core group of five stays together as long as expected and decides cases as ideologically conservatively as expected, they will distinctly and clearly shift the Court to the right over the next decade or so. A Court majority has the institutional ability and constitutional authority to do just that. A glimpse at the agenda of Justice Thomas, the Court's most conservative member ever since his arrival, provides some perspective on what that might mean. And for progressives, it's a devastating prospect. Of course, the five numerical minority justices have already voted to topple *Roe* and decimate affirmative action, something Thomas desired from his earliest days on the Court.[10] From there, these justices could continue to act as a formidable bloc, voting together to augment religious rights, limit access to the ballot box, enhance gun rights, curtail congressional power, broaden presidential power, and undercut the administrative state. In his concurring opinion in *Dobbs*, Thomas suggested other possibilities as well, urging his fellow justices to "reconsider all of this Court's substantive due process precedents, including *Griswold* [right to privacy/contraception], *Lawrence* [sexual intimacy between consenting same-sex adults], and *Obergefell* [marriage equality]."[11]

The United States may now be facing these kinds of precedent-shattering rulings coming from a majority of justices who fit the definition of a numerical minority justice—and who are in fact the only five numerical minority justices in the history of the Supreme Court. Further still, three of these five justices were appointed by a minority president. Arguably, these facts undermine the democratic legitimacy of the Supreme Court. And if the Court does tread the conservative path outlined above, it threatens to ignite a constitutional conflagration unlike any other in American history, particularly if progressives control the other two branches of government.

*

We have ended up with numerical minority justices for a variety of reasons, one of which is structural and written into the Constitution itself: the command that every state have two senators. When this compromise between small and large states was crafted in 1787, the least populated states did not have as much proportional power as they do today. So, the two-senators-per-state rule was not as disproportionate as it is today. At the nation's founding the most populous state, Virginia, was approximately twelve times larger than the least populous state, Delaware. Today, California's population is nearly *seventy* times larger than Wyoming's. And that gap is expected to widen year after year for the foreseeable future. In any case, population difference mattered less in 1787 because state legislatures—not the voters—were entrusted with the authority to select senators to serve in the nation's capital. In other words, the framers did not design the Senate to be a democratic institution in the way we think of it today. That changed with the 1913 ratification of the 17th amendment, which instituted the popular election of senators.[12] But in at least one way—population per senator—the Senate was more representative in 1787 than it is today.

With two senators per state it's not surprising that close votes produce "numerical minority" results: if the margin in a Senate vote is slim, we should expect skewed results with regard to the number of votes a narrow majority of senators received in their most recent elections compared to those in opposition because it is simply not possible for a senator from a state with the population of Wyoming to come close to winning the same number of votes as a senator from a densely populated state like California.

Likewise, many pieces of legislation approved by a narrow margin in the Senate have undoubtedly been supported by a majority of senators who won fewer votes in their most recent election than did those in opposition. But legislation is different from judicial nominations. Legislation also requires approval from the population-apportioned House of Representatives. And if the vote is close, the president's signature (or acquiescence) is required.

Rather than legislation, presidential appointments to the executive branch are perhaps a better comparison to Supreme Court nominations. In those confirmation votes the Senate acts without the aid of the House. And again, these nominees may secure confirmation with a majority of senators who won fewer votes than those in the opposition. But there is an obvious difference here too. Executive branch appointees serve at the pleasure of the president and rarely stay for extended periods of time. For example, over the course of American history, James Wilson holds the record as the longest-serving member of the cabinet. He was secretary of agriculture for sixteen years (1897–1913), under four consecutive presidents. Judicial appointments last a lifetime or until the judge or justice decides to retire. And judges and justices tend to stay on the bench for many years, even decades. For example, in the case of the Supreme Court, the twelve justices appointed during the divided government era—the period between 1968 and 2000 when one party (usually Republicans) held the White House and the other (usually Democrats) controlled Congress—averaged more than twenty-six years, and one (Clarence Thomas) is still serving. The shortest tenure of that dozen was just over seventeen years. The longest was nearly thirty-five years, well more than double Mr. Wilson's time as the head of the Department of Agriculture. Seven presidents occupied the Oval Office during that justice's time on the high bench. Two justices who retired in the 1990s after a similarly lengthy stint on the Court served during eight presidencies. The record, dating back to the nineteenth century, is ten. Moreover, justices are deciding to stay longer than they have in the past. In fact, Donald Trump seemed to celebrate this possibility when he announced the appointment of Neil Gorsuch, suggesting his nominee might serve on the Court for a half century.

Rules always change outcomes, whether in politics or in sports. Democrats argue that the disproportionate power of smaller states in the Senate (and the Electoral College) has unfairly affected their ability to shape the Court's membership and resulted in the prevalence of numerical minority justices. Republicans respond by pointing out that Democrats understood the rules of the nation's electoral system, and in recent years chose to run on a message that attracted a great share of votes in the more populous states but far fewer in the sparsely populated ones. It's unlikely that Democrats were complaining about this system in the mid-1930s when they held seventy-six of ninety-six Senate seats—or, for that matter, during the era of divided government when they effectively limited the ability of Republican presidents to move the Court to the right. So, they shouldn't blame the presence of five numerical minority justices on a system that has been in place for well over a century, since the ratification of the 17th amendment.[13]

Democrats might respond by arguing that the system is inconsistent with the principle of "one person, one vote," which has only been the law of the land since 1964.[14] And it is unclear why votes in one state should be worth more than those in another. The system is the result of a compromise at the constitutional convention, a necessity at the time to secure a nation's bond but one inconsistent with today's understanding of democracy. Democrats might also highlight that the rules have changed to make a numerical minority justice more likely. Before 2017, it essentially took the support of sixty senators to prevent a filibuster and confirm a nominee for the Court. After Republicans altered the rules with the Gorsuch vote, it now takes just a simple majority.

Regardless of which political "side" we are on, it is clear that political polarization has combined with the Senate's equal representation system to produce a politics of choosing and confirming justices that is historically unique and that has now produced a Court unlike any other—one that has the only five numerical minority justices in the nation's history. For their part, progressives are right to wonder, given the political ideology of the senators who voted to confirm these numerical minority justices, if the system today doesn't subvert the idea that the Court "follows the election returns" in line with the principles of majoritarian democracy.

✶

Let's use the Senate's vote on Neil Gorsuch to take a closer look at the profiles of the states represented by senators supporting and opposing him and to highlight the political base backing his nomination. States fall into three categories: (1) those represented by senators who both supported Gorsuch, (2) those represented by senators whose votes on confirmation differed, and (3) those represented by senators who both opposed him.

The red and blue states are markedly different (table 2.2). The red states had the highest percentages of 2016 Trump voters, native-born Americans, and evangelical Protestants. The blue states had the lowest percentages in those categories. The purple states were in the middle. In three other areas, the blue states were the most urban, educated, and supportive of abortion rights. The red states had the lowest percentages in those three categories. Once again, the purple states were in the middle.

The only category that is inconsistent with these clear divisions is the percentage of white residents—that's because many of the more conservative, rural, and Trump-supporting states are in the South and have high African American populations. While the blue states are still the least white, the red states are in the middle of this category. The purple states are the whitest. Nevertheless, these percentages belie the reality in the Senate. African Americans typically vote in overwhelming numbers for the Democratic nominee in Senate contests in the South. But those candidates rarely win. For example, at the time of the Gorsuch vote, there were just three Democratic senators from

TABLE 2.2. Differentiating the States

Categories	23 Red States	9 Purple States	18 Blue States
% Trump Vote	**57**	49	39
% Native-Born	**94**	92	87
% Evangelical Protestants	**33**	24	18
% White	78	**83**	73
% Urban	67	74	**81**
% Bachelor's Degree or More	26	29	**34**
% Supporting Legal Abortion	45	55	**61**
% of Nation's Population	35.7	21.0	**43.1**

Highest percentage for each category is in **bold**.

the eleven traditional southern states.[15] Thus, with nineteen of the twenty-two seats in the hands of the GOP, the voice of southern African American voters—despite their sizeable numbers—was nothing more than a whisper in the United States Senate when it voted to confirm Gorsuch for a lifetime appointment on the Court.

Similarly, senators from blue states—despite representing the most people, with 43.1 percent of the nation's population—have been consistently disregarded in the current polarized age of American politics, and structurally disadvantaged by our current system for choosing and confirming justices. Their voices may be loud, but in the end, they are all but ignored. This is, as we'll see in the coming chapters, much different from the past, when substantial Senate opposition typically did undercut a High Court nominee's confirmation chances. In fact, for most of American history, few nominees who confronted substantial Senate resistance won confirmation.

★

Concerns and questions about the Supreme Court's place in our democracy are not new. Even before numerical minority justices became a majority of the Court, citizens and scholars alike questioned whether granting nine unelected wise men and women lifetime tenure to make law-altering and life-affecting decisions fit with the notion of democracy. In 1962, with the publication of *The Least Dangerous Branch*, Alexander Bickel reshaped thinking about the Supreme Court's position in American democracy, especially in the legal academy.[16] Bickel argued that judicial review created a "counter-majoritarian difficulty" for the democratic system of government in the United States.[17] The counter-majoritarian difficulty is actually two questions rolled into one phrase. The first is empirical: does the Court act in a counter-majoritarian fashion—that is, consistently strike down legislation or executive orders passed or issued by government officials elected by democratic majorities? The second question is a normative one: if the Court does issue decisions that can properly be described as counter-majoritarian, is it in accordance with an American conception of democracy?

Even before the publication of *The Least Dangerous Branch*, political scientists had focused their sights on the first question and argued that the counter-majoritarian force allegedly created by the Court was actually quite weak. As noted earlier, in 1960 the political scientist Robert McCloskey published a slim volume, *The American Supreme Court*, that includes a disproportionately large and powerful observation. In the book's epilogue, McCloskey argues that the Court has rarely "lagged far behind nor forged far ahead of America." Instead, it has typically stayed in line "with the mainstreams of American life and seldom overestimated its own power resources."[18] By his reasoning the Court was not an independent body, eager to strike down legislation at every turn. Instead it was part of the national governing regime, usually working in concert with the other branches of government.

The American Supreme Court is one of the early contributions to "regime politics theory," which gives explanation and understanding to the idea that the Supreme Court is a component of the national governing regime. It asserts that despite the Court's insulation from electoral politics, it advances the interests of the victors of the democratic process. The origins of the theory date back to the 1950s when traditional legal scholars and political scientists were both struggling to understand how the Court's 1954 decision in *Brown v. Board of Education* fit with American democracy.[19] Opposing the traditional "legalistic" view that the Court sits to protect minorities from majority tyranny, Robert Dahl, a democratic theorist, argued in 1957 that in reality the Court usually operated as an arm of the national governing alliances that historically dominated politics in the United States. For Dahl, the Court is seldom in conflict with the political (majoritarian) branches of government, and usually "operates to confer legitimacy, not simply on the particular and parochial policies of the dominant political alliance, but upon the basic patterns of behavior required for the operation of a democracy."[20]

To reach this conclusion, Dahl relied on what is known as the realignment theory of partisan change.[21] While he never specifically mentioned realignment theory, it is implied throughout his work. Its clearest articulation comes in his concluding comments:

> National politics in the United States, as in other stable democracies, is dominated by relatively cohesive alliances that endure for long periods of time. One recalls the Jeffersonian alliance, the Jacksonian, the extraordinarily long-lived

Republican dominance of the post–Civil War years, and the New Deal alliance shaped by Franklin Roosevelt. Each is marked by a break with past policies, a period of intense struggle, followed by consolidation, and finally decay and disintegration of the alliance. Except for short-lived transitional periods when the old alliance is disintegrating and the new one is struggling to take control of political institutions, the Supreme Court is inevitably a part of the dominant national alliance.[22]

So, for Dahl, the political alliances that develop after electoral realignments ensure that the Court will not significantly alter the policy outcomes of democracy—or at least not for long. Given the institutional weakness of the courts, the frequency of high bench vacancies, and the president's power to fill those empty seats with like-minded nominees, it would be improbable that the Supreme Court could, "for more than a few years at most, stand against any major alternatives sought by a lawmaking majority."[23] As the political scientist Jonathan Casper summarized, since "national politics in this country is generally dominated by relatively *stable* alliances of political interests, the Supreme Court—whose members are socialized by the same forces as are others active in politics and whose membership is selected by representatives of these political interests—is itself typically a member of such stable coalitions."[24]

Three years after the publication of Dahl's article, McCloskey, a Court scholar, advanced his similar line of argument in *The American Supreme Court*.[25] While McCloskey did not thoroughly explain the Court's historical alliance with the political branches, he seemingly agreed with Dahl when he wrote: "This is not to suggest that the historical Court has slavishly countered the public pulse, assessed the power relationships that confronted it, and shaped its decisions accordingly. The process in question is a good deal more subtle than that. We might come closer to the truth if we said that the judges have often agreed with the main current of public sentiment because they were themselves part of that current and not because they fear to disagree with it."[26]

In the 1970s the political scientist Martin Shapiro took this regime politics argument to another level. He wrote that successful judicial activism following the New Deal was a direct result of the election of 1932. For Shapiro, the Warren Court "received broad support because, a decade or two after the New Deal, it finally moved to incorporate service to the New Deal victors into constitutional law, just as Congress and the presidency earlier had incorporated such service into statutory law." Thus, "the Supreme Court got away with its activism because it was activism on behalf of the winners not the losers of American politics."[27] More than a decade later, he expanded on this view: "The voting realignment of 1932 led to a realignment of constitutional law that was completed by 1942. The Republican Court had served Republican clients. . . . The new Democratic Court was united in its determination to end this service to Republicans." In Shapiro's telling, "the only significant element in the New Deal Democratic coalition that the [Court] did not serve was conservative southern whites." He added: "But nobody in the New Deal was really fond of them anyway."[28]

So, Dahl the democratic theorist and Shapiro and McCloskey the Supreme Court scholars argued that independent judicial policy-making rarely takes place. That's because, as Dahl argued, it is "somewhat unrealistic to suppose that a Court whose members are recruited in the fashion of Supreme Court justices would long hold to norms of Right or Justice substantially at odds with the rest of the political elite."[29] For him, except in those rare instances of transition, Bickel's concern that a counter-majoritarian Court was in conflict with American democracy was all but moot.

This conclusion was at variance with academic lawyers, who generally stressed the normative aspect of the counter-majoritarian difficulty, and many of whom, by appealing to political theory, purported to have "solved" it.[30] Such an exercise did not interest Dahl. He did not wish to expend his energy on "proving that, even if the Court consistently defends minorities against majorities, nonetheless it is a thoroughly 'democratic' institution."[31] For him, "to affirm that the Court *ought* to act in this way is to deny that popular sovereignty and political equality *ought* to prevail in this country. . . . *[N]o amount of tampering with democratic theory, can conceal the fact that a system in which the policy preferences of minorities prevail over majorities is at odds with the traditional criteria for distinguishing a democracy from other political systems.*"[32]

Dahl was determined to show how democracy was viable when the Court, in applying vague provisions like the due process clauses, makes judgments that shape policy. For him, if the Court "flagrantly opposes the major policies of the dominant alliance,"[33] it will seriously jeopardize its legitimacy. But then again, that only happened on rare occasions.[34]

Just as the Court cannot for long operate in a counter-majoritarian fashion, new legal criteria can likewise be incorporated into its decisions. With a stable national political alliance and a regular appointment process, new justices may arrive at the Court with new legal ideas explicitly or implicitly approved by the president and the Senate. And "within somewhat narrow limits set by the basic policy goals of the dominant alliance, the Court *can* make national policy." If it acts outside these limits or "at times when the [national] coalition is unstable with respect to certain key policies," the Court acts only "at very great risk to its legitimacy."[35] While many have criticized various aspects of Dahl's analysis,[36] his (and McCloskey's) conclusion that judicial decisions are extensions of the dominant political regime is well supported.

Yet the current fractured state of American politics is significantly distinct from the political environment Dahl and McCloskey were observing. In their works, both assumed the presence of enduring political regimes whose leaders attain and hold office with decisive—even landslide—electoral victories.[37] They drew their conclusions in times when the popular vote and the Electoral College results were in alignment and the same party typically controlled the White House and the Senate. Today, in contrast, the popular vote and the Electoral College results are not always in alignment. While the Democratic candidate has won the popular vote in seven of the last eight presidential elections—from 1992 to 2020 with the exception of 2004—Republicans have appointed six of the nine justices. Moreover, five of those six—the five numerical minority justices—won confirmation narrowly, with at least forty-two senators in opposition. Three of them secured their seat on the Court with forty-eight senators voting against confirmation, the most ever for a successful nominee. And two of those three were appointed by a minority president.

Chapters 3 and 4 show how, for the vast majority of American history, such substantial opposition to a nominee in the United States Senate would have doomed his or her candidacy. But that is no longer true. These basic facts suggest that McCloskey's conclusion might no longer apply, or at least might be called into question. We may very well have a Court that "stray[s] very far from the mainstreams of American life."[38] And if that is so, we must question how much democratic legitimacy it possesses.

3

An Electoral-Confirmation Connection and the Historical Rarity of a Contested Justice

Eight minutes. That's all it took for the Senate to confirm one of its own, South Carolina's Jimmy Byrnes, once it received his nomination from President Franklin D. Roosevelt on June 12, 1941. Senate tradition held that any man who had made his way into that body was also worthy of a seat on the Supreme Court. In fact, FDR had taken advantage of this senatorial chivalry four years earlier when he chose Alabama's Hugo Lafayette Black, known at the time as one of the Senate's "most radical" members, as his first nominee. Black's confirmation took a bit longer than Byrnes's did—but not much. Named on a Thursday, he won confirmation—despite noteworthy displeasure from several fellow southern senators—the following Tuesday.[1]

The Senate didn't always confirm nominees so speedily (and it certainly doesn't do so today). It took the longest time in 1916, when considering the nomination of Louis Brandeis. President Woodrow Wilson had stunned the political world by naming Brandeis to a high bench vacancy. Critics objected to his work as a "people's lawyer," a progressive crusader against the economic elite. Former president and future chief justice William Howard Taft was said to be "livid" at the selection, describing it as "one of the deepest wounds that I have had as an American and as a lover of the Constitution." He trashed Brandeis as a "muckraker . . . a socialist . . . [and] a hypocrite . . . who is utterly unscrupulous." To Taft, Brandeis was "a man of infinite cunning . . . of great tenacity of purpose, and . . . of much power for evil."[2] Imbued with the spirit of anti-Semitism, opponents also targeted Brandeis's Judaism. But they couldn't convince enough conservative Democrats to break with their fellow partisan in the White House. One hundred and twenty-five days after receiving his nomination, the Senate confirmed Brandeis, forty-seven to twenty-two.

These dramatically different confirmation timelines show how the Senate's role in the confirmation of justices has shifted over the course of American history.[3] This chapter considers the link between the ballot box and Supreme Court confirmations. It considers how presidents who performed well at the polls fared with their nominations in comparison to those who won narrow victories or who weren't elected at all. And it shows that for much of American history the power of the ballot box has held true. Presidents with impressive election wins had less trouble getting their nominees confirmed. This is as it should be if elections matter. This reality held true until, as I discuss in chapter 4, the divided government era when electorally dominant presidents struggled to shape their Court in their own image. And then, as I discuss in chapter 5, it changed again at the beginning of the twenty-first century when electorally weak Republican presidents with the support of a GOP-controlled Senate took advantage of the nation's polarization to construct a *more* ideologically driven, conservative Court.

For much of American history, and in dramatic contrast to the current trend, few nominees who faced significant opposition in the Senate became Supreme Court justices. They simply weren't confirmed.[4] Brandeis was an anomaly—one of only of eleven contested justices over two centuries of High Court appointments (about 10 percent).

But today, the power of dissent in the Senate has all but evaporated. With the filibuster gone, as long as a president of the same party selects a clear ideological ally the majority will dismiss even a substantial minority of dissenting senators without a second thought. As a result, eight of the Court's nine members—89 percent—are "contentious justices," meaning that they secured their seats only after a contested confirmation vote. This, of course, includes the five numerical minority justices discussed in chapter 2. (I define a confirmation vote as "contested" or "contentious" when at least 25 percent of voting senators opposed the nomination.[5]) In short, the once powerful voice of significant Senate dissent no longer carries much weight. It's like a car alarm on a busy city street, heard but ignored. The popular perception that the Supreme Court nomination process is too polarized and "politicized"—that confirmation is more difficult than in the past—is simply not true. Polarization, ironically, has made confirmation of ideologically extreme nominees more likely, not less. In the past, these types of nominees would not have ascended to the bench. Today, confirmation is typically not in question.

✶

Figure 3.1 clarifies whether presidents who performed well at the polls experienced relative ease in securing confirmation for their nominees, com-

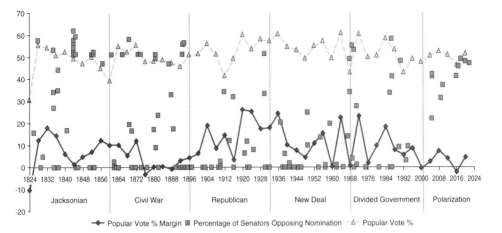

FIGURE 3.1. Presidential Popular Vote and Supreme Court Nominations, 1824–2022

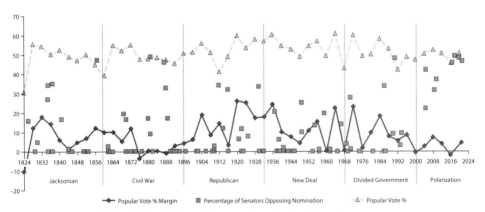

FIGURE 3.2. Presidential Popular Vote and Supreme Court Confirmations, 1824–2022

pared to those who won narrow victories or weren't elected at all. It shows three things: (1) the dotted line displays the successful presidential candidate's popular-vote percentage from 1824—the first election in which the popular vote mattered—to 2020; (2) the solid line shows the percentage of a successful presidential candidate's popular-vote margin of victory, again from 1824 to 2020; and (3) the small squares represent each Supreme Court *nomination* during this period. The location of each square correlates with the year of the nomination and the percentage of senators opposing it.[6] Figure 3.2 also shows the overall popular-vote percentage (dotted line) and the percentage margin of victory for all elected presidents from 1824 to 2020 (solid line). But compared to figure 3.1, the squares represent only Supreme Court *confirma-tions*; that's why there are fewer squares in figure 3.2 than in figure 3.1; the missing squares represent those nominees the Senate didn't confirm. Once again, the location of the square is correlated with the year of the nomination and the percentage of senators opposing it. Both figures are also divided into six historical periods, which will be explored further in this chapter and in chapters 4 and 5.

Four things are quite clear from the historical record. First, for much of American history, when a nominee was out of line with the interests of the Senate—for whatever reason—one of three things occurred that kept the president's choice off the Court: the Senate tabled the nomination and took no further action, rejected the nominee in a vote, or essentially forced the president to withdraw the nomination given the likelihood of defeat.[7] For long stretches of time few nominees who encountered conflict in the Senate reached the Court, as is made apparent by comparing figures 3.1 and 3.2.

Second, as Robert Dahl suggests, one political party was typically domi-nant at the national level and the presidents representing that party were able to secure easy confirmation of their selections for the Court, usually with little or no opposition in the Senate. Yet this was not always the case. As is shown in figures 3.1 and 3.2, the most contentious periods in the Senate for Supreme Court nominees correlated with presidential weakness at the polls, in terms of both the overall popular vote and the margin of victory. Specifi-cally, the data show that during eras of close presidential contests, such as the later Civil War period, Court nominees faced more contentiousness in the Senate. This indicates that ease or difficulty in the confirmation process did correlate with the ease or difficulty of the president's election.

This does *not* mean that every president who won a narrow victory was destined to witness his Supreme Court nominees face difficulty in the Senate. Nevertheless, elections did matter. Most importantly, in the 132-year period between mid-1837 and 1969 (table 3.1), presidents who won election *narrowly* were more than twice as likely to have their nominees face a contentious Sen-ate than those who won decisively (41.7 percent to 19.6 percent).[8] They were also twice as likely to see those contested nominees denied a seat on the Court (25 percent to 12.5 percent). This makes sense. We would expect more elec-torally dominant presidents to have an easier time leaving their imprint on the Court. But even those presidents who won easily in their first campaign could not rest on their electoral success. If they made an appointment during the election year at the end of their first term (or soon after the election) and the presidential race that year was close, the Senate was very likely to con-test their choice (table 3.2). Nearly half of the contested and failed nominees

TABLE 3.1. Nature of Appointing President's Victory and Senate Treatment of Supreme Court Nominees, 1837–1969

President's Victory	Total Number	Contested	Percent Contested	Failed	Percent Failed	Confirmed	Percent Confirmed
Decisive	56	11	19.6%	7	12.5%	49	87.5%
Narrow	24	10	41.7%	6	25.0%	18	75.0%
Unelected	21	12	57.1%	12	57.1%	9	42.9%
Total	101	33	32.7%	25	24.8%	76	75.2%

TABLE 3.2. Senate Treatment of Supreme Court Nominees Appointed by Electorally Dominant Presidents, 1837–1969

President's Victory	Total Number	Contested	Percent Contested	Failed	Percent Failed	Confirmed	Percent Confirmed
Decisive	48	6	12.5%	4	8.3%	44	91.7%
Election Year	8	5	62.5%	3	37.5%	5	62.5%

appointed by electorally dominant presidents faced the Senate in such a situation, and those who did were not confirmed 37.5 percent of the time. Again, this makes sense. Presidents in the midst of difficult reelection fights—even if they won handily the first time—should expect a more aggressive Senate. Unelected presidents—those endorsed not by the vote but by fate—had by far the toughest time securing confirmation for their High Court nominees (table 3.1). Once more, the power of the ballot box holds. Without the benefit of the legitimacy bestowed by voters in a democracy, unelected presidents should not expect to leave a lasting legacy in the form of lifelong judicial nominations.

Third, nominations made at the end of a partisan period, when a political regime's authority was in steep decline, were more likely to be contested in the Senate. In fact, during the period from mid-1837 to 1969, more than half of the nominees named by presidents who had won easily—six of eleven—were nominated at an era's end. And half of those six ended in failure.

Fourth, the power of a decisive victory would stand out even more if not for President Ulysses S. Grant's testy relationship with the Senate. Despite two comfortable electoral victories, the Senate treated some of his nominees with scorn, rejecting or forcing the withdrawal of three out of eight. As we will see, this was likely connected to the expansion and then contraction of the Court during the presidencies of his two predecessors, Abraham Lincoln and Andrew Johnson.

These charts and figures all reveal one thing: the importance of Senate objections to Supreme Court nominees for much of American history. While the president possesses the sole authority to select jurists for the high bench, the Senate's voice has nevertheless been powerful. I suggest that this reality enhanced the democratic legitimacy of the president's Court choices, particularly after the ratification of the 17th amendment in 1913 when the power to select senators shifted from state legislatures to voters. When Senate discontent mattered, it wasn't only the president who was shaping the Court. The president and a majority of senators were collaborating in the effort. The Senate's substantial role in the selection process may also help explain why the Court has usually been in alignment with the political branches of American national government, and why, as Robert McCloskey observed, it "seldom overestimated its own power resources."[9]

So, for significant portions of American history, the assumptions Dahl published in 1957 seem correct: electoral realignments produced enduring political regimes that typically afforded presidents the freedom to successfully put jurists of their liking on the Court. Taking each of these six historical periods one by one, we will see nuances of this electoral-confirmation connection.

Jacksonian Era (1824–1860)

The Jacksonian period, between 1824 and 1860, is easily the most distinct from the others.[10] During this time, nearly two-thirds of nominees faced a contentious Senate—far more than in any other period of the four under review here (table 3.3). And many of them did not become justices. Even so, it still holds true that presidents who were narrowly elected, unelected, or faced a tough reelection fight after a decisive win had the most difficulty securing confirmation for their nominees (table 3.3).[11] Moreover, while President Andrew Jackson undoubtedly had more difficulty with his nominees than should have been hypothesized based on his substantial electoral victories, the Senate ultimately confirmed all of them.[12] Contentiousness did not translate into failure, although he did need to nominate Roger Taney twice. Jackson's appointments are also unusual because he selected two men for the Court after the election of 1836, which his vice president, Martin Van Buren, won decisively. And notably, both nominees were named to newly created seats. Since some senators objected to the Court's expansion from seven to nine members, the vote was likely closer than it would have been if they were filling traditional vacancies.[13]

The president who had the greatest difficulty in securing confirmation for his nominees during this period was John Tyler, the first vice president to assume the presidency due to the death of his predecessor. Tyler had been part

TABLE 3.3. The Confirmation Electoral Connection: Nature of Appointing President's Victory and Nomination Result

Era	President's Victory	Total Number	Contested	Percent Contested	Failed	Percent Failed	Confirmed	Percent Confirmed
Jacksonian	Decisive	13	7	53.9	2	15.4	11	84.6
	Narrow	5	2	40.0	2	40.0	3	60.0
	Unelected	13	11	84.6	11	84.6	2	15.4
	Total	31	20	64.5	15	48.4	16	51.6
	Election Year	2	1	50.0	1	50.0	1	50.0
Civil War	Decisive	13	3	23.1	3	23.1	10	76.9
	Narrow	15	7	46.7	4	26.7	11	73.3
	Unelected	4	1	25.0	1	25.0	3	75.0
	Total	32	11	34.4	8	25.0	24	75.0
	Election Year	0						
Republican	Decisive	20	4	20.0	1	5.0	19	95.0
	Narrow	0						
	Unelected	2	0	0.0	0	0.0	2	100.0
	Total	22	4	18.2	1	4.5	21	94.5
	Election Year	4	2	50.0	0	0.0	4	100.0
New Deal	Decisive	18	2	11.1	2	11.1	16	89.9
	Narrow	4	1	25.0	0	0.0	4	100.0
	Unelected	0						
	Total	22	3	13.6	2	9.1	20	90.9
	Election Year	2	2	100.0	2	100.0	0	0.0

of the Whig ticket with William Henry Harrison in 1840. However, after only thirty-one days in office, President Harrison died. Tyler faced difficulty right from the start as his detractors derisively referred to him as "His Accidency." Ultimately, he was only able to put one jurist on the Court, even though two vacancies opened up during his time in office. He nominated five men in total (two twice and one three times). In addition to the fact that he was unelected, all of these nominations took place in the election year of 1844 or in his final days in office in 1845. By that point, Tyler was a defeated man. In fact, he was not even his party's candidate in the 1844 race, since he had broken with the Whigs three years earlier. Instead, his main adversary among the Whigs—Henry Clay—headed up the ticket. And Clay lost to the Democratic candidate, James K. Polk, in a close race. Given this set of circumstances, we should expect the Senate to deny Tyler's choices for the Court. Millard Fillmore, who assumed the presidency after the death of Zachary Taylor, confronted the same problem as Tyler. And like Tyler, he struggled to get his selections confirmed, succeeding in only one of four attempts. Also like Tyler, he was not the Whig candidate in the next election in 1852, a race the Democrat Franklin Pierce won decisively.

When the Senate contested a nominee in the Jackson era, confirmation was usually denied. Of the twenty contested nominees, only four joined the Court. President Jackson named three: Taney (1836 Senate vote); Philip Barbour (1836); and John Catron (1837). President James Buchanan chose one: Nathan Clifford (1858). A divided Senate also confirmed Jackson nominee William Smith in 1837, but he declined to serve, citing "inadequate pay." Notably, all of Jackson's nominees who confronted conflict in the Senate did so near the end of his presidency. In fact, the Senate votes on Barbour, Smith, Catron, and the second Taney took place during the election year of 1836 or after Jackson's presidency had already ended. Jackson nominated Catron and Smith to fill the two new seats literally on his last day in office. A loyal Van Buren allowed both nominations to stand.[14] The contested confirmation of Clifford occurred in the final throes of the Jacksonian regime, after a weakened Buchanan nominated him to replace Benjamin Curtis, who had resigned from the Court to protest its decision in *Dred Scott*.[15] While Buchanan was only in the middle of his first term after a decisive election victory, presidents making an appointment at the end of a partisan period should expect to face a combative Senate.

Civil War Period (1860–1896)

In the Civil War period (table 3.3) the Senate contested just over one-third of nominees (34.4 percent). Actually, in terms of Supreme Court nominations and confirmations, the years between the election of 1876 and the conclusion of the

Civil War period with the election of William McKinley in 1896 perhaps most closely resemble the polarized politics of the twenty-first century. During these two decades presidential election after presidential election resulted in narrow victories in which the winning candidate never received more than 50 percent of the popular vote, including two times when the victor lost that vote. High Court nominees confronted a confirmation gauntlet as the Senate contested seven of seventeen nominees. But even before this time of close presidential contests, senators contested and rejected President Ulysses S. Grant's choices at an unusually high rate—three of his eight—for a president who had won election so decisively. Grant's difficulty with his Supreme Court selections was similar to Andrew Jackson's. Notably, in both instances, the Congress had recently expanded the Court. But also, like Jackson, and despite his difficulties, Grant was able to remake the Court, ultimately filling all five vacancies. Perhaps the Senate's hostility to Grant was a remnant of Congress's attitude toward his predecessor, Andrew Johnson. Deeply detested by Republicans in Congress, Johnson was not only impeached but also denied any chance of placing a nominee on the Court, despite two vacancies. As the political scientist Henry Abraham writes, "it is doubtful that the Senate would have approved God himself had he been nominated by Andrew Johnson." Abraham has a point. After the death of Justice John Catron in late May 1865, Congress passed legislation to shrink the Court from ten to eight, both to forestall a Johnson selection and to enhance the power of the Lincoln justices.[16]

In the entire Civil War period there were eleven contested nominations, and only three survived the Senate to take a seat on the high bench. The others had no action taken on their nomination, were rejected by the Senate, or were withdrawn by the president.[17] The three contentious justices were Stanley Matthews (1881), Lucius Lamar (1888), and Melville Fuller (1888). Rutherford B. Hayes first nominated Matthews as a lame-duck president in 1881, but the Senate took no action. Hayes's fellow Republican, James Garfield, the victor of the close presidential election of 1880, re-nominated Matthews in the first days of his presidency. Senators objected to the choice once again, but nevertheless he was confirmed by the narrowest of margins, twenty-four to twenty-three. The Senate confirmed President Grover Cleveland's choices of Lamar and Fuller in the election year of 1888, a contest the Republican Benjamin Harrison won even though Cleveland, a Democrat, captured the popular vote.

Republican Era (1896–1932)

With the election of William McKinley in 1896 and the dominance of the GOP over the next thirty-six years (the Republican era), Supreme Court

nominees faced a friendlier Senate en route to confirmation. Only four nominees confronted a contentious confirmation process (table 3.3). Three won
confirmation—Mahlon Pitney (1912), Louis Brandeis (1916), and Charles Evans Hughes (1930)—with approximately one-third of the voting senators in
opposition each time. The other—John J. Parker—suffered defeat in the Senate. As in the previous periods, the general principles I outlined above held
true: President Taft nominated Pitney in the last full year of his presidency,
the same year he finished third in the presidential election of 1912. President
Wilson chose Brandeis in the next presidential election year, and while he
won reelection, he did so by the narrowest margin of any victor during the
Republican era (49.25 percent of the popular vote, beating his opponent by a
3.14 percent margin). During this period of landslides, Wilson also won only
52.2 percent of the electoral vote. And if he had lost the state of California—
which he won by less than 4,000 votes (.38 percent)—he would have lost the
presidency. In all other elections during these years, the winning candidate
captured at least 60 percent of the popular vote, and more often than not
more than 70 percent of the Electoral College delegates.

Notably, the Brandeis vote was the first contested confirmation in the constitutionally reconstituted Senate. Beginning in 1913, after the ratification of
the 17th amendment, senators were elected directly by the voters of their states
rather than by state legislatures, and this may have made the difference for
Brandeis's confirmation. In naming Brandeis, Wilson had failed to follow the
tradition of "senatorial courtesy," which called for the president to "get approval
from, or at the very least notify, the two senators from the nominee's home
state. In Brandeis' case, Wilson did neither." One of Massachusetts' senators
was the conservative Republican Henry Cabot Lodge, who detested Brandeis's
and Wilson's politics. According to the historian David Dalin, "Lodge's position of influence as the senior senator from the nominee's state would probably
have brought about Brandeis's defeat had Lodge invoked the rule of senatorial
courtesy. But to the surprise of many of his Senate colleagues . . . [he] did not
do so." Lodge might have chosen this path of least resistance because, with the
17th amendment in place, he would face voters for the first time and, as Dalin
suggests, "may have feared the political repercussions in the upcoming Senate
election of November 1916." Lodge had "strongly opposed" the amendment,
but its ratification meant "he would have to campaign for the support of newly
enfranchised voters, including many Catholics and Jews." One of his close advisors certainly cautioned him against publicly opposing Brandeis, suggesting that by doing so he would endanger his future in the Senate. And indeed,
his opponent in the race—the charismatic former Boston mayor John "Honey
Fitz" Fitzgerald—applauded "Wilson's nomination of Brandeis, as did most

of the city's Irish Democrats." While Lodge did vote against confirmation, by choosing this quieter form of opposition he sufficiently minimized the issue and won the election by just over six percentage points.[18]

President Herbert Hoover nominated Hughes and Parker at the end of the era, and, significantly, just as the economic devastation of the Great Depression was beginning to take its toll on the nation. To critics, Hughes had served the very interests responsible for the nation's economic ill health and widespread unemployment. Senator George Norris of Nebraska, a progressive Republican, noted in opposing his confirmation, "no man in public life so exemplifies the influence of power combinations in the political and financial world as does Mr. Hughes." Norris was also unnerved by the fact that Hughes had left his seat on the Court to run for the presidency in 1916 and now sought to return to that tribunal. To him, this maneuvering threatened to reduce the Court "to the level of a political machine . . . [which would] inevitably encourage and stimulate political activity on the part of judges of the Supreme Court."[19] Hughes won confirmation despite notable ideological opposition from both Democrats and Republicans.

On the heels of Hughes's narrow confirmation victory, President Hoover, in a bid to build support in the South, nominated forty-five-year-old appeals court judge John J. Parker of North Carolina following the death of Justice Edward Sanford on March 8, 1930. As they had done just weeks earlier with Hughes, liberals sought to use the Parker nomination to attack the president. And this time, they succeeded in denying Hoover his choice for the Court by a vote of thirty-nine to forty-one. The Senate's rejection of Parker briefly interrupted an extended period of successful confirmations. It had been thirty-six years since the Senate had voted to deny a nominee a seat on the high bench—and it would be thirty-eight years before it would do so again.

New Deal Period (1932–1968)

Just as the Republicans had excelled in the elections of previous eras, Democrats dominated the New Deal era. Wilson was the only Democrat elected president during the Republican era—as a result of a divided GOP in 1912—and, similarly, five-star general Dwight D. Eisenhower would be the only Republican elected during the New Deal era. Even more so than in the previous era, landslides defined presidential elections in these years. In seven of the nine elections between 1932 and 1964, the victor won more than 80 percent of the electoral votes.

In turn, and following the axiom that power at the ballot box historically supported successful nominations, Supreme Court selections faced little hostility in the Senate. Only three nominees encountered sufficient opposition to meet the definition of a contested confirmation vote: one who barely met the contested figure of 25 percent of senators in opposition, and two named in the final days of a fading era.[20] The Senate's treatment of Abe Fortas—and by proxy, Homer Thornberry—in 1968 ushered in an era of conflict that would redefine the selection and confirmation processes, so it's worth examining that failed nomination in greater detail.

By the late 1960s, Americans had begun to question where the Earl Warren–led Supreme Court was taking their country. While a few years earlier the Warren Court had strong approval ratings—even after announcing some deeply unpopular opinions—a Gallup poll taken in early summer 1968 showed that was no longer the case. In fact, a majority of Americans now viewed the Court in negative terms for the first time since Gallup began asking them their opinions on it. Only 33 percent of respondents rated the Court as "excellent" (8 percent) or "good" (25 percent); 54 percent rated it as either "fair" (31 percent) or poor (23 percent).[21]

Gallup conducted the poll after another decision came down from the Court that altered its balance: Chief Justice Warren decided to retire from the center chair. Soon after the assassination of Robert Kennedy in his home state of California in early June 1968, Warren concluded that his old nemesis, former Vice President Richard Nixon, would likely capture the White House. So, to prevent Nixon, a fellow California Republican, from naming his replacement, the seventy-seven-year-old Warren strategized that it would be best for him to announce his resignation at that moment. President Lyndon B. Johnson still had seven months left in office. Surely, that was enough time to fill the vacancy. Some senators quickly suggested that Johnson should not name Warren's successor, asserting that he should instead leave the decision to the winner of the 1968 presidential race, which Johnson had declined to contest. But the president was not the type to allow such an opportunity to pass him by. He nominated Associate Justice Abe Fortas to replace Warren as chief, and Fifth Circuit Court of Appeals Judge Homer Thornberry to fill the expected vacant Fortas seat. Before moving to the judiciary, Thornberry had served in the House of Representatives, succeeding Johnson in his Texas Hill Country seat after the future president successfully sought the Senate in 1948. By choosing two men he was close to, the president opened himself up to attacks of cronyism. And his critics took advantage of that opening. But cronyism was not the sole focus of their discontent.

In attempting to elevate Fortas to chief, President Johnson was pursuing what was at that time a proven method of selecting Supreme Court justices.

Ever since Franklin D. Roosevelt had an opportunity to name eight men to the high bench,[22] Democratic presidents had chosen close associates to fill Court vacancies (more on this in chapter 9). These were nominees who reflected the appointing president's ideological views on constitutional matters and had helped advance his administration's cause prior to being selected. These jurists were a different breed of justice than those of today. And while senators occasionally raised questions or concerns during their confirmations, none had faced any serious threat of defeat.

That's how things unfolded in the early days after Johnson announced the Fortas and Thornberry appointments. For example, a July 13, 1968, *New York Times* editorial confidentially explained how confirmation matters would ultimately play out. "A few Republican senators, playing a losing game, are making a futile effort to block the appointment" of the president's two choices for the Court. "When all is said and done, they will be confirmed."[23]

But the *Times*'s confident prediction would prove wrong. Southern Democrats and conservative Republicans, displeased with the work of the Warren Court and eager to aid Richard Nixon on the campaign trail, went on the attack. In four days of hearings, the critical senators effectively put the Warren Court on trial by way of their questions for Fortas, targeting the Court's recent groundbreaking doctrinal shifts, particularly in the area of criminal law.[24] Since Fortas would still remain on the Court even if the Senate rejected his elevation to chief, he often refused to answer out of concern that he might hear a case on the matter. But sometimes that approach just made matters worse. As summer turned to autumn, support for the Fortas nomination slowly fell apart, undoubtedly aided by the work of South Carolina senator Strom Thurmond, the former Democrat who had bolted from his party to seek the presidency in 1948 on the segregationist States-Rights ticket before joining the GOP in 1964. Pat Buchanan, a Nixon aide, explains one particularly effective maneuver—dubbed "the Fortas Film Festival"—that helped to undermine the nomination: "Strom's office came up with the idea of inviting senators to a closed room for a viewing of *Flaming Creatures*, a transvestite pornographic film that Fortas, alone of the justices, in *Jacobs v. New York*, had ruled did not violate obscenity laws. Senator after senator went to the room, watched the film, and emerged shaken, to vote against elevating to chief justice any jurist who regarded this a legitimate form of entertainment."[25]

As the presidential campaign wore on, the Senate waited. Finally, on the first day of October, it held a vote on the nomination. With forty-three senators supporting a filibuster and only forty-five calling for a vote, Fortas's bid to become the next chief abruptly ended. Johnson withdrew the nomination the next day. Since it occurred in the closing moments of the New Deal period, the Fortas defeat fits with the principles outlined above—principles that were, even at this point, losing their applicability and explanatory power.

Johnson had hoped to secure a liberal Court for the foreseeable future. But his Democratic Party was deeply divided on the right path for the Court. By blocking Fortas, the Senate majority—with an eye toward a Nixon victory— effectively aided in moderating the Court. It secured the Court's move to the center eight months later when it confirmed now President Nixon's choice for chief justice, Warren Earl Burger. Burger was considered a "law-and-order" conservative with a moderate record on civil rights. He was decidedly more conservative than Homer Thornberry most likely would have been had he made it onto the bench.[26]

This one appointment profoundly altered the ideological makeup of the Court. Beginning in 1937 and continuing to the Court's most recent term, the political scientists Andrew Martin and Kevin Quinn have estimated an ideological score for every justice in every year. Their scores range from the most liberal of −7.748 for William O. Douglas in the term beginning in 1975 to the most conservative of 4.511 for William Rehnquist, also in the 1975–76 term.[27] The ideological middle sits at zero. In part, this scoring allows Martin and Quinn to show the ideological change on the Court over time as new justices take their seats and new issues emerge. If Fortas had made it to chief, the Court's swing, or median, justice would most likely have been Thornberry (assuming he secured confirmation), since he was expected to vote along moderately liberal lines.[28] In comparison, a Burger-led high bench made Byron White, a John F. Kennedy appointee, the swing justice with a 1969–70 Martin-Quinn rating of .102. White replaced William Brennan in that role. Brennan was much more liberal, with a 1968–69 rating of −1.127.[29]

This alternative path was highly significant for the Court. In the eighty-five years of Supreme Court decision-making Martin and Quinn have analyzed, no year-to-year change compares to the switch from 1969 to 1970. Not only does the swing justice move more than a full point on their scale in this single year (something that had never happened before and has not happened since); White's positive rating also meant that the middle of the Court was now on the conservative side of the ideological dividing line. With the exception of one brief interruption, it has remained there ever since.[30]

In the nearly three-quarters of a century between 1894 and 1968, the Senate had rejected only one Supreme Court nominee. It had only contested four others, one by the narrowest terms possible. But with the Fortas nomination, that changed. In the year and a half between October 1968 and April 1970, the Senate would essentially block four presidential choices for the Court: Fortas in 1968; Homer Thornberry by denying Fortas the center chair, also in 1968; Clement Haynsworth in 1969; and G. Harrold Carswell in 1970. And in 1971, it would contest the nomination of William Rehnquist.

What happened to change the politics of the confirmation process? Put simply, after many years of sitting on the sidelines, with only occasional objections from small groups of senators, the Senate reasserted itself in the confirmation process. It did so because it no longer shared presidential thinking on the desired ideological direction of the Court, and it had the ability to moderate judicial selections at the highest level. Initially, this moderating influence was a reaction to the liberalism of the Warren Court. Then, it was in response to the desire of Republican presidents to pursue a more conservative constitutional path. Finally, at the end of the divided government era in the 1990s, concerns over confirmation tempered a Democratic president's desire to choose an outsider similar to Earl Warren, even though his party controlled the Senate.

★

For most of the nation's history, the relationship between senate and president around Court nominees was accurately characterized by power of the ballot box, as electorally dominant presidents had an easier time securing confirmation for nominees than those elected by narrow margins, and a much easier time than those who ascended to the presidency due to their predecessor's death. Moreover, nominations made soon after or in the midst of a close election were more likely to be contested and defeated.[31] But, as discussed in chapter 4, when the Senate blocked Richard Nixon's second choice to fill Fortas's empty seat, it began to act in a fashion that defied these principles. Previously, even narrowly elected presidents like Nixon did not have two nominees rejected for a single seat. The Senate's action was even more notable in that its negative vote on that second nominee came nearly a year and a half after the last election. The only other president to experience such a fate was Grover Cleveland, nearly three-quarters of a century earlier. But that was at the end of a partisan era—when nominees traditionally face uphill confirmations battles—not at the beginning of one.[32] The Senate's challenge to Nixon did not stop there. In late 1971, with the next presidential election in sight, liberal critics successfully dismissed two of his choices before he even had a chance to officially announce them. They objected once again when he nominated a conservative ideologue in Rehnquist. Liberals pursued this positioning despite clear indications that it was hurting them with at least some of their traditional constituencies. And indeed, the following November, the Democratic presidential candidate, the progressive Senator George McGovern of

South Dakota, would be pasted at the polls in a campaign that highlighted judicial issues. From a historical perspective, the size and the success of the Senate's opposition to Nixon's choices were highly unusual. And this meant that the link between the president's electoral performance and the Senate's treatment of Supreme Court nominees that had held for approximately 132 years—from mid-1837 to 1969—was losing its significance. Presidential election success and the Senate's approach to Court nominees had gone hand in hand, but this axiomatic relationship was fading.

More than a decade later, that reality was confirmed as Ronald Reagan—another landslide election victor—saw his nominee for chief contested, even though Associate Justice Rehnquist's shift to the center chair would not alter the ideological balance on the Court. The following year, Reagan saw Robert Bork, a nominee who *would* alter that balance, suffer one of the most decisive confirmation defeats in the history of Supreme Court nominations. And as with Nixon's choice for the Fortas seat, Senate opponents didn't appear to be willing to let up until the president sent them someone who was not so threatening to the decisions they cherished. With Anthony Kennedy, Reagan did just that.

By the time George W. Bush made his first appointment in 2005, it was as if the selection process was taking place in the DC Comics world of Htrae, where everything is the opposite of what it's supposed to be. As we will see in chapter 5, election results seemed no longer to matter, as the Senate contested all but one of the nominations after the turn of the twenty-first century. Conflict was the default, and an electorally weak, one-term, minority president had a greater impact on the Court's composition than either of the two two-term presidents who preceded him, both of whom won a popular-vote victory—one decisively—less than two years before they made their two successful selections. And while they each had a third nominee denied a seat on the Court, the electorally weak, one-term, minority president succeeded with all of his choices, including one confirmed mere days before he lost reelection by four and a half percentage points. Given this development, it is right to wonder about the democratic legitimacy of a Court constructed in such a fashion, especially if it ushers in a new era of constitutional decision-making.

4

How a Resurgent Senate Tamed the
Judicial Desires of Electorally Dominant Presidents

Election night, 1984. This was not to be one of those long election evenings that stretch into the next morning as the votes are tallied and the candidates anxiously await the outcome. It was not like the election night of 2000, when CBS's Dan Rather famously said the race was "tight as the rusted lug nuts on a '55 Ford . . . Spandex tight."[1] Once the results started coming in it was clear that Ronald Reagan would win reelection over Democrat Walter Mondale in a landslide. The map on the TV screen was a sea of red as Reagan won everywhere except Mondale's home state of Minnesota—which he lost by just under 4,000 votes (.18 percent)—and a small speck in the east representing the overwhelmingly Democratic District of Columbia. It was the second forty-nine-state victory for the GOP's candidate in a mere twelve years. En route to his reelection in 1972, Richard Nixon had become only the fourth presidential candidate in American history to capture more than 60 percent of the popular vote. In 1984, Reagan came up just short of that mark, at 58.8 percent. Moreover, the GOP retained control of the Senate, a chamber it had captured for the first time in over a quarter of a century four years earlier.

Republicans dominated presidential elections during the two decades from 1968 to 1988. Of the six races in those years, Republicans won five—four by overwhelming margins. Indeed, the Democratic nominee won a total of just fifty-four states in those six elections.[2] If the Watergate-affected election of 1976—the only one a Democrat won—is excluded, the figure falls to thirty-one states, an average of just over six states per race. And in each of these six races, a significant aspect of the Republican nominee's appeal, especially for southern whites and northern Catholics, was his positioning on judicially focused social issues. Despite these extraordinary results, at the end of the divided government era assessments of Republican efforts to alter Supreme

Court doctrine highlighted failures rather than successes, particularly on those politically salient social issues. At one point Republican presidents had named ten justices in a row, yet conservatives were still deeply displeased with the Court's doctrinal product.

What happened? Why didn't the Supreme Court follow the election results in the same way it had in the past? At the very end of the New Deal era, the politics of Supreme Court confirmations began to change. That change was driven by a United States Senate—most often in Democratic hands—newly willing to challenge the ideological direction in which presidents—most often Republicans—wanted to take the Court. While these Republican presidents had been dominant at the ballot box, they had not constructed a political regime like those of the past. One result was divided government. Another was a divided GOP. And as Republican presidents sought to move the Court to the right, Senate Democrats—and often a fair number of Republicans—resisted. They did so by contesting or rejecting nominees and/or forcing the selection of more moderate ones, resulting in a Court less conservative than promised by these Republican presidential victors. Nevertheless, it's incorrect to say these presidents failed. While its decisions certainly didn't satisfy movement conservatives who were most committed to disrupting existing constitutional thought, the Court was undoubtedly more ideologically conservative at the end than at the beginning of the era.[3] It was also connected to majoritarian politics, as most of those who joined the high bench during these years did so after being proudly named by the president and overwhelmingly—if not unanimously—supported by the Senate. Finally, according to Gallup, it was a Court highly respected across the land.[4]

✶

Including Abe Fortas, who officially belongs in the New Deal period, presidents made seventeen nominations to the High Court between 1968 and 1994. Democrats made three; Republicans fourteen.[5] The Senate rejected four of those nominees, and another had his name withdrawn. Twelve won Senate approval, two after a contested confirmation. While Republican presidents made most of the selections, the story was much the same for the sole Democratic president who had a chance to fill an empty seat. During this era, with few exceptions, the Senate's confirmation process ensured that the president—no matter the party—was unable to select his most ideological option for a Court vacancy. Republican presidents in particular yearned for a more ideologically friendly Court, but their efforts were largely thwarted by the Senate. In all but three of the twelve successful nominations during the divided

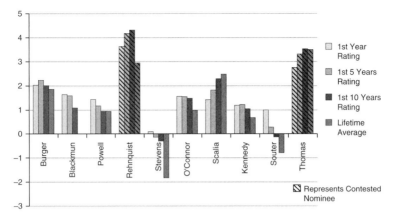

FIGURE 4.1. Estimated Ideologies (by Martin-Quinn Scores) of Republican-Appointed Justices, Divided Government Era

government era, presidents made a more moderate choice among the leading contenders, mostly due to concerns over Senate confirmation. Moreover, in the cases where the nominee suffered defeat in the Senate or was forced to withdraw,[6] the eventual justice most assuredly moved the Court closer to its ideological middle than the appointing president had hoped when he made his initial selection. To be sure, each time the Senate rejected a nominee, there was always at least one other issue undermining his candidacy: as Fortas's close relationship with President Johnson, Clement Haynsworth's ethics, G. Harrold Carswell's qualifications, and, to a much lesser extent, Robert Bork's inauthentic "confirmation conversion" into a moderate.[7] But, as the political scientist John Massaro explains, these were by and large ideological votes.[8] Liberals voted one way, conservatives another. Party affiliation mattered less, particularly in the first three of these votes.

Notably, the evidence suggests the Senate was quite good at evaluating the ideology of Republican nominees during the era of divided government. Of course, there's no way of knowing how the rejected nominees would have decided cases if they had made it onto the bench. But the judicial behavior of the two Republican-appointed justices who survived a contested confirmation gives some indication. Those two justices—William Rehnquist (who experienced two conflictual confirmations) and Clarence Thomas—were easily the two most conservative members of the High Court during this period.[9] Figure 4.1 shows ideological ratings of all the Republican-appointed justices of the divided government era for their first year, first five years, and first ten years, as well as for their entire tenure as a justice.[10] Republican nominees who faced a contested confirmation are denoted by hatch marks in figure 4.1; those who did not face such opposition were more liberal—some dramatically so—during both their early years and their entire tenure on the high bench.

Apart from the first two justices of the divided government era—Warren Burger and Harry Blackmun—the Senate contested and more often than not defeated nominees who were expected to move the Court substantially to the right (table 4.1).[11] It contested all nominees after Burger and Blackmun who were expected to be or who actually were in their first year *four places or more* to the ideological right of the justice they were replacing. For example, in his last term, Justice Thurgood Marshall was the most liberal justice according to Martin-Quinn scores (position 1). After surviving a contested confirmation, Clarence Thomas replaced him. In his first year on the bench—and ever since—Thomas was the most conservative justice (position 9), a difference of eight positions. None of the nominees who were *less* than four places to the ideological right of the justice they were replacing were contested during this period. This held true for even those perceived to be more conservative at the time of their nominations (e.g., Powell, Scalia, and even Stevens) based on Segal-Cover scores.[12] Senate liberals chose not to challenge Burger and Blackmun because they were expected to be moderates on civil rights. At that time, their perceived overall conservatism didn't matter so much. (In Blackmun's case this perception also turned out to be wildly inaccurate.) These vacancies had been created by the departures of Earl Warren and Abe Fortas, two leading liberals. So, it would have been unreasonable to expect a conservative like President Richard Nixon to name a jurist who did not move the Court to the right. Still, given Blackmun's ideological scores (figure 4.1), by defeating Carswell—and perhaps Haynsworth as well—the Senate likely prevented Nixon from moving it even further to the right.

During the divided government era, presidents appointed three different types of nominees. They can be described as objectionable ideologues, confirmable choices, and acceptable ideologues.

✳

"Objectionable ideologues" were quite simply nominees who were perceived as ideologically extreme and were either rejected by the Senate or withdrawn by the president. The two presidents most committed to changing the Court in this era, Republicans Richard Nixon and Ronald Reagan, each put forward two such nominees.

Nixon's first choice for the Court, Warren Burger, sailed through fairly placid confirmation waters. His next two choices, however, contended with stormy Senate seas and were ultimately defeated. Senate liberals held back their

TABLE 4.1. Nominee Type, Ideology, and Ideological Movement, Divided Government Era

Nominee	Nominee Type*	Senate Vote	Segal-Cover Score	Departing Justice's Ideological Location	Ideological Location of New Justice (1st Yr)	Location Difference btw Departing & New Justice	Departing Justice's Ideological Score (Last Yr)	New Justice's Ideological Score (1st Yr)	Ideological Score Difference btw Departing & New Justice
Burger	PP	74–3	0.115	2	9	7	−1.4	2	3.4
Haynsworth	SI	45–55	0.16	3		6**	−1.3		
Carswell	SI	45–51	0.04	3		7**	−1.3		
Blackmun	C	94–0	0.115	3	8	5	−1.3	1.6	2.9
Powell***	S/C	89–1	0.165	7	6	−1	0.7	1.4	0.7
Rehnquist***	I	68–26	0.045	4	9	*5*	0	3.6	3.6
Stevens	PP	98–0	0.25	1	3	2	−7.7	0.1	7.8
O'Connor	S/C	99–0	0.415	6	7	1	0.7	1.5	0.8
Scalia	SI	98–0	0	8	8	0	2.1	1.4	−0.7
Bork	I	42–58	0.095	5		4**	0.8		
Ginsburg	I	NV	0	5		4**	0.8		
Kennedy	C	97–0	0.365	5	6	1	0.8	1.2	0.4
Souter	C	90–9	0.325	2	5	3	−3.7	1	4.7
Thomas	SI	52–48	0.16	1	9	*8*	−4.4	2.8	7.2
Ginsburg	C	96–3	0.68	4	4	0	0.6	−0.2	−0.8
Breyer	C	87–9	0.475	2	4	2	−1.9	−0.3	1.6

Defeated or withdrawn nominees in *italics*.

*Nominee types: C = clear compromise, I = ideologue (without political symbolism), PP = presidential preference, S/C = symbolic and considered confirmable, and SI = symbolic ideologue.

**The outer limits of what was possible based on Segal-Cover score.

***While they were appointed at the same time, Powell filled the Black seat and Rehnquist the Harlan seat. To highlight their ideological impact, I have switched that placement here.

opposition with the Burger nomination but pounced on Nixon's choice to replace Fortas, who (as discussed below) had resigned under a Nixon administration–advanced impeachment threat in mid-May 1969. Nixon's choice to fill the Fortas seat was not announced until near the end of summer, but inside the White House the president made clear his desire for "a white southern conservative federal judge under age sixty." Nixon was pursuing his "southern strategy," hoping to appeal to white southerners disgruntled with the Democratic Party (particularly those who supported the third-party candidacy of George Wallace in 1968). He ultimately chose Clement Haynsworth, a Fourth Circuit Court of Appeals judge from South Carolina. Many in Washington perceived Haynsworth as the choice of one of the leaders of the anti-Fortas forces, Senator Strom Thurmond, who also hailed from South Carolina.[13] And while Segal and Cover rate Burger (and Blackmun) as slightly more conservative than Haynsworth (table 4.1), Nixon's opponents in the Senate didn't see it that way. Instead, liberal senators—both Democrats and Republicans—viewed Haynsworth's ideology through the lens of civil rights.[14] And from this perspective Haynsworth was clearly more conservative than Burger. But at the time, it wasn't considered acceptable for a senator to publicly oppose a nominee purely on ideological grounds. There had to be something else, so Haynsworth's critics raised concerns about his ethics. In truth, when the Senate rejected him, it did so in a largely ideological vote.[15]

Nixon responded to the defeat by naming another southerner, G. Harrold Carswell, whose rating was more conservative than both Haynsworth's and Burger's. But again, the Senate—this time raising questions about the nominee's qualifications—rejected Nixon's nominee in a largely ideological vote.[16] It may have been unfair to Nixon's two rejected nominees—Haynsworth in particular[17]—to highlight ethical and qualification concerns in blocking their path to the high bench, but Senate liberals were unwilling to risk the Court's commitment to civil rights at a time of great uncertainty and unrest. Nixon thought the Senate rejected his choices because they hailed from the South, but given the easy confirmation of Virginia's Lewis Powell in 1971, it seems far more likely that opposing senators from both parties were motivated by genuine ideological unease about these "southern strategy" selections.[18] While Democratic control of the Senate meant more difficulty for Haynsworth and Carswell, both also fell victim to a divided GOP as Republican senators from more liberal states opposed their nominations: 40 percent opposed Haynsworth, and 32 percent opposed Carswell.[19] Of course, there's no way of knowing how Nixon's rejected southerners would have decided cases if they had made it onto the bench. But with Blackmun, the justice who eventually filled the Fortas seat, senators of all ideological stripes confirmed a jurist who undoubtedly helped to thwart the Court's move to the right on a host of issues. So, after casting aside his objectionable ideologues, Nixon capitulated to the Senate by naming Blackmun, thereby increasing the chance of a Court less conservative than many expected when he won election.

In 1987, when another Nixon justice, Lewis Powell, decided to retire from the bench, the Court had moved sufficiently to the conservative side of the ideological divide that he had assumed the mantle of the swing justice. This vacancy, therefore, presented President Ronald Reagan with a perfect opportunity to move the Court further to the right, and he sought to fill the seat with an ideological movement conservative. Reagan first nominated DC court of appeals Judge Robert Bork (Segal-Cover score of .095) to fill the Powell vacancy. The reaction from the Left was immediate and unequivocally critical, and an epic battle unfolded in the Senate. Indeed, when he heard Reagan's choice, Massachusetts Senator Ted Kennedy raced to the Senate floor to deliver a searing and memorable attack on Bork's brand of jurisprudence and what his confirmation would mean for the Court's decision-making and the nation as a whole: "Robert Bork's America is a land in which women would be forced into back alley abortions, blacks would sit at segregated lunch counters, rogue police could break down citizens' doors in midnight raids, school children could not be taught evolution, writers and artists could be censored at the whim of government, and the doors of the federal courts would be shut on the fingers of millions of citizens for whom the judiciary is—and is often the only—protector of the individual rights that are the heart of our democracy."[20]

The Reagan White House readied for the fight. But it was at a disadvantage. Democrats had retaken control of the Senate after the 1986 elections. Therefore, to secure Bork's confirmation, the White House had to ensure that Republicans backed Bork and convince conservative, mostly southern, Democrats to support him as well.

In the end, the first effort was successful. Compared to the Haynsworth and Carswell votes, Republicans largely supported their president's nominee. Just six GOP senators opposed him.[21] Southern Democrats, however, mostly rebuffed Reagan's ideological lure, as only one of the sixteen supported the nomination. Southern Democrats opposed Bork largely because of two factors: Republican advances in the South and the growing importance of the African American vote to Democratic success. While historically a region of comfortable general election victories for the Democratic Party, the rise of Republicanism in the South produced unprecedented stress for Democratic candidates seeking the Senate during this time. In fact, in 1980 southern voters helped the GOP take back the Senate—with a 53–47 majority—for the first time since 1954. While only two decades earlier Democrats had solidly controlled all twenty-two of the South's Senate seats, they now held only twelve.[22] To succeed in future elections Democratic candidates knew they had to alter their course.[23]

This was highly problematic for Robert Bork. Bork's ideology appealed to the traditional conservatism of white southerners, but he was not a southerner. Southern Democratic senators had overwhelmingly supported Rehnquist, who like Bork was a conservative ideologue from outside the South, in both his nominations. But things were different for them now.[24] In the 1986 Senate elections, Democratic candidates, working under new electoral math that emphasized moderation and biracial coalitions, won each of the South's seven races, powering their party's return to the majority.[25] And in 1987 the Bork vote emerged as "a 'litmus test' issue" for their Black constituents. It is easy to understand why. Bork was a well-known critic of the 1964 Civil Rights Act, the 1965 Voting Rights Act, and the Supreme Court ruling upholding the idea of "one person, one vote." These last two were essential for southern African Americans to secure the right to vote. Perhaps most alarming, in 1963, with the Civil Rights Act on the horizon, Bork had written that the prospect of forcing white business owners to serve African American customers was "a principle of unsurpassed ugliness."[26] Thus, while Bork's conservatism might have appealed to southern Democratic senators in the past, they now understood that a vote to confirm him would likely mean substantial constituent discontent. As the Democrat Senator John Breaux of Louisiana put it: "You can't vote maybe."[27] And in the end all but one voted "nay." Moreover, only one other Democrat joined that southerner as the Senate easily blocked Bork's confirmation, forty-two to fifty-eight.[28]

Much like Richard Nixon's choice of another (even more) conservative nominee after the Senate's rejection of Haynsworth, Ronald Reagan was not interested in retreating after the Bork defeat. Instead, he nominated Douglas Ginsburg, a forty-one-year DC court of appeals judge with a more conservative rating than Bork. In fact, at zero, he had the lowest rating possible.[29] Ginsburg's nomination, however, quickly derailed after revelations of his recreational use of marijuana as a Harvard Law School professor.

Instead of searching for yet another ideologue after Ginsburg's forced withdrawal, Reagan chose the more moderate Anthony Kennedy, a Ninth Circuit Court of Appeals judge. Kennedy had been the runner-up to Ginsburg after the Bork defeat largely because movement conservatives wondered about his commitment to their cause.[30] But with Ginsburg out, the president concluded that it was time to move on. As one reporter explained, "Reagan has finally yielded to the imperative of winning in the Senate. After the fiasco of Judge Douglas H. Ginsburg, he had to abandon his preference for a tamper-proof ideologue in the Robert H. Bork image."[31]

As with Haynsworth and Carswell, there is no way of knowing how Robert Bork would have voted if he had won Senate confirmation, although his post-nomination writings suggest he would have pursued a very conservative path.[32] For his part, after withdrawing his nomination Ginsburg stayed on the DC court of appeals for another twenty-four years and continued to vote in a solidly conservative fashion.[33] It is unlikely that either would have voted in the moderately conservative way Justice Kennedy did during his more than three decades on the high bench. According to Martin-Quinn scores, Kennedy was the swing justice for nearly two-thirds of the terms he served, and even crossed over to the liberal side of the ideological divide for two terms. These same scores suggest that over the course of his tenure he was less conservative than Reagan's other two additions to the Court, the movement conservative Antonin Scalia and Sandra Day O'Connor, who like Kennedy caused unease among those most committed to the conservative cause when President Reagan chose her in 1981 (see figure 4.1 and table 4.1).[34]

*

During the divided government era, there were nine occasions when the appointing president selected a more moderate nominee over a pure ideologue. These were "confirmable choice" nominees. At times, the president himself favored the more centrist selection from the start of the process, either because he strategically thought such a nominee advanced his electoral prospects or because his own views tended toward judicial moderation. But most of the time these choices were driven by a desire to avoid a confirmation battle in the Senate, out of a concern that such a fight would be electorally and legislatively damaging. Apart from Nixon's nominees, all these choices—by both Democratic and Republican presidents—fell between .250 and .750 on the Segal-Cover scale, meaning they were perceived as ideologically moderate when they were selected. And all nine won confirmation by overwhelming margins. In fact, the Senate confirmed four of the nine unanimously, and none had more than nine senators oppose them.

These nine confirmable choice nominees can be further divided into three types (table 4.1): two were chosen based on the appointing president's view of an ideal justice (Warren Burger and John Paul Stevens); two were symbolic selections thought to advance the president's electoral interests (Lewis Powell and Sandra Day O'Connor); and five were clear compromises based on confirmation concerns (Harry Blackmun, Anthony Kennedy, David Hackett Souter, Ruth Bader Ginsburg, and Stephen Breyer).

When President Richard Nixon introduced Warren Burger as his choice for chief justice, he beamed with pride, telling the audience his choice for "the most important nomination that a president of the United States makes during his term of office." With wavy white hair, Burger even looked the part. Nixon explained why the selection was so significant. "When we consider what a Chief Justice has in the way of influence on his age and the ages after him, I think it could fairly be said that our history tells us that our Chief Justices have probably had more profound and lasting influence on their times and on the direction of the nation than most Presidents have had."[35] Given the success of Nixon's "law-and-order" campaign for the presidency, Burger was perfect for him. During his thirteen years on the DC court of appeals, Burger, a Minnesotan, had earned a reputation as a judge who took a tough line on criminal law matters. But on civil rights, his record was more moderate.

Given Burger's record on the most politically salient judicial issues of the day, it would have been difficult for liberals in the Democrat-controlled Senate to oppose him. Two public opinion surveys had made clear why it was unwise to challenge a law-and-order judge even the editorial writers at the *New York Times* described as "moderately liberal" on civil rights and other noncriminal justice matters. A January 1969 Gallup poll revealed that 74.4 percent of respondents thought courts did not treat criminals "harshly enough." A paltry 1.9 percent thought courts were "too harsh" in dealing with criminals. Another Gallup poll, begun the day after Burger's nomination, showed 52 percent of respondents thought "conservatives" should fill vacancies on the Supreme Court. Only 25 percent thought "liberals" should be selected for them. Senate liberals had little reason to oppose Burger. Democrat Lee Metcalf of Montana, a liberal with a reputation as one of the Senate's "constitutional scholars," noted: "He's a better appointee than I had any right to expect. . . . Who knows, he might even be another Warren."[36] With reactions such as Metcalf's, Burger's confirmation was a comfortable one. After six weeks of consideration, the Senate confirmed him by a vote of seventy-four to three. However, he did not become another Warren. Rather, he was very much the type of justice Nixon expected, voting in a consistently conservative fashion during his seventeen years in the center chair (see figure 4.1 and table 4.1).

In 1975, William O. Douglas—the longest-serving justice ever and easily the most liberal since 1937[37]—retired from the bench. To replace him, Gerald Ford decided on a selection process that "placed a premium on professional considerations," more in line with the one used by President Dwight Eisenhower than with the one used by his immediate predecessor, Richard Nixon. In fact, Ford's process might best be described as anti-Nixonian, given that he sought to name "a nominee whose professional reputation put him outside the place of partisan political controversy."[38] And unlike his Republican successor in the White House, Ronald Reagan, Ford thought it was a "mistake" to choose a nominee based "on ideological grounds."[39] But as the political scientist David M. O'Brien writes, "even if Ford wanted to make an ideological appointment, he was in a poor position to do so. As an 'accidental president,' he had no pretense of claiming an electoral mandate and faced Democratic majorities in Congress." Ford was "determined to name a respected moderately conservative jurist in order to avoid the kind of political conflict that ensnarled Nixon's two ill-fated nominees," Haynsworth and Carswell.[40] The conservative Pat Buchanan thought the president should have chosen Robert Bork. But Buchanan understood Ford's reasoning for avoiding such an ideological choice, as he wanted to avoid a controversial nominee.[41] In the end, the president selected Seventh Circuit Court of Appeals Judge John Paul Stevens, and the Senate unanimously supported him after a relatively easy confirmation process. Almost immediately, Stevens veered from the moderate conservatism Ford expected of him, and in the 1976–77 term he crossed the ideological dividing line to the liberal side. When he retired in 2010, he was the most liberal justice on the bench, and had been so for nearly two decades.[42]

With symbolic selections, presidents had most often focused on the categories of geography, ethnicity, race, and religion to score political points with their Court nominees. Nixon's first attempt at a symbolic selection came with his nominations of southerners Haynsworth and Carswell. Even though both were defeated in the Senate, the Nixon administration nevertheless believed—for good reason—that those choices were politically beneficial, based on the reaction in the South.[43] In 1971, when Alabama native Hugo Black—the only southerner then serving—retired from the bench, President Nixon once again sought to select a southerner. This time he chose Lewis Powell of Virginia, who was widely considered to be "confirmable" because he was a well-respected attorney with moderate views on civil rights. Powell's age—sixty-four—and questionable health also meant he was not expected to serve for very long. While Powell's Segal-Cover score of .165 seems quite conservative, this rating was in fact the least conservative of all of Nixon's six nominees, and again, the Senate's view of a nominee's ideology at the time was more specifically focused on his commitment to civil rights. True to expectations, Powell's confirmation was a smooth one, with just one senator voting against him.[44] Also true to expectations, he was not a conservative ideologue. During his tenure on the bench, he voted in a remarkably consistent, moderately conservative fashion. In the last three terms of his tenure, the Court had moved sufficiently to the right to make him its swing justice.

He is perhaps best known for his decision in *Regents of the University of California v. Bakke*, in which he concluded—in contrast to his conservative brethren in dissent—that race-based affirmative action programs were constitutionally permissible if properly constructed.

The next symbolic selection added a new category to the traditional ones. Late in the 1980 presidential campaign, after advisors grew alarmed about an emerging gender gap that might threaten his path to victory, Republican nominee Ronald Reagan vowed that if elected he would nominate the first woman to the Supreme Court. Earlier, President Nixon had seriously considered the idea, believing it was an electorally smart strategy. In making his commitment "to make history," Reagan was hoping Nixon was right.[45] The new president kept his promise when, somewhat surprisingly, the seventy-year-old Justice Potter Stewart announced his retirement just five months after Reagan's inauguration day.

Sandra Day O'Connor, the front-runner for the seat, did not live up to the ideological hopes of conservatives, and in particular social conservatives. O'Connor, a judge on the second highest court in Arizona, had endorsed the Equal Rights Amendment and as a state legislator had voted to liberalize abortion laws and to expand the availability of contraception.[46] In fact, even before Reagan made his decision, conservatives denounced the possibility of an O'Connor appointment.[47] Despite this simmering conservative dissent, Reagan nominated O'Connor. In response to the news, Republican Senator Jesse Helms of North Carolina said he was "skeptical" of the nomination. Moral Majority leader Jerry Falwell thought it was "a disaster." The National Right to Life Committee believed it was "a repudiation of the Republican platform," and pledged an all-out fight to block O'Connor's confirmation. At the other end of the ideological spectrum, Democratic Congressman Morris Udall of Arizona concluded that O'Connor was "about as moderate a Republican as you'll ever find being appointed by Reagan." Massachusetts Senator Ted Kennedy declared the nomination "a major victory for women's rights."[48]

With his fiercest critics supporting the nomination and his closest allies expressing concern, Reagan worked hard to bring conservatives into line. He succeeded, as O'Connor sailed through the Senate without a dissenting vote, making her the first woman on the Court. Politically the Reagan White House considered the appointment a striking success.[49] But to movement conservatives in the Reagan Justice Department, O'Connor became "known derisively as an '80 percenter.' Though generally conservative, she deserted the administration at crucial moments."[50] Indeed, she spent about 40 percent of her twenty-five years on the Court as its swing justice. Most notably, she authored the 1992 plurality opinion in *Planned Parenthood v. Casey*, which upheld the right of a woman to terminate a pre-viability pregnancy announced in *Roe v. Wade* nearly two decades earlier.

Richard Nixon struggled mightily to fill the Fortas vacancy. Indeed, it would take him nearly a year to find a nominee the Senate was willing to confirm. With the Haynsworth and Carswell nominations Nixon had allowed his opponents to define the debate as one about protecting civil rights. Consequently, the Senate rejected these two symbolic ideologues. As noted above, on his third try he chose a different course by selecting the confirmable Harry Blackmun, a judge on the Eighth Circuit Court of Appeals. Senate liberals viewed Blackmun, like Burger, as a moderately conservative jurist who was unlikely to challenge the Warren Court's path-breaking civil rights decisions. And with good reason. The two men had known each other since kindergarten, and Blackmun had even served as best man at Burger's wedding. They became known as the Minnesota Twins and had the exact same Segal-Cover rating (.115). But the Senate was not focused on ideology in general; instead, the protection of civil rights, specifically, defined the debate. And as one newspaper account noted, Blackmun's opinions "stamp him as a moderate on civil rights and civil liberties issues . . . [and] more conservative on criminal suspects' constitutional claims."[51] Blackmun faced little resistance in the Senate, winning confirmation unanimously. Once on the Court, however, Blackmun charted his own path. Right from the start he was more liberal than the chief justice, although still the second most conservative member of the Court until the arrival of William Rehnquist in early 1972. He is most well known for authoring *Roe v. Wade* in 1973, a task given to him by Burger, who strategically joined the majority to control the writing assignment.[52] By 1977, Blackmun had moved sufficiently to the left to be the Court's swing justice. Two years later he crossed the ideological dividing line to become a liberal. When he retired in 1994, just one other justice—John Paul Stevens—voted in a more liberal fashion than him.[53]

After Douglas Ginsburg's withdrawal, Ronald Reagan decided to select a nominee unlikely to face a confirmation fight in the Senate. His choice was Ninth Circuit Judge Anthony Kennedy. Conservatives in the Reagan Justice Department raised concerns about Kennedy, fearing he might be another "80-percenter," like O'Connor. Justice Department memos highlight questions conservatives raised about his commitment to their principles. For example, in a memo outlining Kennedy's jurisprudence, Steve A. Matthews, Deputy Assistant Attorney General for Judicial Selection, found that "some of the most disturbing aspects of Judge Kennedy's jurisprudence" were with his use of "novel claims of constitutional protection." Perhaps foreshadowing Kennedy's precedent-altering LGBTQ-rights opinions in *Lawrence v. Texas* (2003) and *Obergefell v. Hodges* (2015), Matthews highlighted the judge's opinion in *Beller v. Middendorf*. For Matthews, Kennedy's *Beller* opinion was somewhat alarming for two reasons. First, he "very grudgingly upheld the validity of naval regulations prohibiting homosexual conduct." And in doing so, he "stated the rule much more narrowly than either the Constitution or precedent required." Second, Kennedy "cited *Roe v. Wade* and other 'privacy right' cases very favorably and indicated fairly strongly that he would not uphold the validity of laws prohibiting homosexual conduct outside the context of the military." To Matthews, "this easy acceptance of privacy rights as something guaranteed by the Constitution is really very distressing."[54]

While it is unknown if President Reagan read this memo, his administration was obviously willing to look beyond conservative concerns about Kennedy. And many who had opposed Robert Bork found Kennedy a refreshing alternative. For example, to the AFL-CIO's Lane Kirkland, "Judge Kennedy—in contrast to Judge Bork—show[ed] no sign of being attracted to eccentric and rigid theories of jurisprudence that would freeze the meaning of the Constitution by referring only to a simplified view of original intent." Rather, Kirkland expected Kennedy to follow a more traditional style of judging, by examining "our historical experiences and our broadly held social values" to give "practical meaning and modern application" to "the Constitution's expansive civil rights and civil liberties guarantees."[55]

Leading social conservatives focused on transforming the courts were not so pleased. For example, the longtime conservative activist Richard Viguerie considered the nomination "a total surrender to the Left."[56] But with Reagan White House opponents like Kirkland expressing support and Republican senators standing by their president, Kennedy won confirmation by a unanimous vote in the Democrat-controlled Senate. Republican strategists were thankful to avoid another Bork battle. Such a choice might have excited and activated the party's base, but it also threatened to offend GOP moderates and independent voters, particularly if the confirmation attracted widespread media attention that portrayed the president as a pawn of ideological zealots. As the political journalist Howard Fineman later noted, a Bork-like confirmation fight "reminds voters, baby boomers in particular, why there are things that they don't like about the Republican Party."[57]

In 1990, George Bush had his first chance to shape the Supreme Court with the selection of a new justice. The vacancy was a significant one. The longtime leader of the liberals, Justice William Brennan, was retiring from the Court. With the Democrats in control of the Senate and with the 1987 Bork defeat still a fresh memory, President Bush understood both the opportunity and the political difficulty of the selection. According to a senior advisor the president wanted "an absolutely unquestioned conservative," but he also wanted a "judge who is not known as having a national position on the abortion issue, who is not hard-core and clear on the issue of *Roe v. Wade*." In other words, it would be better if the nominee's views on *Roe* were "a little fuzzed-up." Robert Dole, the Senate minority leader, agreed: "If you have to have someone who wants to overturn *Roe versus Wade*, it's going to be a blood bath."[58]

After considering the possibilities, Bush chose David Hackett Souter, a First Circuit Court of Appeals judge. Unlike Bork, Souter had left little track record on the most important judicial issue of the day. The political scientist David Yalof explains: "In the twenty-two years since he had left private law practice, Souter had altogether avoided the subject of abortion rights, having never given a speech, written a law review article, or taken a public position of any kind on the correctness of *Roe v. Wade*. Thus, by the administration's way of thinking, Souter was the 'anti-Bork.'" The president settled on Souter, hoping he would be a "stealth conservative."[59] Souter's Segal-Cover score was .325 (table 4.1), placing him slightly to the right of Kennedy but well to the left of Bork and Ginsburg. Bush's choice pleased the Senate, which confirmed Souter ninety to nine.

Understanding Bush's "blank slate" strategy and with assurances from the president's chief of staff, John Sununu, who like Souter hailed from New Hampshire, conservative activists were "cautiously optimistic" about the selection. For example, Viguerie said "it appears that the president has kept his promise to appoint conservatives to the Supreme Court. Unfortunately, we won't know for sure until Justice Souter has been on the bench for a year or so."[60]

Within two years, conservatives knew more, and they were sorely disappointed. As one critic from the Right put it near the end of Souter's time on the bench, "a Republican president replaced William Brennan with a Brennan clone."[61] Most notably, in 1992 Souter joined with Reagan appointees O'Connor and Kennedy to uphold a more limited right for women to obtain an abortion in *Casey*. But Souter was different from O'Connor and Kennedy. He was easily more liberal than those two moderate conservatives (figure 4.1 and table 4.1). Over time he became a consistent member of the liberal bloc. Never a fan of living and working in Washington, the sixty-nine-year-old Souter retired in 2009 after nineteen years on the bench, a comparatively short term by today's standards. "It was true that Souter wanted to return to New Hampshire," the legal journalist Jeffrey Toobin explains about the justice's decision, "but the reasons were harsher, and uglier, than a simple longing for the White Mountains. He abhorred the views of [Chief Justice John] Roberts and [Associate Justice Samuel] Alito. Souter didn't like what the Republican Party—his party—was doing to the Court, or to the country."[62] The need to find a nominee with an ideology the Bush White House was not entirely certain of displays the power of the Senate during the divided government era. That power was also apparent for the one Democratic president to appoint justices to the high bench during this period, but it would not extend into the twenty-first century.

✳

During the divided government era, only two Democratic candidates won the presidency: Jimmy Carter in 1976 and Bill Clinton in 1992 and 1996. However, there were no vacancies during Carter's four years in the Oval Office, resulting in a twenty-six-year gap between selections of a justice by a Democratic president.[63] Before deciding on his first nominee, President Clinton considered an array of possibilities in a process that stretched on for three months. Clinton was enamored with the idea of naming a leading politician—in the tradition of Earl Warren—and seriously considered New York Governor Mario Cuomo and former Arizona governor and then Interior Secretary Bruce Babbitt.

The president was not really interested in appointing a liberal ideologue, and his ultimate selection of Ruth Bader Ginsburg—a DC Circuit Court of Appeals judge—was viewed as a moderate choice with a Segal-Cover score of .680. In fact, because of her criticism of *Roe* (see chapter 8), liberal women's rights groups did not champion Ginsburg's candidacy, even though she had played a major role as an activist attorney who advanced the cause of gender equality. Even with that background, she was expected to face a friendlier Senate than either Babbitt or Cuomo. And once President Clinton had an opportunity to speak with Ginsburg, he reportedly "fell in love" with her and her story of successfully rising through the ranks of the male-dominated legal world.[64] True to expectations, Ginsburg won easy confirmation, ninety-six to three. During her time on the Court, she moved to the left of the ideological divide, and at the end of her life was most frequently the Court's second most liberal justice.

A year after the Ginsburg nomination, President Clinton had another opportunity to fill a seat on the Court. Similar to the process with the first vacancy, Clinton began by focusing on finding a "big-name politician," like Senate majority leader George Mitchell, who had recently announced he would not seek reelection. But Mitchell did not want to complicate Clinton's healthcare agenda in Congress and refused the nomination. Babbitt was considered again, but he was at odds with some western senators, including Republican Orrin Hatch of Utah, who was an influential member of the Judiciary Committee. Although the Democrats controlled the Senate, according to Yalof, the president "hoped to find a candidate who could be easily confirmed without upsetting the administration's delicate relations with Congress." In the end, Clinton chose the candidate who had been the runner-up to Ginsburg the year before—Stephen Breyer, the chief judge on the First Circuit Court of Appeals. Like Ginsburg, White House insiders viewed Breyer as a choice who would win easy confirmation. He had worked on Capitol Hill for the Senate Judiciary Committee and had the support of key committee members, including former chair Ted Kennedy and Hatch.[65] His confirmation was uneventful, as senators approved him eighty-seven to nine. After taking his seat on the Court, Breyer voted in a consistently moderately liberal fashion. In this sense, he has voted as expected.

✶

There were exceptions to the kinds of nominees I've described thus far—those that were expected to move the Court to the right and were nevertheless confirmed by the Senate. I call these nominees "acceptable ideologues." If Nixon's template for nominees was to favor electoral goals and pragmatism over ideology, then President Reagan's was to advance movement conservativism on the Court. Unlike Nixon, Reagan (and his advisors)—particularly in his second term—believed that the conservative political movement was sufficiently strong that they did not have to worry so much about being punished at the polls if they tried to create a deeply conservative Court.[66] The Robert Bork and Douglas Ginsburg nominations fit with this "movement template," as do the three choices here. The first of these, however, was not originally a Reagan selection, but one made by the less ideologically focused Nixon. In fact, I refer to the selection of William Rehnquist as Nixon's "accidental ideologue."[67] While the president would have preferred a nominee who packed a political punch, the changing confirmation dynamics led him to change course (more on this in chapter 6). He chose Rehnquist largely based on his credentials rather than his unflinching commitment to conservatism. In contrast, fifteen years later, President Reagan chose to elevate Rehnquist to chief precisely because of his record on the Court as a movement conservative.

En route to deciding on Lewis Powell of Virginia to fill one of the vacancies open in the autumn of 1971, Nixon toyed with a range of symbolic possibilities for the second seat, including another southerner, a woman, and an "ethnic Catholic." Frustrated by the reaction to a trial balloon list of six possible candidates—who were dismissed as "not so supreme"—Nixon decided instead to focus on quality over political symbolism.[68] The result was William Rehnquist. Even though he was serving in the Nixon Justice Department as assistant attorney general in the office of legal counsel, the president did not know him. And despite Nixon's desire to score political points with his selections, Rehnquist was symbolically insignificant. In fact, the president complained that he was a "damn Protestant," and even joked that his future justice should get a sex change.[69] But Rehnquist had a reputation for being a committed conservative with a sharp mind. And after criticisms that the president favored mediocrity over excellence, Nixon decided against a symbolic choice. He would use the mediocrity label against his enemies in the Senate by selecting a nominee with impressive credentials. Concerned with what they viewed as Rehnquist's extreme conservatism, Senate liberals contested the nomination. But unlike the failures with Haynsworth and Carswell, the Nixon White House was able to convince Senate Republicans to support the choice.[70] Most southern and border state Democrats went along as well.[71] In a comparatively close vote for the time, the Democrat-controlled Senate confirmed Rehnquist sixty-eight to twenty-six. And while Nixon initially chose Rehnquist to counter claims that he favored mediocre jurists for the Court, after the future chief justice won Senate confirmation the president instructed his attorney general "to emphasize to all the southerners that Rehnquist is a reactionary bastard."[72] In this sense, although Nixon had selected Virginia's Lewis Powell as his "southerner," he wanted to use the Rehnquist choice to appeal to voters below the Mason-Dixon Line as well.

When President Reagan sought to elevate Rehnquist to chief in 1986, success was once again dependent on nearly unified Republican support combined with some southern Democratic support. In fact, barring a filibuster, a unified Republican majority could confirm him without any Democratic support.[73] As they had in 1971, Senate liberals contested Rehnquist's nomination. While they preferred that Rehnquist not occupy the Court's center chair, their main objections were defined by his ideology and not his location on the bench. In particular, Rehnquist's Senate detractors, led by Ted Kennedy, thought the future chief justice was too far to the right to lead the Court. As Kennedy declared, Rehnquist's "own record of massive isolated dissent" demonstrated that "he is too extreme on race, too extreme on women's rights, too extreme on freedom of speech, too extreme on separation of church and state, too extreme to be Chief Justice."[74] It was true that Rehnquist was so eager to advance the conservative cause that he often wrote alone in dissent, earning the moniker "the lone ranger." And according to the Martin-Quinn scores, Rehnquist was easily the most conservative justice to serve since 1937. In fact, he remains the only justice to score above a 4.0 rating for a term. And he earned that score for eleven straight terms (from 1973–74 to 1983–84).[75] But the campaign against Rehnquist was geared more toward denying him the opportunity to serve as chief justice—since he would retain his seat on the high bench if the Senate didn't approve his elevation—and on highlighting to the public the Reagan administration's brand of judicial thinking.[76] As the constitutional scholar and soon-to-be Yale University President Benno C. Schmidt Jr. wrote at the time: "the question is whether [Rehnquist's] reactionary constitutional vision is so out of touch with that of his colleagues and the temper of the times that all his powers of intellect and personality cannot overcome the essential isolation that has been the overriding characteristic of his service on the Court to date."[77]

At the time, however, ideology alone was still not sufficient to undermine a nominee's candidacy. So, in addition, Rehnquist's liberal critics highlighted the fact that he owned property with constitutionally invalid restrictive covenants, had as a clerk to Justice Robert Jackson written a memo of dissent for the historic *Brown* decision in 1954, and had as a young man participated in voter suppression (a charge he denied).[78] In the end, Rehnquist was able to adequately deflect these criticisms to win confirmation in another contested vote, sixty-five to thirty-three. Significantly, Republicans largely held together, with only two of the fifty-one in their ranks voting in opposition. Southern Democrats overwhelmingly supported him as well.[79] Even so, it was a close vote and Rehnquist earned the distinction of becoming the chief justice with the highest number of senators opposing his confirmation, a record that stands to this day.

Reagan's decision to elevate Rehnquist was a turning point in Court nominations. Reagan's choice of Rehnquist was different from Nixon's because he chose the sitting associate justice for purely ideological reasons. Nixon was not thinking in these broad ideological terms, preferring a more targeted strike at the most politically unpopular aspects of the Warren Court revolution. In addition to choosing Rehnquist for his indisputable commitment to conservativism, Reagan—and key players in his administration believed (incorrectly) that he would not shift to the left if he moved to the Court's center seat.[80] The following year, Reagan chose Bork and Ginsburg for similar ideological reasons. But things had changed by that point. Most significantly, in the 1986 midterm elections Democrats regained control of the Senate. They could now block—or "Bork"[81]—a nominee selected solely because his views challenged mainstream constitutional thought.

While Rehnquist's elevation was an example of a president deciding against a symbolic selection in hopes of advancing conservative doctrine, there were two other occasions during this era when symbolism and ideological purity aligned. In both cases, the appointing Republican president was able to name a very conservative nominee who secured confirmation. The first occurred in

1986 when President Reagan chose Antonin Scalia for the vacancy created by
Rehnquist's elevation to chief. Reagan had compromised with his selection of
O'Connor, but now in his second term, he displayed a keener commitment to
conservative constitutional change.

The choice to fill the Rehnquist vacancy came down to two candidates:
Scalia and Bork. Both were leading conservative thinkers sitting on the DC
court of appeals who were expected to transform their ideas into doctrine
if selected and confirmed for the high bench. Scalia had the advantage of
being younger and healthier. Bork had more extensive administrative experience, particularly given his service as solicitor general in the Nixon and
Ford administrations (and his brief tenure as acting attorney general after the
"Saturday Night Massacre"[82]). The White House thought Scalia would have
an easier time winning Senate confirmation, in part because he would be the
first Italian American ever appointed to the Court.[83] The Scalia biographer
Joan Biskupic writes, "Scalia's personal story as the son of a Sicilian who had
come to America through Ellis Island, in the shadow of Bartholdi's Statue of
Liberty, was captivating." Inside the White House, Pat Buchanan made the
electoral case for naming Scalia: "He is an Italian-American, a Roman Catholic, who would be the first ever nominated—a tremendous achievement for
what is America's largest ethnic minority, not yet fully assimilated into the
melting pot—a minority which provides the GOP its crucial margins of victory in New Jersey, Connecticut and New York."[84] For his part, Scalia believed
that his ethnicity made a significant difference in the Senate's unanimous vote
for his confirmation. He spoke on the issue in a documentary about Italian
Americans:

> You know, I was confirmed 98 to nothing. Okay. I hope some of that is because
> I was so doggone well qualified. But I later came to understand that a lot of
> it was simply because it meant so much to Italian Americans because of this
> Mafioso thing that they have hung around their neck; it meant so much to
> them to have an Italian American on the Supreme Court. Many of the sena-
> tors who might otherwise have voted against me came from states with a large
> Italian American population. I'm sure they were aware of it. I think for Ital-
> ian Americans, given what they most abhor, which is their identification with
> crime and the mafia, I wouldn't be surprised if they would be more proud to
> have an Italian American justice than to have an Italian American president.
> It meant an awful lot to them.[85]

Scalia was the first nominee to receive the most conservative Segal-
Cover score possible: a .000.[86] But Senate liberals, focused more on resisting
Rehnquist's elevation to chief and the political costs of blocking the path of

an Italian American to the high bench, chose not to put up a fight. Once on the Court, Scalia lived up to his reputation as a conservative of the first order. However, according to the Martin-Quinn scores, he was never the most conservative justice on the Court. That distinction belonged to Rehnquist during Scalia's early years, and then to the last Republican appointee of the period, Clarence Thomas.

In 1991, President George Bush spied an opportunity. In filling the vacancy created by the retirement of Thurgood Marshall, the first and only African American justice, the president figured he could circumvent a confirmation process that seemingly demanded the selection of a moderate who was acceptable to the Democrat-controlled Senate. Bush calculated that if he chose well, he could nominate a steadfast but still confirmable conservative. He decided on Clarence Thomas, a forty-three-year-old DC court of appeals judge whom Bush termed "the best qualified" person for the job. The choice greatly pleased conservatives concerned about the last two Republican selections, Kennedy and Souter. Thomas, an African American from Georgia, had earned a reputation in Washington as an unflinching conservative ideologue.[87] From a strategic perspective, the choice was designed to put the Democrats on the defensive, since the Bush White House believed liberals would be wary of opposing just the second Black American ever named to the Court. And even if they did vote against Thomas, conservative southern Democrats, who were more ideologically inclined to support him, would not be eager to join them because of the large Black constituencies in their states. In other words, the changing nature of southern politics, which had hurt Bork's chances at confirmation, might just help Thomas's Senate fortunes. Ultimately this strategy succeeded, as senators confirmed Thomas in one of the narrowest margins in history, fifty-two to forty-eight.[88] Notably, nine of the eleven Democrats supporting him were southerners. Another was from the border state of Oklahoma. In short, Thomas's race and ideology allowed these southern Democrats to maintain, and possibly expand, the biracial coalitions that had elected them to office.[89] They weren't prepared to pass on that chance. Ever since he took his seat on the high bench, Justice Thomas has met and even exceeded conservative expectations with his decisions. According to Martin-Quinn scores, he has been the most conservative justice every term of his tenure, some years by a substantial margin.

✱

Rehnquist, Scalia, and Thomas, however, were the exceptions that prove the rule. For much of the divided government era, presidents did not choose ideologues for the Court, deciding instead on nominees who would have an easier path to Senate confirmation and at times also to advance their electoral prospects and legislative priorities. Ideology certainly mattered on these occasions, but it did not dictate the choices.[90] Despite the hopes of conservative supporters, Democratic control of the Senate during much of this era, and GOP fragmentation in the early part of it, meant that Republican presidents could not pursue a straight ideological course. In this sense the Senate effectively moderated the Court toward the "mainstreams" of American values and away from movement conservative ideology, even when presidents had won substantial electoral victories.

There is no doubt that the justices appointed by Presidents Ronald Reagan and George H. W. Bush pushed the Court to the right. Nevertheless, even with their five additions to the high bench, and Reagan's elevation of Rehnquist, the Court did not deliver the type of conservative doctrine many of their supporters had hoped for. Indeed, when the Rehnquist Court came to an end on September 3, 2005, with the death of the chief, commentators offered mixed assessments of its success in pursuing conservative ends. To most, while the nearly twenty years of the Rehnquist Court represented a clear advance of conservative principles, it nevertheless fell short of achieving an ideologically consistent doctrine.

In considering the limited nature of the Rehnquist Court's conservatism, scholars from both ends of the ideological spectrum have focused on the divide among its Republican-appointed members. For example, Mark Tushnet—a constitutional scholar from the Left—argued that the "two types of Republican" justices drove this result. To him, the Rehnquist Court's "divisions meant that conservatives prevailed—more or less—on issues associated with the Republican Party's effort to scale down the size of government, while losing rather consistently on the social issues—abortion, gay rights, and affirmative action—that animated an important part of the party's base." Social conservatives' "actual accomplishments have been meager because they [were] thwarted, not by activist liberals or by Democrats but by Republicans uneasy about the Republican cultural agenda."[91] In analyzing six (largely social) "battleground issues," Richard E. Morgan—a constitutional scholar from the Right—largely agreed with Tushnet's conclusions about the extent of the social conservative failure and its political origins. Morgan even put a date on the conservative demise: June 29, 1992. "On that day the long-awaited decision in *Planned Parenthood v. Casey* was handed down, explicitly reaffirming the core holding of *Roe v. Wade*," that a woman has a constitutional right to terminate an unwanted pregnancy. "With this decision," he concluded, "the conservative constitutional insurgency . . . ended in a virtual rout." To Morgan, the reason for this result was clear. "The *blame* belongs mainly to the

presidents who nominated the Rehnquist Court's wavering justices."[92] The
political scientists Jeffrey Segal and Harold Spaeth reach a similar conclusion
in discussing President Ronald Reagan's impact, specifically. They write,

> Few Presidents had the potential opportunity to influence the Supreme Court
> that Ronald Wilson Reagan did. The conservative Republican reached out again
> and again to social conservatives, calling for the return of school prayer and
> the overruling of *Roe v. Wade*. Fate *smiled* upon the fortieth President, granting
> him four appointees to the High Court and hundreds of appointees to the lower
> federal courts. Yet the Supreme Court he left was no more conservative than
> the one he inherited. Moreover, despite his appointments, the twentieth century
> ended with school prayer unconstitutional and *Roe v. Wade* the law of the land.[93]

Unfortunately, just about everything Segal and Spaeth write in the quote
above is inaccurate. First, Reagan only added three new members to the
Court, not the four they imply. Rehnquist just switched seats after his elevation to chief. That move, of course, did not afford the president an opportunity to alter the Court's ideological makeup.

Second, starting from the presidency of Franklin D. Roosevelt, nearly every president (or combination of presidents due to the death or resignation
of the first) who served two terms had more vacancies to fill than Reagan did.
While there was not a single vacancy in FDR's first term,[94] in the eight years
of his second and third terms he was able to replace seven of the justices.[95] In
the next two terms—FDR's final few months before his death and the entirety
of Harry Truman's presidency—there were four vacancies on the Court. In
Dwight D. Eisenhower's two terms there were five Court vacancies, as there
were during the eight years of the Richard Nixon and Gerald Ford presidencies. The only two-term period with just three vacancies—like Reagan—
occurred during the presidencies of John F. Kennedy and Lyndon B. Johnson.
And in fact, each of those presidents named two men to the Court. However,
one of LBJ's choices filled the seat of one of JFK's justices who resigned from
the high bench after just three years of service.[96] Significantly, the three retiring justices during the JFK and LBJ years were three of its four most conservative members in the 1960–61 term, thereby allowing these liberal presidents
a prime opportunity to push the Court to the left.[97] But in Reagan's case, the
fact that the three retiring justices were three of the four most conservative
members of the Court in the 1980–81 term meant that he had no such opportunity.[98] So, compared to other administrations that preceded him, it would
be far more accurate to write that "fate" *frowned* "upon the fortieth president."

Third, despite the conservative nature of the retiring justices, according to
the Martin-Quinn scores the Supreme Court was noticeably more conservative

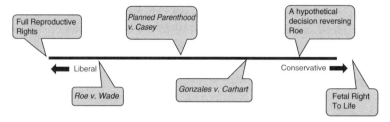

FIGURE 4.2. Range of Ideological Possibilities for Court Decisions on Abortion

when Reagan left the White House than when he entered it. Specifically, at the end of the 1980–81 term, the swing justice's rating was a .168. Eight years later, at the end of the 1988–89 term, the swing justice's score was a 1.057, a shift of almost an entire point to the conservative side of the ideological spectrum. To be sure, this was due to the movement of Byron White—the swing justice in both years—to the right during the 1980s. Nevertheless, it is factually incorrect for Segal and Spaeth to conclude that "the Supreme Court [Reagan] left was no more conservative than the one he inherited." Those words unduly discount the possibility that the Reagan Justice Department's litigation strategy convinced justices like White to endorse its positions. It also ignores the fact that the two Reagan justices appointed during Republican control of the Senate were more conservative than the retiring justices they replaced during their tenures on the high bench (O'Connor and Scalia for Stewart and Burger, respectively). And the third, appointed under a Democratic Senate, was only slightly more liberal than the man he succeeded (Kennedy for Powell).

Of course, Segal and Spaeth were right to conclude that "the twentieth century ended with school prayer unconstitutional and *Roe v. Wade* the law of the land." But their characterization of the religious establishment and abortion doctrines ignores the real gains made by conservatives in those areas of the law. Morgan makes the same mistake. Writing in 2006, he seemingly disregards the Rehnquist Court's notable advances in the nearly decade and a half after 1992, the year he marks as the end of the "conservative constitutional insurgency." Those doctrinal shifts certainly did not go as far as politicians like Reagan had promised, but the march toward the conservative end goals continued at a steady pace as the divided government era ended and the period of polarization began. For example, in a 2016 article, Thomas Keck and I illustrated the progress conservatives made in undermining the right to choose, even though *Roe* still stood.[99] As figure 4.2 shows, Rehnquist Court decisions on abortion clearly restricted a woman's right to choose.

It is clear why the Court advanced a more conservative position on abortion but did not go so far as to overturn *Roe* before Donald Trump named three new justices. As this analysis of the individual nominations shows, Republican presidents rarely sought to name the most ideologically pure nominee during the divided government era. Even Reagan—who was easily the most committed to movement conservatism—nominated two non-ideologues in O'Connor and Kennedy. While it is easy to assess the ideological advance of a Court via an analysis of an administration's selections—especially with the advent of the Martin-Quinn scores—presidents do not often operate in such a simplistic space. Instead, presidential policies toward the judiciary are typically far more sophisticated than a blind pursuit of ideological purity.[100] A variety of things matter in deciding whom to choose for the Court. Ideology is one item, but not the only one.

It also mattered that eight of the ten Supreme Court vacancies filled by Republican presidents during this era occurred when Democrats held control of the Senate. Only two of the eight justices who ultimately occupied these seats could accurately be defined as conservative ideologues (Rehnquist in 1971 and Thomas twenty years later), and both had to survive a contentious confirmation. Significantly, neither faced a filibuster as Fortas did in 1968.[101] But the filibuster was still a possibility then—unlike today.

In other words, Senate resistance was a highly significant moderating force during the divided government era. It meant that Republican administrations devoted to pushing the Court to the right would be limited in their ability to succeed. But this was not just a tale of divided government. Liberal forces in the GOP helped defeat every nominee rejected by the Senate during this period. Specifically, between 13 and 40 percent of senators from the president's party voted against those three confirmations.[102] For the only Democratic president to make High Court appointments, the Senate also played a moderating role. Even though his party controlled fifty-seven and then fifty-six seats in that chamber when he named those nominees, President Bill Clinton feared a potential filibuster if he chose a liberal ideologue. He decided against doing so with both selections.

Earlier in the twentieth century, presidents were able to shape the Court more successfully largely because of party dominance, just as the regime politics literature would hypothesize. But by the time of the Ronald Reagan and George Bush presidencies, such dominance no longer existed. Even though they both won the White House with decisive victories, their pursuit of a more conservative Court coincided with either divided government or narrow Republican majorities in the Senate. In turn, their success was bound to be more limited.

With this in mind, McCloskey's 1960 argument that the Court "seldom strayed very far from the mainstreams of American life" is an accurate description of the justices' work during the era of divided government. The justices advanced some movement conservative ideas, but on a more limited basis than its fiercest advocates desired. It also took some liberal turns, particularly on pressing social issues such as marriage equality. Indeed, the very criticism from the Right about the Rehnquist Court's limited conservatism helps make the case that the justices neither "lagged far behind nor forged far ahead of America."[103]

But this alignment that McCloskey suggests between the Court and the country was about to change, as Senate influence over who would sit on the High Court took a turn. With the confirmation of the first numerical minority justice, Clarence Thomas—supported by a majority of senators who had garnered fewer votes in their most recent elections than those in opposition—a new politics of Supreme Court confirmations was on the horizon. Presidents would need to be less concerned about pleasing senators from the opposing party, and more focused on making sure those in their own party were sufficiently satisfied with their choices for the Court. And in time, they would no longer need to worry about the filibuster, allowing one unified party—no matter the size of the Senate majority—the ability to dictate the course of constitutional law despite a lack of support from the majority of voters.

Polarized Politics and the Court's Legitimacy Paradox

Everyone—even her opponent, Donald Trump—thought that Hillary Rodham Clinton, the former first lady, New York senator, and secretary of state, would win the presidency in 2016.[1] But as the results started rolling in on election night, the inevitability of a Hillary Clinton presidency came undone. Trump scored three extremely narrow victories in states where Democrats were thought to have constructed a "blue wall" to guard against a red Republican onslaught. The reasons for Trump's wins in Michigan, Pennsylvania, and Wisconsin—all by less than 1 percent—will be dissected and debated for years to come. But those victories meant that despite Clinton's 2.8-million-vote lead in the popular vote, the Manhattan real estate developer and reality TV star would become the nation's 45th president, and would consequently have the opportunity to shape the Supreme Court with at least one—and likely more—appointments.

President Trump would ultimately fill three vacancies on the Court. And unlike presidents from the divided government era, Trump did not consider choosing a compromise candidate, either for symbolic purposes or in an attempt to appeal to Senate Democrats. To the contrary, what's particularly striking about the makeup of the Court's current conservative majority in comparison to the Burger and Rehnquist Courts is that it's been largely constructed during a period of *weak* Republican performance in presidential elections. Republican candidates did extraordinarily well in the six presidential contests between 1968 and 1988—they won five of them, four by clear or near landslides. Yet, since these Republican presidents usually faced a Democratic Senate (with the power of the filibuster) and/or a divided GOP, they were unable to construct Supreme Courts that satisfied their party's deepest conservative desires.

Compare that record to the last eight presidential races—from 1992 to 2020. As noted earlier, Republican presidential candidates have lost the popular vote in seven of those eight contests. The highest percentage a Republican nominee received was the only GOP popular-vote victory of the eight, when George W. Bush captured 50.7 percent of the vote in 2004. Nevertheless, with the benefit of our Electoral College system, a more ideologically cohesive GOP Senate majority, and most recently, the end of the filibuster for Supreme Court nominees, Bush and Trump were able to successfully appoint jurists expected to be much more conservative than most of the Republican-appointed justices of the divided government era.

In other words, *weaker* Republican performance at the presidential polls combined with the Senate's confirmation of numerical minority justices has produced *greater* success for conservatism on the Supreme Court. It's the Court's legitimacy paradox: weaker claims to democratic legitimacy have yielded a *more* ideologically driven, conservative Court. Dahl's thesis that the Court is not an institution "in which the policy preferences of minorities prevail over majorities" seemingly no longer applies.[2] The tie between democratic majoritarianism and the Court's doctrinal commitments has been severed.[3] This is unprecedented. Past Supreme Courts have simply not been constructed in such a fashion, making this Court unlike any other in American history.

*

After the confirmation of Stephen Breyer in 1994, the Supreme Court went unchanged for close to eleven years, the longest period of time since the early part of the nineteenth century (when there were two fewer justices).[4] Then, on the first day of July 2005, Justice Sandra Day O'Connor announced her retirement. Chief Justice William Rehnquist died two months later, on September 3. With the Senate in the hands of the GOP, Republican President George W. Bush had an opportunity to shift the Court to the right. To fill the O'Connor vacancy, Bush first chose John Roberts, a judge on the DC court of appeals. But after Rehnquist's death, the president withdrew Roberts's name for that seat and re-nominated him for the Court's center chair. Working under the unwritten rules of the previous era, Bush then searched for a symbolic nominee who was both conservative and easily confirmable. He settled on White House counsel and fellow Texan Harriett Miers. Her nomination, however, did not go well—to say the least. Indeed, the treatment of Miers by members of the president's own party would redefine the politics of choosing and confirming justices for the Supreme Court, favoring ideological certainty over all else. In this sense, the ill-fated Miers nomination represents the best example of a confirmation process divorced from majoritarian politics. Bush, the only Republican president to win the popular vote in the last twenty-eight years of elections—from 1992 to 2020—chose a nominee who had bipartisan backing in the Senate less than a year after he had won reelection. Nevertheless, Miers was upended by a group of unelected conservatives. The president then begrudgingly named a conservative ideologue—Samuel Alito—who only secured confirmation with the support of senators who won fewer votes in their most recent elections than those in opposition. Seventeen years later, Alito would author the opinion overturning *Roe*, despite widespread popular support for that ruling and, according to many legal experts, its status as a "super-precedent"—meaning the justices had repeatedly reaffirmed it over many years.[5]

✳

George W. Bush apparently agreed with the appraisals that the Rehnquist Court had failed to deliver the doctrine conservatives desired. Thus, as president, he sought to change the Court by filling the two vacancies with unflinching conservatives. According to the legal journalist Jan Crawford Greenburg, the president was almost obsessed in this moment with avoiding the misstep his father had made fifteen years earlier with the selection of David Souter.[6]

Conservative activists, who had been told to trust the first President Bush's choice, were angry when Souter proved to be nothing like the rock-solid conservative they'd been promised. They considered the Souter nomination "one of the most inept political decisions of any modern-day president."[7] So, even before he became president, the younger Bush set out to distinguish himself from his father by identifying the Court's two most conservative members, Justices Antonin Scalia and Clarence Thomas, as models to guide his own selections.[8]

Such thinking was a godsend to movement conservatives. To them, Souter wasn't the only problem. O'Connor and Kennedy were also clear Republican failures, deserters of their declared revolution in constitutional law.[9] But now, in 2005, with Republicans in control of the Senate and a conservative in the White House, most on the Right assumed the jurists this President Bush would choose would be much different. They would be ideologically reliable conservatives that Republican senators could support with unbounded enthusiasm. By this time conservatives also believed the electoral math had changed in their favor. Unlike Nixon, who was concerned that a broad-based attack on the Court's liberalism would decimate his party's electoral chances, by the Reagan years many in the GOP—although certainly not all—thought the party could weather conservative decisions overturning *Roe* and other liberal rulings. By the beginning of the twenty-first century, many Republicans had grown even more confident, believing an ideologically aggressive conservative Court would actually *enhance* their party's odds at the polls.[10]

For conservatives, 2005 was a heady time in Washington. President Bush had just won reelection by capturing over 62 million votes—more than any other presidential candidate in the nation's history—and had won fifteen states with more than 59 percent of the vote. He had done so, moreover, not by pandering to the "swing" voter but by pursuing a "base strategy" that highlighted a conservative message designed to turn out ideologically sympathetic supporters in record numbers.[11] It was a strategy Donald Trump would take to a new level in winning the presidency in 2016 (see chapter 10). Following Bush's reelection in 2004, talk of a Republican realignment akin to that of 1896 filled the political air.[12] In addition to Bush's victory, Republicans now controlled fifty-five Senate seats and nearly 54 percent of the House of Representatives. Democrats appeared to be on the ropes, especially considering that six Democratic senators represented states Bush had won decisively. With those seats in hand, Republicans would command a filibuster-proof margin in the Senate.

Given this level of success at the polls, conservatives were not in the mood to compromise. After trusting previous Republican presidents only to be disappointed once their nominees became justices, they were disinclined to give Bush the leeway they had afforded his father, even though it was widely assumed the president was committed to their cause. With his first selection of John Roberts (with a Segal-Cover score of .120), conservatives thought the president had scored big. In their eyes, once confirmed a Justice Roberts would easily make the Court more conservative than it had been with O'Connor. But then Chief Justice Rehnquist died, and the Bush White House had to find a second nominee.

The president acted swiftly on one of the seats, shifting Roberts's nomination from the associate slot to the chief justice position. As the search for another nominee began, Bush appeared quite concerned about one of the few criticisms of his decision to replace O'Connor with Roberts, a white man. As none other than O'Connor herself put it, Roberts is "good in every way, except he's not a woman."[13] First Lady Laura Bush concurred, saying she thought her husband should appoint a woman to the Court. The *New York Times* reported that the first lady's comments were actually a reflection of the president's own thinking—namely, that he understood the political symbolism of not replacing O'Connor with a woman the first time and was now focusing his search on finding a conservative who could fill the bill. (Bush later confirmed the veracity of this story in his memoir.)[14] In the *Times* story, unnamed Republicans listed the reasons why choosing a woman was wise. These included:

Democrats would have more difficulty "demonizing" a female nominee; the confirmation process would be easier because Democrats would be less harsh in their attacks; and given that there was only one woman remaining on the Court, it was the politically astute thing to do.[15]

Within the White House counsel's office, staff lawyers were struck by the president's focus on diversity. As Greenburg writes, "Those lawyers—typically smart young conservatives who'd clerked for Thomas or Kennedy or Scalia or Rehnquist and opposed affirmative action like their former bosses—often were surprised to see the premium Bush put on diversity. 'I don't see any women on here,' Bush would say, with displeasure, if a list of executive branch nominees had only male names." And after Rehnquist died, the president took a similar stance for potential choices for the Court, rejecting the advice of lawyers in the counsel's office who urged him to select the runner-up to Roberts, Samuel Alito.[16] Thinking politically, the president wanted either a woman or a minority. As his chief of staff, Andy Card, put it bluntly, "No white guys."[17] Bush's thinking may have confounded conservatives in the White House, but it should not be surprising. Put simply, Bush was not exclusively focused on ideology. Although he truly believed Miers was deeply conservative, he privileged the potential political impact of his selection. In this sense, he was acting under the governing principles of the previous era of divided government.

A review of the pool of potential candidates, however, made clear that the choices were limited. In the end, the president settled on Miers, who was overseeing the search for a second nominee and was unaware that she was even being considered for the position until Bush had nearly made up his mind. Miers—and many others—had good reasons for not thinking she was a leading candidate. She had had a successful legal career but did not possess the credentials of John Roberts or Samuel Alito (or any of the others who were seriously considered for the first vacancy). But to the president, this lack of a track record was not important because he knew Miers, knew "her heart," knew "her character."[18] As he put it, she was "tough as nails," a "pit bull in size six shoes."[19] In his mind, there was no chance she would drift to the left like O'Connor, Kennedy, and Souter. Greenburg elaborates on the president's thinking, and how much he had Justice Souter on his mind when he made his decision:

> Beyond the political expediency, Bush was also satisfied that she was capable. After all, his legal advisers had assured him she was qualified for the job. And . . . Bush knew his friend was smart and tough enough to remain steadfast

under pressure. . . . It's impossible to overstate how much the last concern drove Bush's thinking on Miers. He was determined not to repeat his father's mistake with Souter. . . . Bush thought Miers was in the mold of Thomas and Scalia, and he could be sure she would stay that way.[20]

Along with his strong views about Miers's conservativism, the president knew that her nomination was unlikely to provoke much of a battle from Senate Democrats. In fact, Senate Minority Leader Harry Reid of Nevada first proposed Miers to Bush, saying, "If you nominate Harriet Miers, you'll start with fifty-six votes," meaning his own and the fifty-five Republicans in the majority. And with Reid's support, the possibility of a Democratic filibuster would be near zero.[21]

Conservative activists, however, didn't seem to care how well the president knew his nominee or how easy her confirmation would be. O'Connor had been the swing justice in her final seven terms on the bench, and they wanted to make sure this choice would shift the balance of the Court to the right. They were not prepared to risk this opportunity on another presidential hunch, on another Bush mistake. Miers was an unknown entity in the Federalist Society, a group of movement conservatives formed in the early 1980s devoted to transforming the law. By "the time of the Miers nomination," notes the political scientist Amanda Hollis-Brusky, "the Federalist Society had created a signaling mechanism within the conservative movement." The message was clear: "If you want to rise through the ranks, we need to know you. And that's what they were all saying about Miers—'We don't know her. She is not one of us.'" Leonard Leo, a longtime staff member and then head of the Federalist Society, was on the team of White House lawyers advising the president on the vacancy, having taken a leave from the organization to join the inner circle of the selection process. He "made it clear to people in the White House that [he] thought her nomination was going to be a heavy lift . . . [with] the conservative community . . . because [they] wouldn't have enough information about her." Leo expected conservatives would take "a wait-and-see approach." But that didn't happen. As he explains, "they ended up coming after her a lot sooner. As opposed to simply being skeptical or agnostic, they became very hostile to the idea soon after the nomination."[22]

In fact, less than two and a half hours after Bush introduced his nominee, William Kristol of the *Weekly Standard* opened the attack by posting a column. "I'M DISAPPOINTED, depressed and demoralized," wrote Kristol. To him, the president had failed to name someone with a "visible and distinguished constitutionalist track record," and instead selected someone with "no constitutionalist credentials." Kristol could not understand why Bush had "flinched from a fight on constitutional philosophy" by appointing someone who "will unavoidably be judged as reflecting a combination of cronyism and capitulation."[23]

While Senate Republicans largely held their fire on the Miers nomination, the conservative effort to block her bid was gaining momentum. "Although the Right tried to phrase its complaints about Miers as a matter of qualifications . . . ," the legal journalist Jeffrey Toobin explains, "for movement conservatives, the problem . . . [was] their own lack of certainty that she would follow their agenda on the Court."[24] Miers was perceived to be clearly more moderate than Roberts, earning a Segal-Cover score of .270 to his .120.[25] The conservative activist Paul Weyrich added Miers to the Republican appointments of John Paul Stevens, O'Connor, Kennedy, and Souter, and explained in perhaps the most straightforward terms that he "had had five 'trust-mes' in [his] long history" in Washington. "I'm sorry, but the president saying he knows her heart is insufficient."[26] Weyrich and other movement conservatives wanted proof of Miers's convictions. But having spent most of her career as a corporate lawyer, she had little to offer.

Of course, in Bush's eyes, he was killing *three* birds with one stone. First, by naming a woman, he was following the wise political course that would provoke little dissent from Democrats, thereby easing her confirmation. Second, he was filling the vacancy with someone who—in his view—was both deeply conservative and highly unlikely to shift to the left once on the Court.[27] Third, the choice would display the "big tent" nature of the Republican Party, potentially attracting female voters to a party that routinely lost the women's vote. Nevertheless, to conservative activists his choice was simply too risky, too much of an unknown quantity to fill the seat of the swing justice. They were tired of crossing their fingers and saying a prayer about a "confirmable conservative." To the fullest extent possible, they demanded ideological purity.

Bush was not prepared to give up on Miers quickly. But outside circumstances began to affect his job performance numbers, and it proved difficult for him to stick by her in the face of such resistance.[28] Unable to command easy conservative support and unwilling to engage in a battle with ideological brethren who were suspicious of his nominee's conservatism and knowledge of the law, the president decided it was time to withdraw her nomination.[29] Three days later, he announced the nominee conservatives wanted all along: Samuel Alito, a judge on the Third Circuit Court of Appeals. Alito was another "white guy" who met the ideological test but who packed little electoral or symbolic punch in the traditional sense. Toobin writes that the president's goal was "to select the most conservative possible Supreme Court justice," one

who would please his ideological base.[30] And this time, by naming Alito—
with a Segal-Cover score of .100—he succeeded.

Bush's decision to surrender to the Right on the Miers nomination is highly
significant if we want to understand the Republican Party during the polarization period, which I define as beginning in 2000 and continuing to this day.
It displays starkly the rise of the staunchest conservatives within the party. In
fact, I argue that 2005 was a high point of conservatism in American politics,
at least since the presidency of Herbert Hoover from 1929 to 1933 and before
Trump's election in 2016.

After the 2004 election conservatives had the upper hand in the Senate,
and they were eager to use their power. Moderate Republicans were said to
be walking on eggshells. Consider, for example, the dilemma Arlen Specter
of Pennsylvania faced soon after Election Day. Specter had responded to a
question about the future makeup of the Supreme Court by suggesting that
the president needed to be cautious if given the opportunity to name a new
justice. "When you talk about judges who would change the right of a woman
to choose, overturn *Roe v. Wade*, I think that is unlikely." In reference to lower
court judges, Specter added: "The president is well aware of what happened
when a bunch of his nominees were sent up, with the filibuster. . . . And I
would expect the president to be mindful of the considerations which I am
mentioning."[31] Following those comments, Specter, a supporter of abortion
rights who had only narrowly fought back a challenger from the Right in
the 2004 GOP primary, quickly became the target of conservatives. As the
expected incoming chair of the Judiciary Committee, conservatives knew he
would have a substantial say in how the Senate treated judicial nominees.
Alarmed by his comments, they were now intent on taking that authority
away, denying him a chairmanship he had long coveted. After two weeks of
lobbying his Republicans colleagues, Specter survived the challenge. But in
that space of time, it became clear that following the 2004 election the dynamics of judicial nominations had changed dramatically. Toobin writes, "in
1987, Robert Bork was defeated because he was too conservative for a Democratic Senate, and Specter still believed that the current Senate might vote
down a nominee who was too conservative. In truth, the bigger risk for a
George W. Bush nominee was if he or she was not conservative enough. To
put it another way, Bork couldn't be confirmed *because* he opposed *Roe v.
Wade*; in 2005, a nominee couldn't be selected *unless* he or she opposed *Roe v.
Wade*."[32] (Notably, four years later Specter switched parties and announced
he would run for reelection as a Democrat. He eventually lost that race in the
Democratic primary, and the conservative Republican who had nearly de-
feated him in 2004—Pat Toomey—captured the seat in 2010.)

✶

In this section, as I did for the divided government era, I'll discuss the nominee type and ideology of all of the Court nominations during the polarization era, beginning with Bush's choice of Roberts in 2005 and continuing through Joe Biden's selection of Ketanji Brown Jackson in 2022. The ideological impact of the new additions to the Court since the turn of the century has been momentous. As illustrated in table 5.1, on every occasion except one (the Miers selection) Republican presidents chose an ideologue, a nominee perceived to be very conservative. Democratic presidents favored symbolism and confirmation safety, avoiding nominees who could easily be labeled liberal ideologues.[33]

After his miscalculation with Miers, it was time for President Bush to move on to another nominee. But before discussing Miers's replacement, it is important to elaborate on the appointment of John Roberts to the Court's center chair. Given Roberts's voting record on the Supreme Court—he's the most moderate of the conservative six (figure 5.1)—and the fact that he attracted the least opposition of any nominee during the polarization era, some might question whether he should be defined as an ideologue or as something else. Indeed, he is a bit difficult to characterize. On the one hand, his Segal-Cover score suggested he would be more conservative than Clarence Thomas when the latter was appointed in 1991. Roberts was also well known in movement conservative circles and had "very strong and long-standing Federalist Society credentials" at the time of his nomination. On the other hand, among movement conservatives Roberts was known as someone who kept his opinions to himself. And inside the Bush White House, there were concerns that he wasn't sufficiently conservative.[34]

President Bush favored Roberts because he clearly stood out among the five finalists he interviewed. And after those interviews, Bush was inclined to select Roberts, even though others in his inner circle supported two alternatives. In the end, as Bush writes in his memoir, a young attorney in the White House helped him think through the decision. He did so by suggesting the president consider who "would be the most effective leader on the Court—the most capable of convincing his colleagues through persuasion and strategic thinking." Bush had the answer. "I believed Roberts would be a natural leader."[35] And with that, he made his decision to nominate the fifty-year-old DC circuit court judge. This focus on leadership is a very interesting development for the president's selection process. As a way of distinguishing between the very conservative finalists, the president focused on a quality that was said to be lacking in his model justices. Specifically, even some on the Right

TABLE 5.1. Nominee Type, Ideology, and Ideological Movement, Polarization Period

Nominee	Nominee Type*	Senate Vote	Segal-Cover Score	Departing Justice's Ideological Location	Ideological Location of New Justice (1st Yr)	Location Difference btw Departing & New Justice	Departing Justice's Ideological Score (Last Yr)	New Justice's Ideological Score (1st Yr)	Ideological Score Difference btw Departing & New Justice
Roberts	I	78–22	0.12	7	6	–1	1.5	1.4	–0.1
Miers	S/CC	*NV*	0.27	5					
Alito	I	58–42	0.1	5	7	2	0.1	1.4	1.3
Sotomayor	S/CC	68–31	0.78	3	3	0	–1.6	–1.6	0
Kagan	CC	63–37	0.73	1	3	–2	–2.9	–1.4	1.5
Garland	CC	*NV*	0.67	7					
Gorsuch	I	54–45	0.11	7	7	0	1.6	1.1	–0.5
Kavanaugh	I	50–48	0.07	5	6	1	0.4	0.6	0.2
Barrett	SI	52–48	0.23	2	7	5	–2.9	1.2	4.1
Jackson	S/CC	55–47	n/a	3	n/a	n/a	–2.1	n/a	n/a

Failed nominees in *italics*.

*Nominee types: CC = confirmable choice, I = ideologue (without political symbolism), S/CC = symbolic and considered confirmable, and SI = symbolic ideologue.

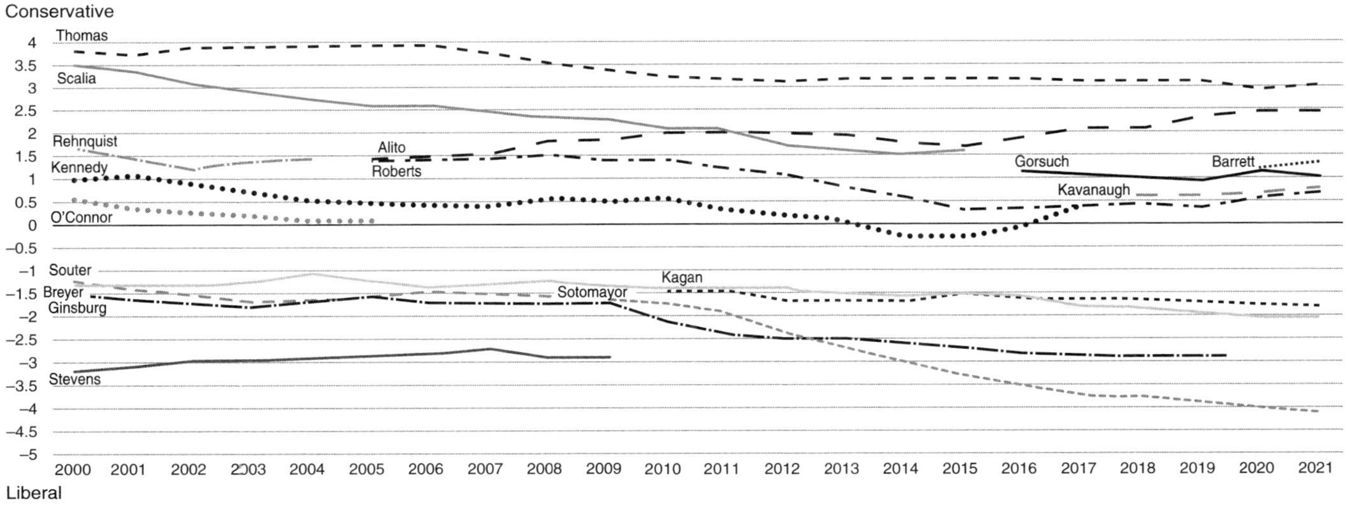

FIGURE 5.1. Estimated Ideologies of the Justices, Polarization Period

had expressed concern that Scalia and Thomas were too often more interested in making a point than in winning a case. Bush thought Roberts would be different, that he would become known for his leadership on the Court, not—like Scalia—for his vicious dissents. Highlighting this attribute made Roberts the clear choice. (In time, the young attorney who suggested that the president focus on leadership in deciding on a nominee would join the Court as well. His name was Brett Kavanaugh.[36])

When the Senate voted on Roberts, it confirmed him by the relatively comfortable margin—at least by polarization-era standards—of seventy-eight to twenty-two. Doubtless this had to do in part with his stellar reputation as an attorney in Washington. As one former Bush advisor put it: "If the president picks Roberts, you can sell him as the nominee who was selected purely on the merits—the quality candidate. He's the best Supreme Court advocate of his generation. Democrats can't attack him." But there were at least two other factors that help explain the relative lack of divisiveness of the confirmation vote. First, when the Senate considered his nomination, there were two vacancies. Notably, beginning in 1968, every time there were two simultaneous vacancies, the Senate contested one—but never both—nominees.[37] These scenarios allowed senators to appear willing both to compromise and to fight for their principles. While the Senate also more frequently (in percentage terms) contested a nominee for chief than for associate in the twentieth century, in this case Senate Democrats chose to target the more conservative Samuel Alito.[38] Second, Roberts was replacing a very conservative justice in William Rehnquist. This mattered. As we saw during the divided government era, the Senate only contested a nominee expected to move the Court significantly to the right. In fact, in replacing Rehnquist Roberts actually made the Court slightly more liberal. His first year Martin-Quinn score was lower than his predecessor's had been in the previous term (table 5.1), and he was the fourth most conservative justice (seat 4) whereas Rehnquist had been the third.[39]

These factors likely convinced some Democrats to support Roberts, but the Senate confirmation vote actually displayed more momentously the arrival of a new politics of confirmation. In the past, senators of the opposing party might have fully supported a nominee like John Roberts, if only to save their opposition for the choice to fill the second vacancy. But in the highly polarized atmosphere of the 2005 confirmation process, the calculation changed. Even though Roberts was the first selection of the newly reelected George W. Bush—who, unlike four years earlier, won both the popular and the electoral college vote in 2004—twenty-two senators opposed the nomination. By historical standards, this was a highly unusual figure. After Franklin D. Roosevelt's appointment of Hugo Black in 1937, every presidential choice to fill the first vacancy on the Court sailed through the Senate with little or no opposition. And unlike Black, Roberts was not expected to vote much differently than the justice he was replacing. Finally, the level of party polarization in the Senate was stark. In the twentieth century, any nominee who confronted that level of resistance (i.e., more than 20 percent) faced bipartisan opposition, even if the number of senators who abandoned the president of their party was small. But in 2005, only Democrats voted against Roberts.

By this time it had become more acceptable for senators to vote against a nominee purely for ideological reasons. Senator Charles Schumer, a Democrat from New York, explained why in a 2001 op-ed: "If the president uses ideology in deciding whom to nominate to the bench, the Senate, as part of its responsibility to advise and consent, should do the same in deciding whom to confirm."[40] When Roberts refused to play along with efforts by Democratic senators to gather more clues about his ideology, Schumer turned to humor to highlight the nominee's avoidance strategy:

> Let me just say, sir, in all due respect—and I respect your intelligence and your career and your family—this process is getting a little more absurd every time—the further we move. You agree we should be finding out your philosophy and method of legal reasoning, modesty, stability, but when we try to find out what modesty and stability mean, what your philosophy means, we don't get any answers.
>
> It is as if I asked you what kind of movies you like. Tell me two or three good movies. And you say, I like movies with good acting. I like movies with good directing. I like movies with good cinematography. And I ask you, no, give me an example of a good movie. You don't name one. I say give me an example of a bad movie. You won't name one. Then I ask you if you like *Casablanca*, and you respond by saying, Lots of people like *Casablanca*. You tell me it is widely settled that *Casablanca* is one of the great movies.
>
> I am making a plea here. I hope we are going to continue this for a while, that within the confines of what you think is appropriate and proper, you try to be a little more forthcoming with us in terms of trying to figure out what kind of Justice you will become.

To laughter, Roberts responded with a direct answer to one of the senator's questions: "First, *Dr. Zhivago* and *North by Northwest*." With regard to his judicial philosophy, the nominee thought the senator wasn't being fair: "I think I have been more forthcoming than any of the other nominees. Other nominees have not been willing to tell you whether they thought *Marbury v. Madison* was correctly decided."[41] Of course, Schumer wasn't really interested in

Roberts's thoughts on a case more than two centuries old and that served as the foundational basis of the Court's authority. He wanted to hear the future chief justice's take on more recent decisions. On that score, Roberts remained coy.

But in 2005, Roberts didn't need to convince a liberal Democrat like Schumer to support his nomination. By this point, nominees faced an entirely different kind of confirmation gauntlet in the Senate than those of the previous century. As Harriett Miers would soon reveal, a Republican-appointed nominee who *might* be too moderate could no longer win confirmation in a GOP-controlled Senate. Senate Republicans didn't mind engaging in a confirmation battle if it meant putting an identifiable movement conservative on the Court. So, it was most important for Roberts to display his conservative stripes. And frustrating Chuck Schumer probably helped his cause.

The confirmation process has changed. It's now far more transparently ideologically laden. There's no need to find some other reason—as there was during the divided government era—to oppose a nominee. And presidents now need to assuage their own party, not the Senate writ large. On the Republican side—and apart from Roberts—this combination has led to the nomination of conservative ideologues who upon winning confirmation fit the definition of numerical minority justices.

As noted earlier, after his misstep with Miers President Bush complied with the wishes of movement conservatives and selected Samuel Alito for the O'Connor seat. Ideological purity eclipsed symbolism. Like Roberts, Alito had strong Federalist Society credentials. But unlike Roberts, there were no concerns about his conservatism in the Bush White House. Notably, Alito's fiercest advocate there was none other than Harriett Miers. As Toobin writes, "in a curious way, the nomination of Alito amounted to Miers's revenge. Miers had been the lone skeptic about Roberts' conservative credentials, only to have her own nomination implode because she could not convince the true believers of her own. So the seat went to Miers's favorite candidate from the beginning, the one who everyone agreed represented a guaranteed conservative voice."[42]

Predictably, the fact that he was an unquestionable conservative ideologue meant that Alito would face a tougher confirmation than Roberts had months earlier. Even if Alito had danced the confirmation dance as well as Roberts—which he didn't—it is unlikely many Democrats would have been willing to support this movement conservative replacement in the same numbers they had for the new chief justice. After all, Alito was replacing the more moderate O'Connor, not the deeply conservative Rehnquist. Even so, with Republicans in control, confirmation was all but assured.

With both the Roberts and Alito votes, more was going on than just the traditional confirmation maneuvering. The politics of judicial nominations—at all levels—were changing. The political scientist Nancy Scherer explains how polarization affected the lower federal court appointment process with what she calls a "theory of elite mobilization":

> Because presidents and senators are so dependent on political activists to mobilize the electorate to turn out at the polls—and key political activists are so dependent on the federal courts to achieve their desired policy outcomes—politicians are now forced to pursue nomination/confirmation strategies that satisfy first and foremost the policy demands of these highly mobilized factions (again, activists concerned with abortion, civil rights, and civil liberties). Simply stated, in the selection and confirmation of lower federal court judges, it is the politicians' pursuit of these policy-oriented strategies—which touch on the most divisive partisan issues of the modern political era—that has led to the heightened politicization of the lower federal courts appointment process. The theory of elite mobilization also explains why politicians expend such an inordinate amount of political capital on the lower federal courts when the issue has no salience with the American electorate. They need to "score points" with key elite constituents.[43]

Such elite action was clearly on display in the Roberts vote. For example, Senate Minority Leader Harry Reid's decision to oppose Roberts's confirmation apparently surprised both the Bush White House and fence-sitting Democrats, in part because Reid was pro-life and represented the then red state of Nevada. After Reid's announcement, the president of the National Organization for Women (NOW), Kim Gandy—referring to a meeting between Reid and liberal advocacy groups—declared: "He got the message loud and clear, didn't he?" Reid admitted as much. In announcing his opposition to Roberts on the floor of the Senate, he noted that he was "very swayed" by arguments made by the leaders of these groups.[44]

Reid's vote suggests that in the increasingly ideologically fractured atmosphere of the nation's capital, any candidate chosen by a president of the opposing party would face a high degree of built-in opposition, no matter the quality of the nominee. However, this new level of contentiousness did not translate into more rejected nominees. In fact, it had the *opposite* effect. The polarization made the very conservative Alito's confirmation *more likely*, not less.

In the twentieth century, every nominee the Senate rejected in an up-or-down vote—all of whom were named by Republican presidents—saw between 13 and 40 percent of GOP senators vote against their confirmation. In fact, in all but one case, about one-third of the president's fellow partisans abandoned his nominee.[45] But in the twenty-first century, with an ideologically cohesive Republican Party in power, a nominee who was appropriately conservative would surely get confirmed with little or no opposition.

Indeed, Senate Democrats could do little to slow Alito's ascent to the Supreme Court. The one possible roadblock was a filibuster, which would require a supermajority of sixty senators. Near the end of the confirmation process, Massachusetts Senator John Kerry—the defeated 2004 Democratic presidential nominee—vowed to do just that. "People can say all they want that 'elections have consequences,'" he wrote. "Trust me, more than anyone I understand that. But that seems like an awfully convoluted rationale for me to stay silent about Judge Alito's nomination." In a later statement, he declared: "Judge Alito's confirmation would be an ideological coup on the Supreme Court."[46] But there was little support in the Democratic caucus for such a fight, perhaps in part because Kerry was issuing these statements while on vacation at a five-star ski resort in the Swiss Alps. In the end, the filibuster effort yielded just twenty-five votes. The group nevertheless included three future Democratic presidential nominees—Barack Obama, Hillary Clinton, and Joe Biden. When the Senate moved to a vote on the nomination itself, it confirmed Alito, fifty-eight to forty-two. Only one Republican—the liberal Lincoln Chafee from the very blue state of Rhode Island, who was facing (and would ultimately lose) reelection in 2006—joined the opposition.[47] Alito became only the second numerical minority justice to win Senate confirmation. And once on the Court, he proved to be the conservative both Republicans and Democrats had expected. Indeed, in the last four terms they were on the Court together, Alito's Martin-Quinn score was more to the right than that of the legendary conservative Justice Antonin Scalia. Only Justice Thomas had a more conservative score. And since Scalia's death, Alito has moved even closer to Thomas (see figure 5.1). Once again, the confirmation politics of the polarization era have yielded justices with arguably less democratic legitimacy who are willing—indeed eager—to pursue a more ideological constitutional course.

*

When Donald Trump announced his three choices for the Court, he spoke the name of only one person in attendance on all three occasions. It was someone who wasn't (and had never been) a Supreme Court justice, or a member of his administration, or a United States senator. She wasn't even a lawyer. Her name was Maureen Scalia, the widow of, in Trump's words, "the late great Justice Antonin Scalia." With his first two nominees—Gorsuch and

Kavanaugh—Trump did note that both had clerked for Anthony Kennedy, in fact during the same term of 1993–94—but he celebrated their connections to Justice Scalia. With Barrett, he chose a former Scalia clerk who hastened to mention at her introduction that "his judicial philosophy is mine, too."[48]

While a professor at the University of Chicago Law School, Scalia had served as the faculty advisor for a group of conservative law students who formed one of the first two chapters of the Federalist Society. (Robert Bork advised the other one at Yale.) And he maintained a close relationship with members of the organization as it grew to become a major force in the conservative legal movement. But more important than his ties to the Federalist Society, Scalia became something of an "intellectual heartthrob to many" young conservatives for his views on the law and his assertiveness in articulating them.[49] Both in the written word and at the speaker's podium, Scalia enjoyed excoriating liberal logic and the idea of a "living constitution" in ways that brought smiles to those on the Right and clenched teeth to those on the Left—or for that matter, in the ideological middle.

So, when word came on February 13, 2016, from the outer reaches of west Texas that the fiery conservative jurist was dead at the age of seventy-nine, it sent shock waves through the legal world. It's unlikely that any other justice appointed to the Court during the Republican dominance of the presidency from 1969 to 1993 will achieve the celebrated status of Antonin Scalia in legal circles, particularly conservative ones. Of the ten justices appointed during those twenty-four years—all by the four Republican presidents who served during that time—Scalia best represented the conservative challenge to the Warren era's constitutional lawmaking.[50] Known for his stinging writing style, keen intellect, and boisterous sense of humor, Scalia helped simultaneously sharpen and soften the conservative criticisms of Warren-era decisions in a way that Nixon-appointed and Reagan-elevated William Rehnquist and the Senate-rejected Reagan nominee Robert Bork could not do. He could rightfully be defined as one of the intellectual founders of the conservative legal movement, and his death meant the Court would undergo a clear break from the past.

On the day of Scalia's death, President Barack Obama still had eleven months left in office. Democrats and Republicans were still in the process of choosing their nominee for the presidential election later that year. What would this mean for filling the vacancy? The picture became clearer mere hours after the world learned of Scalia's death when Senate majority leader Mitch McConnell of Kentucky vowed that he and his fellow Republicans in the upper house of Congress would resist any and all efforts by the Democrat in the White House to fill the empty seat. Later that evening, at a Republican

presidential debate, Donald Trump, leading in the polls for the GOP nomination, endorsed McConnell's strategy: "I think it's up to Mitch McConnell
and everybody else to stop [President Barack Obama's expected nominee to
replace Scalia]. It's called delay, delay, delay."

Scalia's death helped to shape the presidential election of 2016, a race won
by Trump with a minority of the popular vote but an electoral college majority (more on this in chapter 10). On his way to the GOP nomination Trump
sought to ease conservative uncertainty about his outsider challenge and his
previous liberal views on a range of judicially centered social issues by pledg-
ing to release a list of names of potential Supreme Court candidates he would
choose from if elected to the presidency. On May 18, 2016, he released a list of
eleven names, but there was a hedge: "The following list of potential Supreme
Court justices is representative of the kind of constitutional principles I value
and, as President, I plan to use this list as a guide to nominate our next United
States Supreme Court Justices." Erick Erickson, a Trump critic from the Right,
dismissed the list. "Like every clause of every sentence uttered in every breath
Donald Trump takes, this is all subject to change. He will waffle, he will back-
track, and he simply cannot be believed."[51] Four months later, in the midst of
the general election and just before the first debate, Trump altered the list,
expanding it to twenty-one. This time, he also made a commitment to select
from those names when making appointments to the Court. "This list is definitive and I will choose *only* from it in picking future *Justices* of the United
States Supreme Court." As Trump explained, the list had been constructed
with the significant aid of the two movement conservative groups most intent on transforming the law in a rightward direction: the Federalist Society
and the Heritage Foundation.[52] While not all that surprising given Trump's
lack of Washington experience, the admission was somewhat stunning from
the perspective of presidential authority over judicial selection at the highest
level. Elite groups like the Federalist Society had gone from a consulting role
with sympathetic administrations to an all but deciding role. This was elite
mobilization at an unprecedented level.[53]

True to his word—this time—when the newly inaugurated President Trump
announced his choice for the Court, he selected Tenth Circuit Court Judge
Neil Gorsuch, a later addition to the list. An analysis of Trump's list of candidates by three political scientists suggested that Gorsuch was among the most
conservative of the group, falling to the right of Justice Scalia before his death.
His Segal-Cover score was a very conservative .11. Another study "estimated
[him] to be more conservative than 87 percent of all other federal judges—the
nation's primary pool of potential Supreme Court justices."[54] Perhaps most

significantly, unlike candidates of the past—like the stealthy Souter—who had largely avoided commenting on hot-button social issues, Gorsuch had written an entire book on the subject of euthanasia. There he had argued that "all human beings are intrinsically valuable and the intentional taking of human life by private persons is always wrong." He added: "Once we open the door to excusing or justifying the intentional taking of life as 'necessary,' we introduce the real possibility that the lives of some persons (very possibly the weakest and most vulnerable among us) may be deemed less 'valuable,' and receive less protection from the law, than others."[55] While Gorsuch did not take a position on abortion in the book, his arguments on euthanasia and his conservative record on the court of appeals suggested to most that if confirmed he would join the anti-*Roe* forces on the high bench. For example, the Supreme Court reporter David Kaplan writes, "in a nuanced disquisition on assisted suicide and euthanasia—issues that had receded from vehement public debate—[Gorsuch] had provided a proxy for a novel, extreme way to think about abortion. . . . Without ever discussing abortion per se, he had sent a signal to a future conservative president like Trump."[56]

With an ideologically cohesive GOP in control of the Senate (52–48), the president knew his nominee would win confirmation. But what if the Democrats decided to filibuster Gorsuch's nomination? Could he get sixty votes? Senate majority leader McConnell was not prepared to let that happen. Under his guidance, the Senate altered the terms of votes on Supreme Court nominees.[57] Following these new rules, it could confirm Gorsuch with a simple majority. In short, the filibuster was gone, obliterated by the so-called nuclear option. In the end, the Senate confirmed Gorsuch fifty-four to forty-five, as three Democrats joined all the Republicans present to provide the extra boost. All three supporting Democrats represented deep-red states that Trump won in 2016 by 19, 36, and 42 percent. And all three were up for reelection in 2018. The close confirmation vote made Gorsuch the first numerical minority justice nominated by a numerical minority presidency in American history. While the sample size is small, Justice Gorsuch has shown he's a worthy—albeit at times slightly more liberal—ideological replacement for Justice Scalia (figure 5.1).[58] Most importantly for movement conservatives, he joined the majority in *Dobbs*, fulfilling one of Scalia's doctrinal dreams.

Eighteen months after his introduction of Gorsuch, Donald Trump had another, more significant opportunity to shift the Court to the right. The Gorsuch appointment, after all, essentially returned the Court to where it had been before Scalia's death, with a conservative replacing a conservative. But at the end of the Court's term in late June 2018, the swing justice for many years, Anthony Kennedy, announced his retirement from the high bench. Once again, President Trump consulted his roster of conservative candidates and selected a name from it. But notably, the list had been revised since his victory over Hillary Clinton. There were still twenty names on it after Gorsuch's was crossed off, but in November 2017 the White House announced the addition of five more names, including DC court of appeals Judge Brett Kavanaugh. One commentator speculated that Kavanaugh had been left off the pre-Election Day list because he was too much of a Washington insider given Trump's promise to "drain the swamp."[59] Whatever the reason, Kavanaugh's name was added in Trump's first year in office and then selected to fill the Kennedy vacancy less than nine months later. According to one study of the ideology of the twenty-five potential nominees on Trump's lists, Kavanaugh was among the rightmost ideologically, one of nine "extreme conservatives." The study's authors predicted that eight of the nominees falling into this group, including Kavanaugh, "would vote about as conservatively as Thomas. In other words, should any get the nod, Thomas (and Alito) would be less isolated on the extreme right." At .007, Kavanaugh's Segal-Cover score supported this conclusion.[60]

Appointing someone with Kavanaugh's perceived ideology to fill Kennedy's swing seat alarmed liberals, to say the least. But with the filibuster gone and Republicans still in control of the Senate—reduced to fifty-one to forty-nine after an unlikely loss in a special election in deep-red Alabama—the odds that Democrats could block the nomination were long at best. Their only hope was that two moderate Republicans, Alaska's Lisa Murkowski and Maine's Susan Collins, would oppose Kavanaugh's confirmation. If just one of them abandoned the GOP ship, then Vice President Mike Pence would be able to break a tie. However, to add to the Democratic unease, three of their own senators had supported Gorsuch the year before, and each of them was in a tough reelection fight in a deep-red state. As the Judiciary Committee held hearings in early September, things proceeded with the sense that Kavanaugh would win Senate confirmation with all but one or two Republicans in the majority and all but one or two Democrats in opposition.

Then, a few days after Kavanaugh testified, news broke that California Senator Dianne Feinstein—the ranking member of the Judiciary Committee—had in her possession a letter from a woman accusing Kavanaugh of sexual assault. Specifically, as the nation would later learn, the anonymous woman accused the judge of attempting to rape her at a house party while they were both high school students at separate DC-area elite prep schools. Four days after that story broke, Christine Blasey Ford, a professor and research psychologist living in California, went public with her accusations. Kavanaugh's confirmation no longer appeared inevitable.

After two weeks of uncertainty about whether and when Blasey Ford would testify and new accusations by two other women about Kavanaugh's behavior, the Judiciary Committee held a single day of additional hearings. However, the Republican chair, Chuck Grassley of Iowa, determined that the committee would only hear from Blasey Ford and the nominee himself. The other charges were essentially dismissed.

Capitol Hill had not seen such confirmation high drama since the same committee heard Anita Hill's accusations of sexual harassment against then Supreme Court nominee Clarence Thomas twenty-seven years earlier. In moving testimony, Blasey Ford told the committee of the moment that altered her life and why she had waited so long to come forward with her story. With a "100 percent" certainty, Blasey Ford identified Brett Kavanaugh as the drunken seventeen-year-old who had attempted to rape her when she was just fifteen. After being forced into a bedroom and "pushed onto the bed," she said Kavanaugh "got on top" of her. Then, he started groping her and trying to take off her clothes. She continued: "I believed he was going to rape me. I tried to yell for help. When I did, Brett put his hand over my mouth to stop me from screaming. This was what terrified me the most, and has had the most lasting impact on my life. It was hard for me to breathe, and I thought that Brett was accidentally going to kill me." She said she only escaped after the nominee's friend, Mark Judge, who was also in the locked room, "drunkenly laughing [with Kavanaugh] during the attack," jumped on the bed. This caused Kavanaugh and Blasey Ford to "topple over," and he "was no longer on top of" her. She used the opportunity to flee from the bedroom and lock herself in a nearby bathroom.[61]

After listening to her, most commentators gave Kavanaugh little chance of survival. As Chris Wallace of the conservative Fox News told his viewers: "This was extremely emotional, extremely raw, and extremely credible. Nobody could listen to her deliver those words and talk about the assault and the impact it had had on her life and not have your heart go out to her." He then added: "This is a disaster for the Republicans."[62]

Later that same day Kavanaugh appeared before the committee to defend himself. Old calendars in hand, he said there was no possibility he was the person who had attempted to rape Blasey Ford. While Kavanaugh admitted to drinking and partying the summer of the alleged incident—repeatedly telling committee members how much he "liked beer"—he said he had never lost consciousness or even forgotten something he had done after a night of drinking. This was significant since Blasey Ford had noted that Kavanaugh was very intoxicated when the attack occurred. Therefore, it was possible he wouldn't remember it.

During his testimony, Kavanaugh was clearly angry. At times, he was yelling. At other times, his voice quivered with emotion. Many of Kavanaugh's doubters suggested that he had become unhinged in his testimony given his aggressiveness toward committee Democrats. Perhaps most significantly, he accused Democratic senators of participating in a "calculated and orchestrated political hit fueled with apparent pent-up anger about President Trump and the 2016 election." To him, it was "revenge on behalf of the Clintons."[63] But Kavanaugh's main goal was not to convince his doubters of his innocence. His audience was the president—who could withdraw his nomination—and the Republican senators who would eventually vote on it. In the end, the members of that audience were satisfied with his performance, or at least had enough doubts about Blasey Ford's accusations—especially since the alleged attack had occurred so long ago—to maintain their support for the nominee. Trump even mocked Blasey Ford during a campaign stop in Mississippi a few days after her testimony.

In the past, Blasey Ford's accusations of sexual assault coupled with Kavanaugh's accusatory denial would likely have spelled doom for the nominee. Recall that in 1987 the Reagan White House forced Douglas Ginsburg to withdraw his nomination after he admitted that he "once smoked marijuana as a law professor at Harvard."[64] In 1991, Clarence Thomas did (barely) survive Anita Hill's charges against him, but that was at a time when sexual harassment was often dismissed, and Hill's allegations did not include attempted rape.[65] In 2018, given the polarized state of American politics, it was unclear if either Blasey Ford's shocking allegations or Kavanaugh's incensed defense would matter at all. We found out after another week's delay to allow the FBI to quickly carry out a limited investigation. Even at this time of heightened awareness about sexual assault, the Senate confirmed him. Just one Republican, Alaska's Murkowski, vowed to vote "no." And one Democrat, Joe Manchin of West Virginia, chose to join those in support.[66] It was the second closest confirmation vote in the 229-year history of the Senate's consideration of Supreme Court nominees, and it meant that a minority president had placed a second numerical minority justice on the nation's highest tribunal—one seen by his opponents as an attempted rapist with an axe to grind. And now, he had the power to wield it.

I'll discuss Amy Coney Barrett's nomination at length in chapter 12; here I will simply note that like Gorsuch and Kavanaugh, most expected her to be another conservative ideologue. Barrett was in the same ideological range as

Justices Alito and Gorsuch, according to the political scientists Lee Epstein, Andrew Martin, and Kevin Quinn. While not a member of their "extreme right" group, they predicted she would be a "reliable conservative voting to limit gay rights, uphold restrictions on abortion, and invalidate affirmative action programs and campaign finance regulations (as Alito has done throughout his career)." Using Alito as a guide, they further predicted she would "reach conservative decisions in 71% of all cases and in 84% of non-unanimous decisions"—nearly the exact opposite of the justice she replaced, Ruth Bader Ginsburg.[67] Barrett's gender made her a symbolic selection as well, with hopes that her nomination—just weeks before Election Day—would aid in the re-election of a president who struggled mightily to attract women voters.

With the Senate in the hands of Republicans, there was little Democrats could do. Barrett was confirmed in comparatively short order by a vote of fifty-two to forty-eight. All forty-seven Democrats opposed her, including West Virginia's Joe Manchin. One Republican up for reelection in a blue state, Susan Collins of Maine, joined them. Wrote Nicholas Fandos of the *New York Times*, "it was the first time in 151 years that a justice was confirmed without the support of a single member of the minority party, a sign of how bitter Washington's war over judicial nominations has become."[68] Her status as a numerical minority justice—the third chosen by a minority president—meant that the Court now had a majority of them. They had been all chosen to chart a very conservative constitutional course, and they would soon join together in doing so.

In addition to illustrating the heightened polarization in the confirmation process, the selection and ultimate confirmation of Justices Gorsuch, Kavanaugh, and Barrett dramatically highlight the importance of outside groups like the Federalist Society and the Heritage Foundation in the judicial selection process. These groups were at the center of the politics of choosing and confirming justices during the George W. Bush years, but during the Trump presidency they essentially took command of the process. In particular, the Federalist Society's Leonard Leo was indispensable in the development of Trump's list and in the selection of Gorsuch, Kavanaugh, and Barrett. Of course, his politics align with those of the president and the Republican Senate majority. Nevertheless, it is fair to conclude that no other unelected individual has played such a prominent role in the construction of the Supreme Court since the election of Franklin Roosevelt, and perhaps in the history of the nation.

⋆

The trend toward more ideological choices and greater partisan opposition was not limited to Republican administrations during this period. Although

the sample size is quite small, President Barack Obama's two successful selections, Sonia Sotomayor and Elena Kagan—with Segal-Cover scores of .780
and .730, respectively—were the most liberal Democratic nominees since
Johnson sought to elevate Abe Fortas to chief in 1968. (Even Merrick Garland,
whom he appointed with the hope that the Republican Senate majority would
consider him an ideological moderate, had a Segal-Cover score of .67.) Still,
Sotomayor and Kagan were perceived to be noticeably closer to the ideological middle than the five justices George W. Bush and Donald J. Trump selected, making them comparatively more moderate. In addition, neither was
thought to be the most liberal of the finalists President Obama considered.
As Toobin writes, Obama "basically had middle-of-the-road ideas about the
Constitution, and he wanted a nominee with similar views." Moreover, "given
the crowded legislative calendar, Obama and his team wanted a no-drama
confirmation."[69] But despite being perceived as comparatively moderate, both
Sotomayor and Kagan encountered a higher level of Republican opposition
than any successful Democratic nominee since the Senate votes to confirm
Grover Cleveland's appointments of Melville Fuller and Lucius Lamar in 1888.[70]

In filling the first vacancy of the Obama presidency in 2009—to replace the
retiring David Souter—the competition came down to Sotomayor and Diane
Wood. Both were court of appeals judges—Sotomayor on the second circuit
and Wood on the seventh. At the beginning of the search, the president favored Judge Wood. She had developed a reputation as a vigorous advocate for
the protection of women's reproductive rights, and a liberal "living constitution" form of judicial interpretation. "Wood," writes the legal journalist Joan
Biskupic, "was a deep thinker who could offer an intellectual counterpoint to
the Supreme Court's conservatives."[71] To top things off, Obama knew her well,
since they were both on the faculty of the University of Chicago Law School.

For her part, Sotomayor had a powerful story of overcoming great odds.
Born in the South Bronx to Puerto Rican parents, she was diagnosed with
type 1 diabetes when she was eight years old. The very next year her father
died of a heart attack, leaving her mother to care for her and her younger
brother. With a focus on education, Sotomayor's mother sent the two to parochial Catholic schools, and—often while working two jobs—went to school
to become a nurse. In time, she was able to move her family out of the "projects" and into the massive middle-class development in the Bronx known
as Co-Op City. Both kids excelled in school, and the future justice earned a
scholarship to Princeton. Years later, she would call herself a "proud affirmative action baby," one who graduated summa cum laude from one of the most
prestigious universities in the nation. After Princeton, Sotomayor attended
Yale Law School. And at the end of her time there, the legendary New York

County District Attorney Robert Morgenthau hired her as an assistant DA in his office. In 1991, based on the recommendation of Democratic New York senator Daniel Patrick Moynihan, President George Bush appointed her to a federal district court in southern Manhattan, and the Senate confirmed her unanimously the following year. Five years later, President Bill Clinton nominated Sotomayor for the Second Circuit Court of Appeals, also in Manhattan. After a long delay, and only after New York Republican senator Al D'Amato pushed for a vote in hopes of appealing to Hispanic voters in his bid for re-election, the Senate confirmed her.[72] But the unanimity was gone. The vote was sixty-seven to twenty-nine, with only Republicans in opposition.[73]

President Obama understood that by choosing Sotomayor he would be making history. He would be appointing a member of America's largest minority group—Hispanics were 45 million strong and a growing part of the electorate—to the nation's highest tribunal. While the symbolic power of making such a selection undoubtedly helped convince the first African American president to select Sotomayor, he was reportedly most impressed by "her personal intensity and her continued connections to her community." Biskupic writes, "the Bronx Latina had not forgotten her roots."[74] Throughout the selection process, Sotomayor had to overcome questions about her intelligence and charges that she had been an arrogant bully on the bench. Even after she was chosen, liberals like the *Washington Post*'s Dana Milbank concluded that Obama had "opted for biography over brains."[75] However, her most learned critic on the Left, Laurence Tribe of Harvard Law School, backtracked once she established herself on the Court. "Simply put," Tribe noted, "I was totally wrong in ever doubting how strong a Supreme Court justice Sonia Sotomayor would be, as I had done when contrasting her with Elena Kagan, whose nomination I favored at the time."[76]

Along with Tribe, there was another influential member of the legal community advocating for an Elena Kagan selection. This one, however, was on the other side of the ideological divide, and a current member of the Court. As David Axelrod, the longtime Obama advisor, tells the story, when the Souter seat came open in 2009, none other than Justice Antonin Scalia pushed for Kagan. According to Axelrod, the conversation occurred when he and Scalia were seated together at the White House Correspondents Association dinner. After speaking for some time, the justice took the opportunity to make his recommendation. "I have no illusions that your man will nominate someone who shares my orientation. But I hope he sends us someone smart." A surprised Axelrod responded: "I'm sure he will." But Scalia had more to say. Leaning in and fixing his eyes on Axelrod's own, he said "in a lower, purposeful tone of voice . . . 'Let me put a finer point on it. I hope he sends us Elena Kagan.'"[77]

Tribe and Scalia didn't get their wish in 2009, but the following year President Obama had another opportunity to fill a vacancy—this time due to the retirement of the Court's most liberal member, John Paul Stevens. And his solicitor general, Elena Kagan, was the clear front-runner. While Kagan—considered a moderate by most—obviously had her supporters, some on the Left were perplexed about why she was leading the pack of potential nominees. "Why do the conservatives always get the conservatives, but we don't get to get the liberals?" Senator Tom Harkin, a Democrat from Iowa, complained. "What the hell is that all about?"[78]

Harkin had a point. Two faculty members at the University of Chicago Law School, William M. Landes and Richard A. Posner (who was also a court of appeals judge), "ranked all forty-three justices from 1937 to 2006 by ideology and found that four of the five most conservative ones [were] on the current court. Even the moderate swing vote, Justice Kennedy, was the 10th most conservative over that period. By contrast, none of the current justices rank[ed] among the five most liberal members."[79] Moreover, if chosen, the moderate Kagan would likely move the Court to the middle, not to the left, since she would be replacing Stevens, its most liberal member. This apparently didn't matter to the president. He was convinced Kagan was the perfect person for the vacancy.

Obama did consider other possibilities, including the liberal runner-up to Sotomayor, Judge Diane Wood, but it is doubtful that anyone else really had a shot. "[C]hoosing Wood meant a fight over abortion in the Senate," and Obama was hoping "to get the justice he wanted without the heartburn." It was an approach that presidents on the Right rarely expressed in the polarization era. Like President George W. Bush's choice of Roberts, Obama also focused on finding a jurist who might be able to convince his or her colleagues in a close vote once on the Court. Writes Toobin, "Obama didn't want someone who could write eloquent dissents. He wanted someone who could *win*."[80] Finally, Kagan was a full decade younger than Wood, and that meant she would likely allow Obama to leave a longer legacy with his Supreme Court appointments.

With fans like Scalia and critics like Harkin, Republicans couldn't complain too much about Kagan. In fact, with fifty-nine Democrats in the Senate, Obama could likely have chosen a much more liberal nominee and still secured confirmation. Even though he didn't, the "elite mobilization" that came to define the judicial selection process in a polarized Washington occurred again. In particular, the National Rifle Association announced that it would not only oppose Kagan, but would also "score" the vote for senators.[81] That meant senators—particularly more moderate Republicans and more conservative Democrats—who wanted an unblemished NRA grade to highlight in their campaign ads would have to decide whether supporting the nominee was worth it. For a Republican, a vote to confirm might even provoke a primary challenge. So even though she was more moderate than Sotomayor and would move the Court closer to the middle, Kagan only won confirmation by sixty-three votes to thirty-seven. One red-state Democrat joined the opposition,[82] and just five Republicans risked voting "aye"—all but one of those five representing states Obama won in 2008. Rigid partisan ideological boundaries had now become the norm in Supreme Court confirmation votes, no matter the type of nominee chosen. As we will see, it was a lesson seemingly lost on Obama when he sought to fill the Scalia seat with an older moderate in hopes of winning a confirmation vote. Put simply, in the confirmation politics of today, a president of one party can do little to move the partisan needle in the eventual Senate vote. We can further understand why by taking a closer look at the decisions of several Republican senators in the Kagan vote.

There was some thought that Orrin Hatch of Utah, a longtime conservative member of the Judiciary Committee who had nevertheless supported both Ginsburg and Breyer, might back Kagan. But Hatch had just witnessed his Utah colleague, Bob Bennett, finish third in a Republican convention to two challengers from the Right, despite having very high approval ratings statewide. (Notably, the eventual winner of that race, Mike Lee, would develop a record that made him the most conservative member of the Senate. And despite his being a Donald Trump critic, the future president added his name to the updated September 2016 list of potential Supreme Court nominees, joining his brother Thomas. In an analysis of those potential nominees, Senator Lee was easily the furthest to the right, projected to exceed even the conservative decision-making of Clarence Thomas.[83]) Taking cues from Bennett's defeat and anticipating a similar challenge in 2012, Hatch chose to oppose Kagan. Indiana's Richard Lugar was also expected to face a tough Republican primary fight in his next election, but he nevertheless voted to confirm Kagan. The results were telling. Hatch easily won his primary, while Lugar lost badly to an unapologetic conservative who considered "compromise" and "bipartisanship" to be slurs.[84] Two of the other Republicans who supported Kagan—Judd Gregg of New Hampshire and Olympia Snowe of Maine—chose not to seek reelection at all, with both citing the rise of polarization as a primary reason.[85] This was the new state of confirmation politics in the US Senate: either support the party's position, step aside, or suffer the consequences. There were few exceptions.[86]

   Consider how differently the Senate has behaved in this era compared to the divided government era. As we saw in chapter 4, the Senate only contested a nominee when he or she was perceived to be very conservative—with a Segal-Cover score of .16 or less—and expected to be four seats to the ideological right of the departing justice. And it didn't even contest those kinds of nominees on every occasion. The Senate minority no longer picks its fights in such a manner (see table 5.1). Every nominee but one—Chief Justice John Roberts—has been contested in the polarization era. Even Kagan, who was expected to be significantly *more moderate* than the departing John Paul Stevens, was contested by the Republican senators in the minority. And the one nominee who was not contested had two advantages. He was replacing the conservative Chief Justice William Rehnquist (with expectations—similar to Kagan—that he would push the Court to the middle), and he was nominated when there were two vacancies.

✶

This polarized confirmation politics helps us understand what happened to President Obama's final choice for the Court, Merrick Garland, the DC court of appeals judge chosen to fill the Scalia seat in mid-March 2016. After Obama chose Garland, Senate majority leader Mitch McConnell refused, as promised, to move on the nomination. Threatened (by McConnell) with primary challenges, few Republicans met with Garland as senators typically do, no hearings were held, and no vote was taken. In short, he was ignored, cast adrift in a non-confirmation process. There was hope in the Obama White House that the Republican Senate would consider Garland, given his age—at sixty-three he was much older than most nominees—and his reputation as a moderate. Better Garland than a younger, more progressive nominee Hillary Clinton might name after her inauguration. As we know, that thinking was grossly incorrect. Despite public opposition to their stonewalling, Senate Republicans held firm.[87] And when Donald Trump captured the presidency, they celebrated in the knowledge that they had prevented the Court from moving to the left.
   In *How Democracies Die*, the political scientists Steven Levitsky and Daniel Ziblatt highlight the Senate's arguably unprecedented treatment of Garland. To Levitsky and Ziblatt, the Senate's handling of the Garland nomination was much more than a slick legislative strategy by a partisan majority:

> [F]or the first time in American history, the U.S. Senate refused to even consider an elected president's nominee for the Supreme Court. As we have seen, the Senate had always used forbearance in exercising its advice and consent in

the selection of Supreme Court justices. Since 1866, every time a president had moved to fill a Supreme Court vacancy prior to the election of his successor, he had been allowed to do so.

But the world had changed by 2016. Now, in a radical departure from historical precedent Senate Republicans denied the president's authority to nominate a new justice. It was an extraordinary instance of norm breaking. Within a year, a Republican was in the White House and Senate Republicans got their wish: a conservative justice nominee, Neil Gorsuch, whom they quickly approved. The GOP had trampled on a basic democratic norm—in effect, stealing a Supreme Court seat—and gotten away with it.

The traditions underpinning America's democratic institution are unraveling, opening up a disconcerting gap between how our political system works and long-standing expectations about how it *ought* to work. As our soft guardrails have weakened, we have grown increasingly vulnerable to antidemocratic leaders.[88]

It's a powerful critique. But are Levitsky and Ziblatt correct in their conclusions about the Senate's treatment of the Garland nomination? I'd suggest that had the alternative happened, and the Republican Senate considered Garland, the confirmation process would have been extraordinarily similar to the way the Senate handled Associate Justice Abe Fortas in the midst of the very divisive election of 1968. Senate critics of the Warren Court—both Democrats and Republicans—excoriated Fortas for his ties to the president and, more importantly, for his liberal decision-making as a justice. Holding off on a vote until the final weeks of the campaign season, they then filibustered his bid for the Court's center chair. To break the filibuster, Fortas needed sixty votes, but he only got forty-five.[89] In short, it wasn't even close.[90] And since Fortas would not be switching seats, there was no reason for the Senate to consider Johnson's nomination of his replacement, Homer Thornberry. The winner of the 1968 presidential election, Richard Nixon, would be the one to replace Earl Warren. A man the chief justice detested would choose his successor.

While Levitsky and Ziblatt do not mention Fortas or Thornberry—surely because the Senate *did* consider the former's nomination—wasn't this another Supreme Court seat stolen from a lame-duck Democrat for a newly (and narrowly) elected Republican?[91] (Publicly, Nixon tried to stay out of the fray, even referring to Fortas as an "able lawyer" and "able justice." But privately, as one of his key campaign aides explained years later, he "wanted the Fortas nomination killed" without leaving "fingerprints on the murder weapon."[92]) If the Senate had held hearings on Garland, wouldn't the Republican majority have toyed with him just as conservative senators from both parties had done with Fortas, using this sitting Supreme Court justice as cannon fodder in a tightly contested election campaign where judicial issues were front and center? The Republican majority in 2016 certainly displayed no willingness to see Garland become a justice, and the confirmation gauntlet can demolish even the hardiest of souls.[93]

I'd suggest that instead of providing new evidence of the pending death of American democracy, the Senate's treatment of Merrick Garland was similar—perhaps even preferable—to its handling of Fortas nearly fifty years earlier, the last time a Supreme Court seat opened during a presidential election year.[94] To be sure, this was not an intended act of mercy. It was instead the flexing of Republican muscle to derail a president they had promised to impede from day one. But in both cases, the Senate's treatment of the nominee should be seen as a political play in hopes of enhancing the electoral prospects of a presidential candidate who would make another choice, someone more to the liking of a majority of senators.[95] And both times the maneuver worked. In fact, given his ultimate resignation, the campaign against Fortas's elevation was both worse for the target and more effective for the aggressors. The decision to ignore Merrick Garland still left him with other options— even if that wasn't part of the Senate Republican plan—and he ultimately won Senate confirmation to become President Joe Biden's attorney general (with Mitch McConnell's support). The Fortas filibuster, on the other hand, led to further investigation: an investigation advanced by eager Nixon administration officials playing "very dirty pool," hoping to rid the Court of another liberal. They succeeded, even though, as the legal historian and Fortas biographer Laura Kalman writes, "in the half century that followed" the associate justice's departure from the Court "it would be clear to most, if not all, who studied the episode" that his behavior had been "indiscreet," but "not criminal."[96] In Levitsky and Ziblatt's terms, it was yet another Supreme Court seat stolen. And when it happened, attorneys in the Nixon Justice Department "opened the bar, [and] poured heartily," raising their glasses in celebration. A joyful president phoned to offer his thanks.[97]

There are, nevertheless, concerns about Senate Republican maneuvering from the standpoint of the Court's democracy gap. The fact that they blocked the choice of a president who had won both the popular and the electoral vote in 2012 combined with the fact that Gorsuch was nominated by a minority president and fit the definition of a numerical minority justice certainly undercuts the Court's democratic legitimacy. This is exacerbated by Gorsuch's participation in a narrow majority committed to rewriting constitutional law.

✶

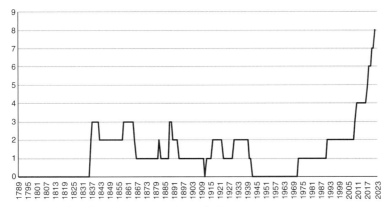

FIGURE 5.2. Number of Contentious Justices Serving by Year

The confirmation process today has undoubtedly reached a new stage of contentiousness. Since George W. Bush's nomination of Harriett Miers in 2005, the Senate has contested every nominee (and the opposition to Roberts almost reached the threshold of a conflictual confirmation). Two nominees—Miers and Garland—have had their names withdrawn without the benefit of a Senate vote of any kind. And five are numerical minority justices, having secured confirmation with a majority of senators who had received fewer votes in their most recent election than those in opposition. Finally, eight of the nine members of the current Court are products of a contentious confirmation. While it is true that confirmation conflict is not unprecedented (it occurred most often in the past when the winning presidential candidate did not receive a majority of the overall vote in a two-candidate race and did not win the popular vote by more than 5 percent), in the first two centuries of the Court the highest number of contentiously confirmed justices to sit together was three (figure 5.2). And that was only for brief periods of time. Table 5.2 lists all the contentious justices, divided by era, for the entirety of Supreme Court appointments. Notably, eight of the nineteen—42 percent—sit on the Court today.

Given that its sources remain, this contentiousness is unlikely to go away anytime soon. We see the ideological hardening of the parties that has produced reflexive opposition to the Supreme Court selections of any president from the other side. This was all but unheard of in the past when ideology alone wasn't considered "acceptable" opposition, and when most nominees received unanimous—or near-unanimous—Senate support. We see parties that, when unified internally, won't break ranks one way or another, and where the struggle—as the Miers nomination so brilliantly illustrates—is intra-party rather than inter-party. We see that this ideological scoring happens—again

TABLE 5.2. List of Contentious Justices, 1789–2022

Period and Justice's Name	Year of Vote	Senate Vote	Percent Opposed
Founding (1789–1824)			
None			
Jacksonian (1824–1860)			
1. Roger Taney	1836	29–15	34%
2. Philip Barbour	1836	30–11	27%
3. John Catron	1837	23–18	35%
4. Nathan Clifford	1858	26–23	47%
Civil War (1860–1896)			
5. Stanley Matthews	1881	24–23	49%
6. Lucius Lamar	1888	32–28	47%
7. Melville Fuller	1888	41–20	33%
Republican (1896–1932)			
8. Mahlon Pitney	1912	50–26	34%
9. Louis Brandeis	1916	47–22	32%
10. Charles Evans Hughes	1930	52–26	33%
New Deal (1932–1968)			
None			
Divided Government (1968–2000)			
11. William Rehnquist	1971	68–26	28%
—elevation to chief	1986	65–33	34%
12. Clarence Thomas	1991	52–48	48%
Polarization (2000–present)			
13. Samuel Alito	2006	58–42	42%
14. Sonia Sotomayor	2009	68–31	31%
15. Elena Kagan	2010	63–37	37%
16. Neil Gorsuch	2017	54–45	45%
17. Brett Kavanaugh	2018	50–48	49%
18. Amy Coney Barrett	2020	52–48	48%
19. Ketanji Brown Jackson	2022	53–47	47%

in an all but unique fashion—through the mobilization of interest groups like the NRA, the Federalist Society, and NOW. Finally, we see an electoral basis to this contentiousness, as primary voters reward candidates who reject all nominees they view as ideologically inadequate, no matter the circumstances. And yet, paradoxically, these developments have made it more likely that a nominee will get confirmed, as opposed to earlier times when substantial Senate opposition across the aisle was a meaningful check.

Perhaps more alarming, increased polarization in the Senate—encouraged by outside groups—has predictably bred increased polarization on the Court. Based on the work of Lee Epstein and three other political scientists, a FiveThirtyEight analysis undertaken just before the Kavanaugh appointment showed an ever-widening gap among the middle five justices. Indeed, at no time since 1953, when the analysis begins, has the ideological divide been as wide as it was at the end of 2017, just *before* the swing justice Anthony Kennedy retired.[98] With the addition of two more Trump conservatives—Kavanaugh and Barrett—and the Biden-appointed Ketanji Brown Jackson, we should only expect this rift to grow.[99]

I argue that as currently constructed, the Roberts Court—with a majority of numerical minority justices—has a looser connection to majoritarianism than did Supreme Courts of the past, significantly deepening the Court's "democracy gap." The electorally dominant political regimes that previously drove presidential success in both the popular vote and the electoral college— often by wide margins—are gone. The Senate's voice, particularly the voice of the minority, has been all but silenced, thanks to the elimination of the filibuster. The result is that five numerical minority justices, three of whom were chosen by a minority president, dominate a conservative majority of six. Despite the fact that its candidates have collected more votes in both presidential and senate elections, nearly all elected members of the Democratic Party have been closed out of the process of choosing and confirming these justices. For this reason, the democratic legitimacy of the Roberts Court is at best uncertain. The Court treads on thin judicial ice. If it continues to pursue an aggressively conservative course, overturning decades-old decisions a majority of Americans still support, it may very well become the most countermajoritarian Court in the history of American democracy. It has already embarked on this path, most especially with the *Dobbs* decision upending *Roe*. The only question is how far will it go? How far will it "stray . . . from the mainstreams of American life," and how often will it "overestimate its power resources"?[100]

PART II

Searching for Wizards of the Law:
How the Rise of the Supreme Elite Further Distanced
the Court from the American People

6

How the Redefinition of Quality Created
a Cookie-Cutter Court

Job posting: The president of the United States seeks applicants for the position of Supreme Court justice. Interested candidates must have graduated from an elite private undergraduate institution (preferably an Ivy League university), earned a JD from an elite private law school (preferably Harvard or Yale), and be around fifty years old. Ideal candidates will be a judge on the Court of Appeals, will have never sought elective office, and will have clerked for a Supreme Court justice. Professional experience in Washington, DC, is a significant plus. Ideological compatibility with the president is a must. All others need not apply.

Certainly, we might think, the potential pool of candidates to be a Supreme Court justice is far larger than the terms of this outlandish, imagined job posting would suggest. The United States is home to well over a million lawyers, easily more than any other country in the world. Surely, a significant share of them are "qualified" to serve on the highest court in the land. But this hypothetical ad is a fairly accurate portrayal of the backgrounds of the nine sitting justices. In fact, some of the qualifications listed in the ad describe nearly all the justices of the last fifty years, after a significant shift in the definition of "quality." The current composition of the Court differs markedly from past Supreme Courts, particularly those from 1900 to 1970. Indeed, it is not only different from past Courts, it is a historical anomaly.

What's strange about the Court's current makeup is that it doesn't need to be this way. Unlike the presidency or the Congress, the Constitution is silent on eligibility for the Court. It speaks of no qualifications for membership at all. Justices need not be native-born citizens, or attorneys, or even a certain age. But despite this presidential freedom to choose, I argue that today's political environment demands the selection of a certain type of nominee from an extraordinarily small pool of potential candidates—what I call the "supreme elite." This is true of both Republican and Democratic presidents, although as I discuss here and in chapters 7 and 8, there are important differences between the two major parties on this matter. The result of this shallow candidate pool is a cloistered, cookie-cutter Court. Given the nation's growth in size and diversity, we might expect the opposite: a Court defined by variety and different traits. But instead, and in a consequential paradox, we have one ever more defined by sameness in a country ever more defined by diversity. With the historic exceptions of ethnicity, gender, and most recently race, the Court is less diverse than it was a half century ago.

This is not to say that today's justices have not worked very hard to reach the Court, nor is it to question their tremendous legal skills and unimpeachable educational qualifications. However, I do question the structure of the selection process that they all successfully traversed, and especially how the politics of the twenty-first century have redefined who is deemed "qualified" for the Court. This has resulted in a collection of justices who are drawn from an extraordinarily small slice of America. The Court is packed full of individuals who have lived dramatically different lives not only from everyday Americans but also from many of the legislators who make the laws they interpret.

In this chapter I'm going to elaborate on the backgrounds of today's justices and compare them to those of the past, and in the next two chapters I'll explore how we got here: why things changed, why only such a remarkably small group of individuals are judged to be eligible for appointment to the Court today, despite the Constitution's silence on that matter and the examples of diverse life experiences among past justices. In chapter 9, I'll examine the importance of the justices' backgrounds and the audiences they seek to please with their work, once again contrasting today's Court with those of the past. Throughout part II, I'll consider the consequences of this shift for the Supreme Court's decision-making and for its legitimacy in our democracy. It is certainly worth considering what it means for the country if constitutional and statutory interpretation at the highest level are undertaken by such a tiny sample of America. Are the justices' deliberations missing certain voices essential to understanding alternative paths forward or differing interpretations of the Constitution? Do they fully comprehend how the law in the books they write affects life in the streets? Does their lack of cultural diversity blur their vision of the Constitution, as some have alleged?[1] Finally, does their extreme outlier status undermine the Court's place in American democracy?

★

There are more than 37,000 high schools—public, private, and parochial—in the United States today. Yet Donald Trump's first two choices for the Supreme Court graduated from the same one: the exclusive private Georgetown Preparatory School (Georgetown Prep), located in the suburbs of Washington, DC, with 2022–23 tuition of more than $66,000 a year for boarding students. Indeed, only three of the justices—Samuel Alito, Elena Kagan, and Ketanji Brown Jackson—attended a public high school. And one of these three—

Kagan—went to the highly selective Hunter College High School in Manhattan.[2] Another—Alito—is the only Republican appointee who did not go to a private or parochial institution at the secondary level.

There are more than 2,500 accredited four-year colleges and universities in the United States. Yet, seven of nine justices earned an undergraduate degree from one of four Ivy League universities: three went to Princeton (Alito, Sonia Sotomayor, and Kagan), two to Harvard (John Roberts and Jackson), and one each to Columbia (Neil Gorsuch) and Yale (Brett Kavanaugh). The other two justices graduated from nationally ranked liberal arts colleges: one (Clarence Thomas) from Holy Cross on the outskirts of Boston and the other (Amy Coney Barrett) from Rhodes College in Memphis, Tennessee.[3] All six of these schools are private. So, unlike the vast majority of Americans who go to college, none of the justices attended a public college or university as an undergraduate.

Finally, there are more than 200 law schools in the United States. Yet, all but one of the justices attended either Harvard (4) or Yale (4). Amy Coney Barrett attended Notre Dame. As with their undergraduate education, none of those justices earned their law degree from a public institution.

The Court today is much different from those of the past. Before 1970, of the forty-one justices confirmed in the twentieth century, only ten— 24.4 percent—attended Harvard or Yale law schools. Seven went to Harvard and three went to Yale. (And at the time there were far fewer law schools than there are today.) The others studied at a range of law schools: from other Ivies such as Columbia and the University of Pennsylvania, to public institutions such as Alabama, the University of California-Berkeley, Indiana, Michigan, and Texas, to lesser-known law schools such as Albany, Cumberland, and Howard, to ones that no longer exist such as Centre and Saint Paul.[4] And four didn't actually go to a law school at all.

I call this shift toward hyper-elite, narrowly similar educational backgrounds the "Hruska switch," after a Nebraska senator, Roman Hruska, who famously—and unsuccessfully—defended the qualifications of one of President Richard Nixon's High Court nominees. On March 16, 1970, President Nixon needed a favor—he needed someone in the Senate to vigorously defend his nominee for the Supreme Court. Just four months into his presidency Nixon had been given a rare opportunity: two vacancies on the Supreme Court, both of which were created by the retirement of liberal justices, just the type of justices Nixon had criticized on the campaign trail. To recall, his first choice of Warren Earl Burger to replace Chief Justice Earl Warren had gone smoothly, as the Senate confirmed the Minnesotan with just a handful of dissenters. His second choice, however, did not go so well. The Senate rejected his selection of Clement Haynsworth of South Carolina to replace Associate Justice Abe Fortas. After that defeat, and even though the southern pool of qualified conservative Republican jurists was quite limited, Nixon was determined to name another southerner to the Fortas seat. Soon after the Haynsworth defeat he settled on G. Harrold Carswell of Florida.

In Washington, the choice was not well received. Opponents of the president criticized the selection for a variety of reasons, but the one that bothered Nixon the most was the characterization of Carswell as "mediocre." The Nixon administration viewed the attacks as a thinly veiled desire by liberals to undermine the president's plans to shift the Court to the right. For example, William Rehnquist, the person in the Justice Department heading up the search for a suitable nominee, angrily denounced two *Washington Post* editorials critical of Carswell's civil rights record. In a written response, Rehnquist sought to expose the true intent of the anti-Carswell campaign exemplified by the editorials. "[W]hat you are really fighting for . . . is the restoration of the Warren Court's liberal majority. . . . In fairness you ought to state all of the consequences that your position logically brings in its train: not merely further expansion of constitutional recognition of civil rights, but further expansion of the constitutional rights of criminal defendants, of pornographers, and of demonstrators."[5]

Nixon was not prepared to surrender to the Left by abandoning Carswell. But it was now a full ten months since the Fortas resignation. So, he marshaled supportive forces in the Senate. Roman Hruska, a senator Nixon briefly considered for the Court vacancy before dismissing the idea due to his age, would lead the charge. And on March 16, Hruska made his case for confirmation to his colleagues on the Senate floor, urging them to accept "Judge Carswell's nomination [as] sound, logical, and desirable." He added that Carswell was "well qualified . . . well suited for the post . . . learned in the law . . . experienced . . . [and] a man of integrity." Other senators echoed Hruska's words. The legal historian Laura Kalman writes that Louisiana's Russell Long, like Rehnquist did in his letter to the *Post*, "waved the bloody shirt of the Warren Court." To him, Carswell was indeed different from a liberal intellectual. He might not be a "brilliant student" like Fortas, but it was time for a change since those justices wrote decisions that wound "up getting us a 100-percent increase in crime." The nation had "had enough of those upside down, corkscrew thinkers." It was time for someone who could "think straight."[6]

If the appeals for Carswell's confirmation had remained on the Senate floor that day, the words spoken there may very well have been lost to history. But as the television cameras rolled, Hruska continued his pitch in an interview, making his notoriously memorable defense of the nominee: "Even if he is mediocre, there are a lot of mediocre judges and people and lawyers. They are entitled to a little representation, aren't they, and a little chance?" A Hruska aide said he meant it as a joke, but no one was laughing.[7]

After Hruska made his comment, a stunning change—the Hruska switch—occurred: all but four of the subsequent nineteen justices appointed (79 percent) attended Harvard Law or Yale Law, including twelve in a row at one point.[8] The same shift toward an Ivy League education occurred at the undergraduate level, albeit less dramatically. Twelve of the forty-one justices appointed in the twentieth century before the Hruska switch attended an Ivy League institution (29.3 percent). Three justices didn't attend college at all. Six attended but didn't graduate. After the switch, the Ivy League figure rose to 58 percent (11 of 19), including seven of the last eight justices (87.5 percent). All the others went to elite private colleges or universities, including three to Stanford, one of the highest-ranked schools in the country today (and then known as the "Harvard of the West").[9] In fact, the last justice to attend a public undergraduate institution was appointed in 1969, the last appointment before the Hruska switch, more than fifty years ago.[10] The last justice to attend a public law school was named in 1957, more than sixty-five years ago.[11]

Part of the explanation for this shift doubtless stems from some of the ways that institutions such as Harvard, Princeton, and Yale have changed since the mid-twentieth century. Once dominated by the wealthy and well-connected—America's aristocracy—these institutions are now far more diverse, more broadly defined, and far more aggressive in recruiting top students from across the nation (and the world). So, while the Ivies' doors may have been shut to some who went on to make their mark on the Court in the past, they are now at least ajar to all.

Nevertheless, the wealthy and well-connected still have an immense advantage at elite institutions. And while these schools strive for inclusivity, inequities persist. As the Yale Law School professor Daniel Markovits writes in *The Meritocracy Trap*, "the richest children, from the best high schools, dominate the student bodies at elite colleges and universities." More specifically, according to a 2017 study, five of the eight Ivy League schools had more students from the wealthiest 1 percent than from the bottom 60 percent.[12]

And those disparities perpetuate themselves for those who seek a law degree. For instance, at Yale Law, Markovits writes, the "student body includes as many and in some years more students from households in the top 1 percent of the income distribution than in the entire bottom half."[13] Consider the exclusivity of an Ivy League education in another way: of the 1.9 million college graduates from four-year institutions in 2020, approximately 13,500 earned their bachelor's degree from an Ivy League school. That's .007 percent.

And again, three of the justices graduated from just one of those schools (Princeton), and two from another (Harvard); two others graduated from two more (Columbia and Yale). In the past, the story was quite different.

✳

In their exhaustive US Supreme Court database, Lee Epstein and her colleagues include a variable about the "general socioeconomic status" of each justice's "family during his or her childhood."[14] As might be expected given the education levels of the five classes they identify—lower, lower middle, middle, upper middle, and upper—for much of American history many of the justices came from the upper-middle and upper socioeconomic rungs of society. In fact, only presidents of the New Deal period appointed more nominees from the three poorest classes of American society than from the two wealthiest (see figure 6.1). This helps explain why, with just one exception, justices from the two wealthiest backgrounds dominated the Court for nearly its first 150 years. President Abraham Lincoln ensured this one exception in 1862, when he nominated Noah Haynes Swayne for the Court; after that nomination, a majority of the sitting justices had been raised in families from the three poorest classes for the first time since the Court's creation in 1789. Lincoln followed up that appointment with three other jurists from humble origins. In fact, none of his nominees came from the upper class, and only one was raised in an upper-middle-class home. With Lincoln's imprint apparent, justices from the three least affluent classes continued to comprise a majority for a dozen years after his death. But Lincoln was unusual with his selections. In the entire Civil War period, nearly 70 percent of appointments came from the two wealthiest classes (figure 6.1). So, a Court majority from the most well-to-do families returned in 1877.

That majority lasted until 1930, when it shifted back with the appointment of Charles Evans Hughes, who was raised in a middle-class home, to the

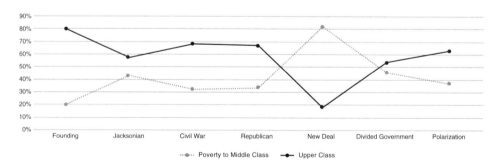

FIGURE 6.1. Justices' Family Socioeconomic Status, by Era (two classes)

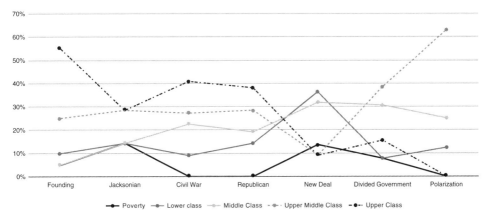

FIGURE 6.2. Justices' Family Socioeconomic Status, by Era (five classes)

Court's center chair. While the dominance of justices from the two wealthiest classes of society ended during his immediate predecessor's presidency, Franklin D. Roosevelt made certain it would not return again in the near future. Like Lincoln, Roosevelt did not appoint any men from the upper class to the Court, and only one from an upper-middle-class family. FDR wanted those who "had come up the hard way," who "knew how the other 90 percent live."[15] Moreover, he appointed two of the seven justices ever to serve on the high bench who were raised in poverty. Two others were part of the lower middle class. The remaining four were from middle-class families. Indeed, for much of the New Deal period (1932–1968), few jurists came from either of the two most prosperous classes (figure 6.2). And Democratic presidents did not choose a single justice who was raised in an upper-class home during this time.[16]

While Nixon's first selection after the Hruska switch (Harry Blackmun) came from the middle class, with his 1971 choices of Lewis Powell and William Rehnquist a new trend started to emerge. Beginning with those 1971 High Court appointments and continuing today, nearly three-fourths—thirteen of the last eighteen—were raised in an upper-middle- or upper-class home. And in 1994, with President Bill Clinton's appointment of Stephen Breyer, a majority of the justices once again came from America's two most affluent classes. That lasted until 2006 when Samuel Alito (middle class) replaced Sandra Day O'Connor (upper middle class). It changed back in 2017 when Neil Gorsuch (upper middle class) filled the seat of Antonin Scalia (middle class). After the confirmation of Amy Coney Barrett (upper middle), six of the nine justices were raised in upper-middle-class homes—the most ever—and one in a middle-class home. Two were children of the two poorest classes: Thomas (lower) and Sotomayor (lower middle). Notably, both of these two faced far more questions about their qualifications during their confirmations than did their fellow justices.[17] Today, after Ketanji Brown Jackson (middle[18]) replaced Stephen Breyer (upper middle), the class background of the justices sits at five upper middle, two middle, one lower middle, and one lower (although see note 18 for more details about Jackson's socioeconomic background).

While recent presidents are certainly not choosing their nominees based on their class background, the redefinition of "quality" after the Hruska switch likely contributed to this shift. Based on what we know about Ivy League admissions, a selection process that highlights where nominees earned their undergraduate and law degrees will in turn increase the likelihood presidents will select someone who has been reared in an upper-middle- or upper-class home. So, it is not the least bit surprising that more justices today—including six of the last nine additions (67 percent)—were raised in upper-middle-class homes. That's strikingly at odds with the overwhelming number of Americans, 86 percent of whom live below that income level.[19]

.   ✶

All but one of the current justices spent significant parts of their pre-Court careers in Washington, DC. The one exception—Sonia Sotomayor—spent her entire pre-Court career in Manhattan. Indeed, a majority of the justices had worked in the Supreme Court building before they ascended to the high bench. Six of them clerked for a justice, snaring a rare ticket to a firsthand experience in constitutional lawmaking. This is a very new development for the Court. Aside from the six former clerks sitting today, only four other justices had previously served in that role in the history of the Court, including the recently retired Stephen Breyer.[20] And three of the six filled the vacancy of the justice they clerked for, including two of the last three.[21]

All but one of the justices served as circuit court judge before ascending to the Court. The one exception is Elena Kagan. And notably, she was selected for a vacancy on the DC court of appeals. However, Senate Republicans delayed consideration of her nomination long enough for President Clinton's presidency to end. Four of the others were judges on that same DC court of appeals before their nomination to the Supreme Court (Thomas, Roberts, Kavanaugh, and Jackson). The four others served on four different courts of appeal: Alito on the third, based in Philadelphia; Sotomayor on the second, based in Manhattan; Gorsuch on the tenth, based in Denver; and Barrett on the seventh, based in Chicago. Notably, Gorsuch and Barrett are the only ones to serve on a circuit court away from the East Coast. Sotomayor and Jackson are the only ones to serve as a district court judge before their nomination to a court of appeals.

Choosing circuit court judges is a relatively new development. In the twentieth-century nominations that predate the Nixon administration, presidents chose a sitting circuit court judge less than a quarter of the time (10 of 43). And President Eisenhower made three of those ten selections.[22] The Senate did not confirm two of the ten nominees. So, before the Nixon administration, eight justices in total were elevated directly from the circuit court. Three others had been circuit court judges before leaving to pursue more appealing posts, all at the behest of the sitting president.[23] These departures suggest that these presidents and future justices did not view being a court of appeals judge as the best training for the high bench.[24] In fact, that view was highlighted in 1957 by Justice Felix Frankfurter, who vociferously made the following case about the selection process:

> The search should be made among those men, inevitably very few at the time, who give the best promise of satisfying the intrinsic needs of the Court, no matter where they may be found, no matter in what professional way they have manifested the needed qualities. Of course, these needs do not exclude prior judicial experience, but, no less surely, they do not call for judicial experience. *One is entitled to say without qualification, that the correlation between prior judicial experience and fitness for the functions of the Supreme Court is zero.* The significance of the greatest among the Justices who had had such experiences, Holmes and Cardozo, derived not from that judicial experience but from the fact that they were Holmes and Cardozo. They were thinkers, and more particularly legal philosophers.[25]

While Frankfurter's argument focuses on all types of prior judicial experience—for instance, Holmes and Cardozo were state court judges—a much-cited study evaluating the first 100 justices—those appointed from 1789 to 1967—bolsters his case with regard to the circuit court judges who went on to become justices. According to that study, none of the thirteen justices who had been circuit court judges were among the "greats" of the twentieth century. (And, for that matter, only one of the nineteenth-century "greats" had been a circuit court judge.) Two of those thirteen were deemed "near greats," but one had left his circuit seat years earlier to pursue other posts, including president of the United States. Four were defined as "failures," including three chosen directly from the circuit court.[26]

The trend toward selecting circuit court judges began just before the Hruska switch. Presidents—particularly Eisenhower and Nixon—began favoring nominees sitting on a circuit court, especially the one in Washington. But even here, their court of appeals experience was limited. One of the three judges Eisenhower chose directly from a circuit court had spent less than a year there before his elevation to the High Court. A second was there for just over a year. The third spent four years there. And all had significant experience outside the judiciary before serving on the court of appeals. In contrast, the eight former circuit court judges serving as justices in 2021 spent more than a *decade* on average in those seats. And many of those justices were chosen in part due to their relative youth. In fact, the average of court of appeals experience has only been lowered recently because Presidents Trump and Biden searched for even younger nominees in replacing Justices Ginsburg and Breyer, both of whom served at least thirteen years on the court of appeals.

While Nixon did nominate four circuit court judges to the high bench—only two of whom were confirmed—he didn't do so because they were court of appeals judges. Indeed, nowhere on the portion of his tapes where he discusses the two 1971 Supreme Court vacancies at length—the recording system was not in place at the time of the earlier vacancies—does he articulate a desire to name a circuit court judge. Rather, he chose his nominees because they checked other boxes important to him.[27] This helps explain why neither of the two men he ultimately chose for the 1971 seats had previously served as a judge. Nevertheless, and however tentative or conditional, his inclination, and Eisenhower's before him, to nominate circuit court judges began a trend that would firmly take hold "in the Ford and Reagan presidencies."[28] In all, since the beginning of the Nixon administration, twenty-one of the last twenty-six nominees have been sitting circuit court judges—that's more than 80 percent. And nearly half of those were members of the DC court of appeals (10 of 21, or 48 percent). The Senate did not confirm all of these nominees. Sixteen of the twenty-one eventually became justices, including seven of those who served in DC. Notably, three of the five nominees who were not court of appeals judges were women. The other two, Nixon's two 1971 choices, were selected early in this period.

In his 2001 year-end report, Chief Justice William Rehnquist expressed concern about a federal judiciary that no longer drew "from a wide diversity of professional backgrounds," believing it could be deprived of its potency. As he wrote, "we have never had, and should not want, a Judiciary composed only of those persons who are already in the public service." To him, a federal judiciary filled with such judges and justices would be too similar to those found in "civil law countries." And those courts, Rehnquist asserted, "simply do not command the respect and enjoy the independence of ours." He then made a plea: "We must not drastically shrink the number of judicial nominees who have had substantial experience in private practice."[29]

In favoring circuit court judges, recent presidents have virtually abandoned choosing judges from other courts: most significantly, state courts. In the last sixty-plus years, only Sandra Day O'Connor was chosen directly from a state court (although David Souter was a member of the New Hampshire Supreme Court before being confirmed for the First Circuit, where he served less than a year). Choosing nominees with state court experience was quite common during the early years of the twentieth century. But soon after that, the practice fell into disfavor. Nevertheless, several justices who served as a judge in one type of state court or another were among the twentieth century's "greats." Frankfurter alluded to two: Oliver Wendell Holmes and Benjamin Cardozo. Two others were "near greats": William Howard Taft and William Brennan.

Sonia Sotomayor, to recall, is the only sitting justice not to have worked in Washington before her elevation to the High Court. Delving more deeply into Washington experience (and leaving aside clerkships), there is a clear partisan division among the justices with regard to pre-Court experience in the nation's capital. Five of the six Republican-appointed justices have worked in the executive branch, four of them in the Department of Justice. (In chapter 7 I'll argue that there is a specific reason for this development: recent Republican presidents' desire to ensure ideological purity and prevent ideological drift.) The two Democrat-appointed justices who worked in Washington had more diverse experiences there. While Elena Kagan worked in the executive branch, she was also special counsel to the Senate's Judiciary Committee for a short time. When not in Washington she mostly worked in Cambridge, Massachusetts, at Harvard Law School, serving as the school's dean for nearly five years before returning to Washington to serve as solicitor general for the Obama administration. Ketanji Brown Jackson spent the vast majority her adult life in Washington, working in private practice (2002–2003 and 2007–2010); as assistant special counsel for the US sentencing commission (2003–2005); as a federal public defender (2005–2007); as vice chair and commissioner of the US sentencing commission (2010–2014); as a federal district court judge (2013–2021); and finally, as a DC court of appeals judge (2021–2022).[30]

With few exceptions, after graduating from law school the justices spent all or significant portions of their working lives in the megalopolis that extends down the nation's northeastern coast, dominated by the country's academic center (Boston), political center (Washington, DC), and cultural and financial center (New York City).[31] Indeed, most could be fairly described as Washington attorneys before their appointment to the court of appeals (four of whom served on that court in DC).

Even though they spent much of their adult lives in the nation's capital, none of the justices have ever run for an elective office. None of them had to put their name on the line for the public's approval on Election Day. None had to ask for a campaign contribution or address a hostile group of constituents. None had to knock on a door to convince a skeptical voter of the rectitude of their positions or the quality of their character. None had to appeal to a majority to retain their position. None needed to please a large group made up of individuals who didn't have the initials J and D after their name.[32]

My point isn't that every Supreme Court justice needs to run for elective office to perform effectively. It is only to underscore that in the past, nominees had much greater experiential diversity. They have included sitting senators, former governors, former members of the House of Representatives, former state legislators, former members of city councils, former mayors of major cities, and even a former president. Notably, this list does not even reach back to the nineteenth century. The justices with this political experience were all appointed in the twentieth century. Some of them went on to distinguish themselves on the bench, earning "great" or "near great" status. Others were abject failures. But service in a democratically elected institution didn't disqualify them for selection to the nation's highest tribunal. Today, apparently, it does.

So, none of the 2023–2024 term justices would likely have passed the so-called biography test, meaning they would be worthy of a biography had they not been appointed to the Supreme Court. In fact, most wouldn't merit an entry in an encyclopedia, or, at the appropriate moment, leaving the native New Yorkers aside, an obituary in the city's *Times*. They lived extraordinarily similar adult lives in hopes of grasping the brass ring on the Supreme Court selection carousel. And in that endeavor, they succeeded.

✴

With regard to religion, the justices overall are quite historically unusual. Most notably, there are only two Protestants—easily the largest religious group in the nation—on the Court. And both are recent additions. In fact, between the retirement of John Paul Stevens in 2010 and Neil Gorsuch's confirmation in 2017, there were no Protestants on the Court at all.[33] This is quite a development, since Protestants dominated the Court's makeup for much of American history. For much of the polarization period, this change meant more justices from two religious backgrounds: Catholicism and Judaism. While Catholics were once "assigned" a single seat on the high bench, there are now six Catholic justices (Alito, Barrett, Kavanaugh, Roberts, Sotomayor, and Thomas). In addition, one of the Protestants, Justice Gorsuch, was raised Catholic.[34] For approximately sixty years of the early and middle part of the twentieth century a single seat was also "reserved" for a Jewish justice, although for two stints there were two Jewish members of the Court.[35] Until Ruth Bader Ginsburg's death in 2020, three of the justices were Jewish. With Stephen Breyer's 2022 retirement, the figure is back down to one (Elena Kagan).

This has created a Court that diverges markedly from those of the past. Its religious makeup has shifted but not diversified. In fact, it's more accurate to say that the 2020 Court was less religiously diverse than it had been in the mid-1990s, after the appointment of Stephen Breyer. At that point, the justices' religious affiliations were as follows: four Protestant (O'Connor, Rehnquist, Souter, and Stevens); three Catholic (Kennedy, Scalia, and Thomas); two Jewish (Breyer and Ginsburg).[36] Even before the Hruska switch in 1970 the Court was somewhat more religiously diverse than in 2020. Although it was overwhelmingly Protestant, there was a Catholic and a Jewish justice (as tradition held). But among the Protestant seven, there was a Baptist (Hugo Black). Justice Black is one of only three Baptists ever to serve on the Court, despite the fact that Baptists are easily the largest Protestant denomination in the United States. There's a fairly straightforward reason for this trend away from religious diversity on the Court. Recent presidents simply haven't paid much attention to religious affiliation when searching for a Supreme Court nominee, except perhaps when it reinforces a nominee's ideology (more on this in chapter 7). On other occasions, it hasn't mattered much (even when we might expect otherwise). For example, in discussing President Bill Clinton's first nomination, the political scientist David Yalof writes that "the fact that [Ruth Bader] Ginsburg was Jewish . . . was barely a factor in the decisionmaking calculus."[37]

✶

In 2016, before the death of Antonin Scalia, four of the nine justices were from four of the five boroughs of New York City (Ginsburg, Kagan, Scalia, and Sotomayor). Another was from central New Jersey, about an hour's drive from New York City (Alito). Two others were from the greater San Francisco area (Breyer and Kennedy). Only one grew up in the South (Thomas). And another was raised in a suburb of Buffalo, New York before moving to a small Indiana city on the far outskirts of Chicago (Roberts). Today, the Court still counts as members two daughters of New York City (Sotomayor and Kagan), and a son of central New Jersey (Alito). The Buffalonian/Indianan (Roberts) and the southerner (Thomas) also remain. One of the new additions (Kavanaugh) grew up in the affluent DC suburb of Bethesda; another (Gorsuch) attended high school in the DC area, although he was born and raised in Colorado. In fact, Gorsuch is the only westerner to serve on the Court since Sandra Day O'Connor's retirement in 2005. The two most recent additions, Amy Coney Barrett and Ketanji Brown Jackson, triple the representation of southern-ers. Barrett and Jackson were both raised in the suburbs of major southern cities—Barrett near New Orleans and Jackson near Miami.

In the past, geography was an essential consideration in the search for a Supreme Court nominee, especially if a president thought the Court did not have proper representation from a particular region. Most famously, as I described earlier, Richard Nixon searched for a southern nominee to success-fully appoint to the Court. After the Senate rejected his first two choices, he succeeded in appointing Lewis Powell of Virginia. Earlier, Franklin Roose-velt sought to appoint a "true Westerner" because even though William O. Douglas hailed from the state of Washington, he had lived his life in the East after arriving in New York City to attend law school. With his final appoint-ment, FDR settled on Wiley Rutledge of Iowa (and previously of Colorado and Missouri), the only one of the nine Roosevelt justices who spent his adult life west of the Mississippi. These are just a couple of examples of presidential attention to geography. Notably, today presidents pay little if any attention to where a potential nominee grew up. It simply doesn't matter anymore.

Linked to the geography of a justice's childhood home is the setting of that home. For example, approximately 60 million Americans live in rural areas of the United States (about 19 percent). But with the exception of Clarence Thomas, none of the justices have lived what might be called "a rural life." For his part, Thomas spent only the first six years of his life in rural Pinpoint, Georgia. In the first grade, his single mother moved him and his brother to Savannah (his sister stayed in Pinpoint). There, as he wrote in his memoir, he faced "the foulest kind of urban squalor" until he and his brother perma-nently moved into his maternal grandparents' home in the Black section of Savannah.[38] He lived there until he left for the seminary in Missouri, but he also spent significant parts of his summers on "the farm," in rural Georgia.

So, as a group, the justices spent much of their pre-college years in urban and suburban settings. Put another way, none spent the majority of those years where the crops are grown, only where they are consumed. Unsurpris-ingly, given the nation's agrarian history, far more justices were raised in a rural setting in the first two centuries of the Court than in the tenure of those sitting today.

★

Recent Supreme Court justices are even roughly the same age. The eight who have made it onto the Court during the polarization era have been between forty-eight and fifty-five years old. The thinking is obvious. A potential nominee who is much older than fifty-five may not serve long enough to leave a legacy. One who is significantly younger than forty-eight has probably not had sufficient time to develop into a superstar of the law. Not surprisingly, presidents have always desired to appoint justices on the younger side. But today, it appears that any potential nominee over sixty is instantly excluded. Moreover, justices are living and serving longer than in the past. The average length of service for the justices appointed during the divided government era was more than twenty-six years (with one still there). Before Justice Kennedy retired in 2018, three justices were over or just weeks short of eighty years old. Only four justices have served past the age of eighty-seven in the history of the Court. One of them, John Paul Stevens, retired in 2010. Another, Ruth Bader Ginsburg, died in September 2020.

Of course, the combination of young appointees and longer service means the Court changes less frequently, and is therefore less open to electorally inspired change—a development that contributes to the Court's democracy gap (see chapter 13). A preference for nominees under sixty years old also means that justices who went on to serve admirably in the past would never have made it onto the Court today. For example, if President Clinton had listened to some of the voices in his White House and chosen someone younger than Ginsburg—who was sixty when he nominated her—she would have never have become "Notorious RBG."[39] Indeed, the list of the eleven twentieth-century justices appointed after the age of sixty includes a striking number of legends of the law: Oliver Wendell Holmes (61), William Howard Taft (63), Charles Evans Hughes (who returned to the Court as chief justice at 67), Benjamin Cardozo (61), and Earl Warren (61).[40] By the time he took his oath of office, Louis Brandeis was just five months shy of his sixtieth birthday. One study that asked experts to evaluate all of the fifty-two justices appointed during the twentieth century ranked Brandeis first; Holmes was a very close second. Cardozo was fifth; Warren seventh. Hughes, who served six years as an associate justice before leaving to pursue the presidency, only to return as chief fourteen years later, was eighth. Taft was thirteenth.[41] The study of the first 100 justices cited earlier ranked those above as "great," with the sole exception of Taft. He was deemed "near great." Only three others appointed in the twentieth century earned "great" status.[42]

✳

Other scholars have already done the work of assessing fully and in detail the characteristics of justices today.[43] This review is intended to highlight essential differences between the justices today *as a group* compared to justices in the past *as a group*, and most especially those of the first seventy years of the twentieth century.[44] At various points, I also note how they differ from the vast majority of their fellow Americans.

While this Court is far less diverse in numerous ways than previous Courts, it is not entirely so. The sitting justices are easily more representative of America's heterogeneity in terms of gender, ethnicity, and race compared to the Court before the Hruska switch. Specifically, there are four women (Sonia Sotomayor, Elena Kagan, Amy Coney Barrett, and Ketanji Brown Jackson)—the most ever. Justice Sotomayor is also the first Hispanic American ever to serve on the Court. And Samuel Alito is the second Italian American justice, although that distinction was certainly not as symbolically significant as it was in 1986 when Antonin Scalia was chosen. On race, the Court stayed the same for fifty-five years. The number of Black justices remained at one from Thurgood Marshall's appointment 1967 to Ketanji Brown Jackson's in 2022. She joins Clarence Thomas, the second ever African American justice, doubling that figure.[45]

Sotomayor and Thomas bring diversity to the Court in other ways as well. Thomas is the only sitting justice raised in poverty—although in his telling, once he moved in with his grandparents as a young child his socioeconomic status was closer to lower middle class.[46] Sotomayor's family was also of the lower middle class. They lived in the "projects" before moving to Co-Op City in the Bronx.[47] As children, both Thomas and Sotomayor spoke a language other than English at home. For Sotomayor, the daughter of Puerto Rican parents, it was Spanish; for Thomas, it was Gullah Geechee, a version of English originating with African slaves.[48] Indeed, Thomas has said it was "difficult for [him] to learn English" and that he "didn't become entirely comfortable with [it] until the late 1980s," just before his appointment to the Court.[49] But while the makeup of the Court has diversified on gender, ethnicity, and race since the early 1970s, it has somewhat counterintuitively become *more* homogeneous in a host of other areas.

My intention in outlining the differences between the Court's current members and those of the past is not to criticize the former. After all, they recognized the selection landscape and then embarked on the necessary career path. Even then, their odds of being chosen for such a coveted seat were exceedingly long, at best. Rather, my argument is that the structure of the selection process itself is deeply flawed, leaving the Court without the eclectic collection of voices that was once at the very center of constitutional lawmaking.

We cannot know what the nation is missing if the doors to the Court are closed for those who are off the "right" path, but history and examples from other pursuits can provide some clues. Malcolm Gladwell's book *Outliers* popularizes scientific research in a variety of areas. In making a point about the predictive quality of IQ tests, Gladwell lists the undergraduate institutions of the last twenty-five American winners of the Nobel Prize in medicine. Predictably, five of the eight Ivies are on the list. But only Columbia appears more than once (it's there twice). Several public universities of varying size and *US News* rank are listed, including Berkeley, Hunter, Illinois, Minnesota, Texas, Washington, and North Carolina. Small liberal arts colleges, such as Amherst, Antioch, DePauw, Gettysburg, Hamilton, Holy Cross, and Union College (Kentucky), are represented. And there are others—some more well known—that devote more attention to STEM research: California Institute of Technology, Case Institute of Technology (now Case Western Reserve), Johns Hopkins, and Massachusetts Institute of Technology (MIT). Notre Dame is the other school on the list.[50]

Gladwell then lists the undergraduate institution of the last twenty-five American Nobel laureates in chemistry. The list is even more varied than the one for medicine. Only three of America's top chemists graduated from an Ivy League school. Two of those attended Harvard. But two also went to the City College of New York. Some were alums of small schools that are not very well known, including Augsburg, Berea, Grinnell, Hope, Ohio Wesleyan, and Rollins. Others went to mid-size and large public universities such as Dayton, Florida, Massachusetts, Nebraska, University of California-Riverside, and Washington State. Once again, some attended more STEM-focused schools: Georgia Tech, MIT (two winners), and Rice. And two attended universities in Canada. Brigham Young University and Stanford are the other schools on the list.[51] "[N]o one would say [these] list[s] represent the college choices of the absolute best high school students in America," writes Gladwell.[52] But they all apparently provide an opportunity to secure a solid foundation from which to build the intellectual capability and scientific creativity necessary to conduct research worthy of a Nobel Prize.

In an article for the *New Yorker* in 2005, Gladwell considers how law schools select their students, and ends up questioning the emphasis on standardized test scores. As he writes:

> In a recent research project funded by the Law School Admission Council, the Berkeley researchers Sheldon Zedeck and Marjorie Shultz identified

twenty-six "competencies" that they think effective lawyering demands—among them practical judgment, passion and engagement, legal-research skills, questioning and interviewing skills, negotiation skills, stress management, and so on—and the L.S.A.T. picks up only a handful of them. A law school that wants to select the best possible lawyers has to use a very different admissions process from a law school that wants to select the best possible law students. . . . This search for good lawyers, furthermore, is necessarily going to be subjective, because things like passion and engagement can't be measured as precisely as academic proficiency.[53]

So, if law schools like Harvard and Yale have a particular focus in selecting their students, as Gladwell and Markovits suggest, it's important to ask if that bias extends to a Supreme Court filled with eight justices who attended those two schools. Do we have a Court packed with excellent law students or excellent lawyers? Or perhaps the better question is: would a selection process less focused on where potential justices attended college and law school and more focused on what they did after earning their degrees produce a Court that better serves the American people and American democracy?

Let's consider these questions by examining two past justices from the middle and latter part of the twentieth century who likely never would have made it to the Court with today's selection process. Critics will certainly say, and rightly so, that I am cherry-picking these jurists. I also focus on two Democratic nominees. But a survey of the lives of Republican-appointed justices such as Oliver Wendell Holmes and Earl Warren would illustrate a similar point. Indeed, the two under review are two of several—if not many—examples of justices who were quite different from those of today. I highlight these two—each of whom would be an extreme long shot for a Court nomination today—not to celebrate their greatness on the Court. While one has been ranked near the top, the other has been deemed a mere "average" justice. The argument, instead, is that in redefining quality after the Hruska switch, we've ended up with a Court arguably less well suited to serve the interests of the American people and American democracy—that, ironically and paradoxically, in our search for "quality" we've ended up with a less qualified Court for our nation.

✳

In 1950 the Court was hopelessly divided. The National Association for the Advancement of Colored People (NAACP) had painstakingly brought cases before the justices for more than a decade in hopes of developing the precedent necessary to constitutionally undercut the "separate but equal" doctrine announced in *Plessy v. Ferguson* in 1896. Now it was asking the Court to finally demolish this most racially discriminatory doctrine. The Truman Justice Department added its voice too, subtly suggesting the Court end *de jure* segregation in the schools. The justices were uncertain, however. Four thought the Court should once and for all strike down *Plessy*, the constitutional foundation of the South's system of white supremacy. Four others thought differently or weren't prepared to act just yet. One sought the middle, hoping to enhance his leverage in the Court's final determination.

During conference, the first justice to articulate a desire to constitutionally decapitate *Plessy* stressed the likely consequences of such a decision. This justice did not shy away from the uproar likely to ensue. According to one report, he suggested that such a precedent-shattering decision would mean the end of "Southern liberalism for the time being." He expected that race-baiting politicians would rise to the fore to fight against the change. Riots would erupt, and "the Army might have to be called out." While his words "scared" the other justices, he was unmoved by the possibilities emanating from southern white rage. Instead, he was "determined to overrule" *Plessy* "on principle."[54] As he stressed to his colleagues that day, segregation was nothing short of "Hitler's creed." The German Führer had "preached what the South believed."[55]

The identity of the justice who spoke these words surely would have surprised many casual observers: Justice Hugo L. Black of Alabama had once been a member of the Ku Klux Klan. But to those who knew better, Black's resistance to the reigning order was not the least bit surprising. As a senator, Black had been a liberal firebrand. One critic called his nomination a presidential "trick to ram the furthest Left-winger available down the Senate's throat"—a judicial Trojan horse. Still another concluded, "Mr. Roosevelt could not have made a worse appointment if he had named [labor leader] John L. Lewis."[56] Indeed, the very selection of Black displayed FDR's determination to choose High Court nominees who challenged the legal status quo. Even Steve Early, the president's chief of staff, could not contain his surprise when he heard the news of Black's nomination, muttering: "Jesus Christ."[57]

As the historian Robert Harrison writes, President Roosevelt looked for justices "who had come up the hard way, who had worked to improve the economic conditions of 'the little man,' and who had deplored the predatory practices and lack of public accountability of financiers, bankers, industrialists, and corporate leaders."[58] Of Roosevelt's nine justices, Hugo Black exemplified these ideals most of all. And while FDR was focused on disrupting the reigning economic order, both he and Black fervently believed "Southern Democracy" prevented the federal government from appropriately responding to the crisis at hand, from improving the economic livelihood of Americans as a whole.[59] Of course, those committed to the cause of racial justice were right to be skeptical. After all, blinded by political ambition, Black had joined the "Invisible Empire," as the KKK was known, in 1923. Significantly, he was the only Klan man running for an open Senate seat in 1926. But it was evident to many racial progressives that he was a different man by the time of his appointment to the Court in 1937. In fact, soon after he won his Senate seat, Black began working against KKK interests. By the time he was up for reelection in 1932, "the Klan actively opposed him." After Black's Klan membership came to light soon after his Senate confirmation as a justice, the NAACP, which had supported his nomination, quickly called on him to resign. But notably, its longtime leader, Walter White, came to his defense. White and Black were in fact close friends. So, the NAACP leader sought to ease those concerns by speaking of his "firsthand acquaintance" with Black. To those willing to listen, White said that "the new Justice's views on racial, economic, and political questions convinced me that Mr. Black would prove to be one of the most valued and able members of the Court." As he would later write about the justice, "the dead hand of tradition was anathema to him."[60]

Born in February 1886 in a log cabin in rural Clay County, Alabama, Black was the eighth and youngest child of parents who had buried their seventh child a few days earlier. The Black family worked their farm with their tenants, and Hugo's father also ran a country store. This was a county "of white yeoman farmers," according to Black biographer Virginia Van der Veer Hamilton. A decade before the turn of the twentieth century, approximately 90 percent of its 16,000 residents were white and 10 percent were Black, "a ratio in direct reversal of the heavy black majorities" in counties where the land was more fertile. When the youngest Black was not yet four, the family moved a few miles down the road to Ashland, the county seat, where his father became a partner in a general store near the courthouse. The move also afforded the Black children more of an educational opportunity, a chief concern of their mother, who loved books and was responsible for bringing a variety of works into the Black household, including those of Victor Hugo, the inspiration for the justice's name.[61]

In Ashland, Black attended public schools, eventually enrolling at Ashland College. Despite its name, according to a Black biographer, "it was no more than a country high school."[62] The future justice didn't stay long enough to earn a degree. After an attempt by two teachers to "whip" him went awry, he left the school.[63] At sixteen, he "was a high school dropout." His family then convinced him to give medical school a try. And despite his lack of educational credentials, Birmingham Medical College accepted him. He stayed for a year, and did well, but concluded that medicine was not for him and from there went to Tuscaloosa and the University of Alabama. Officials admitted him but determined he should begin as a freshman in the liberal arts college. Black thought his previous studies qualified him for sophomore status. Frustrated by their decision, he headed over to the law school instead, which did not require an undergraduate degree to enroll in its two-year program. With just two faculty members, the offerings were obviously limited, so Black filled out his schedule with courses in other parts of the university, particularly in history, literature, and political economy. In 1906, he was awarded a Bachelor of Laws degree—one of seven in his graduating class to earn the highest honors.[64] While Black excelled in Tuscaloosa, "in truth," writes the legal scholar Noah Feldman, his "formal education was . . . not very extensive at all. . . . Although he was not, strictly speaking, an autodidact in the sense of Abraham Lincoln, he believed his education was his own more than a product of the University of Alabama."[65]

At just twenty years old Black was now ready to begin his career in law. The most notable experiences of his early years in the law came with a move to Birmingham after his office in Ashland burned down. After a few years as a solo practitioner representing all sorts of clients—in fact, just about anyone who came through his door—Black landed a position as a police court judge. Sometimes hearing as many as 100 cases in a single morning, he became a heroic figure in a humorous series written by a local reporter, providing him the public attention he desired. The defendants in his court were primarily African Americans "arrested for drinking, using dope or shooting craps, thievery or vagrancy, fighting or marital disturbances." Black found the experience extremely valuable, noting soon after he resigned that it had afforded him "broad insight into human nature."[66]

Black did not stay away from public office for long. Two years later he ran for Jefferson County prosecutor as a reformer and won. In that position he challenged the status quo in many southern county jails. In particular, "he moved against the [Bessemer] jail after" realizing that the "assembly-line stream of confessions that came from it" were the result of "prisoners, usually black, being mercilessly beaten until they confessed to whatever charge had been lodged against them." His time as a prosecutor profoundly shaped his views on criminal justice. "Over a half century later," one of his biographers writes, "the millions of Americans who observed Black's reading of passages from his great opinion in *Chambers v. Florida* [during a CBS broadcast] *condemning* confessions *incommunicado*, were really witnessing the closing part of a process of development that had begun long before, at the Bessemer jail."[67] Indeed, even near the end of his life, Black could not read his words from that 1940 opinion unanimously overturning the conviction of four African

American tenant farmers forced to confess to a murder they did not commit without tears welling up in his eyes and "streaming down his face." Here are some of his words:

> Today, as in ages past, we are not without tragic proof that the exalted power of some governments to punish manufactured crime dictatorially is the hand-maid of tyranny. Under our constitutional system, courts stand against any winds that blow as havens of refuge for those who might otherwise suffer because they are helpless, weak, outnumbered, or because they are nonconforming victims of prejudice and public excitement. Due process of law, preserved for all by our Constitution, commands that no such practice as that disclosed by this record shall send any accused to his death. No higher duty, no more solemn responsibility, rests upon this Court than that of translating into living law and maintaining this constitutional shield deliberately planned and inscribed for the benefit of every human being subject to our Constitution—of whatever race, creed or persuasion.[68]

∗

By the 1930s the Great Depression was breaking the backs of everyday Americans, particularly those in Birmingham, one of the worst-hit cities nationwide. By virtue of winning the all-important Democratic primary several months earlier, Black knew he would soon secure a second term in the Senate. Still, he wanted to get a better understanding of the economic despair gripping the "Magic City." So he set up an office and invited his constituents to stop by to speak with him. Feldman continues with the story:

> When Black arrived at 9:00 a.m., hundreds of unemployed people had crowded the lobby of the federal building. Black's nephew Hollis, who was helping him in the campaign, was worried they would riot if Black reneged on this promise to meet them individually. Hollis hastily scribbled down numbers on scraps of paper to be handed out to the crowd. Taking them in numerical order, Black saw each in turn. For four full days, Black listened to the men. Ranging from farmers to court clerks to businessmen, there were, Black said, "my oldest and best friends." And they were desperate. "Some . . . were threatening suicide if they didn't get a job."[69]

Black biographer Roger K. Newman adds: "The Depression traumatized Black. He agonized when broken and dispirited men and women, with sacks wrapped around their feet for shoes, stopped him on the street to beg for government jobs." The Depression in Birmingham meant that "the self-reliant lost their reliance, the independent became dependent on others, the proud went into shock. The terrible suffering hit Black as few other things could." In early December 1932, mere weeks after those countless conversations with his constituents, a newly elected Black introduced the thirty-hour work week bill, a "remarkably simple" piece of legislation designed to limit the numbers of hours a single individual could work in order to ensure others a paycheck as well. If his bill became law, Black predicted it would create 6 million jobs.[70] While it passed the Senate in early 1933, the Roosevelt-supported National Industrial Recovery Act soon supplanted it. And Black's bill ultimately died in the House.

The evidence suggests that Black's pre-Court experience consistently influenced his decision-making as a justice, so much so that one of his biographers titled his book *Hugo Black of Alabama: How His Roots and Early Career Shaped the Great Champion of the Constitution.*[71] Elsewhere Michael Paris and I argue that Black's experience with the Klan likely shaped his near absolutist views on free speech. While he was a committed defender of pure speech, he viewed dissent defined by conduct differently. We suggest that distinction provides clear "evidence of his understanding of the ability of groups like the Klan to suppress democracy through their actions."[72]

So, in 1950, when Black articulated to his brethren his determination to decimate *Plessy* despite his expectation of violent outbreaks, he spoke from experience. And, indeed, the politics of "massive resistance" consumed the South after *Brown*, negating much of the Court's work for a time. White hate hit Black personally as well. After *Brown*, the justice only returned home to Birmingham with the protection of a bulletproof vest. Old friends abandoned him. Members of a country club first booed and then banned him. His only son concluded it was best to leave the state after white defiance upended his once thriving legal career. The state's voters, nearly all white since African Americans were shut out of the voting booth, now detested him. His fellow Alabamians, who had twice elected him to the US Senate with more than 80 percent support, now tarred him as "Judas." The state Senate even "resolved that Black's remains must never be buried in Alabama's sacred soil."[73] But Hugo Black pushed on, forcefully articulating a vision for the South free from the sins of segregation. Writing in 1975, Richard Kluger concluded that Black's tenure as a justice would "prove [that] the black man never had a better friend on the Supreme Court than this lean, courtly son of the Deep South."[74]

Accolades like Kluger's abound for this first Roosevelt justice. He is easily identified as one of the few "great" justices: a revolutionary thinker who, after some initial struggles on the Court, found his voice and helped to transform American law by extending long-cherished rights to those who had been denied them.

But the modern-day version of Hugo Lafayette Black, if there is one, would have little to no chance for a spot of the high bench. The "quality" of such a nominee would be an open question. His educational and legal background would elicit ridicule and mockery on nomination day.

⋆

"Thurgood's coming!" Those two words brought excitement to African American communities throughout the South. Typically, NAACP lead attorney Thurgood Marshall was traveling to a locale after a tragic event—a lynching or some other travesty of justice. This was before he led the NAACP's effort to constitutionally decimate southern segregation. In these years, his biographer Gilbert King writes, "Marshall fought countless battles for human rights in stifling antebellum courthouses where white supremacy ruled." Usually traveling alone, he would board a train from New York, and ride "southward, closer and closer to benighted towns billeting hostile prosecutors, malicious police, and the Ku Klux Klan."[75] Once he arrived, he would attempt to ensure that the law on the books was carried out, to press local authorities to afford due process to an African American accused of a crime, or to pursue proper prosecution if the victim had been Black. Success was usually far from certain, but still Thurgood Marshall went.

No justice could match Thurgood Marshall's experiences before arriving on the Court. Born into a lower-middle-class family—his father was a railroad porter and his mother a teacher—he attended historically Black Lincoln University in Pennsylvania. Eager to return to his hometown of Baltimore to pursue a law degree, Marshall was denied the opportunity because of his race. The University of Maryland Law School did not accept African Americans in 1930. So instead, Marshall attended the historically Black Howard University School of Law in Washington, DC. After graduating from Howard first in his class, Marshall worked for a short time as a solo practitioner in Baltimore. Here he began his long association with the NAACP, working with his mentor at Howard, Charles Hamilton Houston, the architect of the campaign to legally dismantle segregated schools in the South.

⋆

Marshall fought what are now legendary battles in the field for the NAACP's cause. And on the night of November 18, 1946, on the outskirts of Columbia, Tennessee, he nearly paid the price.

Angry white men were gathering down by Duck River. There was going to be a lynching that night. The victim had been identified and was under arrest, sitting in the back of an unmarked police car between two armed officers on the false charge of drunken driving. The officers who had stopped the vehicle—both state patrolmen and Columbia police—had instructed the three men the suspect was traveling with to continue on their way to Nashville while they took their friend back to the station house for processing. But the police cruiser didn't go directly to the station. Instead, it headed toward the river. When it came to a stop, one of the officers noticed the headlights of another car behind them. The travel companions of the man under arrest had ignored the police request to keep driving. Instead, they turned around to follow the police car. Once it entered the woods, they feared the worst. And now, they stood ready to prevent a lynching.[76]

The man under arrest in the rear seat of the police car was Thurgood Marshall. Gilbert King tells us why Marshall knew what was about to happen to him: "Marshall knew that the Ku Klux Klan in Columbia was deeply entrenched in the local police; he knew its members served as sheriffs and magistrates. He had read the NAACP reports. This wasn't the Klan of 'cowardly hood', rather, it 'wears cap and visor, and shining badge. . . . It is the LAW. It arrests its stunned victims, unlisted." Marshall must have been filled with fear and trepidation, knowing what happened thirteen years earlier near that very same spot. King continues: "Looking out the window of the [police] sedan, [Marshall] could see the cedar trees as the headlights flashed across them. It was under a cedar tree just down the road that hundreds of townspeople had gathered around young Cordie Cheek in his last living moments. They had watched and cheered as officials pulled down Cordie's pants and castrated him before forcing him up a stepladder and hanging him. Pistols were passed around the crowd; they were fired until all the bullets were gone."[77]

Marshall was in Columbia that night because he had just finished defending two men accused of shooting at police officers during a race riot in February 1946. Marshall was too sick to attend an earlier trial that had resulted in the acquittal of twenty-three of twenty-five African Americans accused of participating in the riot. Held in a neighboring county, an all-male all-white jury had delivered the stunning acquittals and recommended a three-year sentence for the two convicted men. The most recent trial, held in Columbia, had concluded earlier that evening. And once again, an all-white jury delivered a surprise. It found one of the two accused Black men "not guilty" of attempted murder. The other was guilty as charged. Marshall had argued that both men were simply defending themselves in the midst of the riot after a white mob entered the Black section of town. "The mob came down there, and the police were in front of the mob when they shot."[78]

Marshall often joked about the violent racism he confronted on his many travels through the South, but his near-death experience by the banks of the Duck River left a clear and indelible mark. Writes Marshall biographer Juan Williams, "he had a newly found fear of white mobs and violent policemen."[79]

So, when *Justice* Marshall considered police brutality cases or those involving law enforcement's participation in extrajudicial violence like lynching, he did not need to imagine the horror of these events after reading a legal brief. They were his lived experiences and those of the individuals he represented. When *Justice* Marshall considered death penalty cases, he knew well of suspects falsely accused of murder. He knew because he had defended them. When *Justice* Marshall considered school segregation cases, he knew firsthand what Black schools looked like throughout the Jim Crow South—that they were often little more than shacks with the sky peeking through dilapidated roofs.[80] And he understood that they were designed not to educate but to denigrate, intended not to lift Black children out of their poverty and segregated persecution but to keep them in "their place." The NAACP's campaign against segregated schools had challenged southern white supremacy at its core, and perhaps no one understood that more than Thurgood Marshall.

That was the main reason President Lyndon B. Johnson wanted Marshall on the Supreme Court. It was one thing to appoint the first Black American to the Court, but Marshall also and more specifically brought with him a deep experience of the pervasiveness of the Jim Crow system and its impact on the nation. Still, Johnson was not prepared to name Marshall from the Second Court of Appeals, where he had served since President John F. Kennedy nominated him and the Senate confirmed him, after a southern-led delay, in the autumn of 1961. The president wanted Marshall first to become his solicitor general, to give up his lifetime appointment as a federal judge to serve as the nation's chief advocate before the Court. To Johnson's mind, the position was "a tryout for the possible first black associate justice of the Court" and an opportunity for Marshall "to prove to everyone, including the President, what he could do." "Just as much as he understood the dramatic possibility of appointing an African American to argue the government's cases before the court," the legal historian Laura Kalman adds, "LBJ early became captivated by the idea of naming the right African American to the Supreme Court after preparing him and the nation for the move."[81] So, he rejected his attorney general's recommendations to keep the Kennedy-appointed solicitor general—the famed Harvard Law professor Archibald Cox—and named Marshall instead. It was important to Johnson to make Marshall an "administration man," and making him his solicitor general would do just that. (Upon retirement from the high bench, Marshall highlighted the importance of his time in that post, noting that "as solicitor general, you're in the dead middle of everything that's legal, and you have your two cents to put in."[82])

After Marshall became solicitor general, many expected Johnson to name him to the high bench once a vacancy opened up. But in the spring of 1967, the Court remained unchanged, so the president decided to force the issue. Johnson phoned Justice Tom Clark to inform him that he intended to make Clark's son, Ramsey, his attorney general. But he added that he would not name Ramsey Clark the nation's top attorney if the justice did not wish to retire. Tom Clark got the not-so-subtle hint and announced his resignation two hours after the president nominated Ramsey to become his next attorney general. LBJ had created space with the intention of making history by naming the first Black justice to the Court.[83]

However, at this point there was some thought that the president ought not to choose Marshall for the vacancy because he hadn't worked as hard as solicitor general as he had as the NAACP's lead advocate. Rumors were circulating that he was "lazy" and too quick to take a drink. And as Kalman explains, there were other African Americans to consider. For example, "William Hastie, who had attended more elite universities, something that never concerned LBJ . . . would carry less political baggage to the Senate Judiciary Committee than did Marshall who symbolized the struggle for black equality. But former Attorney General Katzenbach told Johnson that Marshall's past provided the very reason that the president must put him on the court."[84] Johnson had other reasons for favoring Marshall over any other possibility. Williams elaborates: "One, the president, genuinely liked Marshall and continued to see him regularly, both for business and to drink and tell stories. Two, Johnson considered Marshall a man in his own image, a person who had worked his way up from the bottom, not a person born to wealth."[85] In fact, despite talk of Marshall's flaws, the president "never seriously considered anyone other than Marshall to succeed Clark."[86] He would name the former lead attorney for the NAACP to integrate the Court. Marshall was deeply proud that he would be the man to break that barrier. Not surprisingly, some southern senators denounced the choice. But Johnson had already lined up the votes.

After his confirmation, when it was time for Marshall to take the oath of office, an old friend volunteered to perform the honors. So, on September 1, 1967, Marshall entered the chambers of the Court's most senior member for a private ceremony to become the 96th justice. Thurgood was now coming to the nation's highest tribunal. And Justice Hugo L. Black would be the one to swear him in.[87]

✴

Thurgood Marshall would be the last jurist to become an associate justice prior to the Hruska switch. Before long, the backgrounds and experiences of new members of the Court would depart dramatically from those they replaced. By the dawn of the twenty-first century the supreme elite was firmly established—particularly for conservatives—and justices like Black and Marshall were an extinct breed. Today's justices may be exceptionally talented, but they have lived lives sheltered from the roughness of a political campaign, the difficulties of the legislative process, and—dare I say—the less pampered environment of a public university. Apart from Justices Thomas and Sotomayor, all have pursued a clear-cut path from undergraduate education, through to law school, to clerking for a court of appeals judge or a Supreme Court justice (usually both), to highly desirable positions in the law. As a group, they have emerged from an exceptionally small sliver of America. It is fair to hypothesize that their deliberations over the components of a case miss certain voices essential to understanding the best path forward or the best interpretation of what the Constitution allows. We might reasonably wonder if they fully understand how the law in the books they write affects life on the streets. Arguably their extremely anomalous, outlier lives—far different from many of their twentieth-century predecessors—undermine the Court's place in American democracy. In reflecting on this argument, consider this question: does it matter that these justices have not had experiences anything close to those of Black during the Depression, sitting for days on end listening to the downtrodden and distraught on the verge of suicide, or to those of Marshall, facing a lynch mob on the banks of Duck River? I suspect it does.

Choosing Right: How Conservative Efforts to Eliminate Ideological Drift Stifled Republican Presidential Choice

When he entered the Supreme Court's robing room for the first time, the newly minted Justice Harry Blackmun spied the other justices. At the time, the high bench included several legends of the law: Hugo Black, William O. Douglas, William Brennan, John Marshall Harlan, and Thurgood Marshall. Mere days after his final term on the bench ended, Blackmun admitted that that scene, nearly twenty-five years earlier, had left him "overwhelmed with feelings of self-doubt and inadequacy over the immense responsibilities before him." To Blackmun, his presence in that room left him "almost desperate," questioning if he belonged there.[1]

Despite this uncertainty, Blackmun was on the leading edge of an emerging trend. Jurists like him would come to dominate the Court. From then until today, there would be no more US senators chosen for the Court, as Black had been; no more chairs of the Securities and Exchange Commission (SEC), as Douglas had been; no more judges chosen directly from their state's highest bench, as Brennan had been; no more Thurgood Marshalls.[2] The Republican presidents who had the opportunity to fill most of the vacancies during this time would increasingly look to jurists like Blackmun: longtime court of appeals judges with Ivy League degrees who were thought to be conservative. And when justices like Blackmun disappointed by moving to the left, additional criteria were added in hopes of preventing ideological drift.

Why did this happen? How did the Court become a domain for only those select few deemed "eligible" to serve—the supreme elite—despite the Constitution's silence on the matter? As we will see, the answer lies mainly in a conservative effort to prevent the ideological drift of justices after they ascended to the high bench. Republican presidents sought to simultaneously deliver the doctrine they had promised and mobilize voters by selecting nominees with ideological rather biographical or geographical appeal. This search for judicial sameness ultimately stifled presidential choice, as presidents increasingly deferred to unelected leaders of movement conservatism to identify the "right" nominees—those tapped on the shoulder for admittance into the supreme elite.

Since Democratic presidents have filled so few seats over the last half century of appointments—naming only five of the last twenty justices and making only six of the last twenty-seven nominations (those from 1969 to 2022)[3]—this is very much a Republican story. But Democratic presidents have played a role as well. And as we will see in chapter 8, with obvious ideological differences, their nominees shared many of the same attributes as those selected by their GOP counterparts.

*

To be sure, change was in the air before the "Hruska switch" described in chapter 6, but I argue that the reaction to the Nebraska senator's appeal for mediocrity was an important moment, and marker, for the transition to a new politics of choosing and confirming justices. Soon after Hruska's comments in 1970, President Nixon came around to the idea that his best chance to get a conservative on the Court was to highlight quality over political symbolism.

Nixon did not come to this decision easily. His appointment of Blackmun a few days after the Senate's rejection of Carswell was based mainly on a desire to secure confirmation of a nominee for the Fortas seat; selecting Burger's "twin" seemingly guaranteed that. The following year, Nixon would try again to score political points with Supreme Court selections.

In September 1971, when two vacancies opened on the Court in the course of a week, President Nixon once again made a play for symbolism, believing it would win him votes for the upcoming presidential election. He decided on two replacements, Herschel Friday and Mildred Lillie. Friday was a southerner and Lillie would make history by becoming the first female justice if confirmed. The two were on a list of six nominees released to gauge how they would be received by the public at large and by decision-makers in Washington. But in fact, the president had already decided on Friday and Lillie. The other four were just decoys. The reaction to the list of six was swift and critical, with many highlighting the "mediocrity" of the choices. In time, members of the American Bar Association's Standing Committee on the Federal Judiciary would vote that neither Friday nor Lillie met their standards for service on the Court—Lillie by a vote of eleven to one.[4] Fearing a repeat of the Carswell debacle, Nixon tacked to an alternative course. Friday and Lillie were out. Nixon now hoped to appoint two southerners, Lewis Powell of Virginia and Tennessee senator Howard Baker. Powell took some convincing but did agree to the nomination. Baker, however, wasn't sure whether he wanted to be a Supreme Court justice or stay in the Senate, so he started avoiding Attorney General John Mitchell's phone calls to stall for time. Thinking Baker wasn't interested, Nixon moved on to William Rehnquist, assistant attorney general for the office of legal counsel. Then, in a fateful phone call, Mitchell relayed to the president that he had finally had a chance to speak to Baker and the young senator was willing to accept the nomination after all. Nixon was taken aback, and for fifty-three seconds he considered his options, without saying a word. In that long moment of silence, he decided. He would choose Rehnquist, with a stellar academic record and a reputation as a serious legal thinker.[5] The selection process would never be the same.

Instead of selecting a candidate based on geography or gender or religion—Nixon considered all three options, roughly in that order[6]—the president chose one based on "quality." As he put it, "the political mileage basically is . . . that we are appointing a highly qualified man." But while "brains not ideology" convinced Nixon to select Rehnquist instead of Baker, as noted in chapter 4, he would sell it differently, telling his aides working to corral southern votes in the Senate to highlight his nominee's right-wing ideology. That strategy showed that Nixon had learned a valuable lesson. Initially, by focusing on finding a *southerner* perceived to be conservative, he first selected a nominee with an ethics issue and then chose one deemed unqualified for the Court. Senate distress over Haynsworth's ethics and Carswell's qualifications provided cover for ideological votes at a time when senators would not publicly oppose a nominee based simply on ideology. But Nixon would not repeat the mistake. To avoid such Senate subterfuge, he and future Republican presidents would search for nominees with clean records, top-tier law degrees, and reputations as conservative ideologues—jurists who would become known as movement conservatives. Nixon's search for a southerner in many ways typified how many of his predecessors often thought about Supreme Court picks—they were vehicles to attract votes by appealing to a desire for geographic representation or to display ethnic, racial, or religious pride. The right choice might help swing a state or an electoral constituency while at the same time advancing an ideology on the Court in line with the president's own.

But in trying to outmaneuver his critics, Nixon had stumbled onto a new strategy that would dominate the selection process for the next half century. Republican presidents would still occasionally make symbolic choices—and sometimes symbolic choices who were also ideologues. But when Senate confirmation dynamics allowed, Republican presidents from that point on would select candidates perceived to be ideologically pure, with credentials difficult to challenge. Political symbolism was secondary. This is why President Reagan's elevation of Rehnquist to chief justice was such a turning point (chapter 4). He was a proven conservative whose electoral advantage for the president was based on *ideology*, not gender, geography, race, or religion.

But rarely did presidents have the ability, as Reagan did with Rehnquist, to examine nearly a decade and a half of decision-making on the high bench. So, in the search for ideologically pure nominees without a High Court track record, Antonin Scalia, appointed alongside the future chief justice, emerged as the prototype. Casting aside the symbolism Scalia brought to the table as the first Italian American, Republican presidents looked to him as the best way to ensure they were choosing well, both to prevent ideological drift and, in time, to convince conservative voters of their commitment to moving the Court further to the right.

*

An examination of Republican presidential choices reveals a de facto checklist designed to eliminate those susceptible to ideological drift. And the items on that list align closely with the professional and ideological characteristics of Scalia before his appointment to the Court.

The list of ideological drifters rolls off the tongues of conservative critics: Harry Blackmun, John Paul Stevens, and David Souter are among the most prominent. They were all jurists appointed by Republican presidents who, once on the Court, proved to be more liberal than expected. Conservatives were so perturbed by this phenomenon that they gave it a name: the "Greenhouse effect." Their idea was that new members of the Court sought to please the liberal Eastern elite and, more specifically, Linda Greenhouse, the longtime Supreme Court reporter for the *New York Times*. In pursuit of this goal they drifted to the left.[7]

Take, for example, the ideological path of John Paul Stevens. When he retired from the Court in 2010, Stevens was the Court's most liberal member by far. That wasn't the type of justice newspaper editorials thought President Gerald Ford had nominated in 1975. While he was not considered an ideologue comparable to Rehnquist, the perception was that Stevens would be a moderate conservative (with a Segal-Cover score of .250). But he quickly tacked left. Indeed, according to the Martin-Quinn scoring of the justices' ideology, Stevens spent only his first year on the conservative side of the ideological divide. For most of his first decade and a half on the Court, he was its third most liberal member. After the retirement of William Brennan in 1990

and Thurgood Marshall a year later, Stevens was the Court's most liberal justice by far, and that continued until his retirement nearly two decades later.

This phenomenon was not new to Washington. Richard Nixon believed
that Justice Potter Stewart had been "twisted by the Georgetown set," and
feared it would happen to his own choices.[8] He even asked Blackmun if he
could resist the pull of the "Georgetown crowd" and the "Washington cock-
tail party circuit." Blackmun assured Nixon that he wouldn't be a victim of
any attempt to influence him.[9] Obviously, from the standpoint of movement
conservatives, that did not turn out to be true. But as I discuss elsewhere, the
president did not wish to wage a full-scale conservative counter-attack on the
Warren Court's judicial liberalism. Instead, he pursued precision maneuvers
to tame it, and in turn to build an enduring Republican electoral alliance.
Nixon did not expect Blackmun to be a conservative ideologue. In fact, if
that had been the perception when he was appointed, it's unlikely the Senate
would have confirmed him. Moreover, there is no evidence that Nixon had
any misgivings about choosing Blackmun. He was proud of the appointment,
and that wasn't true for all of his nominees.[10]

Some also point to Sandra Day O'Connor and Anthony Kennedy as victims of the Greenhouse effect. But the Reagan Justice Department considered
both to be "eighty-percenters," likely to agree with the president's positioning in
four out of five cases (chapter 4). While they may have been too moderate for
conservatives—especially on key social issues like abortion and gay rights—
President Reagan knew the risk in appointing them. In O'Connor's case, to fulfill a campaign promise, Reagan chose symbolism over ideological purity from
a shallow pool of candidates. He did so even though the Senate was in Republican hands for the first time since the mid-1950s. With Kennedy, he wanted
to secure the confirmation of a new justice before his presidency ended.

David Hackett Souter usually gets the most attention in discussions about
the Greenhouse effect. In fact, the phrase "No more Souters" became a rallying cry for movement conservatives, particularly during the George W.
Bush administration, intent on making sure the president chose right. But
interestingly, Souter's Segal-Cover score was slightly more conservative than
O'Connor's or Kennedy's (.325 to O'Connor's .415 and Kennedy's .365). Liberals even labeled him a "stealth" nominee out of concern that his nonexistent
record of writings on the most salient issues of the day would mean he would
be a staunch conservative once on the Court. So, from a conservative perspective, what went wrong?

The answer to this question goes back to the 1986 appointments of Rehnquist for chief and Scalia for the associate slot. Recall that in his second term

in office, President Reagan was more committed to imposing his conservative imprint on the Court than he had been in his first term, which was defined by his choice of O'Connor and a go-slow strategy on social issues. He appointed his longtime confidant, Edwin Meese, to be attorney general. Once in place, Meese set out to advance the president's constitutional vision in the courts. Chief Justice Warren Burger's retirement in 1986 created an unexpected opportunity to reshape the Supreme Court. And central to the thinking in the White House in its search for a replacement was to subvert the Greenhouse effect. With Blackmun and Stevens frustrating conservative goals, Reagan wanted assurances—especially with the Senate in Republican hands—that his second-term appointees would deliver conservative doctrine for years to come. Not surprisingly, he looked to Rehnquist as an example. Specifically, members of the White House—including the president—determined "that sitting judges or justices who had a clearly articulated philosophy were the most likely to remain steadfast to their views."[11] No one had done so more than Rehnquist, and he had done it for fourteen years at the highest level of the federal judiciary.

But Blackmun and Stevens had also been judges before assuming their seats on the high bench. And perceptions about their ideology turned out to be deeply flawed. Moreover, Rehnquist had not been a judge when Nixon selected him for an associate seat in 1971—he was a high-level member of the Justice Department. So, two more items were added to an emerging de facto checklist when searching for an ideal nominee for an open seat: (1) recent professional experience *in Washington*, and (2) work in a *Republican administration*. (Preferably, the two would go together.)

Favoring professional experience in Washington wasn't a new idea for presidents searching for a like-minded nominee. Of FDR's nine justices, all but one was working in Washington at the time of his appointment to the Court. Four were part of Roosevelt's administration; two were US senators; and two were members of the federal judiciary.[12] The one exception was hardly an exception at all. Felix Frankfurter, a close advisor to the president, was said to be one of the most influential men in Washington (while still residing in Cambridge, Massachusetts).[13] All the appointees of Presidents Roosevelt, Truman, Kennedy, and Johnson had extensive experience in Washington prior to joining the Court, and most were members of the appointing president's administration or close advisors to him when they were chosen (chapter 9). Republicans Eisenhower, Nixon, and Ford, however, did not follow that Democratic precedent. In fact, only one of Eisenhower's five nominees had recent Washington experience, and that was for just over a year as a judge on the DC court of appeals.[14] Only two of Nixon's six nominees—Burger and Rehnquist—had worked in the nation's capital. And each had experience in the Justice Department. Notably, according to the assessments of their ideology during their years on the high bench, they were Nixon's two most conservative justices, and Rehnquist was the more conservative of the two.

President Reagan's next three choices were similar to the 1986 version of Rehnquist. Scalia, Robert Bork, and Douglas Ginsburg had all served in a Republican administration in Washington. All were current members of a federal court in Washington, namely the DC court of appeals. And all were deemed conservative ideologues (with Segal-Cover scores of .000, .095, and .000, respectively). Only Scalia offered any electoral advantage.[15]

There was something else the three had in common. While at the University of Chicago, Scalia had been the faculty advisor for a new group of conservative law students called the Federalist Society. As we know, there was only one other chapter at the time, at Yale. Its faculty advisor was Robert Bork. Ginsburg also had ties to the group, and before his appointment to the federal bench he had served in the Meese-led Justice Department, which was considered "a Federalist Society shop."[16] Indeed, it was members of that very Justice Department who urged the selection of Ginsburg over the more moderate Anthony Kennedy after the Senate rejected Bork in 1987. They won out, but soon thereafter Ginsburg was forced to drop out of consideration after admitting that he smoked marijuana "once as a college student in the 60s, and then on a few occasions in the 70s."[17] Just over a year earlier First Lady Nancy Reagan had launched her "Just Say No" campaign to combat the use of drugs by children. So, the president was not eager to stand by the pot-smoking Supreme Court nominee. Even his support in the Justice Department fell away. Officials there were reportedly fearful "he would become known as the 'marijuana judge.'"[18]

Once on the Court, Scalia emerged as an intellectual force. Brandishing a bandolier of rhetorical bullets, he would fire off questions to attorneys appearing before the justices, transforming the Court's oral arguments into Socratic-style law school classes and often eliciting ripples of laughter from the typically staid crowd in attendance.[19] Compared to the wooden Rehnquist, Scalia was a charismatic defender of conservative principles both from the bench and in public. His mix of wit and wisdom endeared him to conservatives (and some liberals as well); soon he surpassed Rehnquist as the embodiment of a Republican president who had chosen correctly—his name became the right answer to a debate question about the ideal justice. Indeed, just by uttering "Scalia," Republican presidential candidates signaled to voters their commitment to the conservative cause. In this sense, he was their judicial North Star.

So, in 1990, with the surprising retirement of the liberal icon William Brennan, President George Bush sought to find another Scalia. And seemingly,
Solicitor General Kenneth Starr fit the bill: a diehard conservative with both
administrative and judicial experience in Washington and close ties to the
Federalist Society. He had served as a judge on the DC court of appeals for
nearly six years before leaving that life-tenure position to become solicitor general in the Bush administration. He had likely done so to enhance
his chances of being selected for a Supreme Court seat. But in discussing
the Brennan vacancy in a White House meeting, with the president in attendance, Attorney General Richard Thornburg declared that Starr was "unacceptable."[20] The feeling among Thornburg's closest aides—Bill Barr (the
future two-time attorney general) and J. Michael Luttig (a former Scalia
clerk[21])—was that Starr was not sufficiently reliable. In other words, he might
potentially fall victim to the Greenhouse effect. As the Supreme Court cor-
respondent Jan Crawford Greenburg writes, "administration officials, especially Barr and Luttig, believed him to be a decent man, but one who could
be maddeningly squishy and unfocused. Those traits could be disastrous in a
would-be conservative Supreme Court justice, making him more susceptible
to drift to the left after the first criticism from liberals in the media and in
academia."[22] With Starr out, the decision came down to either David Hackett
Souter of New Hampshire or Edith Jones of Texas. Administration officials
thought Jones, a forty-one-year-old conservative ideologue on the Court of
Appeals for the Fifth Circuit, would face a much tougher confirmation battle
before the Democratic Senate. So, once assured of his conservatism by assessments of his judicial record and by former New Hampshire governor and
White House Chief of Staff John Sununu, Bush was willing to take a chance
with Souter. It apparently didn't matter to the president that the future justice
had spent most of his life in New Hampshire before his recent appointment
to the First Circuit Court of Appeals in Boston. And while he had worked for
an attorney general, it was at the state level. He also was not connected to the
Federalist Society.

So, while the Bush administration did consider the potential for ideological
drift when it dismissed Starr in favor of Souter, it ignored or de-emphasized
several characteristics shared by previous Republican-appointed justices who
stayed true to their conservative principles once on the Court. This proved
to be problematic for advancing conservative interests. Like Stevens, Souter
took up a position on the liberal side of the ideological line soon after assuming his seat on the high bench. According to the Martin-Quinn scores, he
spent just three terms on the conservative side of that line. For the rest of his
tenure, his ideological scores were very close to those of Ruth Bader Ginsburg

and Stephen Breyer, Bill Clinton's two appointees. He never reached the liberalism of John Paul Stevens, however.

Signs of Souter's potential liberalism emerged quite quickly, even as early as his confirmation hearings in the Senate.[23] So, the following year, when another liberal icon, Thurgood Marshall, retired from the bench—because, as he explained, "I'm old . . . and coming apart"—the Bush administration was ready with a nominee few doubted was a committed movement conservative. Like Scalia, Clarence Thomas had administrative experience in Washington before his recent appointment to the DC court of appeals. He also had strong ties to the Federalist Society and a JD from Yale. He was truly thought to be a can't-miss pick from a conservative standpoint. And, indeed, he was.

A Republican president wouldn't make a Supreme Court selection for another fourteen years, but a checklist for choosing right was clearly emerging. In assessing past choices, the essential attributes to prevent ideological drift were becoming apparent. Consider the six appointed after Nixon won the White House in 1968 who did not live up to movement conservative standards: Blackmun, Powell, Stevens, O'Connor, Kennedy, and Souter. Except for a single year Stevens spent clerking at the Court, none of them had ever worked in Washington until they arrived at the high bench. None of them had worked in a Republican administration. None had served on the DC circuit court. None of those appointed after its formation had strong ties to the Federalist Society. Contrast that with those who were deemed sufficiently conservative or who didn't have the opportunity to display their ideology as a justice because they were never confirmed: Burger, Rehnquist, Rehnquist for chief, Scalia, Bork, Ginsburg, and Thomas. All had experience in a Republican administration in Washington, and with the exception of Rehnquist's initial appointment as associate justice, all had served on the DC court of appeals or the high bench (in the case of Rehnquist's elevation for chief).

Moreover, beginning with Scalia, all had either graduated from or taught at Harvard or Yale law schools. The two non–Ivy League law graduates—Bork and Ginsburg—attended the University of Chicago, but Bork would later teach at Yale and Ginsburg at Harvard.[24] This heavy preference for Harvard and Yale is somewhat curious for leaders of a party that typically denounced the East Coast elite. For example, when discussing the two 1971 vacancies with Attorney General John Mitchell, Nixon commented, "You've seen a lot of Harvard men around, they're soft in the head. And they don't work as hard."[25] But several of Nixon's nominees or possibilities—specifically Carswell and his list of "mediocrities"—had been criticized as unthinking ideological hacks. So, whether Nixon liked it or not, he understood that a Harvard or Yale law degree told a different story to the public, and, perhaps

more importantly, to members of the Senate.[26] Finally, there was the Federalist Society connection. Again, beginning with Scalia, the most conservative
Republican nominees had strong ties to the group. Those who were thought
to have drifted left once on the Court did not.

✶

To summarize, here are the items on the seven-point checklist—roughly in
order of importance—designed to inoculate against ideological drift. As explained here and displayed in table 7.1, Scalia and Thomas checked all seven
boxes. None of the others did.

1. Perception as a conservative ideologue (Segal-Cover score of .160 or less)
   Scalia's score of zero is the most conservative possible. Somewhat surprisingly, Thomas's score is noticeably higher at .160.[27]
2. Professional experience in Washington (excluding a clerkship)
   Both Scalia and Thomas held several positions in Washington before
   taking seats in the federal judiciary. Scalia's non-judicial DC experience
   spanned from 1971 to 1977; Thomas's from 1979 to 1990.
3. Experience in a Republican presidential administration
   Scalia worked in both the Nixon and Ford administrations, including the
   Ford Justice Department. Thomas came to Washington to work for Republican Senator John Danforth of Missouri. He then served in both the
   Reagan and Bush administrations, most prominently as chair of the Equal
   Employment Opportunity Commission for nearly two terms.
4. Court of appeals judge
   President Reagan appointed Scalia to the court of appeals in 1982. President Bush did the same for Thomas in 1989.
5. Strong ties to the Federalist Society
   Scalia was the faculty advisor for one of the first two chapters while a professor at the University of Chicago Law School. He continued to have a
   close relationship with the organization's leaders throughout his life. The
   legal scholars Michael Avery and Danielle McLaughlin list Thomas as a
   member of the Federalist Society and write that that his nomination to the
   high bench was one of the organization's "greatest successes."[28]
6. Harvard or Yale Law graduate or faculty member
   Scalia graduated from Harvard Law in 1960. Thomas graduated from Yale
   Law in 1974.
7. Judge on the DC court of appeals
   Both Scalia and Thomas were members of this court until their appointment to the nation's highest tribunal.[29]

The items on this list are based on the backgrounds of the most conservative Republican-appointed justices of the Reagan/Bush years—those who

TABLE 7.1. The Emerging Anti-Drift Checklist, Divided Government Era

Nominee	Perceived Ideology	Washington Experience	Administration Experience	Court of Appeals Judge	Harvard or Yale Law	Federalist Society	DC Court of Appeals Judge	Total
Blackmun	x			x	x	~		3
Powell					x	~		1
Rehnquist	x	x	x			~		3
Stevens				x		~		1
O'Connor						~		0
Rehnquist	x	x	x	x*	x		x*	5
Scalia	x	x	x	x	x	x	x	7
Bork	x	x	x	x	x	x	x	7
Ginsburg	x	x	x	x	x	x	x	7
Kennedy				x	x			2
Thomas	x	x	x	x	x	x	x	7
Souter				x	x			2

Failed nominees in *italics*.

*Associate Justice of the Supreme Court.

~Federalist Society was still in its infancy at the time of nomination.

did not drift decisively to the left once on the high bench. The ideological "success" of Scalia and then Thomas essentially generated this blueprint for Republican presidents of the polarization era. Indeed, both George W. Bush and Donald Trump promised to appoint more justices like those two. Three additional characteristics were shared by nearly all the Republican-appointed selections of the polarization period. One of these characteristics was absent from both Scalia's and Thomas's resumé, and the other two they both shared. The missing characteristic is a clerkship with a Republican-appointed justice. Apart from Samuel Alito, all the justices appointed by Republican presidents in the polarization period previously clerked with a Republican-appointed justice. (Alito clerked for Third Circuit Court Judge Leonard Garth. He interviewed for a clerkship with Justice Byron White—a Democratic appointee— but didn't get an offer.[30]) The first shared characteristic is their Catholic faith. Beginning with Scalia, all of the Republican-appointed justices have been Catholic, or—in one case, Neil Gorsuch—previously identified as Catholic (table 7.2).[31] The second is relative youth. Beginning with Scalia, all Republican-appointed justices have been fifty-five or younger, some substantially so. So, the updated anti-drift list would include these three additional items:

8. Clerkship at the Supreme Court
   This is the one exception for both Scalia and Thomas. Neither clerked for a judge or Supreme Court justice.
9. Strong ties to Catholicism
   A graduate of a Jesuit high school and Jesuit Georgetown University, Scalia was a deeply devout traditional Catholic who considered the priesthood and preferred attending a Latin mass. Thomas attended a Catholic parochial school as a child. At sixteen, he transferred to Saint John Vianney, a minor seminary, "to prepare for the priesthood." From there, he attended Immaculate Conception Seminary in Missouri. After his first year, he decided against the ministerial life.[32] He then transferred to the Jesuit College of Holy Cross to complete his undergraduate degree.
10. Relative youth
    At the time of their nominations, Scalia was fifty years old, Thomas just forty-three.

I suggest that the first two characteristics on this second list are less important than the first seven because more than being driving factors in the selection process, they are experiences and values shared by the small group of individuals committed to movement conservativism who stood out sufficiently to warrant consideration for a Court appointment.[33] Nevertheless, the high number of former clerks chosen for the Court recently does display the successful development of the conservative legal movement: no more do

TABLE 7.2. The 10-Point Anti-Drift Checklist, Polarization Period

Nominee	Perceived Ideology	Washington Experience	Administration Experience	Court of Appeals Judge	Federalist Society	Harvard or Yale Law	DC Court of Appeals Judge	Supreme Court Clerk	Catholic	Age (55 or younger)	Total
Scalia	x	x	x	x	x	x	x		x	x	9
Thomas	x	x	x	x	x	x	x		x	x	9
O'Connor										x	1
Kennedy				x		x			x	x	4
Souter				x		x				x	3
Roberts	x	x	x	x	x	x	x	x	x	x	10
Miers		x	x								2
Alito	x	x	x	x	x	x			x	x	8
Gorsuch	x	x	x	x	x	x		x	x	x	9
Kavanaugh	x	x	x	x	x	x	x	x	x	x	10
Barrett	x	x		x	x	x		x	x	x	7

Failed nominees in *italics*.

Model justices in **bold**. Non-movement conservative justices in ***bold italics***.

Republican presidents need to take chances on unknown entities, as Nixon did. And while the Catholic Church does espouse positions that often align with those of movement conservatives, there is no evidence of a judicial Opus Dei (even though conspiracy theories about one abound).[34] After all, the three Republican-named nominees who were not confirmed—Robert Bork, Douglas Ginsburg, and Harriet Miers—were not Catholic.[35] And the most liberal member of the high bench, Sonia Sotomayor, is Catholic as well.

Age has always been an important factor for presidents making a lifetime appointment. But more than others, Republican-appointed justices beginning with Scalia have been noticeably younger, with an average age of just over fifty years old.[36] The average age for the Democrat-appointed justices during this time was over fifty-four years old.[37] Youth certainly didn't matter for all the Republican presidents' choices during these years; the rejected Bork and the withdrawn Miers were both sixty. On the other hand, the other withdrawn nominee, Douglas Ginsburg, was just forty-one. Adding those ages in, the average age of all Republican *nominees* after and including Scalia was just over 51.[38] Including the appointed-but-not-confirmed Merrick Garland, the average age for all Democratic nominees during this period is an even 56, nearly five years older than their GOP counterparts.[39]

One additional characteristic that is likely not related to ideological drift, but nevertheless has been shared by all the Republican-appointed justices since and including Scalia, should not go unnoted. None have ever served in elective office. In at least one case the pursuit of elective office didn't exclude a potential nominee, since Miers was elected to the Dallas city council for one two-year term. But as we'll see, this is another example of how she was a much different type of nominee, one outside the "supreme elite."

This list for a "right" nominee was crystallizing in the 1990s and early 2000s. But it wasn't clear to all. Indeed, the checklist didn't become fully actualized until the second term of the George W. Bush presidency. In fact, President Bush's attempt to circumvent this checklist with the selection of Harriet Miers displays in the most profound terms just how important it was for movement conservatives. It also displays their power to block a presidential nominee with too few checks on this anti-drift checklist. For these reasons Bush's choice of Miers—although thwarted—was the most illuminating selection in the polarization period. And in a stunning irony, it was precisely Bush's success in marshaling social conservatives to the polls in the 2004 presidential election that made the Miers choice so susceptible to Senate backlash over her quality and ideology.

Even after conceding to the conservative checklist, Bush still didn't fully embrace it. He was clearly frustrated by his inability to select outside the "judicial fraternity."[40] Nevertheless, the failed Miers nomination made clear that in order to be worthy of elevation to the high bench during a Republican administration, a potential nominee had to be a member of the conservative supreme elite. And to achieve this status, a nominee had to check a minimum number of boxes on the anti-drift checklist—seven of the ten boxes in table 7.2, by my count. Indeed, this list so dominates the selection process for a Republican administration that it significantly constrains presidential choice of Supreme Court appointments.

Undoubtedly the checklist continues to evolve. Indeed, in a sign of the maturation of the movement and the rise of conservative alternatives, the last Republican nominee, Amy Coney Barrett, did not have a connection to Harvard or Yale. By this point in the development of the conservative legal movement, a Notre Dame degree may have actually meant more than one from Harvard or Yale. As the political scientists Amanda Hollis-Brusky and Joshua C. Wilson explain, "Notre Dame's law school has done significant work not only to become one of the nation's elite law schools, but also to become arguably the nation's elite *conservative* law school."[41] Like America's politics, legal education has become increasingly ideologically polarized, helping to drive the division on courts across the land. In this context, Barrett's law school credentials certified her ideological commitments to those wary of ideological drift.

Barrett also offered something her most recent Republican-appointed predecessors didn't. She was a woman. With voters already casting their ballots in the 2020 election, the fact that she would replace another woman and be appointed by a president facing a massive—unprecedented—gender gap was highly significant to her selection. She would become only the second Republican-appointed woman on the Court, named nearly four decades after the first female justice, Sandra Day O'Connor, took her seat. Notably, O'Connor had been the last justice appointed by either a Republican or a Democrat who had not attended Harvard or Yale for law school. She attended Stanford Law in Reagan's California.[42] In between the two appointments, the seven Republican-appointed justices were men.

*

The year between July 4, 2004, and July 4, 2005, was a prolific one for right-wing firebrands writing books about the Court. Phyllis Schlafly, the famed anti-feminist, started them off by publishing *The Supremacists: The Tyranny of Judges and How to Stop It* on that first date. Next, the televangelist and onetime Republican presidential candidate Pat Robertson released *Courting Disaster: How the Supreme Court Is Usurping the Power of Congress and the People* in September 2004. Then came a book by the radio talk show host

Mark Levin in February 2005. Ignoring the two women on the high bench, he titled it *Men in Black: How the Supreme Court Is Destroying America*. A month later, Roy Moore, the twice-ousted Alabama Supreme Court chief justice—once before the book's publication and once after—and future failed Senate candidate released *So Help Me God: The Ten Commandments, Judicial Tyranny, and the Battle for Religious Freedom*. Finally, the radio talk show host Mark I. Sutherland's edited volume, *Judicial Tyranny: The New Kings of America?* was published on July 4, 2005.[43] Sutherland's volume was a collection of essays and speeches by several social and religious conservative activists, including Schlafly and Moore. Former Reagan administration Attorney General Edwin Meese provided a very brief opening chapter, which concluded with "we have a constitutional crisis at the present time."[44]

Each of these five conservatives no doubt had the 2004 election in their sights or in their rearview mirror when they decided to author or edit a Supreme Court–focused book. The Court had remained unchanged for over a decade, Chief Justice Rehnquist was a very ill man, and Justice O'Connor was eager to retire,[45] so many expected the winner of the 2004 race to reshape the high bench, especially if it was Senator John F. Kerry of Massachusetts, the Democratic nominee. Moreover, unlike many presidential campaigns,[46] judicial issues were a centerpiece of the discussion. Soon after the exit poll results were revealed, commentators even began referring to it as the "moral values" election.

So, when Sandra Day O'Connor announced her retirement the following July, Court watchers expected Bush to appoint a nominee in the mold of Scalia and Thomas, as he had suggested he would do on the campaign trail.[47] Thomas was the last justice a Republican president had appointed, and after this nearly fifteen-year drought, Bush's father's two justices weighed heavily on his mind. As he explained in his memoir: "I knew how proud Dad was to have appointed Clarence Thomas, a wise principled, humane man. I also knew he was disappointed that his other nominee, David Souter, had evolved into a different kind of judge than he expected." In a press conference the day after the Miers nomination, Bush stressed his concern about the potential for ideological drift: "I know her well enough to be able to say that she's not going to change, that twenty years from now she'll be the same person with the same philosophy that she is today."[48]

Bush first decided on John Roberts to fill the O'Connor seat (chapter 4). But after Chief Justice William Rehnquist died in early September, he withdrew that nomination and re-nominated Roberts for the Court's center chair. Bush then selected the sixty-year-old Harriet Miers for the associate vacancy. He had chosen Miers over Priscilla Owen, a former Texas Supreme Court justice whom he nominated for the Fifth Circuit Court of Appeals early in his presidency but who wasn't confirmed until May 2005. As Bush explains, he decided against Owen because "a number of senators, including Republicans, told me the fight would be bloody and ultimately she would not be confirmed." He moved on to Miers partly based on a suggestion from "consultations on Capitol Hill" that he consider "picking a lawyer from outside the bench," and Miers specifically.[49] Significantly, Harry Reid, the Democratic leader in the Senate, pushed Bush to choose Miers. The idea intrigued the president: "She had been a legal pioneer in Texas—the first woman president of a major Texas law firm, the Dallas Bar Association, and the State Bar of Texas. She had been elected to the Dallas City Council, directed the Texas Lottery Commission, and served nearly five years in top White House positions. There was no doubt in my mind that she shared my judicial philosophy and that her outlook would not change. She would make an outstanding justice."[50]

Bush shared the idea of Miers with members of the White House selection group, which included Federalist Society head Leonard Leo (on leave from the organization). As discussed briefly in chapter 5, the reaction was mixed. "Some thought she would be a good choice," Bush remembered. "Others argued that it was too risky to pick someone with no established record on the bench, or that we would be accused of cronyism. Several told me bluntly that she was not the right choice." Leo was in the latter group, cautioning (to recall) that a Miers selection would be a "heavy lift" with movement conservatives.[51] But significantly for the president, no one told him "to expect the firestorm of criticism" from conservative supporters that was eventually unleashed. The negative reaction, as noted earlier, was fast and furious, led by the *Weekly Standard*'s William Kristol. Bush was taken aback, writing in his memoir: "on the Right, initial whispers of disbelief turned into howls of incredulity . . . [from] the wolves of Washington."[52] They focused mainly on Miers's lack of experience and her unknown "judicial philosophy."

According to Bush, "another argument against Harriet . . . went largely unspoken." It highlights the weight movement conservatives placed on the components of the anti-drift checklist—even those items previously near the bottom (and therefore ostensibly less important). Writes Bush: "How could I name someone who did not run in elite circles? Harriet had not gone to an Ivy League law school. Her personal style compounded the doubts. She is not glib. She is not fancy. She thinks hard before she speaks—a trait so rare in Washington that it was mistaken for intellectual slowness. As one conservative critic condescendingly put it, 'However nice, helpful, prompt, and tidy she is, Harriet Miers isn't qualified to play a Supreme Court justice on

The West Wing, let alone to be a real one.'"[53] That disdainful nugget of conservative condemnation came from the columnist Ann Coulter. In the full
column, Coulter makes the case for choosing from the supreme elite: "Being
a Supreme Court justice ought to be a mind-numbingly tedious job suitable
only for super-nerds trained in legal reasoning like John Roberts." Coulter
dismissed Miers's defenders who argued that "the GOP is not the party which
idolizes Ivy League acceptability as the criterion of intellectual and mental
fitness." To her, in choosing a Supreme Court justice conservatives should be
"looking for lawyers with giant brains to memorize obscure legal cases and
to compose clearly reasoned opinions" on specialized areas of the law. Coulter, who received her bachelor's degree from the Ivy League school Cornell
before attending the University of Michigan for law school, thought elite college conservatives would be most prepared for the intellectual combat they
would face once they arrived at the Court. As she writes: "Conservatives from
elite schools have already been subjected to liberal blandishment and haven't
blinked. At top universities, you come face to face with Satan's minions every
day, and you learn all their little tropes and tricks. These are right-wingers
who have fought off the best and the brightest the blue states have to offer. . . .
They aren't waiting for a pat on the head from Nina Totenberg or Linda
Greenhouse. To paraphrase Archie Bunker on honest Italians, when you find
a conservative from an elite law school, you've really got something." While
Coulter's suggestion that leading liberal thinkers only come from Democratic
states is a head-scratcher,[54] the broader point was clear: presidents ought to
only consider supreme elites for the high bench.

There was more to the unease with Miers than just her lack of elite credentials or supreme elite status. Robert Bork expressed his disquiet bluntly: "We
don't know whether she'll rule with Scalia and Thomas." When then asked
if he was certain "what kind of justice" the recently confirmed John Roberts
would be, Bork admitted that he was worried there, too. But he added: "Well,
we know that John Roberts is an extraordinarily capable attorney, far more so
than the average or even the high-average run. And we do know that he has
intimate knowledge of constitutional law and philosophy and we do know
that as a young man he expressed conservative views when he was working
in the Reagan administration."[55] Of course, Miers was working in the Bush
White House at that moment, and the president had assured his fellow conservatives of her commitment to their cause. But that didn't seem to matter. Members of the supreme elite were worthy of trust; those who weren't
just weren't.

Indeed, it is striking how little regard conservative critics had for a president fresh off the only Republican popular-vote victory since his father's win

sixteen years earlier. "He was elected to represent the American people, not be dictator for eight years," Coulter wrote. In her eyes, it wasn't really for Bush to decide on the next justice, even though he won the race that created the opportunity to push the Court rightward. Coulter thought instead that another entity should make the choice:

> Among the coalitions that elected Bush are people who have been laboring in the trenches for a quarter-century to change the legal order in America. While Bush was still boozing it up in the early '80s, Ed Meese, Antonin Scalia, Robert Bork, and all the founders of the Federalist Society began creating a farm team of massive legal talent on the Right. To casually spurn the people who have been taking the slings and arrows all these years and instead reward the former commissioner of the Texas Lottery with a Supreme Court appointment is like pinning a medal of honor on some flunky paper-pusher with a desk job at the Pentagon . . . while ignoring your infantrymen doing the fighting and dying.[56]

Coulter's overheated rhetoric might suggest that she was an outlier among conservative intelligentsia, but she wasn't. In addition to the quickly critical William Kristol, David Frum, Jonah Goldberg, Laura Ingraham, Charles Krauthammer, Andrew Sullivan, and George Will jumped in, each adding to the "drumbeat of doubt" surrounding Miers's quality and ideological reliability.[57] Still other conservative voices joined in the criticism, including Gary Bauer, Pat Buchanan, Rush Limbaugh, Phyllis Schlafly, and Paul Weyrich. Bork echoed anxieties about Bush's failure to select from the supreme elite, telling Tucker Carlson that the Miers choice "was a disaster on every level . . . it's kind of a slap in the face to the conservatives who've been building up the conservative legal movement for the last twenty years."[58]

Clearly, the fact that Miers was not part of the conservative legal movement mattered more than the Bush selection team expected. Even Leo was surprised by the speed of the conservative reaction. By 2005, more than having attended the "right" law school, it was important to be a known and trusted commodity in conservative legal circles. Setting Miers aside, consider President Bush's friend and attorney general Alberto Gonzales. While Gonzales was a Harvard Law graduate, he was not a Federalist Society regular. And although lawyers in the White House viewed him as "a hundred percenter," conservatives outside the administration did not. In an interview, Bork repeated a quip to me that summed up their view: "'Gonzales' is Spanish for 'Souter.'"[59] Movement conservatives were suspicious of Gonzales because of his role in moderating the Bush Justice Department's litigation campaign. Specifically, as White House counsel, he—along with longtime Bush advisor and political strategist Karl Rove—successfully pushed for a limited rather than an aggressive attack on affirmative action in the noteworthy University of Michigan cases. Gonzales and Rove had done so in hopes of "expanding the Republican base to include minorities."[60] Moreover, earlier in his career, when he was a justice on the Texas Supreme Court, Gonzales had provoked scorn from Christian evangelical leaders with his decision to allow a minor to obtain an abortion based on his reading of the state's judicial bypass law.[61] Understanding movement conservative skepticism about Gonzales, White House lawyers convinced the president not to even consider him for the Court in 2005, thus denying Bush the historic and symbolic score of naming the first Hispanic American justice.[62]

With Miers, however, Bush chose another untrusted nonentity in movement conservative circles. To her critics on the Right, she was a mere crony, untested and unwanted.[63] In a *Wall Street Journal* op-ed, Bork elaborated on why this mattered so much:

> Only a commitment to originalism provides a solid foundation for constitutional adjudication. There is no sign that [Miers] has thought about, much less adopted, that philosophy of judging. . . . The Senate is asked, then, to confirm a nominee with no visible judicial philosophy who lacks the basic skills of persuasive argument and clear writing. . . . By passing over the many clearly qualified persons, male and female, to pick a stealth candidate, George W. Bush has sent a message to aspiring young originalists that it is better not to say anything remotely controversial, a sort of "Don't ask, don't tell" admonition to would-be-judges. It is a blow in particular to the Federalist Society, most of whose members endorse originalism.[64]

It was also clear with the Miers nomination that conservatives were not willing to defer to the president as they had previously. In fact, they sought to undercut his authority to choose. George Will, a conservative commentator far more respected in Republican circles than Coulter at the time, made the following curious claims:

> The president's "argument" for her amounts to: Trust me. There is no reason to, for several reasons. He has neither the inclination nor the ability to make sophisticated judgements about competing approaches to construing the Constitution. . . . Furthermore, there is no reason to believe that Miers's nomination resulted from the president's careful consultation with people capable of such judgements. . . . In addition, the president has forfeited his right to be trusted as a custodian of the Constitution . . . [because] he signed the McCain-Feingold law expanding government regulation of the timing, quantity and content of political speech.[65]

Bush initially dismissed such criticisms as reactions to his willingness to choose someone different than the typical nominee—someone outside the "judicial monastery."[66] And he was confident of confirmation, as were some of his critics.[67]

There was reason for his optimism. As noted, some Democrats, including Minority Leader Reid, were pleased with the choice. And Bush thought he had sufficiently addressed conservative distress over Miers's ideological reliability by personally vouching for her commitment to the cause, and by providing not-so-subtle hints that she would vote to overturn *Roe v. Wade*. Not a single Republican senator echoed the scorn of conservative commentators, and many "generally praised" the choice. Some, however, remained silent.[68] And that meant something. While support (or silence) in the Senate held despite the initial flurry of insults from the Right, soon Miers's lack of a track record and her vague answers to questions in meetings with senators intensified worry about her ideological purity. Furthermore, concerns about her competence intensified. For example, after meeting with Miers, Republican Arlen Specter, chair of the Judiciary Committee, made a disparaging comment about her command of the law. Referring to practice sessions where nominees are grilled with questions as though they are before the Judiciary Committee, Specter said: "She needs more than murder boards. She needs a crash course in constitutional law."[69] In fact, Miers did perform poorly before the murder boards, reportedly providing "uncertain, underwhelming responses."[70] So, with doubt defining her nomination, it was doomed.

In another sign of presidential weakness, instead of putting up a fight the Bush White House simply surrendered, making him the first president to do so since the nineteenth century.[71] Contrast that decision with those of Presidents Nixon and Reagan, who pushed for votes on the Senate floor with nominees destined for defeat. Nixon even made an impassioned plea about his prerogative as president: "What is centrally at issue in this nomination is the constitutional responsibility of the president to appoint members of the Court—and whether this responsibility can be frustrated by those who wish to substitute their own philosophy or their own subjective judgment for that of the one person entrusted by the Constitution with the power of appointment. The question arises whether I, as president of the United States, shall be accorded the same right of choice in naming Supreme Court justices which has been fully accorded to my predecessors of both parties."[72]

Bush's fight was different—it was an intra-party conflict with movement conservatives who had been consistently disappointed by the choices of Republican presidents focused on ensuring confirmation. So, surrender didn't mean ideological defeat for Bush as it had for Nixon and Reagan. As long as he chose a nominee from the supreme elite, a GOP majority in a deeply fractured Senate would surely vote to confirm.

And soon after Miers's withdrawal, Bush did just that by naming Samuel Alito to fill the O'Connor vacancy. The choice was based on the recommendation of none other than Harriet Miers. Alito checked eight of the ten boxes on the anti-drift checklist (table 7.2). Miers had checked just two. And as expected, even though Senate Democrats aggressively contested his nomination, Alito won confirmation with near-unanimous Republican support.[73] By conceding to movement conservative forces, Bush highlighted the diminished capacity of a Republican president to fill a Supreme Court seat on his own terms. Unlike his recent GOP predecessors, including a newly inaugurated Reagan who named O'Connor in the face of social conservative fury, he had little choice.

While Harriet Miers never made it to the Court, I argue that her appointment is deeply revealing about the state of the Supreme Court selection and confirmation processes for GOP nominees in the polarization period. The search for quality initially began as a means to ensure the confirmation of Republican-named nominees before a Democratic Senate in 1970. But by 2005, quality had expanded to encompass to the extent possible an ideological guarantee: an assurance that a nominee would join forces with Scalia and Thomas once on the Court. So, while Miers may very well have been as conservative as President Bush promised, his decision to choose someone who was not a member of the movement conservative club made the selection suspicious.

Miers's failed bid displays vividly the dominance of judicial sameness in the Republican effort to secure a conservative majority on the Supreme Court. This sameness significantly reduced the danger of more Souters and enhanced the likelihood of a "true" conservative majority and the desired doctrinal developments. As in Cold War spy tradecraft, where the possibility of a secret agent becoming a turncoat was acute, every candidate is viewed suspiciously. Only the well-tested are worthy of an assignment.

So, while Republican presidential candidates recite the familiar refrain to appeal to conservative voters in caucuses and primaries, promising more Scalias and Thomases, even without such commitments their options are extraordinarily limited. And as we'll see in part III, Donald Trump, first as a candidate and then as president, essentially ceded control of the selection process to movement conservative groups like the Federalist Society and the Heritage Foundation. Trump would eventually release four Federalist Society–approved lists of potential nominees—two before Election Day 2016 and two as president. The forty-six names, in total, included individuals with diverse backgrounds, some of whom were certainly not among the supreme elite—not even close. But when it came time to select the actual nominees, the significance of the anti-drift checklist was obvious. Gorsuch checked all but one of the boxes, Brett Kavanaugh all ten, and Amy Coney Barrett seven (table 7.2). And those last two choices, as noted, weren't on either of Trump's two pre–Election Day lists. They were added nearly a year into his first term, with the prospect of Justice Anthony Kennedy's retirement on the horizon and talk of "draining the swamp" a faint echo from another time.

Democratic Presidents and the Avoidance of Confirmation Conflict

The president had reportedly winnowed his list down to two, perhaps three. One candidate in particular was attracting lots of attention because she was much different from those selected in the past half century. She had a blue-collar background, had been the first in her family to attend college, had earned both her undergraduate and law degrees at public universities, had never clerked for a judge (let alone a justice), and was not a sitting member of a court of appeals but a federal district court judge. Before her nomination to that post, she had been a state court judge. She had never lived in Washington. In fact, few there knew her. And she had faced adversity unlike many others, including losing her police officer father to gunshot wounds when she was just fourteen.[1] A leading Senate critic of the president urged him to nominate her and predicted substantial bipartisan support if he did.[2]

Her primary contender, in contrast, was educated at Harvard and Harvard Law, had clerked for the very justice retiring to create the vacancy, and was a current member of the DC court of appeals. She had spent nearly all of her adult life in Washington and had already been confirmed by the Senate three times. She was even related by marriage to a former Speaker of the House and vice-presidential nominee.[3] And at fifty-one, she was five years younger than her out-of-the-box competitor.

If you are not already aware of the ultimate choice, it should be clear from the previous two chapters which candidate the president selected. President Joe Biden, a veteran of many confirmation battles as a member and sometime chair of the Senate Judiciary Committee, may have toyed with the idea of nominating the unconventional J. Michelle Childs, but in the end he did not dare veer from the well-worn path traveled by so many of his predecessors.

He selected Ketanji Brown Jackson instead, and in doing so, definitively reaffirmed the power of the supreme elite.

∗

Compared to their counterparts in the Republican Party, Democratic presidents and allied legal forces exhibited a less developed, more ad hoc appointment strategy during the years of Republican dominance over the selection process. Patterns are less pronounced or distinctive with such a small sample size—again, just five of the last twenty justices (six of the last twenty-seven nominees). Nevertheless, several characteristics of those appointments distinguished them from those made by Republican presidents. While Republicans sought to develop a way to prevent ideological drift, the three Democratic presidents during this time focused on different factors. First, Bill Clinton, Barack Obama, and Joe Biden sought safety (see chapters 4 and 5). They selected nominees most likely to win confirmation, which was particularly important for Clinton and Obama since the filibuster was still in place.[4] All of them pursued safety first even though they enjoyed Senate Democratic majorities at the time they made their selections. In fact, in the case of Obama's first nomination, Democrats held a sixty-seat filibuster-proof majority.[5] Contrast that with their Republican counterparts, who typically appointed a conservative ideologue when the GOP held the Senate (and even sometimes when it didn't). Second, in contrast to their Republican counterparts, Presidents Clinton, Obama, and Biden sought out nominees who were more diverse in terms of ethnicity, gender, race, and (to a lesser extent) professional experience. Finally, all three thought seriously about making an unconventional choice for the Court—someone outside the liberal supreme elite. But as we'll see, it was not to be.

As an alternative, each chose nominees who exhibited what President Obama called "judicial empathy." As he noted in announcing Elena Kagan for the Court, that meant a nominee who had an "understanding of law, not as an intellectual exercise or words on a page, but as it affects the lives of ordinary people."[6] In his memoir, Obama dismissed conservative charges that judicial empathy translated into the appointment of "woolly-headed, social engineering liberals who cared nothing about 'objective' application of the law." To him, conservatives "had it upside down. It was precisely the ability of a judge to understand the context of his or her decisions, to know what life was like for a pregnant teen as well as for a Catholic priest, a self-made tycoon as well as an assembly-line worker, the minority as well as the majority, that was the wellspring of objectivity."[7] Obama's interest in an alternative inspired blatant exaggeration. Specifically, when he announced Kagan's nomination, he stressed that he had "reached beyond the so-called 'judicial monastery'" in making the selection. But he picked his solicitor general, who was a former Harvard Law dean and former nominee for the DC circuit court. As one commentator pointed out, such a selection "hardly reaches outside the Ivy League, East Coast legal elite."[8] Even a decade after the event, as his recollection in his memoir highlights, Obama's positioning was defensive, with a sharp eye on Republican dissent. The roots of progressive displeasure with the courts, then, lay not only with the GOP but also with these Democratic presidents. More often than not they did not use these appointments to advance a strategy of extending liberal principles in law, but rather to protect already-won gains.

While they often succeeded in this goal, Clinton, Obama, and Biden did not offer dramatically different alternatives from Republican presidents with regard to educational background and pre-Court experience. Instead, they highlighted quality in much the same way their Republican counterparts had after the Hruska switch. Restated, these choices were not in the vein of those made by Franklin D. Roosevelt or Lyndon Johnson. Consider that all six Democratic nominees had earned their undergraduate degree from an elite private university. Two went to Harvard, two to Princeton, and one each to Cornell and Stanford. Five attended Harvard Law, the other Yale Law.[9] All but one was a court of appeals judge before being nominated to the high bench. None had ever been elected to office. Indeed, aside from ideology, they were quite similar to Republican-appointed counterparts—members of the supreme elite on the other side of the left-right divide.

While the liberal checklist is neither as well developed nor as binding as its conservative counterpart, it nevertheless includes several important items: the perception of a moderately liberal ideology rather than a liberal firebrand;[10] a connection to Harvard or Yale law schools; a clerkship for a liberal justice; Washington experience (other than service as a clerk); a position either in the Senate or the executive branch under a Democratic administration; and a judgeship on the court of appeals. As suggested above, all but one of the five Democratic selections during this period checked off most if not all of these boxes (table 8.1). Stephen Breyer and Merrick Garland checked all six, Ketanji Brown Jackson five. Although Jackson was a federal public defender and President Obama nominated her—and the Senate confirmed her—to become vice chair of the United States Sentencing Commission, she did not work for a Democratic administration or Senate office. Elena Kagan checked off five boxes as well, having been denied a court of appeals judgeship by a Senate running out the clock on the Clinton presidency. Ruth Bader

TABLE 8.1. Shared Characteristics of Democratic Nominees, Divided Government and Polarization Periods

Nominee	Perceived Ideology	Senate or Administration Experience	Washington Experience	Court of Appeals Judge	Harvard or Yale Law	Supreme Court Clerk	Total
Ginsburg	x		x	x	x		4
Breyer	x	x	x	x	x	x	6
Sotomayor	x			x	x		3
Kagan	x	x	x		x	x	5
Garland	x	x	x	x	x	x	6
Jackson	x		x	x	x	x	5

Failed nominee in *italics*.

Ginsburg checked four boxes. She was not a Supreme Court clerk, nor had she worked in the Senate or the executive branch. Sonia Sotomayor checked only three, which confirms her outsider status. Although she did work for Robert Morgenthau, the Democratic district attorney for New York County (Manhattan), she did not clerk for a justice.[11] She also didn't work in the Senate or for a Democratic administration. In fact, until she joined the High Court, she had never worked in Washington.

Diversity was certainly a defining feature of these selections. Clinton appointed only the second woman ever to serve on the Court (Ginsburg). Obama named the third and fourth (Sotomayor and Kagan), Biden the fifth (Jackson). Sotomayor was also the first Hispanic justice. Jackson was the first Black woman. And four of the six Democratic nominees during this period were Jewish (Ginsburg, Breyer, Kagan, and Garland), although little was made of that fact at the time of the nominations.

Nevertheless, the appointments were historically significant. As noted earlier, for much of the twentieth century, there had been one seat "reserved" for a Jewish justice. President Nixon disrupted that tradition after Abe Fortas resigned from the Court in 1969. The so-called Jewish seat would remain vacant until Ruth Bader Ginsburg's confirmation in 1993. Although similar to the prevalence of Catholic appointees by Republican presidents, the nominees' Judaism was not a motivating factor in these selections. For example, as one administration official told members of the press corps at the time of the Ginsburg nomination, "it was something that if you find the right person and that person happened to be Jewish, then you could say you fill the Jewish seat. But really, it was not a driving factor. There were a number of people on the list that were Jewish, many more that were not Jewish."[12] The opposite was true regarding ethnicity, gender, and race. The search for a woman was usually intentional, as was Obama's decision to name the first Hispanic

justice and Biden's to select the first Black woman. These choices were made
to score political points with communities of voters that had both supported
the appointing president and offered possibilities to enhance the Democratic Party's electoral performance. But given that four of the six nominees
were Jewish, the potential electoral benefits of a symbolic Supreme Court
selection—with the clear exceptions of Sotomayor and Jackson—were obviously de-emphasized. And unlike their Republican counterparts, they did not
offer an electoral appeal based on ideology. Indeed, at least in the cases of
Clinton and Obama, the entire enterprise of Supreme Court selections appears to have been given less attention compared to Republican presidents of
the same era.[13]

As noted above, these three Democratic presidents prioritized confirmation success in selecting their nominees for the Court. In fact, even the very
conservative Justice Antonin Scalia expressed support for two of the nominees just before their selection. As described in chapter 5, he advocated for
Elena Kagan to longtime Obama confidant David Axelrod. He didn't get his
wish at that particular time, but he would the following year. The other Democratic nominee that pleased Scalia was his good friend Ruth Bader Ginsburg. The justice told the story in her book, *My Own Words*: "When President
Clinton was mulling over his first nomination to the Supreme Court, Justice
Scalia was asked a question to this effect: 'If you were stranded on a desert
island with your new Court colleague, who would you prefer, Larry Tribe or
Mario Cuomo?' Scalia answered quickly and distinctly: 'Ruth Bader Ginsburg.' Within days, the president chose me."[14]

To better understand the circuitous Supreme Court appointment strategy
of two of these three Democratic presidents, let's consider more closely the
three individuals they either nominated or hoped to name, beginning with
the very first empty seat in 1993.

✶

On December 20, 1992, the plane was said to be waiting. But it would never
take off. New York Governor Mario Cuomo stepped in front of a gaggle of
press to tell all those interested that he would not flying to New Hampshire to
file papers to participate in the state's first-in-the-nation primary. As in 1988,
he would rebuff widespread calls for him to enter the 1992 race for the Democratic presidential nomination. Unconvincingly, he said he needed to stay in
Albany to work on the state's budget.

Eighteen months later the newly inaugurated Democratic President Bill
Clinton was looking for a different, unusual Supreme Court pick. In a cha-
otic process lasting three months, Clinton publicly procrastinated over whom

to name to replace the retiring Justice Byron White. The political scientist Henry Abraham writes that Presidents Reagan and Bush "made a total of eight nominations in half that time."[15] The difference may have been an artifact of the Democrats' inconsistent strategy on High Court selections in this period or because a Democratic president had not had the opportunity to choose a justice in over a quarter of a century. Whatever the case, Mario Cuomo was first on Clinton's list. Nicknamed Hamilton-on-the-Hudson, Cuomo was the Democrats' most articulate defender of progressive values during the 1980s; for liberals, he was the Dr. Jekyll to the Mr. Hyde of Ronald Reagan. Before pursuing elective office—first unsuccessfully, for mayor of New York City—he had risen to prominence as a defender of homeowners' rights and as a mediator in a politically tense dispute over a low-income public housing development. Now in his third term as governor of New York, he was someone whose voice liberals believed would undercut conservative thinking from the likes of his fellow Italian American, Antonin Scalia.

While Cuomo and Scalia had grown up mere miles apart in Queens, New York, they had pursued divergent career and ideological paths. Cuomo, who spent many hours in his parents' mom-and-pop corner grocery store, attended the local Catholic college, the Vincentian St. John's University. After a promising career in baseball was cut short when he was hit in the head by a wild pitch, Cuomo returned to St. John's for law school. He was closer to the streets than Scalia, who as the son of a college professor attended the more prestigious Jesuit Georgetown University in Washington, DC, before moving on to law school at Harvard. Unlike Scalia, who was a conservative from the crib, Cuomo would be a jurist who, in FDR's words, knew "how the other 90 percent live."[16] If both were on the high bench, liberal imaginations envisioned a clash of two intellectual titans. And Cuomo, known for his sharp elbows during pickup games on the basketball court, was expected to show no mercy as a player on the highest court in the land. A "dramatic, transformative choice like Cuomo" deeply appealed to the president. As he put it: "Mario will sing the song of America. It'll be like watching Pavarotti at Christmastime."[17]

But just like the plane that waited in vain for Cuomo's presidential bid, so would President Clinton. At literally the eleventh hour—fifteen minutes before the president was scheduled to call the governor to offer him the nomination—Cuomo phoned George Stephanopoulos, senior advisor to the president, to say he had decided to stay in Albany. "The president shouldn't call me," Cuomo told Stephanopoulos. "I feel that I would not be able to do what we all need, including supporting the president politically. I surrender so many opportunities of service if I take the Court. I feel that I would

abandon what I have to do. . . . It would be untrue to myself."[18] Clinton never
made the call.

*

With Cuomo out, Clinton finalized his decision to nominate Ruth Bader
Ginsburg the following day. She was "arguably the seventh choice," according to one count.[19] Indeed, if not for a dithering governor, a bad meeting,
a deeply devoted husband, and a president who ignored her age, Ginsburg
would never have made it on the Supreme Court at all. Yet, at the time of her
death in mid-September 2020, she was easily the most celebrated of the justices, particularly among the liberals. That, however, was not the case when
she was appointed in June 1993. In fact, some of the liberal groups that champion her today did not even support her candidacy back then.

Before Ginsburg, Clinton had apparently settled on a candidate backed
by Massachusetts Senator Ted Kennedy. It came down to a meeting with the
president and the Kennedy-supported Stephen Breyer. The meeting, however, did not go well. Breyer was recovering from a bicycle accident and fresh
off a long train ride from Boston. As one person put it, the two just didn't
connect. That provided Ginsburg an opportunity. Her name had originally
been part of a long list of about fifty, but it did not make it onto the short list
until very late in the process.[20] There were at least three strikes against her.
First, the president had seemingly dismissed her after hearing she was a "cold
fish."[21] Second, White House aides wanted the president to select someone
younger than the sixty-year-old Ginsburg.[22] Finally, and most importantly,
some progressives thought she wasn't sufficiently liberal, particularly on the
issue of abortion.

But the supportive letters and phone calls for Ginsburg kept coming in to
the White House. They were generated by her husband Marty, a well-connected
Washington tax attorney and Georgetown Law professor. "Marty's minions
ginned up so many letters," Linda Hirshman writes, that "no one at the White
House could read them all."[23] Marty was also a friend of a key player in the selection process, White House counsel Bernard Nussbaum. But the president
still wasn't convinced, telling Senator Daniel Patrick Moynihan, who was calling him every day to push for Ginsburg, "the women are against her."[24]

Indeed, liberal interest groups, which had gained prominence during the
successful effort to block Robert Bork's confirmation in 1987 and the near
defeat of Clarence Thomas in 1991, were not great fans of Ginsburg. Although
she had garnered comparisons to Thurgood Marshall for her groundbreaking
legal advocacy for women's equality, that work was downplayed—somewhat
astonishingly—in the selection process. This was due to the political salience

of the abortion issue. Significantly, less than two weeks before Justice White announced his retirement, Ginsburg had given a Madison Lecture at New York University School of Law in which she had dared to criticize *Roe v. Wade*.[25] Progressives did not appreciate her take. In fact, "for the feminists and lawyers listening to her Madison Lecture, RBG's argument felt like a betrayal. At dinner after the lecture, Burt Neuborne remembers, other feminists tore into their old friend. 'They felt that *Roe* was so precarious, they were worried such an expression from Ruth would lead to it being overturned.' "[26] Defenders of Ginsburg were a bit perplexed by this opposition, given her take on *Roe* in the lecture. Significantly, she did not criticize the result in *Roe*. She criticized the reasoning and timing of the decision. One of her biographers, Jane Sherron De Hart, explains: "Taking issue with grounding the right to abortion in privacy rather than equality . . . Ginsburg . . . also questioned the sweep of *Roe v. Wade*, arguing that the law is best changed in 'measured motions' rather than in 'doctrinal limbs too swiftly shaped' (and hence unstable). Had the Court simply ruled on the more extreme Texas law at issue, giving the states more time to liberalize their laws, some of the discord, she suggested, might have been averted."[27]

But because she had offered an alternative view on *Roe* at a time when it was thought to be hanging by a doctrinal thread, pro-choice advocates charged her with disloyalty to the women's movement. Pushed by Moynihan, who spent a lifetime thinking for himself, she had apparently gone too far. Added to liberal consternation, as a member of the DC court of appeals Ginsburg had joined with her conservative brethren Robert Bork 85 percent of the time when they served together, compared to just 38 percent with a fellow President Jimmy Carter appointee. A ruling Ginsburg joined rejecting a Women's Equality Action League's case added fuel to the fire, resulting in a "palpable lack of enthusiasm" from women's groups.[28] But after the bad meeting with Breyer and the end of Cuomo's tease, Clinton set aside his uncertainties and decided on Ginsburg. At this late date in the process, her age clearly mattered little to him.

And whether intended or not, Ginsburg's Madison Lecture likely smoothed her path through the confirmation process. After all, some had a different view of her position on abortion. For example, President Clinton expressed concern she was too close to "the cultural Left" on the issue.[29] To liberal critics, her Madison Lecture emphasized—to their frustration—her willingness to consistently articulate a judicial philosophy based on incrementalism. But that philosophy made it easier for Republican senators to support her. The fact that she had a conservative friend and fan on the Court undoubtedly helped as well.

Despite all the things pushing against her nomination, Ginsburg, as a DC court of appeals judge with two Ivy League degrees and extensive experience at both the American Civil Liberties Union (ACLU) and Columbia Law School, was undoubtedly part of the liberal supreme elite and a Washington insider at the time of her nomination. But for a president trying for an unconventional choice, she fit the bill of a nominee different from the runner-up. In the final vote, the Senate confirmed her ninety-six to three. There has not been a more lopsided vote since.

*

Justice Antonin Scalia did not intend to leave the Court at a time when, as he put it, he might be replaced "by someone who immediately sets about undoing everything I've tried to do." That much was obvious, and he told his interviewer in typical Scalia style, "I shouldn't have to tell you that. Unless you think I'm a fool"[30]

But when the justice died on February 13, 2016, President Barack Obama, the liberal Democrat in the White House, had an unexpected opportunity to shape the High Court. With nearly a year left in his presidency, surely Obama would be able to name a replacement for Scalia. Republicans, however, controlled the Senate. And their leader—Senator Mitch McConnell of Kentucky—was determined to block any Obama selection.

With vain hope, the president nevertheless moved forward with a nomination, choosing Merrick Garland, a centrist judge on the DC court of appeals. In selecting Garland, the White House's thinking was quite clear. At sixty-three, Garland was one of the oldest nominees ever put forward for an associate justice post. At that age, he wouldn't be able to serve as long as a typical justice. Combined with his moderate positioning, Republican senators just might be convinced to consider and confirm him.

However, the strategy didn't work. Senate Republicans were unmoved by the selection of the deeply respected Washington insider. As promised, they effectively ignored Garland, with most refusing even to meet with him in their offices. They did so all the while insisting that the next president—who eventually proved to be Donald J. Trump—should fill the vacancy. They benefited from the fact that Democrats—most notably then senator Joe Biden—had made similar (albeit hypothetical) arguments in the past.[31]

Did Obama believe that if he chose Garland McConnell would change his mind and allow the nomination to proceed through the Senate? The majority leader certainly gave no hint that he would do such a thing. And Trump, leading in the GOP presidential primary polls at the time, was cheering McConnell on. But the Garland choice doesn't make much sense unless Obama believed that Republican senators would succumb to public displeasure and at least give Garland a fair hearing. And indeed, many Americans were outraged by the Senate majority's treatment of Garland. For example, an early May 2016 poll showed that nearly 70 percent of voters nationally, including 59 percent of Republicans, thought the Senate should both hold hearings on the Garland nomination and schedule an up-or-down vote on his confirmation.[32] Some even thought the Senate's refusal to consider Garland was a threat to the fundamentals of American democracy (see chapter 5). But despite Democratic objections, Senate Republicans held tight on Garland, effectively nullifying the nomination. To them, his selection was almost like a mirage.

★

Would it have been preferable for President Obama—as the Democrats sought to appeal to the working-class voters flocking to the Trump candidacy in early 2016—to pick from the Hugo Blacks, Earl Warrens, and Thurgood Marshalls of today? State school kids from humble backgrounds who, through smarts and grit, reached the pinnacle of the American legal system and who died as legends of the law—those who weren't presented with a path to the "supreme elite" the day a thick envelope arrived at their homes from Cambridge, Massachusetts or New Haven, Connecticut, or even the environs of Palo Alto, California. We'll never know the answer to that question. The possibility doesn't appear to have received serious consideration in the Obama White House.[33]

We do know that the president—a graduate of Ivy League Columbia and Harvard Law—chose another member of the supreme elite. After graduating from Harvard College, Garland simply moved quads to attend law school there. After earning his JD, he clerked for Judge Henry Friendly of the Second Circuit Court of Appeals and then for Justice William Brennan at the Supreme Court. Over the next decade and a half, he alternated between important positions in the Department of Justice—including a stint as a federal prosecutor—and at a venerable Washington, DC, law firm. In 1995, President Bill Clinton nominated him for the DC court of appeals. After a Senate delay, Clinton nominated him again in 1997. The Senate confirmed him by a vote of seventy-six to twenty-three in March of that year. When President Obama chose him for the high bench in 2016, he was that appellate court's chief judge, with nearly two decades of service. Like Justice Breyer, he checked all six of the boxes on the liberal Supreme Court checklist (table 8.1). And like three of the four previous Democratic nominees, he was Jewish. So, Garland's religion was unlikely to sway many voters in the upcoming election.

Indeed, on the campaign trail the Garland nomination didn't offer much for the Democratic nominee, Hillary Clinton. In the final debate of the 2016 presidential race, less than three weeks before Election Day and when millions were casting early ballots, the very first question, traditionally when the most eyes were glued to TV screens, dealt with the Supreme Court. But in speaking about the Court vacancy and the Senate's obstinacy toward Obama's choice, Hillary Clinton didn't even mention Merrick Garland's name. Some interpreted this refusal to say his name as unwillingness to commit to advancing his nomination should she win the presidency.[34] Either way, to her Garland was "the nominee that President Obama has sent to [the Senate]."[35] It was hardly a rallying cry to get voters to the polls.

This was not a first. Clinton hadn't mentioned Garland's name in the previous debate either. She did discuss what type of person she would choose for the Court if given the opportunity. But her description did not fit the nominee Obama had selected just months earlier. Specifically, Clinton said she wanted to appoint nominees "who have real-life experience, who have not just been in a big law firm and maybe clerked for a judge and then gotten on the bench, but, you know, maybe they tried some more cases, they actually understand what people are up against."[36] Garland had tried cases while in the Justice Department, but in several other ways he diverged from Clinton's ideal nominee. After all, he had also worked for a big law firm, clerked for a celebrated judge and Supreme Court justice, and been on the federal bench for nearly two decades. Finally, he didn't represent the diversity that Clinton highlighted on other occasions when speaking about potential choices for the high bench.[37] Perhaps for all these reasons she didn't take the opportunity to say that she would stick with his nomination if she won the election. She apparently never decided what she would do if she did win.[38]

In choosing Garland, Obama played into Republican hands. Instead of using the opportunity to choose a symbolic nominee who might have motivated progressive voters in the way Brett Kavanaugh and Amy Coney Barrett did for the GOP in 2018 and 2020, he chose someone Republicans could effectively snub, diminishing the potential for scoring electoral points with his selection. Garland's resumé was undoubtedly impressive, but his career had taken the traditional route to the Court—one that was decidedly different from the ideal Hillary Clinton stressed in her answer to the debate question. Had Obama chosen an alternative path, accepting the near certainty McConnell would stick with his strategy of resistance, Clinton might have been better able to use the Senate's intransigence to rally voters to the polls in the same way Nixon did in the South after the defeat of Clement Haynsworth and G. Harrold Carswell.

So, instead of pushing against the liberal "supreme elite," Presidents Clinton and Obama—and later Biden—solidified a path trod by Republicans after the Hruska switch. They spoke about choosing a justice of a different type. And Clinton certainly tried to do so. Obama chose Sotomayor, who while no doubt part of a liberal "supreme elite," checks the fewest boxes (table 8.1). As promised, Biden focused on selecting the first Black woman for the Court. But he did not choose the most unconventional jurist on his final list.

In the end, all three, while celebrating justices like Warren and Marshall, ignored the rich tradition of Democratic choices for the Court. In doing so, they likely undermined their ability to appeal to voters and/or move the Court to the left. Instead they played a defensive game, crossing their fingers and hoping to ward off the most serious challenges to decisions like *Roe*.

Given the confirmation politics of today, it may be difficult to find out-of-the-box selections, and perhaps even harder to secure confirmation for them. But recall, in all five cases where a Democratic president successfully filled a high bench vacancy in the last half century, he did so with a Democratic majority in the Senate. In one case that majority was filibuster-proof; in another it was just one vote shy of sixty.[39] The last nomination was the only time the Democrats held a bare majority, but by that point the filibuster was a thing of the past.

And compared to President George W. Bush, Presidents Clinton, Obama, and Biden were not that limited by their own allies. They simply chose an appointment strategy that highlighted confirmation safety, with a nod to diversity and empathy. Scoring political points was an afterthought on all but two occasions: Obama's selection of Sotomayor, and Biden's choice of Jackson to fulfill a pledge made in the midst of the 2020 presidential election.

How the Selection of Unknown Voices with Different Audiences Transformed the Court into a Judicial Aristocracy

How did a middle-aged woman, born and raised on the Upper West Side of Manhattan, who had never fired a gun in her life suddenly become a hunter? It's a story Justice Elena Kagan recounts often, and it begins soon after President Barack Obama nominated her to replace John Paul Stevens in 2010. As Kagan tells it, the origins of her willingness to go hunting came at the end of a long day of the so-called courtesy visits with individual senators a Supreme Court nominee typically makes in hopes of winning confirmation.

During these meetings, as Kagan explains, senators—sometimes alone and sometimes with staff—"take the opportunity to talk to you about things they are concerned about." And while "everybody thinks number one on the list is . . . abortion," in her case that issue was easily "dwarfed by the concern" about her "views on gun rights and guns." Since senators understand they will not get an answer to a question about Supreme Court precedent, "they try to find different ways of exploring the same areas." Kagan made eighty-two courtesy visits, and in her telling, "one after another after another—Democrats and Republicans" would ask her a string of gun-related questions to try to glean some information about her views on the second amendment. "Do you own any guns? I would say, no. Has anybody in your family ever owned any guns? I would say, no. Have you ever hunted? No. Does anybody in your family hunt? No. Do any of your friends hunt?"

Kagan found these attempts at discovery "really pretty pathetic." Then, during a visit with a senator from Idaho, Kagan took a different approach to the barrage of second amendment questions. She understood the importance of this issue for the senator and his constituents, and the serious "concern that I could never understand the place of guns and gun culture in the lives of the people of his state." So, she essentially invited herself to the senator's ranch to go hunting with him. But once those words came out of her mouth, as Kagan tells it, a "look of abject horror came over his face." Realizing that she "had gone a little bit too far," she offered an alternative, making the following promise: "If I'm lucky enough to be confirmed, I will ask Justice [Antonin] Scalia, whom I knew to be a very avid hunter, to take me hunting." After she joined the Court, now Justice Kagan relayed the story to her new colleague, Justice Scalia. He happily obliged in helping to keep her promise—they went on numerous hunting trips together before his death (in the midst of a hunting trip) in early 2016.

In a speech in 2004, Justice Clarence Thomas spoke about a particular activity he loves—something he described as "an important part of my life . . . my avocation." He added: "It allows me a sense of freedom . . . [and] helps me do my job better." That thing might come as a surprise to readers. The most senior justice on the Supreme Court today was speaking about RVing. He was talking about taking trips in his recreational vehicle—although he's quick to point out that he travels in a Motor Coach, not an RV—with his wife and grandnephew, sometimes overnighting in Walmart parking lots. He elaborated: "The world I live in is very cloistered. The bulk of my adult life has been spent in Washington, D.C. RVing allows me to get out and see the real America. In RV campgrounds, you wave at everybody and they wave back. We're all here for the same reason. The best people in the country can be found in RV campgrounds."[1]

Justice Thomas has continued his RVing, and when asked about it more recently, he recounted with delight his travels across the back roads and byways of America. In a 2016 interview he offered a bit more insight into why he enjoys it so much. "I grew up in Georgia, and the thing about segregation . . . it created fear; that you couldn't talk to each other. You couldn't go anyplace. So, the fear in Georgia was I couldn't go to small towns. . . . And I wanted to see small towns; to see our country. And now that I can do that without fear, we thought that we would do it." He continued, with joy filling his voice: "But most of all you see the citizens of this country. An RV park is very very democratic, with a small d. It is some of everybody there. . . . Everything about it, I love it. This is a great country. We've done about 40 states. Met a lot of people. Been a lot of places. It's freedom for me." Then he touched on the relevance of those trips for his position as a justice: "It shows you the constituency for the Constitution. It shows you it's not this city [Washington, DC]. It's not the people who are doing all the talking and all the prevaricating. It's just a person camping out of the back of his motorcycle who wants to be left alone; who wants to enjoy his country; who wants to raise his family or her family, and they're just friendly. . . . I think that it has shown me a part of the country that you wouldn't normally see."[2]

In another interview, Justice Thomas spoke about how these trips prevent him from being consumed by the "self-importance" of Washington, allow him "to have something in common with people from totally different backgrounds," and keep him "normal" rather than "insulated or isolated" from the country. He spoke of having a conversation—his anonymity intact—with a retired postal worker at Poncho's Pond, an RV park in Ludington, Michigan. For Thomas, that chat, a couple of hours in length, "was one of [his] great experiences." And, since he began his travels in 1999, conversations like that one have "been replicated hundreds of times all over this country."[3]

Kagan's hunting story highlights one of the questions about judicial decision-making animating this chapter. Thomas's traveling tales illuminate another. First, how much does biography and life experience matter to a Supreme Court justice's voting behavior? Second, does understanding the justices' individual audiences provide us with a sharper sense of their potential doctrinal path?

As Kagan suggests, all the senators who asked her about owning a gun were really trying to glean from her background an understanding of how she might rule on second amendment cases. From their perspective, a justice familiar with guns was more likely to appreciate their value to many Americans, and therefore unlikely to constitutionally constrict the newly discovered individual "right to bear arms."[4] The fact that she was from New York City didn't necessarily provide an answer. After all, the hunting-loving Scalia, who wrote the 2008 *District of Columbia v. Heller* opinion, was also from New York City. But unlike Kagan, he had extensive experience with guns. As a boy, he hunted rabbits with his grandfather during summer vacations on Long Island. And he attended a military-style, Jesuit, single-sex high school in lower Manhattan that required every student to participate in junior ROTC, which meant carrying his rifle on the subway back and forth to his home in the outer borough of Queens.[5] Sometimes when Justice Kagan tells this story her words suggest that all those senatorial questions, even if her promise to take up hunting as a hobby did not fundamentally alter her views on the second amendment, were nevertheless important to her understanding of the issues at hand. As she explained in one interview: "I actually quite liked hunting, which I think, you know, some of my East Coast friends are horrified about. But it was a good lesson. You know, this is a big country. And we grow up in so many different ways, and what's second nature to me, you know, somebody else can't imagine doing and vice versa." So, for her, hunting was an opportunity to "learn from . . . the experiences" of others.[6] It was similar to another lesson she said she learned while clerking for Justice Thurgood Marshall: that "behind law there are stories—stories of peoples' lives as shaped by the law, stories of peoples' lives as might be changed by the law."[7] So, by understanding the experiences of everyday Americans—even better, by living them—a justice would be better positioned to ensure that the letter of the law reflected the reality of life.

In trying to understand the motivation of judicial decision-making, legal scholars and political scientists look to many possibilities, including a keen focus on a justice's audience. Some totally ignore audience, positing that unelected justices with life tenure have the necessary independence to pursue their own ideological interests, unencumbered by appeals to any audience but themselves.[8] Others, such as those who investigate ideological drift, clearly view the justices as affected by the consumers of their decisions, whether public opinion generally or specific subsections of American society. Thomas's affinity for the RV lifestyle indicates a yearning to connect with a constituency that we might not expect for a justice of the Supreme Court.

Do biography and notions of audience matter to how the justices make decisions? I ask this question to draw and underscore a contrast between Supreme Courts of the past and the one of today. Specifically, I compare the justices appointed during the New Deal era with those appointed during the two most recent eras, of divided government and polarization. I focus on appointees of the dominant party since they defined these time periods. During the New Deal era, Democratic presidents selected sixteen of the twenty-one justices (76 percent). Since Richard Nixon's first appointment in 1969, Republican presidents chose fifteen of twenty justices (75 percent); ten of twelve (83 percent) during the divided government era, and five of eight (63 percent) during the polarization era.[9]

I argue, based on the work of other scholars, that both biography and audience matter greatly. And by contrasting the justices of the last two periods with those of the New Deal era, we are better able to understand how the divide between the Court and both the American people and American democracy has grown deeper.

✶

It has become commonplace, usually at the introduction ceremony or the beginning of a confirmation hearing, for nominees for the High Court or their supporters to convey aspects of their lives that suggest a connection to everyday Americans. There seems to be a need, almost an imperative, for this exercise. For example, Stephen Breyer noted that during the early part of his life, he "joined the Boy Scouts," worked "as a delivery boy," dug "ditches for the Pacific Gas & Electric Company," and "mixed salads up" for a San Francisco city camp. He added that his mom didn't "want him to spend too much time with his books." Samuel Alito spoke about the "unpretentious down-to-earth" neighborhood of his youth. He then compared it to what he experienced as a student at Princeton. "I saw some very smart people and very privileged people behaving irresponsibly, and I couldn't help making a contrast between some of the worst of what I saw on the campus and the good sense and the decency of the people back in my own community."[10] Translation: While I attended an Ivy League school, I'm not one of them. Amy Coney Barrett spoke about her everyday life after being introduced by President Donald Trump, noting: "While I am a judge, I'm better known back home as a room parent, carpool driver and birthday party planner."[11]

In introducing himself to the nation, Brett Kavanaugh made it sound like he was a middle-class kid who had made it big. He spoke of how his teacher mom left the classroom when he was ten to attend law school; of how his dad attended law school at night while working full time. He spoke of his "Jesuit high school," his love of sports, and his role as coach for his daughter's basketball team.[12] He said not a word about attending Yale as an undergraduate and a law student. President Trump had taken care of that. He did mention that his mom was a judge but didn't specify her court.[13] He also didn't mention that his father was a full-time lobbyist in Washington while he attended law school. Nor did he mention that his "Jesuit high school" was a nationally ranked prep school that very few Americans could afford. When asked during the hearings about his admission to Yale, he said he had "no connections" to the school, despite the fact that his grandfather was a Yale graduate. During the confirmation period, President Trump inflated Kavanaugh's record at Yale, saying he thought he was first in his class both as an undergraduate and at the law school.[14] But that was not true. Kavanaugh finished approximately in the second quartile of his undergraduate class, earning *cum laude* status— a position that would not likely get him admitted to Yale Law School today.[15] As for the president's assertion that Kavanaugh was first in his class at Yale Law, that is simply not possible, since the school does not award traditional grades or rank its graduates.[16]

It is not surprising that a president and his team would seek to accentuate the accomplishments of their nominees—to showcase their intellect and experience. But for me, the stories nominees tell to humanize themselves to a nation that is most likely seeing their face for the first time are more revealing. They are usually designed to convey a kinship with everyday Americans, and an understanding of how the law affects everyday life. For his part, Kavanaugh said this explicitly: "My mom taught me that judges don't deal in abstract theories; they decide real cases for real people in the real world." He then provided a specific example of how his mom's work had left an indelible impression on him:

> Fifty years ago this week, in September 1968, my mom was 26 and I was 3. That week, my mom started as a public-school teacher at McKinley Tech High School here in Washington, D.C. 1968 was a difficult time for race relations in our city and our country. . . . I vividly remember days as a young boy sitting in back of my mom's classroom as she taught American history to a class of African-American teenagers. Her students were born before *Brown versus Board of Education* or *Bolling versus Sharpe*. By her example, my mom taught me the importance of equality for all Americans—equal rights, equal dignity, and equal justice under law.[17]

Notably, Kavanaugh didn't mention some of the defining episodes of his legal career—he didn't mention his work in the Kenneth Starr–led investigation of President Bill Clinton or his role in the *Bush v. Gore* case that helped to decide the 2000 presidential election in favor of the candidate he would soon work for in the White House. Instead, he curiously highlighted his recollections of a classroom a half century earlier, when he was a very young boy. The choices of what to include and exclude in his introduction to the nation were no doubt linked to the task at hand: winning confirmation in a Senate with a narrow Republican majority. With respect to his work as a justice, most would probably say that personal history would make a difference for all justices; but despite the substantial attention to biography at the time of nomination, from both Democratic and Republican appointees, some justices, particularly those on the Right, dismiss its importance.

Justice Antonin Scalia clearly dismissed the importance of background and diverse experiences in a characteristically seething dissent in *Obergefell v. Hodges* (2015). He said biography shouldn't matter. But he added one important caveat: as long as justices behaved as justices were supposed to.

Obergefell dealt with the issue of same-sex marriage, and Scalia believed the majority had erred in its decision, which effectively constitutionalized such unions, by short-circuiting democracy. "A system of government that makes the People subordinate to a committee of nine unelected lawyers does not deserve to be called a democracy," Scalia wrote. He then summarized parts of the backgrounds of the nine members of the Court at the time, leaving out some aspects and making some questionable assertions:

> Judges are selected precisely for their skill as lawyers; whether they reflect the policy views of a particular constituency is not (or should not be) relevant. Not

surprisingly then, the Federal Judiciary is hardly a cross-section of America.
Take, for example, this Court, which consists of only nine men and women,
all of them successful lawyers who studied at Harvard or Yale Law School.
Four of the nine are natives of New York City. Eight of them grew up in east-
and west-coast States. Only one hails from the vast expanse in-between. Not a
single Southwesterner or even, to tell the truth, a genuine Westerner (California does not count). Not a single evangelical Christian (a group that comprises
about one quarter of Americans), or even a Protestant of any denomination.
The strikingly unrepresentative character of the body voting on today's social
upheaval would be irrelevant if they were functioning as *judges*, answering the
legal question whether the American people had ever ratified a constitutional
provision that was understood to proscribe the traditional definition of marriage. But of course the Justices in today's majority are not voting on that basis;
they say they are not. And to allow the policy question of same-sex marriage to
be considered and resolved by a *select, patrician, highly unrepresentative panel
of nine* is to violate a principle even more fundamental than no taxation without representation: no social transformation without representation.[18]

When Scalia was in dissent in a politically salient case, which happened
quite often, it was not unusual for him to charge the majority with acting as
a "super-legislature"—i.e., making policy—even if he didn't always use those
words. His search for the original meaning of the Constitution or a statute
under review meant that it was necessary for him and his allies to "find the
law" as those who advanced an aspirationalist or evolving interpretation—
the idea of a living Constitution—did not. Scalia believed the justices in the
Obergefell majority were making policy instead of interpreting the Constitution. But, of course, he knew very well that judges and justices often "make
policy," whether they are conservative or liberal, originalists or evolutionists.[19]

In advancing this argument about the nature of a good judge, Scalia was
parroting Justice Felix Frankfurter. In 1957, in making a case against the necessity of judicial experience prior to ascent to the high bench (as discussed
in chapter 6), Frankfurter noted:

> The search should be made among those men, inevitably very few at any time,
> who give the best promise of satisfying the intrinsic needs of the Court, no
> matter where they may be found, no matter in what professional way they
> have manifested the needed qualities. . . . Selection wholly on the basis of
> functional fitness not only affords the greatest assurance that the Court will
> best fulfill its functions. It also will, by the quality of such performance, most
> solidly establish the Court in the confidence of the people, and the confidence
> of the people is the ultimate reliance of the court as an institution.[20]

Like Frankfurter, Scalia suggested he viewed the Court as a lawyer and a judge. But he knew the game. And he well knew he was advancing a view that wasn't true. Presidents don't choose justices simply based "their skill as lawyers." Presidential perception of "whether they reflect the policy views of a particular constituency" is highly relevant to the ultimate selection. Put simply, the construction of the Court is a deeply political enterprise. But in *Obergefell* (and in a host of other decisions) Scalia argued that justices ought to be disconnected from the representative facets of American democracy. In conflict with Oliver Wendell Holmes—who famously wrote "the life of law is not logic, but experience"—Scalia pleaded with his fellow justices to ignore experience. Originalism should rule the day.[21]

For these same reasons, biography didn't matter much to him. So, when asked about how his devotion to Catholicism shaped his thinking on the bench, Scalia had a simple and straightforward answer. It didn't. Or at least, he hoped it didn't. Of course he had "religious views." But he "was not authorized to impose those on this society." They ought "not to play any role" in his judging. Another time, he said his Jesuit education and Catholic faith had "nothing to do with how I decide cases."[22] To him, if a judge was acting properly, biography was quarantined from the interpretation of a statute or the Constitution. It is a view that others on the Right have adopted, including Justice Kavanaugh: "A judge must be independent and must interpret the law, not make the law. A judge must interpret statutes as written. A judge must interpret the Constitution as written, informed by history and tradition and precedent. In deciding cases, a judge must always keep in mind what Alexander Hamilton said in *Federalist 83*: 'the rules of legal interpretation are rules of common sense.' A good judge must be an umpire—a neutral and impartial arbiter who favors no litigant or policy."

Kavanaugh's analogy of the judge as umpire was not an original one. But it clearly clashes with the lessons he said he learned from his mother about judging: namely, that "real people" are behind the cases they decide. When an umpire calls a pitch a strike or a batter out, there are real consequences for that player, too. But it's not supposed to influence the call. Of course, others disagree with the idea that judges are unaffected by their personal histories. In 1973, Thurgood Marshall wrote a dissent in *US v. Kras* expressing this view:

> It may be easy for some people to think that weekly savings of less than $2 are no burden. But no one who has had close contact with poor people can fail to understand how close to the margin of survival many of them are. A sudden illness, for example, may destroy whatever savings they may have

accumulated, and, by eliminating a sense of security, may destroy the incentive to save in the future. A pack or two of cigarettes may be, for them, not a routine purchase, but a luxury indulged in only rarely. The desperately poor almost never go to see a movie, which the majority seems to believe is an almost weekly activity. They have more important things to do with what little money they have—like attempting to provide some comforts for a gravely ill child. . . . It is perfectly proper for judges to disagree about what the Constitution requires. But it is disgraceful for an interpretation of the Constitution to be premised upon unfounded assumptions about how people live.[23]

Thurgood Marshall often sought to emphasize the importance of the individuals affected by the law, and his *Kras* dissent is just one example. Through his stories, he conveyed the same idea: for example, he knew from personal experience (chapter 6) that the law needed to protect those alleged to have acted outside of it. If it didn't, someone might be lynched. One of his former clerks writes about how Marshall recounted his near lynching on the banks of Duck River: "By bringing the shadow of death into the room, he had reminded us all of the stakes. . . . And whenever the Supreme Court heard a case involving the rights of criminal suspects, he'd remind us that he was the only Justice who'd ever been in handcuffs—or sat on the wrong side of an interrogation table."[24] He understood how the law worked (or didn't) in ways the other justices couldn't.

During the New Deal era, presidents sought to select these types of justices, based on the expectation that their upbringing and personal histories would define their decision-making. By understanding the issues through their own life experiences, they were more likely to reach the "right" result. The idea that personal biography is deeply significant to judging has a rich history. Indeed, biographers of Supreme Court justices pursue their subject believing that an individual's biography matters. Why else devote countless hours to conducting interviews and reading through documents in some dusty archive? Perhaps the better question for a biographer is whether a justice's background and experiences are determinative of his or her judicial behavior, or if they simply influence it. In writing of Roger Brooke Taney, the legal scholar Fred Rodell's take on this question is clear: "There is not one of his decisions as Chief Justice—from his years nipping at the Marshall-nurtured rights of Northern capitalists to his ill-fated last-ditch effort to hold the dike for slavery—but can be traced, directly or indirectly, to his big-plantation birth and background."[25] In his book, *The Enigma of Clarence Thomas*, Corey Robin pursues a similar course, tracing many of the justice's judicial opinions to the Black nationalism he embraced in his college years.[26]

Joan Biskupic, a Supreme Court reporter and author of several biographies of justices, considers a similar question: "Is personal biography judicial destiny?" In answering it in three different books, she argues that Scalia's experience in the executive branch in post-Watergate Washington shaped his views on the erosion of presidential power and defined his combativeness toward Congress, and that O'Connor's time as a state legislator honed her ability to count votes and conditioned her to work out compromises.[27] In writing about Sotomayor, Biskupic contends that her history of breaking barriers as a Puerto Rican kid from the Bronx defined her views on race. Biskupic highlights one particular case, *Schuette v. Coalition to Defend Affirmative Action*, which "echoed with [Sotomayor's] personal story."[28] In denouncing the conservative majority's take on affirmative action, the justice wrote with power in *Schuette* (and seemingly in reference to personal experience):

> Race matters. Race matters in part because of the long history of racial minorities' being denied access to the political process. . . . Race also matters because of persistent racial inequality in society—inequality that cannot be ignored and that has produced stark socioeconomic disparities. . . . And race matters for reasons that really are only skin deep, that cannot be discussed any other way, and that cannot be wished away. Race matters to a young man's view of society when he spends his teenage years watching others tense up as he passes, no matter the neighborhood where he grew up. Race matters to a young woman's sense of self when she states her hometown, and then is pressed, "No, where are you really from?" regardless of how many generations her family has been in the country. Race matters to a young person addressed by a stranger in a foreign language, which he does not understand because only English was spoken at home. Race matters because of the slights, the snickers, the silent judgments that reinforce that most crippling of thoughts: "I do not belong here."[29]

In an essay titled "Biography Is Destiny," the legal scholar Earl M. Maltz agrees with Biskupic about the importance of a justice's background: "Judicial biographies are an indispensable resource for those of us seeking to understand the structure of constitutional law. The evolution of this structure is determined by the interacting views of the shifting groups of nine individuals serving on the Court over time. *Each individual's position reflects a unique set of influences and experiences.* Judicial biographies provide detailed accounts of these influences and experiences, thereby deepening our knowledge of the forces that ultimately shape Supreme Court jurisprudence."

Maltz adds that "more traditional modes of constitutional scholarship tend to focus only on certain parts of the Justices' biographies to the exclusion of other significant influences on the development of their views."[30] In making this point, Maltz discounts the explanatory power of not only "purely doctrinal descriptions of Supreme Court opinions," but also analyses that "emphasize the political backgrounds and views of the Justices as the primary determinants of judicial decisionmaking." He adds: "The views of judges are not shaped only by legal theory and political ideology, but by the totality of their life experiences."[31]

With the last reference, Maltz is no doubt reflecting on the work of political scientists who advance the "attitudinal" model. This model focuses exclusively on ideology to explain judicial behavior. In a much-quoted two-sentence summary of their argument, the attitudinalists Jeffrey Segal and Harold Spaeth write: "[Chief Justice] Rehnquist votes the way he does because he is extremely conservative; Justice Marshall voted the way he did because he was extremely liberal."[32] Other political scientists advance the strategic model, which views the justices as slightly more complex in their thinking, suggesting that they are rational actors weighing a variety of factors when reaching decisions in the hopes of advancing their own interests.[33] In more recent work, the political scientist Matthew Hall adopts a psychoeconomic approach to understanding judicial behavior, positing that "in order to establish *what justices want*, we must first determine *who they are*."[34] While Maltz believes only judicial biography captures the full picture of a justice, all of these models actually reinforce his main conclusion: biography matters.[35] The political science scholarship, of course, focuses on specific characteristics of a justice's background, while Maltz explores the entirety of it. But the conclusion is the same. And who gets chosen in the selection process significantly determines how the Court decides its cases.

As discussed in earlier chapters, this was certainly the view during the New Deal era. A nominee's biography was expected to matter. He wouldn't have been chosen otherwise. Recall Roosevelt's insistence on choosing justices who had come up "the hard way." He also didn't favor nominees with prior judicial experience—only one of his nine appointees had been an appellate judge (and that was his final choice for an unexpected vacancy). Indeed, putting ideology aside, it is unlikely that any of today's justices would have made a Roosevelt short list for Supreme Court selection. Today's justices all took a decidedly different path to the Court after the Hruska switch, a change that has accelerated during the polarization era. Specifically, Republican presidents have chosen jurists who were strikingly similar to each other in hopes of ensuring their long-term commitment to conservatism on the bench. Democratic presidents have responded in kind, although their selections have been more varied. The result is a cookie-cutter Supreme Court with justices coming from a tiny sliver of America, chosen from the supreme elite on both sides of the ideological divide, making the Court of today distinct from those of yesterday.[36]

✶

If Supreme Court justices of today come from a particular niche of the nation, then arguably they also speak to their own particular niches—their own audiences. Consider a speech given in a large banquet room in a Boston hotel in February 2005. There is no video of the speech or recording of the words spoken then and there. But those in attendance tell of a wild scene. At the podium, Elena Kagan, then dean of Harvard Law School, stood ready to address student members of the Federalist Society gathered there from across the country. She began with words of admiration: "I love the Federalist Society." She then paused. And repeated the line once more: "I love the Federalist Society." Upon hearing the noted liberal dean articulate such sentiment, the audience rose and roared with delight. Kagan then added: "But, you know, you are not my people."[37]

Kagan's final line suggests that justices (or potential justices, in this case) have "people" they wish to satisfy. The idea sounds perfectly reasonable. The life of a justice can be a confined, cloistered one, as Justice Thomas has noted. Indeed, the nature of the position has deterred some from seeking an appointment, resulting in their names being taken off presidential lists.[38] The legal scholar Neal Devins and the political scientist Lawrence Baum argue that a justice's audience is quite important—that only by understanding a justice's audience can we understand his or her voting behavior, because justices "care greatly about the esteem in which they are held." According to Devins and Baum, justices "are far more likely to care about their reputation among the elite audience they come from and interact with than their reputation among the general public." For them, elite opinion matters more than public opinion. Although each does not have equal weight, "the key elite audiences for Justices are the legal profession, academia, news media, political groups, and personal social circles."[39]

In the not so distant past the justices who assumed their seats on the high bench were closely connected to the political regime that put them there. Of justices appointed during the first two-thirds of the twentieth century, some had been part of the appointing president's administration, serving as members of the cabinet or in influential positions of power. Others were close advisors to the president. Still others were trusted allies in Congress or governors of large states. Some even continued to interact with the appointing president after they joined the Court.[40] Several were considered serious contenders for the presidency. Indeed, one left the Court to nearly capture the White House. And, of course, another had been president before joining the Court as chief justice. Notably, few had significant judicial careers before their appointment to the high bench. Even fewer were sitting judges at the time of their nomination. Rather, they were men of politics—what I call "administration men." Generally, this meant that they met the following three conditions: they served in the appointing president's administration (or an earlier presidential administration of the same party); they were known to the president (either because he appointed them to another position previously or considered them an important advisor, or because they were a congressional ally); and they had more extensive experience in the executive branch (or in Congress) than in the federal judiciary. More importantly, it meant that they cut their teeth in the policy and political arenas and were conditioned to advance the governing regime's principles and strengthen and extend its authority. These were not legal "super-nerds" like those Ann Coulter described (see chapter 7). In his seminal 1957 article, the political scientist Robert Dahl highlights the nature of these choices:

> Justices are typically men who, prior to appointment, have engaged in public life and have committed themselves publicly on the great questions of the day. As Mr. Justice Frankfurter has recently reminded us, a surprisingly large proportion of the justices, particularly of the great justices who have left their stamp upon the decisions of the Court, have had little or no prior judicial experience. Nor have the justices—certainly not the great justices—been timid men with a passion for anonymity. Indeed, it is not too much to say that if justices were appointed primarily for their "judicial" qualities without regard to their basic attitudes on fundamental questions of public policy, the Court could not play the influential role in the American political system that it does in reality play.[41]

All but two justices appointed by Democratic presidents during the New Deal era were members of the national governing alliance before appointment to the Court (table 9.1). At the very least, the appointing president knew them at a distance. Sometimes he knew them quite well. And he presumed they were committed to the New Deal regime's governing principles and its continued success. Two of the justices were not officially part of an administration or a congressional ally. But both Felix Frankfurter and Wiley Rutledge supported the New Deal in significant ways. In fact, Frankfurter was considered one of FDR's most trusted advisors, and he sent scores of recent Harvard Law grads to Washington to work in the rapidly expanding executive branch. The president also offered Frankfurter the solicitor general position, but the future

TABLE 9.1. Pre-Court Experience of Democrat-Appointed Justices and Failed Nominee, New Deal Period

Justice	Appointing President	Administration Man	Position at Nomination	Previous Notable Positions in Government
Black	Roosevelt	Yes	US Senator (AL), 1927–37	
Reed	Roosevelt	Yes	US Solicitor General, 1935–38	General counsel for Federal Farm Board, 1929–32; General counsel for Reconstruction Finance Corporation, 1932–35; Special assistant to the attorney general, 1935
Frankfurter	Roosevelt	Yes	Law professor/presidential advisor	Assistant US attorney, Southern District of New York, 1906–9; Law officer of the Bureau of Insular Affairs (War Dept.), 1911–14; Special assistant to the secretary of war and judge advocate general (War Dept.), 1917–18; Assistant to secretary of labor, 1918–19
Douglas	Roosevelt	Yes	SEC Chair, 1937–39	Member of the SEC, 1936–39
Murphy	Roosevelt	Yes	US Attorney General, 1939–40	Assistant US attorney, Eastern District of Michigan, 1919–20; Mayor of Detroit, 1930–33; Governor/High Commissioner of the Philippines, 1933–36; Governor of Michigan, 1937–39
Stone	Roosevelt	No	Associate Justice, 1925–41	US Attorney General, 1924–25
Byrnes	Roosevelt	Yes	US Senator (SC), 1931–41	US Congressman (SC), 1911–25
Jackson	Roosevelt	Yes	US Attorney General, 1940–41	General counsel, Internal Revenue Bureau, 1934–36; special counsel, SEC, 1935; assistant attorney general, 1936–38; US Solicitor General, 1938–39
Rutledge	Roosevelt	Yes	Appeals Court Judge (DC), 1939–43	
Burton	Truman	Yes	US Senator (OH)	Mayor of Cleveland, OH, 1935–40
Vinson	Truman	Yes	US Secretary of Treasury, 1945–46	US Congressman (KY), 1923–29, 1931–38; appeals court judge (DC), 1938–43; director of the Office of Economic Stabilization, 1943–45; federal loan administrator, 1945; director of War Mobilization and Reconversion, 1945
Clark	Truman	Yes	US Attorney General, 1945–49	Special assistant, DOJ, 1937–43; assistant attorney general, 1943–45

(continued)

TABLE 9.1. (continued)

Justice	Appointing President	Administration Man	Position at Nomination	Previous Notable Positions in Government
Minton	Truman	Yes	Appeals court judge (7th), 1941–49	US Senator (IN), 1935–41; administrative assistant to the president, 1941
White	Kennedy	Yes	US Deputy Attorney General, 1961–62	
Goldberg	Kennedy	Yes	US Secretary of Labor, 1961–62	
Fortas	Johnson	Yes	DC lawyer/presidential advisor	Assistant director, SEC, 1937–39; general counsel for Public Works Administration, 1939–40; director of the Division of Power (Interior Dept.), 1941–42; undersecretary of interior, 1942–46
Marshall	Johnson	Yes	US Solicitor General, 1965–67	Appeals court judge (2nd), 1961–65
Failed Nominee				
Thornberry	Johnson	Yes	Appeals court judge (5th), 1965–78	US Congressman (TX), 1949–63; federal district court judge (TX), 1963–65

justice thought it best to stay out of the spotlight and work behind the scenes. Rutledge was not as close to Roosevelt. But as a law professor, he was a vocal advocate of the president's Court-packing plan and a committed New Dealer.

The audience for New Deal–era justices, then, was clear: it was the political regime with which they were aligned. Recall Martin Shapiro's conclusion that the Warren Court "got away with its activism because it was activism on behalf of the winners not the losers of American politics." In other words, the justices were selected to serve the interests of the political coalition that put them in place, and they did so. These were administration men first and foremost, but that did not make them "yes" men.[42] As Justice Robert Jackson tells it, FDR only asked him once about a Court opinion, and that was during a poker game.[43] In fact, justices of the New Deal era were often divided in their decision-making. They did not march in lockstep to advance the interests of the appointing president, and at times some of them upset the appointing president with their decisions. For example, President Truman famously called Justice Tom Clark that "damn fool from Texas" after learning of his decision in the 1952 steel seizure case.[44] But that just emphasizes the point: this arrangement was not about the president always getting his way. Removed from partisan politics, the justices would make their own decisions; nevertheless, as I've written elsewhere, a president's policy toward the judiciary helped to "forge the institutional mission of the Court" at particular historical moments. And presidents like FDR—those whom the political scientist Stephen Skowronek calls "reconstructive presidents" because they possess far more authority and capacity for action than others—have the greatest ability to "reorder the judiciary" and serve "as the mainspring of constitutional change."[45]

In turn, during the New Deal period, justices were chosen based on their service to the Democratic political order and the president's belief that they would continue to serve it well once on the Court. Some of their decisions were destined to divide, since the justices considered many of the most politically sensitive issues of the day—issues that exacerbated the New Deal coalition's internal cleavages or even split it entirely. At times they came down on opposite sides, asserting their differing opinions on the constitutionally acceptable course of action. As Shapiro writes: "the history of the Court at its activist peak in the 1950s and 1960s, and even into the 1970s, is actually the history of a political institution working out the implications of the victory of the New Deal coalition and the dominance of the New Deal consensus."[46] The same might be said of today's Court—that it is working out the implications of Republican success in presidential and senatorial elections. But there's an important difference. The dominance is gone. Again, Republicans have lost the popular vote in seven of the last eight presidential elections, and the Court's five most conservative members are numerical minority justices. Yet this conservative core has moved ahead as though they are advancing the interests of a dominant regime, when they clearly are not.

Importantly, this process of working out the meaning of a political coalition or consensus was not a creation of the Roosevelt era. In discussing the history of the Supreme Court, Robert McCloskey elaborates on the roots of this arrangement: "Our courts and, even more important, our legislatures have been shaped by the understanding that the judiciary will help in charting the path of governmental policy. A rough division of labor has developed from that understanding, for it is assumed that the legislature can focus largely on the task of 'interest representation,' while passing on to the courts a substantial share of the responsibility for considering the long-term constitutional questions that continually arise."[47] Dahl makes a similar point: "The Supreme Court is not . . . simply an agent of the alliance. It is an essential part of the political leadership and possesses some bases of power of its own, the most important of which is the unique legitimacy attributed to its interpretations of the Constitution."[48]

Under these terms, if the structural components of a regime are powerful, being a justice is not about being an autonomous voice untethered to the democratically elected branches of power. It's about deciding on the most vexing questions that come before the Court based on the regime's principles, not one's individual ideology. In such an arrangement, the Court's democracy gap is narrow—the justices' decisions are an extension of the dominant democratically elected entities that put them in place. The justices themselves are independent, but not isolated.

This may nevertheless mean that the Court acts in a way that is electorally destructive to the very coalition that constructed it. For example, in *Brown v. Board of Education*, the Court—with five Roosevelt and three Truman justices—delivered a decision that helped tear asunder the New Deal coalition. Nevertheless, sitting at the "apex of a federal branch of government," to borrow a phrase from Justice Robert Jackson, the justices unanimously believed that the constitutional eradication of segregation was necessary, indeed vital to the interests of the nation they helped lead.[49] Power emboldens. And in *Brown*, although uncertain of the consequences, the justices were committed to employing whatever power they had at their command. Anchored to a dominant political regime and the democratic legitimacy it provided them, they believed it was their responsibility to act against segregation at long last.

And after they did, they were not alone. With many excruciating delays, the other branches of the federal government added their authority to the cause of ending southern segregation. Presidents of both parties stepped in to enforce the Court's desegregation orders and eventually champion the advancement of civil rights. Congress offered its powerful hand as well, most especially by passing the 1964 Civil Rights Act and the 1965 Voting Rights Act. There were surely days when the justices felt abandoned by members of the other branches, but in time the regime's forces aligned.

*

In today's Washington culture, it would be all but unimaginable that a president might pop over to a private home to play "no-limit Texas Hold'em" on a standing poker night and discuss a Court vacancy with a sitting Supreme Court justice. Yet during the Roosevelt years the president often played poker with Justices William O. Douglas and Jackson. The general rule was no discussion of the affairs of the nation. But according to Douglas, on one particular night—at Treasury Secretary Henry Morgenthau's house—"FDR was in a serious mood, anxious" to be asked about a vacancy on the high bench. If Douglas's memory is to be believed, the justice was not bold enough to ask the president whom he was going to appoint to the seat. So, he asked him whom he wasn't going to appoint. The president "threw back his head and laughed in his typical robust way."[50]

Douglas was referring to a 1942 vacancy created by the resignation of Jimmy Byrnes. A former senator from South Carolina, Byrnes had been on the high bench for barely a year. But he felt he could better aid the nation and the war effort in the White House—the epitome of an administration man. The vacancy meant that Roosevelt would appoint an eighth justice, not counting his elevation of Harlan F. Stone to chief. Aside from George Washington, no president has appointed more. The choice apparently came down to two men: Learned Hand, a legendary Second Circuit Court judge, and Wiley B. Rutledge, a lesser-known DC court of appeals judge whom Roosevelt considered for earlier vacancies, particularly two that went to Frankfurter and then Douglas, both in 1939. When Rutledge lost out on the second spot, the president appointed him to the DC court of appeals instead.

Hand had his celebrated intellect and an aggressive Justice Frankfurter on his side. With America at war, FDR was also interested in appointing a Republican to help balance out the Court after his first seven additions to it.[51] Hand was a progressive Republican of the first order. Rutledge, who had spent much of his adult life west of the Mississippi River, had geography on his side, since Roosevelt had yet to appoint a "true" westerner. At forty-eight, he was also more than two decades younger than the seventy-one-year-old Hand. And the age of the justices was an essential aspect of the president's critique of the Court during his "packing" efforts in 1937. Additionally, as the legal scholar Gerald Gunther writes in his exhaustive biography of Hand, FDR was choosing between warring factions of the Roosevelt Court:

> The central issue . . . [was] whether judicial restraint—broad deference to leg-islative resolutions of policy debates—should be the across-the-board posi-tion of the justices as to *all* types of laws, or whether there should be some-thing of a double standard under which the justices would keep their hands off economic regulations and at the same time scrutinize more carefully those laws attacked as impinging on personal liberties. All the New Deal justices agreed that the hands-off attitude was appropriate for economic laws, but they differed sharply about the proper approach to individual-rights cases. The Frankfurter wing insisted that a double standard was inappropriate; ju-dicial deference to majority rule should govern even when the challenged law curtailed personal rights, not only when economic interests were threatened. Justices [Hugo] Black and Douglas, argued just as vehemently that a more ac-tivist, interventionist role for the Court was appropriate when personal rights sought protection. This battle over contending philosophies was at its peak in 1942, when the Byrnes vacancy arose.[52]

After hearing that the chief justice—who was first appointed to the Court by the Republican Calvin Coolidge—was recommending Rutledge, Attor-ney General Francis Biddle set up a meeting to hear him out.[53] He then met with the Court's leading liberals, Black and Douglas. Both were "enthusiastic about Rutledge."[54] By the poker night Douglas recalls, Roosevelt had made up his mind.[55] He would make an appointment that advanced the power of the Court's liberal faction and furthered Frankfurter's descent into dissent.

In many ways, Rutledge was least like FDR's other justices, given that he did not serve in the administration, the president did not know him well, and he was a sitting court of appeals judge. But he had "a long record of personal support for FDR, a predictable judicial philosophy of liberal activism, and the prospect of a long tenure on the Court." Hand's support for the president's administration was more in doubt. As Gunther writes, "Roosevelt was not acquainted with Hand, but he knew enough about him to recognize that he was no ideological crusader. Hand was a probing skeptic, a judge committed to independent, reasoned decision making."[56] He was also a product of the federal judiciary, having served there for more than three decades. Rutledge had only come to the federal bench three years earlier (and that was at the behest of the president). He viewed his position as a justice as an administra-tion man, committed to advancing FDR's cause, as is clear in his words to the president when he began his service as a justice: "On my first day here, I want you to know you have been very much in my thoughts. I shall not try to put them down. But please know I shall try to serve, giving to the large task you have assigned me the best effort of which I am capable. If, in some way, they may help to establish more firmly the democratic institutions which you fight to keep, and to create through out the world, it will make me glad. May God bless and keep you."[57]

These words convey the nature of the administration men selected for the Court during the New Deal period. In general, these justices believed they had retired from politics, but not from the affairs of state. In turn, it was not uncommon for them to participate in matters outside the Court, both formally and informally. And a few even chose to unretire from politics (or at least explored the idea).[58]

Choosing administration men was not an entirely new phenomenon. In fact, the legal scholar Tracey E. George writes, promotions from the federal bench "were rare in the nineteenth century: only six of the fifty-seven Justices appointed before 1900 [just over 10 percent] had served on the lower federal courts." Because of the low number and "limited authority of district and circuit courts . . . Presidents were less likely to promote from within the federal judiciary than to look outside the courts, particularly for party faithful, to fill open seats on the High Court." Things "changed dramatically at the turn of the twentieth century," soon after Congress expanded the size and authority of the federal courts.[59] But even during this time, the numbers are not overwhelming. Specifically, in the thirty-three-plus years of the twentieth century before FDR's inauguration, only one-third of the justices (six of the eighteen) had previously served as a federal judge (two at the district level and four on a circuit court).[60] And one of those six was not a judge at the time of his selection for the high bench. Indeed, most of the Republican era (1896–1932) nominees could easily be defined as administration men, most notably former president William Howard Taft. In addition, several continued to have interests outside the Court after they became a justice. Charles Evans Hughes left the Court in 1916 to become the Republican presidential nominee, and also served as secretary of state from 1921 to 1925. Owen Roberts considered leaving the Court to run for president in 1936; also, as a justice, he headed up the commission to investigate the attack on Pearl Harbor.

Justices today generally do not fit the description of administration men or women. Justice Kagan is the closest, having served for the president who chose her and never in the federal judiciary. But that was largely due to the fact that her nomination to the court of appeals stalled in the Senate at the end of the Clinton administration. Justice Thomas is the nearest Republican-appointed justice, given that he served in both the Reagan and George Bush administrations and only briefly on the court of appeals. In a striking illustration of the move away from administration men and women, Senate opponents tried to use Kagan's and Thomas's lack of experience on the federal bench as an argument for why they should not be confirmed for the nation's highest tribunal.[61] The other seven sitting justices either didn't serve in the executive branch or spent more than a decade away from it (mostly as court of appeals judges) before appointment to the nation's highest tribunal.

★

These pre-Court experiences have implications for a justice's audience. Consider the following. Justice Samuel Alito's office at the Supreme Court sits just across the street from the US Capitol. The three Senate office buildings are even closer to the Court, while the three House buildings are a bit farther away. Yet Justice Alito so detests legislators that he admits to crossing the street to avoid them on Capitol Hill.[62] Alito is not alone among the justices in his distaste for Congress. Recall from chapter 5, in his highly charged testimony before the Senate Judiciary Committee, Brett Kavanaugh, hoping to save his nomination following allegations of attempted sexual assault, unleashed his rage at the Democrats on the dais. He called the efforts to deny him a seat on the High Court "a calculated and orchestrated political hit . . . a circus . . . [and a] grotesque and coordinated character assassination." Then, he issued what sounded to some like a threat: "And as we all know, in the United States political system of the early 2000s, what goes around comes around."[63]

The increasing hostility of the confirmation process has undoubtedly played a role in how justices view Congress, especially since very few of them had any experience in the legislative branch before they tried to secure confirmation, usually first for a court of appeals judgeship.[64] Thus, their defining experience with Congress has been through the nomination process. Consider also that the two most recent Democratic presidents, Barack Obama and Joe Biden, opposed all the sitting Republican-appointed justices they had an opportunity to vote on as senators.[65]

But in addition to the coarsening of the confirmation process, the nature of the nominees changed during this period. Beginning with Richard Nixon's presidency in 1969 and the Hruska switch a year later, nominees were no longer selected for their closeness to the appointing president or their service in his administration or in Congress. Increasingly they were chosen for their *perceived* ideology and *presumed* "quality." The latter requirement almost always meant they were selected from the court of appeals. Indeed, all but one of the last fourteen justices were elevated directly from that federal bench.[66] But the move away from administration men was more evolutionary than revolutionary. And for this reason, it's important to separate the divided government era from the polarization era.

Notably, four of the ten Republican-appointed justices of the divided government era—Warren Burger, William Rehnquist, Antonin Scalia, and Clarence Thomas—were lesser versions of the New Deal period's administration men. They worked in the executive branch in Washington, although none held cabinet-level positions like some of their New Deal counterparts (table 9.2). All four were also appointed to the federal judiciary in the nation's capital, either directly to the Supreme Court or first to the DC court of appeals. Two of the four failed nominees during this time—Robert Bork and Douglas Ginsburg—had a similar profile. They both served in the executive branch and as a DC circuit court judge.[67] On all but one occasion, the four Republican presidents during these years—Nixon, Ford, Reagan, and George Bush—only chose different types of nominees—individuals who did not come close to fitting the definition of an administration man or woman—when (1) their options were more limited due to confirmation concerns (John Paul Stevens and David Souter), (2) they had a desire for a politically symbolic selection (Clement Haynsworth, G. Harrold Carswell, Lewis Powell, and Sandra Day O'Connor), or (3) after the defeat of a nominee befitting the administration man label (Anthony Kennedy). (The selection of Harry Blackmun is the exception. He was chosen after Nixon's two unsuccessful attempts to name a southerner.[68]) This suggests a continuing desire on the part of these presidents to choose nominees at least somewhat connected to their administrations.

Still, the four administration men of the divided government era were different from their New Deal counterparts. For example, only Rehnquist and Thomas served in the administration of the president who appointed them to the Court. And even so, neither knew the president well. In fact, Nixon famously flubbed Rehnquist's name—calling him "Rehnchberg"—and once criticized him for dressing like a "clown." Thomas notes that he had only one "very brief" private conversation with a "distracted" Bush before his nomination to the Supreme Court.[69] Indeed, most of the Republican-appointed divided government–era justices served—often for significant lengths of time—as court of appeals judges before elevation to the high bench. Two of the exceptions—Lewis Powell and William Rehnquist—were chosen early in this period, named on the same day in late 1971. At that point, the bench for potential conservative Supreme Court nominees was not very deep. The other exception—Arizona's Sandra Day O'Connor—was a sitting state court judge chosen by President Reagan to fulfill his campaign promise to appoint the first female justice. Again, the pool of potential nominees was quite shallow at the time.

TABLE 9.2. Pre-Court Experience of Republican-Appointed Justices and Failed Nominees, Divided Government Era

Justice	Appointing President	Administration Person	Judgeship at Nomination	Years as Court of Appeals Judge	Notable Position(s) in the Federal Executive Branch	Other Notable Positions in Government
Burger	Nixon	Partially*	Court of appeals (DC)	13.2	Assistant attorney general for the Civil Division, 1953–56	
Blackmun	Nixon	No	Court of appeals (8th)	10.7		
Powell	Nixon	No	N/A	N/A		
Rehnquist	Nixon	Yes	N/A	N/A	Assistant attorney general for the Office of Legal Counsel, 1969–71	Supreme Court clerk (Jackson)
Stevens	Ford	No	Court of appeals (7th)	5.1		Supreme Court clerk (Rutledge)
O'Connor	Reagan	No	Arizona court of appeals	N/A		Arizona assistant attorney general, 1965–69; Arizona State Senate, 1969–75; Maricopa County superior court judge (Arizona), 1975–79
Scalia	Reagan	Yes	Court of appeals (DC)	4.1	General counsel, Office of Telecommunications Policy, 1971–72; Chair of the Administrative Conference of the US, 1972–74; Assistant attorney general for the Office of Legal Counsel, 1974–77	
Kennedy	Reagan	No	Court of appeals (9th)	12.7		
Souter	Bush	No	Court of appeals (1st)	0.4		New Hampshire attorney general, 1976–78; NH superior court judge, 1978–83; NH Supreme Court justice, 1983–90

Thomas	Bush	Yes	Court of appeals (DC)	1.6	Assistant secretary for civil rights, US Department of Education, 1981–82; Chair of the US Equal Employment Opportunity Commission, 1982–90	Missouri assistant attorney general, 1974–77; legislative assistant, US Senate, 1979–81
Failed Nominees						
Haynsworth	Nixon	No	Court of appeals (4th)	12.4		
Carswell	Nixon	No	Court of appeals (5th)	0.6	US attorney, Northern District of Florida, 1953–58	Federal District Court judge, Northern District of Florida, 1958–69
Bork	Reagan	Yes**	Court of ppeals (DC)	5.4	US solicitor general, 1973–77; Acting attorney general, 1973–74	
Ginsburg	Reagan	Yes	Court of appeals (DC)	1	Deputy assistant attorney general for regulatory affairs, 1983–84; Administrator for Information and Regulatory Affairs, OMB, 1984–85; Assistant attorney general, antitrust division, 1985–86	Supreme Court clerk (Marshall)

*I define those who had a significant administrative post, but spent more time on the court of appeals than in the executive branch prior to Supreme Court appointment, as "partially" administration men or women.

**While Bork served slightly more time in the federal courts than in the executive branch prior to his nomination, given his position as acting attorney general and his role advising the Nixon administration before joining it, he is best described as an "administration man."

⋆

The five Republican-appointed justices of the polarization period had still fewer ties to the administration of the appointing president (table 9.3). It is difficult to describe any of them as an administration man or woman. In fact, none served under the president who appointed them. Three did serve in earlier Republican administrations but then spent many years—more than thirteen, on average—on the court of appeals. After serving in the executive branch, Chief Justice Roberts might have followed a similar path. But the Senate held up his 1992 nomination to a seat on the DC court of appeals. So instead, he went into private practice in Washington, but he was never far from the Court.[70] During those years Roberts frequently argued before the justices. Combined with his appearances as a government attorney, he argued before them thirty-nine times, putting him in rare company. He was nominated a second time for the DC court of appeals by George W. Bush in 2003, and this time the Senate confirmed him. The fifth Republican-appointed polarization-era justice, Amy Coney Barrett, did not serve in the executive branch at all.

So, while the Republican-selected justices of today were certainly chosen for their presumed ideological compatibility with the appointing president, they went to the Court with far fewer political connections to the governing regime than justices of the past. Their comparatively long service on the court of appeals and their clerkships for federal judges and justices meant that they were mainly conditioned in the judiciary, not the executive or legislative arena. In fact, given their clerkships with conservative justices, it's fair to say that they have been groomed for the Court by the justices themselves. Additionally, three of the five worked in the solicitor general's office while in the federal government. Because that office interacts closely with the High Court, the solicitor general is often referred to as "the tenth justice." In other words, even their executive service has a judicial bent to it. Devins and Baum suggest that the nature of their pre-Court experience may affect their behavior as justices. "Legal elites may be even more important to Justices in the current era than in past eras, because the Justices who have been appointed to the Court in the past half century typically come from careers in law rather than politics."[71]

Today's Republican-appointed justices are best described as ideological allies rather than administration men and women.[72] (The Democrat-appointed justices are not much different, but again my focus in this chapter is on the former.[73]) In fact, it is rather stunning from a historical perspective that Republican-appointed justices are likely more closely aligned with the Federalist Society than with the executive branch of the federal government. While

TABLE 9.3. Pre-Court Experience and Affiliations of Republican-Appointed Justices and Failed Nominee, Polarization Period

Justice	Appointing President	Administration Person	Judgeship at Nomination	Age at Court of Appeals Nomination	Years as Court of Appeals Judge	Clerkships	Federalist Society	Years at DC Law Firm	Notable Positions in the Federal Executive Branch
Roberts	W. Bush	No	Court of appeals (DC)	37/48	2.3	Friendly, *Rehnquist*	Yes	1986–89; 1993–2003	Special assistant to the attorney general, 1981–82; associate White House counsel, 1982–86; principal deputy solicitor general, 1989–93
Alito	W. Bush	No	Court of appeals (3rd)	39	15.8	Garth	Yes	None	Assistant US attorney (NJ), 1977–81; assistant solicitor general, 1981–85; deputy assistant attorney general, 1985–87; US attorney (NJ), 1987–90
Gorsuch	Trump	No	Court of appeals (10th)	38	10.7	Sentelle, *White*, *Kennedy*	Yes	1995–2005	Principal deputy associate attorney general, 2005–6
Kavanaugh	Trump	No	Court of appeals (DC)	38	12.4	Stapleton, Kozinski, *Kennedy*	Yes	1997–98; 1999–2001	Solicitor general office attorney, 1992–93; associate counsel in the Office of the Independent Counsel, 1994–97, 1998; White House associate/senior associate counsel, 2001–3; White House staff secretary, 2003–6
Barrett	Trump	No	Court of appeals (7th)	45	3	Silberman, *Scalia*	Yes	1999–2002	
Failed Nominee									
Miers	W. Bush	Yes	N/A	N/A	N/A	None	No	None	White House staff secretary, 2001–3; White House deputy chief of staff for policy, 2003–5; White House counsel, 2005–7

Supreme Court Clerkships in *italics*.

four of the five served in a Republican administration, all had spent significant time on the federal bench by the time of their selection for the Supreme
Court. Moreover, Federalist Society head Leonard Leo arguably (and extraordinarily) has had more influence on who sits on the Supreme Court during
the polarization era than have its elected Republican presidents, George W.
Bush and Donald J. Trump. With his selection of Harriett Miers, President
Bush challenged the power of movement conservatives, and lost. With the
release of his Federalist Society–approved lists, then-candidate Trump acqui-
esced to these forces even before he entered the Oval Office.

Movement conservatives expect that close ties between rightly chosen
justices and the Federalist Society will both shape and constrain their voting behavior once they are on the high bench. In discussing Justices Scalia,
Thomas, Roberts, and Alito, Devins and Baum note that their conservative
voting "probably stems from more deeply rooted conservatism," but they add
another factor. "Equally telling, once these Justices joined the Court, the conservative movement . . . continue[d] to serve as an important reference group
for them. Unlike earlier periods (when elite social networks were dominated
by liberals), conservative Justices on the Roberts Court have had links with
like-minded people and groups that would support and reinforce the Justices'
conservative stances on the issues that came before the Court."[74]

Devins and Baum note that other scholars reinforce their conclusions. The
political scientist Amanda Hollis-Brusky also emphasizes the importance of
the Federalist Society serving as a "competing judicial audience, so these justices and judges don't need to seek the applause of the liberal, Establishment
media." In an interview with Hollis-Brusky, Steven Calabresi, a cofounder
of the Federalist Society, goes so far as to suggest that the Federalist Society
"absolutely helps keep" conservative justices "in check." He elaborates by asserting that the justices definitely "notice" criticism "by law schools, journalists, and conservative think tanks like the Federal Society. . . . They may or
may not be persuaded by it but I think they know it's out there and I think it
is something of a check on them."[75]

The polarization of American society has added another component to
the mix. Devins and Baum explain:

> Justices increasingly come to the Court with strong ties to conservative and
> liberal elites; ties that they maintain as Justices. . . . More fundamentally, Jus-
> tices are like other Americans in that the circles of friends and acquaintances
> around them are more likely to have homogeneous ideological orientations
> than was true in prior eras. As a result, Justices are reinforced in the ideologi-
> cal tendencies that they bring to the Court. In this new world, the ideological
> content of Justices' votes and opinions is less susceptible to change than it was

in the preceding period. Democratic appointees are liberals who interact with other liberals; Republicans are conservatives who are oriented toward other conservatives.[76]

The case of Justice Thomas is particularly interesting with regard to the concept of a polarized audience. According to Devins and Baum, in his early years on the Court the young justice worked to construct a "world apart from his critics." So, he agreed to appear "at law schools with relatively conservative orientations and focused his attention on news media with similar orientations."[77] In 2010, he stated that he was now focusing on speaking at law schools in the circuit he oversaw.[78] But the 11th circuit covers the states of Alabama, Georgia, and Florida—three states that were deep red, solidly red, and purple at the time. In addition, in his first twenty-two terms none of the law clerks Thomas hired—almost 100 in total—had not first worked for a Republican-appointed court of appeals judge. When he broke that extraordinary record, he did so by hiring "a clerk who had been president of the Yale Federalist Society."[79] And importantly, Thomas deeply values his clerks. As he noted in an interview, "the best part of the job [is] hanging out with my law clerks. They're energetic, they're fun . . . they're smart, they're hardworking, they're dedicated."[80] Finally, Thomas has suggested that he has sealed himself off from those assessing his work, noting that he was unaffected by contempt or praise. In his telling, his road from poverty to the Court was a "providential" one, the result of an inexplicable string of "miracles." So, "there's nothing that the critics can either give me or take away that's of value to me." To him, "what really matters is whether or not you do what you are called to do." Quoting Mother Theresa, he added: "It's always between God and me." But for a man who claims this to be the case, he refers to his detractors frequently in interviews, and to "the beatings" he took from them.[81]

Justice Thomas has also sought to counter a presumed lack of cultural diversity that several commentators on the Right highlighted as a reason for the Court's less-than-conservative record during the Rehnquist and early Roberts years. For example, writing in 2002, Robert Bork noted: "The Court as a whole lists heavily to the cultural left." To him, "no matter how many justices are appointed by Republican presidents, the works of the Warren Court and the victories of the ACLU are not reversed." Instead, the Court is the most "elite institution in America," in that it is most often "ahead of the general public in approving, and to a degree enforcing, the vulgarization or proletarianization of our culture."[82] Justice Scalia complained similarly, suggesting in a 1996 gay rights case that the majority has reached "the resolution favored by the elite class from which the Members of this institution are selected."[83]

Devins and Baum argue that Bork and Scalia had a point. To them, the liberal leaning of the "elite social community in Washington, D.C. . . . helps to explain the unexpected moderation or liberalism of many of the Justices who were appointed by Republican presidents between 1953 and 1990."[84]

While none of those justices are sitting on the Court today, given the lives most of the current justices have lived—educated at the Ivies, serving for years on the federal bench, and residing mostly in the Northeast corridor—they may still veer toward the elite version of the proper doctrinal path, whether conservative or liberal. Justice Thomas has openly challenged this impression as it applies to him and has worked to counter it at the Court through the clerks he hires.

While he did attend Yale Law (in fact, Bill and Hillary Clinton were his classmates there), he insists he is not part of the "new or faux nobility." Speaking at the University of Florida Law School in 2010, he elaborated on his thinking: "I'm from the sovereign state of Georgia. I grew up in those woods just off 95. And there is absolutely no way I can claim or now act as though I'm from a different background." As we already know, Thomas does not hold Washington in high regard. So, when possible, he seeks refuge from the "cloistered" world of the nation's capital in America's RV parks and Walmart parking lots. Indeed, as noted above, he finds great value in doing so. Should we be surprised that the Court's most senior justice seeks escape from the environs of Washington, DC? After all, Thomas is a man accused of serious sexual indiscretions before a captivated national television audience during his Senate confirmation; a man who headed home from those hearings to "curl up in the fetal position"; a justice known for *not* asking questions from the bench; a famous man who avoids the limelight, who seemingly longs to be just another guy in an RV park. As quoted above, he believes "the best people in the country" are found there, and that his interactions with them help to inform "what I do and the way I look at things."[85] In a documentary about his life he added: "I come from regular stock and I prefer that. I prefer being around that."[86] Ostensibly, his RV journeys connect him with "regular stock" and rebut the idea that the justice only seeks to appeal to a conservative audience.[87]

But RVers have traditionally been older, whiter, wealthier, and far more likely to be married with adult children compared to the average American.[88] While I could find no data on the political affiliation of RVers, their demographic characteristics suggest they would be notably more conservative than the rest of the nation's population. So, the folks Thomas runs into at places like Poncho's Pond are more likely to agree with his positions and celebrate his ideology than those at Washington's Kennedy Center or, for that matter, a local DC-area movie theater.

In addition to these anti-elite attitudes and practices, Thomas has aggressively sought to hire clerks from non-elite law schools to enhance cultural diversity at the Court. He explains why: "We have allowed qualifications to be defined by where you go to school. . . . People say the Ivy Leagues have the better kids. . . . I don't believe they have a monopoly on intelligence. I also don't believe they have a monopoly on the best kids to clerk. This is a big country . . . I have a preference, actually, for non–Ivy League law clerks simply because I think clerks should come from a wide range of backgrounds." Not surprisingly, his clerk choices haven't come without criticism. For example, one year when he chose recent graduates from Creighton, George Mason, George Washington, and Rutgers, some in elite legal circles belittled them as "third-tier trash"—TTT for short.[89] Such snarky scorn speaks to—and perhaps confirms—concerns many conservatives have toward the elite colleges and universities in America.

This worry, according to Yale Law Professor Daniel Markovits, is not without merit. For him, elite universities seek to remold their students. Meritocracy "inclines elites to chauvinistic contempt or even cruelty regarding inequalities that cannot be cast in terms of identity politics." Even politicians, both Democrats and Republicans, "show open contempt for the middle and working classes."[90] Middle-class students will find it difficult to emerge from elite institutions unchanged. The insults will not cease for the few admitted "into their caste." Such behavior is central to "their meritocratic ideals and their business models," which "require elite universities to overwrite their middle-class students' original identities and make them elite." Writing about his own institutions, Markovits adds: "It would be offensive almost beyond belief for Yale Law School to tell its black students, 'Come study with us, and we will make you white.' But Yale—for structural reasons that it cannot avoid—openly proposes to erase its first-generation professional students' middle-class identities."[91]

The selection of Amy Coney Barrett (see chapter 12) may be some indication of a broadening of the conservative supreme elite that Justice Thomas has helped advance. While Barrett ticks off many of the items on the anti-drift checklist (chapter 7), she did not attend an Ivy League school for either her undergraduate degree or her law degree. And while she did graduate from an elite law school (and later taught there), Notre Dame is intentionally more conservative than Harvard or Yale.[92] At the same time, she is further from an administration person than any of her Republican-appointed colleagues, having never spent a single day serving the nation or a state in the legislative or executive realms (either officially or as an advisor). Whether these factors will matter for her judicial behavior remains to be seen, although she has already established a very conservative voting record. If that continues to prove true, she may very well join other Republican-appointed justices in advancing the conservative agenda to an extent never seen before.

Thomas may be particularly unusual with his treks across America and his isolation from wider sectors of the legal world, but all of the conservative justices have close connections to the Federalist Society; its members are said to be their "people." And if Devins and Baum are correct, all will seek to remain in good standing with that group as they sit together on the Court for years to come. The justices of the Supreme Court are no longer administration men and women and are increasingly disconnected from the other branches of government. They come from a tiny segment of society, and those in the majority appear eager to please a slightly larger—but still infinitesimal—group of conservative attorneys unelected and unknown to the voting public. As I have stressed, these justices are much different from those of the past, and now we should consider the consequences of this shift for American democracy.

✳

The replacement of justices who are administration men and women with ideological allies has produced at least one highly significant development: enhanced autonomy for the justices. Coupled with the audience, this may help explain why the Court has increasingly ventured out on its own, issuing decisions constitutionally disrupting congressional action and overturning decades-old decisions like *Roe* and *Bakke*. In other words, if the justices' audiences are no longer the political regime that put them in place, we are more likely to see them pursue a course designed to satisfy the audiences they do care about.

The political scientist Keith Whittington's judicial-review-of-Congress database provides evidence for how this development has played out in recent years with regard to federal legislation. Consider that of the ninety-nine Supreme Court terms between 1896 and 1994, there were only three in which the justices issued more decisions constitutionally invalidating a federal law than upholding one. But now the Court does so routinely. Specifically, in the twenty-five terms between 1995 and 2019, that happened twelve times. In the entirety of the polarization era (2000–2022), when the Court "substantively reviewed the constitutionality of a provision or application of a federal law," it struck it down more often than it upheld it (52.2 percent to 47.8 percent).

In the first 211 Court terms—from 1789 to 1999—that figure was much different—23.3 percent to 75.7 percent. This change displays a clear hostility on the part of the Court toward Congress and the president who signed the legislation (assuming he did).[93]

This is not to say that a Supreme Court closely linked to the larger political regime is without grounds for concern or criticism. As Ran Hirschl has argued, "judicial empowerment through constitutionalization is best understood as the product of strategic interplay" between groups that include "threatened political elites, who seek to preserve or enhance their political hegemony by insulating policy making in general and their policy preferences in particular from the vicissitudes of democratic politics" and "judicial elites . . . [who] seek to enhance their political influence."[94] Presidents of the United States admit as much, often saying that among the most important decisions they make while in office are the justices they choose for the Supreme Court. Long after the presidents have departed the political scene, those justices continue to influence the law of the land. Consider Justice Douglas, the holder of the Court's endurance record. Appointed by President Roosevelt in 1939, he served until 1975, more than thirty years after FDR died. This longevity means that it can be difficult for a new regime to oust the remnants of the previous one, as entrenched justices persist in implementing their views despite the democratic choices of the voters. Of course, that is what FDR confronted during the early part of the New Deal, and it is what instigated his doomed Court-packing plan.

The end of administration men or women ascending to the high bench nevertheless means that the justices of today are far more separate from the elected branches than were their predecessors, even if they are ideologically aligned with a particular political party. Coupling this development with the choice of individuals who seek to appeal to a very limited ideological audience has resulted in a Court that may not "follow the election returns," unless we are referring to the returns of a Republican party primary. Indeed, today's Court is set to deliver decisively the social conservative agenda that will in many (although certainly not all) cases be inconsistent with the positions of a majority of Americans. If it does so, it will often be upsetting long-standing "settled" law, as it did in the 2022 *Dobbs* decision. And if this occurs, it will result in a Court that is truly counter-majoritarian.

*

In the period immediately after its creation, the Supreme Court all but belonged to the aristocracy of American society. "Sons of members of the gentry class," writes the political scientist John R. Schmidhauser, had a "virtual monopolization" on "the top judicial offices" at the federal level.[95] Change came slowly to the Court, but in time the backgrounds of the justices grew more economically diverse, although they still skewed to the affluent. It's fair to ask if a new judicial aristocracy has emerged today, one based not just on socioeconomic background, but on several characteristics necessary to enter the supreme elite. And one not just about the justices themselves, but about their isolation from the elected branches of our democracy.

The typical justice appointed in this century was most likely reared in an upper-middle-class home, attended a private or parochial high school, and then went off to an elite undergraduate institution—most likely an Ivy.[96] After that, in all but one case, they moved on to Harvard Law or Yale Law.[97] (If a conservative, the typical justice's association with the Federalist Society began either in law school or soon thereafter.) Next, the justice did a stint as a clerk, first for a court of appeals judge and then most likely at the Supreme Court.[98] From there, depending on which party controlled the presidency, the typical justice took a position in the administration in Washington, most likely at the Justice Department (and most commonly in the Office of the Solicitor General[99]), or went to work at a Washington law firm.[100] If he or she was shut out of the administration in Washington, the typical justice waited until the electoral winds changed before seeking a post in the executive branch—again, likely in the Justice Department.[101] The final stop before elevation to the high bench was a court of appeals judgeship.[102] For two of the Democratic appointees, they first served as a district court judge before ascending to that seat. For all but one of the justices, the nomination to the federal judiciary came before their fortieth birthday.[103] For the typical justice, service as a federal judge was longer than the time spent in the executive branch, most likely by many years.[104] Finally, the typical justice dismissed any thoughts of running for elective office. The path to power was through appointment, not the ballot box.

There is a long tradition of highlighting the independence of the federal judiciary in American politics. But as McCloskey and Dahl argue, historically such suggestions have at best been exaggerations, if not outright falsehoods. Throughout American history, the Supreme Court has been filled with individuals who have been active participants in the elected branches of government at the time of appointment. Some of them were well known even to the casual observer of politics.

Today, that is no longer true. Before their appointment to the Supreme Court, today's justices were unknown entities to the general public. They largely lived lives at a distance from everyday Americans because the current selection model highlights membership in a cloistered supreme elite, not personal experience closest to the people; the justices are also products of an independent unelected federal judiciary, not administration men and women from the democratically elected executive and legislative branches of government. In dismissing judicial claims of "legislative superiority"—the idea that "justices are better legislators than the members of Congress and state legislatures"—court of appeals Judge Richard Posner made a similar point. Writing in 2008, before the appointment of Sonia Sotomayor, he noted:

> Except for Justice Thomas, the current Justices of the Supreme Court grew up in privileged circumstances and do not rub shoulders with hoi polloi. Sheltered, cosseted members of the upper middle class, and, most of them quite wealthy, the Justices are less representative of the American public than elected officials are. They also lack ready access to much of the information that elected officials obtain routinely in the course of their work. They have much smaller, less specialized staffs, and as lawyers they have professional biases and prejudices that can distort their legislative judgements. Cocooned in their marble palace, attended by sycophantic staff, and treated with extreme deference wherever they go, Supreme Court justices are at risk of acquiring an exaggerated opinion of their ability and character. In a democratic society of great size and complexity, it is difficult to justify giving a committee of lawyer aristocrats the power not just to find or apply the law and make up enough law to fill in the many gaps in the law that is given to them, but also to create out of whole cloth, or out of their guts, large swathes of law that as a practical matter they alone can alter.[105]

The consequences of this new selection model may be dramatic for American democracy. Justices of the past had close ties to the elected political leadership, which provided the decisions they handed down more democratic legitimacy. They were more part of the dominant governing regime than a distinct autonomous force perceived to be ideologically sympathetic to a particular party momentarily in power. And this difference, although seemingly subtle, affected how they ruled. As McCloskey wrote in 1960: "the facts of the Court's history impellingly suggest a flexible and non-dogmatic institution alive to such realities as the drift of public opinion and the distribution of power in the American republic."[106]

Today, we apparently have something different: a Supreme Court more isolated than ever, more removed from the results of democracy, more replete with justices largely unknown to the president who appointed them. It is fair to wonder if it has become a judicial aristocracy unmoored from the electoral foundations that give American democracy its legitimacy.

To be clear, I am not suggesting that the sitting justices are undeserving of their positions. Instead, I am arguing that it is imperative for our nation's democracy that presidents draw from a broader bench of individuals for consideration on the Court. All justices do not need to emerge from the same mold—the upper-middle-class Ivy-educated former Supreme Court law clerk who worked in the Justice Department before nomination to the court of appeals by the age of forty—or a close approximation of it. The nation is not best served by a cookie-cutter Court.[107] Significantly, expanding diversity of experience does not need to undercut a commitment to expanding ethnic, gender, and racial diversity. Indeed, it may actually aid it.

Here and in chapters 7 and 8 I've suggested that the way in which the Court is currently constructed undermines its democratic legitimacy. In part III, I consider another possibility: even if the Court is far more aristocratic and more isolated from the elected branches of government than its twentieth-century predecessors, might we find in our electoral politics a new source of democratic legitimacy for today's Court?

Legitimacy on the Campaign Trail:
Can Electoral Success by Judicially Focused
Candidates Reduce the Court's Democracy Gap?

The Court Issue and the Presidential
Election of 2016

Franklin D. Roosevelt's speech in Baltimore on October 25, 1932, had called for him to denounce the Four Horsemen of the Republican leadership—"Destruction, Delay, Deceit, and Despair"—in straightforward terms. It read: "After March 4, 1929, the Republican party was in complete control of all branches of the government—the Legislature, with the Senate and Congress; and the executive departments." But the words on the page were not enough for an enthusiastic Roosevelt, so he veered from the prepared text: "and I may add, for full measure, to make to complete, the United States Supreme Court as well."[1] Controversy ensued. As they had done in response to Progressive Party candidate Robert La Follette's assaults on the Court in 1924,[2] Republicans were quick to attack Roosevelt's "demagogue" appeal. To his critics, his improvised line was a "slur" on the Court. They added: "to weaken respect" for that institution "is to destroy the foundations of law and order." The Republican incumbent, Herbert Hoover, questioned FDR's "deeper implications": "Does it disclose the Democratic candidate's conception of the functions of the Supreme Court? Does he expect the Supreme Court to be subservient to him and his party? Does that statement express his intention, by his appointments or otherwise, to attempt to reduce that tribunal to an instrument of party policy and political action for sustaining such doctrines as he may bring with him?" While some Democrats were alarmed at the Republican onslaught, Roosevelt was unmoved, telling Senator Jimmy Byrnes of South Carolina—a future Roosevelt Supreme Court selection—he had meant what he said, "and whatever is in a man's heart is apt to come to his tongue." He added, "I shall not make any explanations or apology for it."[3]

The controversy surrounding Roosevelt's speech helps illustrate why for much of American history the Supreme Court was not a topic for campaign discussion. Only on rare occasions did it become a centerpiece of candidate appeals to the voters. Of course, things have changed in recent elections. In the last four national elections—2016, 2018, 2020, and 2022—the Court generally and judicial issues specifically have been featured in presidential and senatorial campaigns. Parts I and II have outlined transformations both in the selection process and in the characteristics and backgrounds of High Court nominees, and I have argued that both major shifts have imperiled the Supreme Court's legitimacy and its alignment with democratic principles.

However, does the fact that the Court and judicial issues are now part of election campaigns sufficiently correct for the lack of majoritarian support for recent high bench confirmations? After all, if successful presidential and senate candidates emphasize a desired doctrinal path and an ideal judicial nominee, then doesn't voter support for these choosers and confirmers of the justices enhance the democratic foundations of the Court itself? Some might suggest that it doesn't: that the current Court is so isolated from the democratically elected branches of government—for reasons I detail in parts I and II—that there is no legitimacy to be gained for it through the electoral process. In short, electorally enhanced legitimacy has been closed off due to the professionalization of the legal community and the independence of the Court. The latter is especially true because the Court's independence has been increasingly celebrated, framed as a normative good that views the judges as impartial adjudicators set apart from the political muck of Washington. In this sense, the Court cannot have it both ways. It cannot celebrate its independence from the political branches—with the justices professing to be mere umpires calling balls and strikes—and simultaneously gain legitimacy from judicial-themed campaigns run by ideologically aligned politicians. Put another way, if the Court is really a judicial aristocracy (chapter 9), it doesn't matter what issues candidates highlight on the campaign trail en route to electoral victory.

It wasn't always this way. The Supreme Court did not always dictate constitutional interpretation. Take, for example, the conflict between President Abraham Lincoln and the Court in the wake of its *Dred Scott* decision of 1857. At this point in American constitutional development, political leaders like Lincoln were unwilling to cede the final word on the interpretation of the Constitution to the justices. As the political scientist Stephen Engel explains: "For Lincoln, the *Dred Scott* ruling was predicated on Democratic electoral success in 1852 and 1856. This claim implied that elections could be taken as evidence of the status of a given constitutional interpretation. If judicial decisions contradicted the principles of the party most recently victorious at the polls, then politicians could legitimately not enforce the decision beyond the claimants until the ruling became more settled."

And that would only happen over time. By grounding constitutional interpretation "in popular sovereignty," Lincoln argued that "law would only be settled if reaffirmed continuously by the majority." For him, "the Constitution's meaning, far from being fixed and singular," was tied to electoral politics. "It followed, first, that multiple equally legitimate constitutional visions could exist, and second, that elections were about constitutional meaning, which ultimately set up each election, not just the Founding ratification itself as a moment of popular sovereignty."[4]

While acknowledging the Court's independence and dominance over constitutional interpretation today has lessened the importance of elections in determining constitutional meaning, I nevertheless argue that the electoral process may confer legitimacy on the Court. I do so based on the evidence that fewer and fewer voters believe the justices when they assert an open-mindedness on the most politically salient issues of the day. According to a 2022 Pew Research survey, "among the overwhelming majority of adults (84%) who say Supreme Court justices should not bring their own political views into the cases they decide, just 16% say they do an excellent or good job" in doing so.[5] After the Court overturned *Roe* in *Dobbs*, a Marquette Law School poll found something similar: 61 percent of respondents thought the Court was motivated "mainly by politics"; 39 percent thought it was motivated "mainly by law."[6] These numbers show that voters understand the importance of elections in the construction of the federal judiciary. They understand that elections have consequences for who sits on those courts. They understand that elections matter for the doctrinal path judges and justices take once on the bench. Indeed, as detailed below, in 2016 one of every five voters said the Court was *the* most important issue determining their vote for president. These voters believed their vote had the potential to shape the Court. In turn, I argue that a successful campaign that highlights judicial issues confers at least some legitimacy on a Court that advances the doctrine—or ideological direction—highlighted by the victorious candidates who later either nominate or confirm a Supreme Court nominee. This is especially true for presidential candidates, but it is present for senatorial candidates as well.

The Court has been more important in recent election years due to three vacancies and two confirmations that occurred during 2016, 2018, and 2020. The political fallout from the *Dobbs* decision continued this trend in the 2022 midterm elections as Democrats sought to exploit voter displeasure over the upending of *Roe*. However, this shift toward more heightened attention to the Court during campaign season is different from the first two shifts I detailed in parts I and II. It is likely to be a passing phenomenon since the Court's membership is likely to be stable for the foreseeable future (chapter 13).

Nevertheless, it raises important questions about the Court's place in American democracy today. It does so by challenging the arguments I have made so far in this book. Indeed, I suggest that it restores at least some democratic legitimacy to the Court. The only question is how much, which I will consider in the pages that follow.

In this chapter, I briefly review the history of Court appointments in presidential campaigns, and then focus on the 2016 presidential race between Democratic nominee Hillary Clinton and Republican Donald Trump as they vied to win the White House and the opportunity to fill the seat of the recently deceased Antonin Scalia. In chapter 11, I consider the 2018 Senate elections, with specific attention to the five red-state Democrats up for reelection in the immediate aftermath of the Brett Kavanaugh confirmation. In chapter 12, the last of this section, I explore the significance of Justice Ruth Bader Ginsburg's death in mid-September 2020, the nomination and confirmation of Amy Coney Barrett soon after that, and Joe Biden's defeat of Donald Trump ten days later. In that chapter and the book's conclusion, I devote some attention to the impact of *Dobbs* on the 2022 midterm elections just over five months later.

✳

When President Donald Trump appointed Neil Gorsuch to the high bench soon after taking office, he alluded to the importance of the Court issue in the 2016 presidential election. "Millions of voters said [the Supreme Court] was the single most important issue to them when they voted for me for president." Exit polls confirmed Trump's conclusion about the electoral significance of his promise to select conservatives for the Court—a promise he fulfilled by choosing Justices Gorsuch, Kavanaugh, and Barrett. "I have always felt that after the defense of our nation, the most important decision a president of the United States can make is the appointment of a Supreme Court justice," Trump elaborated. "Depending on their age, a justice can be active for 50 years and his or her decisions can last a century or more and can often be permanent."

In reality, however, there are few races for the presidency in American history where the Court played any notable role at all. The legal historian Christopher Schmidt writes: "One of the lessons of history is that presidential candidates rarely find enough advantage in discussing the Court to make it a central issue of their election campaigns. The Supreme Court has always been an unwieldy and risky campaign issue."[7] Since Franklin D. Roosevelt's election in 1932, the Court was most prominent during the elections of 1936, 1968, 2004, 2016, and 2020.

In 1936, the Supreme Court had recently constitutionally decimated much of the New Deal legislation signed into law by President Roosevelt during his first term, so his race for reelection was primed to be one in which the justices were at the center of the campaign. As noted above, Roosevelt had not shied away from criticizing the Court during his 1932 campaign, although his attack was only an incidental, improvised remark. Things were sure to be different and more purposeful in 1936. After all, as president, FDR had more forcefully criticized the justices after they issued decisions striking down key components of his first New Deal. Most famously, he said the Court had returned the nation to the "horse-and-buggy" era with its unanimous constitutional destruction of the National Industrial Recovery Act on the last Monday in May 1935—a.k.a. "Black Monday."[8]

Curiously, however, during the 1936 campaign FDR stayed "largely silent on the Court question," the presidential historian William Leuchtenburg writes.[9] Instead, the president's allies took up the case, repeatedly mentioning the work of the Court on the campaign trail. Perhaps more significantly, Republicans consistently defended the justices' New Deal–destroying decisions. Consequently, some construed Roosevelt's historic rout of the GOP's Alf Landon as an endorsement of the president's constitutional vision and a rejection of the Court's attack on the New Deal.[10]

In fact, many scholars have suggested that this interpretation of the election results provided the president with the confidence—even arrogance—to unleash his Court-packing plan a few weeks after his second inauguration.[11] While the bill ultimately suffered defeat in the Senate, that only came after the Court altered course in two fundamental ways. First, in the famous "switch in time that saved nine," it ushered in the constitutional revolution of 1937 by upholding the legislation in the president's second New Deal and, a year later, outlining its future role in protecting the channels of democracy and the rights of "discrete and insular minorities" in footnote 4 of *United States v. Carolene Products* (1938).[12] Second, a string of vacancies in Roosevelt's second term allowed him to "pack" the Court without the need for legislation to increase its size from nine. Specifically, in just twenty-nine months, the Senate confirmed five new justices, providing the president with the Court majority he had long desired.

*

While Roosevelt's surrogates took the lead in questioning the justices during the 1936 election, Republican Richard Nixon and third-party candidate George Wallace issued Court-based attacks themselves in the 1968 race, particularly on the racialized "law-and-order" issue. The final stages of the general election of 1968 were carried out with the knowledge that the next president would have a Supreme Court vacancy to fill due to Chief Justice Earl Warren's pending retirement and the Senate's successful filibuster of Associate Justice Abe Fortas's nomination for the center chair. Indeed, President Lyndon B. Johnson's attempt to elevate Fortas helped spotlight the Court in the race. A month after the Senate ended that bid, Nixon won the three-candidate contest. While the winning margin was narrow, the results were telling. The combination of Nixon's votes with those of Wallace, an even harsher Court critic, totaled nearly 57 percent.

As had happened in FDR's second term, several vacancies opened up in Nixon's first term. In addition to Warren's center seat, the new president would have an opportunity to fill three others. And while he stumbled mightily with his attempts to win confirmation for his nominees, he ultimately succeeded in leaving his imprint on the Court. Specifically, the Senate confirmed four new justices in just over thirty months. In the 1970 midterm elections the president sought to use the Senate's defeat of his two southern selections to advance the Republican cause. Vice President Spiro Agnew led the way, attempting to link Democratic candidates to the liberal decisions of the Warren Court. Laura Kalman writes that Agnew "and 'his unabridged Webster's dictionary' traversed the Midwest and West maligning 'pusillanimous pussyfooting,' 'the vicars of vacillation,' 'the nattering nabobs of negativism,' and 'the hopeless, hysterical hypochondriacs of history.'" In doing so, as I write elsewhere, "Agnew attempted to appeal to Americans alienated by alternative attitudes with alliterative articulations attacking the apparent arrival of the Age of Aquarius."[13]

In his race for reelection in 1972 Nixon would again focus on the Court in his campaign, particularly on the issue of busing to achieve school desegregation. Aided by a Democratic nominee from the left of the party, Nixon won a forty-nine-state landslide, capturing 60.7 percent of the popular vote. Of course, his second term would become mired in the Watergate scandal, which ultimately forced his resignation. Gerald Ford, who assumed the vice presidency after Agnew's resignation due to a scandal of his own, would ultimately replace Nixon in the Oval Office and finish out his term. In 1975, he filled the fifth Supreme Court vacancy of the Nixon-Ford years, finalizing a majority for a new era.

✳

In the post–Election Day analysis, commentators were quick to label the 2004 presidential race the "moral values" election. Several recent court decisions on such politically salient social issues as abortion, affirmative action, school prayer, and same-sex marriage helped to define this very ambiguous phrase.[14] And the focus on those issues appeared to aid the incumbent's re-election effort. Most commentators highlighted "moral values" in the 2004 race for three reasons. First, in responding to an exit poll question about the most important issue of the election, more voters said "moral values" than any of the other six choices. And the substantial majority of those who did—so-called values voters—supported the victor, President George W. Bush. Second, religiously conservative voters—many of them values voters—reportedly turned out in unprecedented numbers, substantially boosting their numbers from four years earlier when Republicans cited their apathy as a reason for Bush's loss of the popular vote.[15] For example, voters who were frequent churchgoers—those who said they attended church more than once a week—increased by 2 percent from four years earlier (from 14 to 16 percent), a notable rise in such a close race.[16] While much of the attention focused on Bush's ability to bring out evangelical Christians to support his candidacy, Bush won the Catholic vote as well, even though his Democratic opponent, John F. Kerry, was Catholic himself. Third, eleven state referenda to ban same-sex marriage passed by wide margins on Election Day. According to those advancing the moral values narrative, these eleven referenda inspired religious conservative voters to go to the polls, feeding their increased turnout. Indeed, Kerry won just two of these eleven states, and both by narrow margins.[17] In Ohio, where a constitutional amendment banning same-sex marriages and civil unions passed by a 24-point margin, Kerry lost by approximately 118,000 votes. And if he had won Ohio, he would have won the electoral college and the presidency.

The Supreme Court of autumn 2004 had been unchanged for over a decade, and most expected that the winner of the election would have the chance to fill a few vacancies. While President Bush did not have the same opportunities Roosevelt and Nixon had to reshape the Court, less than a year after his reelection he did successfully appoint two justices who have helped push the Court to the right. Perhaps more importantly, if a hypothetical President Kerry had successfully replaced those two justices—the moderate conservative Sandra Day O'Connor and the very conservative William Rehnquist—the Court would have had a liberal majority for the first time in thirty-five years. The conservative bloc would have been reduced to just three justices. To emphasize again, elections matter.

★

These three elections highlighted the Court issue, but they are notable exceptions historically. This changed in the last two presidential elections and the midterm elections of 2018 and 2022. Driven by the death of two justices—one

conservative and one liberal—in presidential election years and the retirement of another—the swing justice—in the summer of 2018, the Court has
received more electoral attention than at any time in recent memory. In 2022,
the recent end of *Roe* put the Court on the tongues of candidates once again.

Antonin Scalia was a legend among movement conservatives, and his
death in mid-February 2016, after three decades on the high bench was a clear
transition for the Court. With the remaining eight justices split between four
conservatives and four liberals, it mattered greatly whether his seat would be
filled by the Democratic president, Barack Obama; the front-runner for the
Democratic presidential nomination, Hillary Clinton; or the eventual Republican nominee, Donald Trump. Indeed, the type of justice to replace Scalia
was destined to have deep implications for the Court's work.

Based on the Martin-Quinn ideological scores, and focusing on the swing
justice—the justice who represents the ideological middle of the Court—it
is clear just how much the election mattered to the direction of the Court,
especially given the Senate's refusal to consider President Obama's nominee,
Merrick Garland.[18] A Hillary Clinton victory and a successful confirmation
of a liberal nominee to replace Scalia would have shifted the swing justice
from Anthony Kennedy (with a 2017–2018 ideological score of .407) to Elena
Kagan (with a score of −1.623 that same year). The last time such a significant ideological shift occurred was during the late 1960s and early 1970s when
Richard Nixon replaced four justices—three of them leading liberals—with
two moderate conservatives and two solid conservatives. Additionally, during the 2016 campaign, many noted the possibility that one or both of the
Court's oldest liberals—Ruth Bader Ginsburg (83 years old at the time of the
election) and Stephen Breyer (78)—or the swing justice Kennedy (80) might
retire during the next president's first term. If Ginsburg and Breyer did retire
following a Clinton victory, liberals would have been virtually assured of a
Supreme Court majority for a generation, assuming successful Senate confirmation. According to Martin-Quinn scores, a majority like that last happened in the mid-1960s and lasted for only a brief period. Alternatively, a
Trump victory followed by the selection of a nominee ideologically similar
to Scalia promised to return the Court to its ideological point before Scalia's
death. Of course, if Donald Trump was elected and Justice Kennedy retired,
conservatives would be able to solidify an ideological majority, likely with
someone more committed to their cause than Kennedy. Considering these
possibilities, a Clinton victory—followed by the retirement of both Ginsburg
and Breyer—might have produced a Court with Kagan as the swing justice
and a relatively youthful five-justice liberal majority. Alternatively, a Trump
victory—followed by a Kennedy retirement—would have produced a Court

with John Roberts serving as the swing justice (with a 2017–2018 Martin-Quinn score of .394). This is where things stood going into the campaign season in autumn 2016. Of course, the latter ultimately transpired. And in addition to Kennedy's retirement, the liberal Ginsburg died just weeks before Election Day 2020, allowing Trump to place a sixth conservative justice on the Court, and making Roberts the fourth most liberal justice, despite his deep conservatism.

Few other elections have offered the possibility of such a clear ideological shift for the Court. Even with this possibility of a dramatic change, the Court's future did not appear to garner as much outward attention as expected in the 2016 presidential campaign.[19] However, by examining the specific judicial issues where a change in the Court's makeup might have altered doctrine, the presence of the Court issue becomes clearer. After all, the makeup of the Court is sometimes implicit in a discussion of divisive issues like abortion and same-sex marriage. It may even come through the mere mention of a name like Scalia. Given the power of such shorthand signaling and coding, further elaboration on a candidate's part may not be necessary, and (as Schmidt points out) may be at odds with the campaign's goals.[20]

Five judicial issues—gun rights, campaign finance, abortion, same-sex marriage, and the constitutionality of the Affordable Care Act—attracted the most attention during the 2016 presidential campaign. Each issue was connected to at least one Supreme Court decision, all of which were decided with just five justices in the majority. In three of those cases Justice Scalia was in the minority. In two of them he joined the majority, including the 2008 gun-rights case, *District of Columbia v. Heller*, which he wrote for the Court.

On April 27, 2008, during a *60 Minutes* interview, the CBS reporter Leslie Stahl read to Justice Scalia a note he had written to Justice Harry Blackmun years earlier, at the end of the 1995–1996 term. It read in part: "I am more discouraged than I have been at the end of any of my previous nine terms. . . . The Court must be living in another world. Day by day, case by case it is busy designing a Constitution for a country I don't recognize." In response to Stahl twelve years later, Scalia confirmed that he had felt that way back then. But he quickly added: "It's been less dire in more recent years."[21]

No wonder Scalia was optimistic in 2008. When that interview aired, he was penning what would become one of his more notable majority opinions for a five-to-four Court in *Heller*—a decision that established for the first time in the nation's history the basis for an individual right to bear arms.

In the seven years between that decision and the beginning of the nomination phase of the presidential race in 2015, the Court had changed little with regard to the presumed lineup of justices on the issue of gun rights. President Barack Obama had named two justices, Sonia Sotomayor and Elena Kagan, but each had replaced a justice (David Souter and John Paul Stevens, respectively) who dissented in *Heller*. And while Obama, as a candidate for the presidency, had announced his support for *Heller*, given their liberal leanings most did not expect Sotomayor or Kagan—despite the latter's newfound affection for hunting—to join Scalia's position as articulated in *Heller*.[22] Scalia's death therefore allowed Republican candidates to highlight the gun-rights issue as an area where a Hillary Clinton–appointed justice might overturn doctrine. And Trump consistently emphasized this issue when discussing the Supreme Court, tying the two together most memorably when he said at a campaign rally in North Carolina:

> Hillary wants to abolish—essentially abolish the Second Amendment. By the way, and if she gets to pick. (CROWD BOOING) If she gets to pick her judges, nothing you can do, folks. *Although the Second Amendment people, maybe there is. I don't know*. But—but I'll tell you what. That will be a horrible day. If—if Hillary gets to put her judges—right now, we're tied. You see what's going on. We're tied 'cause Scalia—this was not supposed to happen. Justice Scalia was going to be around for ten more years at least and this is what happens. That was a horrible thing. . . . *If you—we can add I think the National Rifle Association, we can add the Second Amendment to the Justices—they almost go—in a certain way, hand in hand*.[23]

Aside from what some viewed as subtly encouraging his supporters to physically harm his opponent, Trump was attempting to link the pursuit of a conservative Court with the protection of gun rights. In essence, Trump was prepping his audience for the use of a code word like Nixon's "law and order" in 1968 and George W. Bush's "culture of life" in 2000 and 2004. It applied to a specific issue or set of issues but was intended to say far more. (However, as we'll see, unlike his two Republican predecessors, when questioned in the final debate Trump was quite willing to elaborate in explicit terms on just what he desired for the Court's doctrine on the most controversial issues of the day.).

The other case where Scalia joined the majority in the five issue areas identified above was the 2010 campaign finance decision of *Citizens United v. Federal Election Commission*. In addition to joining the majority opinion, written by Kennedy, Scalia authored a concurring opinion. He did so principally to respond to portions of Justice Stevens's dissent that argued the Court's majority opinion was inconsistent with the ideals of originalism. Taking exception to this charge, Scalia concluded in the following terms:

> The Amendment is written in terms of "speech," not speakers. Its text offers no foothold for excluding any category of speaker, from single individuals to

partnerships of individuals, to unincorporated associations of individuals, to incorporated associations of individuals—and the dissent offers no evidence about the original meaning of the text to support any such exclusion. . . . A documentary film critical of a potential Presidential candidate is core political speech, and its nature as such does not change simply because it was funded by a corporation. . . . We should celebrate rather than condemn the addition of this speech to the public debate.[24]

Given that Republicans generally celebrated the *Citizens United* decision while Democrats lamented it, it is not surprising that Secretary Clinton and Senator Bernie Sanders condemned it during the nomination phase of the election.[25] Clinton also consistently and specifically emphasized her desire to overturn *Citizens United* when discussing the Supreme Court during the general election campaign.

Justice Scalia was well known for his biting dissents, including his opinion in the 1992 abortion case of *Planned Parenthood of Southeastern Pennsylvania v. Casey*. This dissent took on a plurality opinion co-written by Republican-appointed justices O'Connor, Kennedy, and Souter. Scalia began his *Casey* dissent by restating his well-known views: "The States may, if they wish, permit abortion on demand, but the Constitution does not *require* them to do so. The permissibility of abortion, and the limitations upon it, are to be resolved like most important questions in our democracy: by citizens trying to persuade one another and then voting." Then he quickly took a scornful tone. After quoting the first line of the Court's plurality opinion—"Liberty finds no refuge in a jurisprudence of doubt"—he added: "One might have feared to encounter this august and sonorous phrase in an opinion defending the real *Roe v. Wade*, rather than the revised version fabricated today by the authors of the joint opinion."[26] With *Casey* and a series of other decisions, the Court slowly restricted the right of a woman to terminate an unwanted pregnancy after the 1973 *Roe v. Wade* decision (chapter 4). But Scalia and his fellow conservatives were never able to cobble together a majority to overturn the essence of *Roe*, despite Republican presidents appointing eight of the twelve new justices from the time of that decision until the 2016 presidential election.[27] Indeed, in 2016, just months after Scalia's death, in *Whole Women's Health v. Hellerstedt*, five of the eight justices affirmed the *Roe* and *Casey* decisions by striking down a Texas law that sought to restrict access to abortion in the name of furthering the state's interest in protecting women's health. Given his past opinions, Scalia would undoubtedly have joined the three conservatives in dissent in that case.

The abortion issue received the most attention during the third and final debate, with Hillary Clinton articulating a stridently liberal position and

Donald Trump providing a full-throated pro-life defense. Assuming she was able to successfully appoint justices to match her rhetoric, a Clinton victory would have put one of the fundamental goals of social conservatives—overturning *Roe*—even further out of reach. Alternatively, with a Trump victory and the appointment of the Scalia-like replacement, that possibility would be more likely, especially if one of the three aging justices in the *Whole Women's Health v. Hellerstedt* majority (i.e., Breyer, Ginsburg, or Kennedy) left the Court during his presidency. As we know, Trump was able to fill two of those three seats after Kennedy's retirement and Ginsburg's death. And in 2022, the Court struck down *Roe* in *Dobbs*.

Same-sex marriage was another area where Justice Scalia held strong views. And in the 2015 *Obergefell v. Hodges* case, where a five-to-four Court held that the right to marry was a fundamental liberty and applied to both opposite-sex and same-sex unions, he authored another cutting dissent. After joining Chief Justice John Roberts's dissent in full, Scalia authored his own opinion—joined only by Clarence Thomas—to, as he put it in his opening sentence, "call attention to this Court's threat to American democracy." Scalia specifically stressed that the majority's decision would likely stifle democratic debate: "Until the courts put a stop to it, public debate over same-sex marriage displayed American democracy at its best. Individuals on both sides of the issue passionately, but respectfully, attempted to persuade their fellow citizens to accept their views. Americans considered the arguments and put the question to a vote." In Scalia's view, the *Obergefell* Court was employing "super-legislative power," and its opinion was "lacking even a thin veneer of law." He continued: "Buried beneath the mummeries and straining-to-be-memorable passages of the opinion is a candid and startling assertion: No matter *what* it was the People ratified, the Fourteenth Amendment protects those rights that the Judiciary, in its 'reasoned judgment,' thinks the Fourteenth Amendment ought to protect."[28] Whether due to *Obergefell* or for other reasons, during the 2016 race same-sex marriage was not as much of a defining issue as it had been in past presidential contests. While Hillary Clinton defended the right and suggested Donald Trump wouldn't, Trump in fact consistently sought to avoid taking a direct position on whether he would push the Court to overturn *Obergefell* (although he certainly made statements that corroborated Clinton's charge).[29] Additionally, at times the issue of how the Court might resolve questions about religiously based refusals of services to same-sex couples was raised, but that was very much a marginal issue in the overall conversation of the campaign.[30]

The final judicial issue that did attract notable attention during the campaign dealt with the constitutionality of the Affordable Care Act (i.e., Obamacare). While seemingly settled after the cases of *National Federation of In-*

dependent Businesses v. Sebelius (2012) and *King v. Burwell* (2015), the issue nevertheless reappeared in the Republican primary campaign. In each of the cases (decided 5–4 and 6–3, respectively) Justice Scalia dissented. In *King v. Burwell*, he wrote separately in what one reporter called a "searing snarky" opinion—one that attracted significant attention for its string of conservative zingers.[31] Scalia accused the Court's majority of performing "somersaults of statutory interpretation" and "interpretive jiggery-pokery," and making an argument that was "pure applesauce." Because the Court had done so much to save Obamacare, he also suggested that "we should start calling the law SCOTUScare."[32] After these cases, most assumed that if conservatives were going to end Obamacare as they had promised, they would need to do so by the legislative route. These two decisions, in other words, had closed off the judicial path. Therefore, the fact that they were raised at all during the campaign was a bit surprising. Nevertheless, criticism of Chief Justice John Roberts's majority opinions in both cases allowed Donald Trump to fend off attacks from his challengers about liberal positions he had once held on politically salient social issues, and to instead put them on the defensive for their support of the Roberts nomination in 2005. As with the issue of same-sex marriage, at times questions of Obamacare's reach into the realm of "religious liberty"—similar to those raised in the Court's 5–4 decision in *Burwell v. Hobby Lobby Stores* (in which Scalia joined the conservative majority)—were given voice during the campaign. But not very often.

These five judicial issues specifically, and the Court issue generally, helped to define the presidential campaign of 2016.

✶

Scalia's death earlier in the day on February 13, 2016, shaped the Republican debate that evening. The highest court in the land now had eight members, four appointed by Democratic presidents and four by Republicans. Before the day was out, Senate majority leader Mitch McConnell of Kentucky vowed that he and his fellow Republicans in the Senate would resist any and all efforts by President Obama to fill the vacant seat, even though the president had nearly a year left in his term.

After a moment of silence in memory of the late justice, the debate moderator, John Dickerson of CBS News, began the questioning with the future of the Court. Most of the GOP candidates assembled in Greenville, South Carolina spoke kindly about Justice Scalia; specifically, about the politics of the appointment process; and in vague generalities about the desire for less divisiveness and the need for a more conservative Court. To applause, Donald Trump, the runaway winner of the recent New Hampshire primary and front-runner according to the polls, endorsed McConnell's strategy of "delay."[33] Texas Senator Ted Cruz, hoping to assume the mantle of the social conservative warrior most committed to appointing movement conservative justices, vowed to make the future of the Court *the* issue of the race. And once given the opportunity, he unleashed rhetoric designed to do just that:

> We are one justice away from a Supreme Court that will strike down every restriction on abortion adopted by the states. We are one justice away from a Supreme Court that will reverse the *Heller* decision, one of Justice Scalia's seminal decisions, that upheld the Second Amendment right to keep and to bear arms. We are one justice away from a Supreme Court that would undermine the religious liberty of millions of Americans—and the stakes of this election, for this year, for the Senate, the Senate needs to stand strong and say, "We're not going to give up the U.S. Supreme Court for a generation by allowing Barack Obama to make one more liberal appointee [*sic*]."[34]

While Republicans largely agreed on the desired direction of the Court's doctrine, that didn't prevent Cruz from going on the attack. Given Trump's front-runner status, he criticized the Manhattan billionaire's previously held liberal positions on social issues such as abortion and his continuing—albeit uncertain—support for funding some aspects of Planned Parenthood.[35]

But Trump seemed prepared for the charge and responded by castigating Cruz for daring to offer kind words about the Republican-appointed Chief Justice of the United States, John G. Roberts. Trump was referring to an op-ed Cruz had penned praising Roberts when he was nominated for the Court in 2005. Writing in the *National Review* soon after President George W. Bush announced Roberts as his choice, the then solicitor general of Texas had called the nominee "brilliant," adding that he "is undoubtedly a principled conservative, as is the president who appointed him."[36] In the February 13 debate, shortly after calling Cruz a "liar" and "a nasty guy," Trump criticized his support of Roberts and included an attack on former Florida governor Jeb Bush—the younger brother of the former president: "Ted Cruz told your brother that he wanted John Roberts to be on the United States Supreme Court. They both pushed him, he twice approved Obamacare." After a few exchanges between Bush and the moderator, Cruz and Trump continued:

CRUZ: I did not nominate John Roberts. I would not have nominated John Roberts.
TRUMP: You pushed him. You pushed him.
CRUZ: I supported . . .
TRUMP: You worked with him and you pushed him. Why do you lie?[37]

This was not the first time Trump had attacked a federal judge. On repeated occasions, he directly challenged—even mocked—judges who disagreed with him, most notably Indiana-born United States district court Judge Gonzalo Curiel, whom he dismissed as biased because, according to Trump, "he's a Mexican."[38] And very early in the race, when Jeb Bush was by far the front-runner for the Republican nomination, Trump criticized Bush for his support of Roberts. He did so by using Twitter, his favorite vehicle for getting his message out. Soon after the second Obamacare decision, *King v. Burwell*, he tweeted: "Once again the Bush appointed Supreme Court Justice [*sic*] John Roberts has let us down. Jeb pushed him hard! Remember!"[39] With Jeb Bush's candidacy—following Trump's predictions—running low on energy, Trump continued the attack on the seemingly less vulnerable Cruz, a Harvard Law graduate who had served as one of Chief Justice William Rehnquist's law clerks in 1996.

Cruz's campaign strategy focused on winning the front-loaded southern primaries. But he was sorely mistaken if he thought his conservative legal credentials and far-right policy positions would lead him to victory in these culturally conservative states rich with evangelical voters. In South Carolina, the first contest in the South, and in the so-called SEC primary, named after the southern-based collegiate athletic conference, Trump outperformed expectations. Specifically, he easily won South Carolina, and then, ten days later, captured five of six southern contests, losing only in Cruz's home state of Texas.[40] With the race moving into more unfriendly territory, Trump's success in so many southern states effectively killed the Cruz campaign.

As he transitioned to the general election campaign, Trump took a decisive step to reassure his conservative doubters of his commitment to advancing their interests. He had promised to release a list of jurists he considered leading contenders for a nomination to the high bench if he had the opportunity to choose Scalia's replacement. And on May 18, 2016, he released that list. Notably, it did not include these three names: Neil Gorsuch, Brett Kavanaugh, and Amy Concy Barrett.

On the Democratic side, the Court was less of an issue. The front-runner Hillary Clinton, denounced the Republican strategy of delaying Senate consideration of Obama nominee Merrick Garland, suggesting that in doing so those senators "dishonor our Constitution." In the first debate after Scalia's death, she added: "we must all support President Obama's right to nominate a successor to Justice Scalia and demand that the Senate hold hearings and a vote on that successor because there are so many issues at stake." She then vowed "to reverse *Citizens United*," promising: "if we can't get it done through the Court, I will lead a constitutional amendment effort to reverse it that way."[41]

Her Democratic opponent, Senator Bernie Sanders, supported her call for the end of *Citizens United*. Their agreement on the issue and their shared hope for a progressive Court meant that they would mainly focus on other concerns to distinguish themselves in the Democratic primaries. Nevertheless, they did differ on gun control. While Sanders was willing to endorse litmus tests for upholding *Roe* and overturning *Citizens United* for his Supreme Court choices, he was not willing to say he would search for jurists ready to overturn the *Heller* decision. Neither was Secretary Clinton. But, as was highlighted in a question in the final debate of the general election, she had said the following in reference to *Heller*: "The Supreme Court is wrong on the Second Amendment." Coupled with her consistent critique during the Democratic primaries of Bernie Sanders's voting record on gun control, voters could certainly have been left with a perception that she thought the Court should reverse its *Heller* ruling.[42]

As the campaign moved from the primary stage to the general election, the Court issue, despite expectations, did not specifically command a great deal of attention. In his acceptance speech at the Republican Party convention, this is all Trump said about the Court: "We are also going to appoint justices to the United States Supreme Court who will uphold our laws and our Constitution." Combining the Court issue and the gun issue once again, he added: "The replacement for Justice Scalia will be a person of similar views and principles. This will be one of the most important issues decided by this election. My opponent wants to essentially abolish the 2nd amendment. I, on the other hand, received the early and strong endorsement of the National Rifle Association and will protect the right of all Americans to keep their families safe."[43]

Hillary Clinton said even less in her speech to the Democratic Party convention: "That's why we need to appoint Supreme Court justices who will get money out of politics and expand voting rights, not restrict them."[44] Furthermore, each articulated similar lines on the campaign trail, with Trump consistently highlighting his list of potential nominees for the Court and promising to protect second amendment rights and Clinton vowing to upend *Citizens United* and protect the right to franchise.

Unlike past Democratic nominees, Clinton chose not to emphasize the possibility that a conservative Court might constitutionally upend *Roe*, except for one brief moment following the release of the *Access Hollywood* video, in which Trump was heard bragging about sexually assaulting women.[45] Instead, both in stump speeches and especially on television ads, Clinton focused on Trump's personal shortcomings: on his multitude of indiscretions and his lack of qualifications to hold the highest office in the land. In a late

September speech in New Hampshire she did briefly address the Court is-sue: "I never thought I'd hear someone running for president, my opponent, who says he wants to appoint Supreme Court justices who would overturn marriage equality and turn the clock back on LGBT Americans, overturn a woman's right to make her own healthcare decisions and reverse that funda-mental right and so much more."[46] It is striking that in discussing the Court, Clinton defended a women's right to choose to terminate a pregnancy in such tame terms, choosing not to use the word "abortion" or even the phrase "pro-choice." Rather, she seemingly referred to a longtime conservative effort to reverse *Roe* as "overturning a woman's right to make her own healthcare de-cisions." In doing so, she was obviously attempting to downplay a divisive issue in a battleground state she likely needed to win to capture the electoral college.

During the debates, however, Secretary Clinton would use much differ-ent, and decidedly more strident, language to defend abortion rights. The Court issue first came up at the end of the second debate. At that point, both candidates slipped into their routine script. Clinton began by agreeing with the audience questioner that the Court was "one of the most important is-sues in this election," before highlighting her call to reverse *Citizens United* and protect the right to franchise. She then added: "I want a Supreme Court that will stick with *Roe v. Wade* and a woman's right to choose, and I want a Supreme Court that will stick with marriage equality. Now, Donald has put forth the names of some people that he would consider. And among the ones that he has suggested are people who would reverse *Roe v. Wade* and reverse marriage equality. I think that would be a terrible mistake and would take us backwards."[47]

For his part, Trump largely dismissed the question. He began with a short statement about Scalia before moving on to his pledge to protect the second amendment. But most of his answer was a response to Clinton's focus on "dark money" in the campaign. He wanted the audience to know just how much of his own money—he claimed "$100 million" he was putting into the campaign.[48] Then he asked why Secretary Clinton wasn't doing the same.

The Court issue received the most noteworthy attention in the third and final debate. Fox News's Chris Wallace started things off with a question about the future of the Court: "The next president will almost certainly have at least one appointment and likely or possibly two or three appointments. Which means that you will, in effect, determine the balance of the Court for what could be the next quarter century. First of all, where do you want to see the Court take the country? And secondly, what's your view on how the Constitution should be interpreted? Do the founders' words mean what they say or is it a living document to be applied flexibly according to changing circumstances?"[49]

Clinton began by giving an expanded version of her answer in the previous debate. Trump responded with a dig at Justice Ruth Bader Ginsburg—she had recently called him a "faker"—before highlighting his recently updated list of possible nominees.[50] The exchange then shifted to the issue of gun control with both candidates emphasizing their differences. Trump reasserted his strong support for *Heller*, and stressed that Clinton was "extremely upset, extremely angry" with that decision. Clinton responded by noting that she was upset because "dozens of toddlers injure themselves, even kill people with guns, because, unfortunately, not everyone who has loaded guns in their homes takes appropriate precautions." She then reassured voters that she "respect[ed] the Second Amendment" and believed "in an individual right to bear arms," but thought that "sensible, commonsense regulations"—like the one the Court struck down in *Heller*—should be allowed in the interests of safety.[51]

Next, Wallace sought to "drill down" on the issue of abortion, inquiring about how far "the right to abortion goes." He then added in a question for Clinton: "You have been quoted as saying that the fetus has no constitutional rights. You also voted against a ban on late term partial birth abortions. Why?" After earlier expressing her strong support for *Roe v. Wade* and criticizing Trump's support for the effort to defund Planned Parenthood—even if it meant shutting down the federal government—Secretary Clinton reiterated her belief that "the United States government should [not] be stepping in and making those most personal of decisions," like those to end a late-term pregnancy. This led Mr. Trump to respond: "Well I think it is terrible. If you go with what Hillary is saying, in the ninth month you can take the baby and rip the baby out of the womb of the mother just prior to the birth of the baby." But Clinton held firm, denouncing Trump for using "scare rhetoric," and restating her position: "This is one of the worst possible choices that any woman and her family has to make. And I do not believe the government should be making it." In contrast to her husband's call for abortion that was "safe, legal, and rare" in the 1990s and Barack Obama's successful avoidance of the issue in 2008 (largely because of the importance of the economy), Hillary Clinton's answer was strikingly liberal, perhaps driven by her confidence in her position in the polls—a confidence that would prove fatal on Election Day.[52]

✶

While the Court issue itself was not as distinctive a feature in the discourse of the campaign during the general election phase as some commentators

TABLE 10.1. 2016 Exit Poll: "In your vote, were Supreme Court appointments . . ."

Answer	Percent of Total	Trump	Clinton	Difference
The most important factor	21	56	41	15
An important factor	48	46	49	−3
A minor factor	14	40	49	−9
Not a factor at all	14	37	55	−18

expected, it was nevertheless quite present in several polarizing social issues. And Donald Trump certainly had reason to believe the issue played a significant role in his victory. Indeed, according to one report, Trump campaign polls indicated that the Court was "a unifying issue for [him] across varying constituencies in the GOP," suggesting it was among his "best weapons against Clinton," one that could even overcome "misgivings about Trump."[53] Those polls showed that voters uncertain about Trump might nevertheless support him precisely because of his commitment to appointing conservative justices. Trump suggested as much at an early August rally in Virginia, telling his audience: "Even if you can't stand Donald Trump, you think Donald Trump is the worst, you're going to vote for me. You know why? Justices of the Supreme Court."[54] He repeated the point a few days later at his North Carolina "second amendment" rally, telling those gathered that they should support him "for no other reason" than his promise to appoint Scalia-like justices to replace those expected to retire in the next presidential term. "This next four years is where you will pick more Supreme Court Justices than anybody has ever had the opportunity to do. Believe me, I'll make you very proud of those Justices every day."[55]

Election Day exit polls echoed the Trump campaign's poll numbers on the Court issue. In answering the question about the importance of Supreme Court appointments in their vote, 21 percent of exit poll respondents said the appointments were *the* most important factor (table 10.1). And 56 percent of those voters supported Donald Trump's candidacy.

As in 2016, it was clear in the 2004 presidential election that the victor would likely have an opportunity to appoint at least one new justice in the next four years.[56] And as in 2016, judicial issues rose to the fore and the Republican nominee captured the White House. Notably, however, George W. Bush identified himself as a born-again Christian and had worked closely with evangelical groups for many years, beginning with his father's 1988 presidential campaign. So, his success with those voters was not all that surprising. Donald Trump's ability to perform so well with evangelical voters in 2016 was more striking, particularly given his difficulty naming books of the Bible and his self-promoted

TABLE 10.2. 2004 "Values Voters" Compared to White Born-Again/Evangelical Christians, 2004 and 2016

State	Value Voters	Percent for Bush	Born-Again/ Evangelical Christians 2004	Percent for Bush	Born-Again/ Evangelical Christians 2016	Percent for Trump
National	22	80	23	78	26	80
Georgia	24	88	35	84	34	92
Iowa	22	87	33	66	34	70
Kentucky	26	93	45	71	53	79
Michigan	19	82	24	71	27	81
Missouri	24	86	35	75	35	73
North Carolina	24	89	36	84	38	81
Ohio	23	85	25	76	33	77
South Carolina	23	88	30	88	44	85

TABLE 10.3. Results in the Deciding States, 2004 and 2016

Deciding State	Bush 2004	Margin–Result	Trump 2016	Margin–Result
Michigan	47.81%	.38% loss	47.25%	.77% win
Pennsylvania	48.42%	3.42% loss	48.17%	.22% win
Wisconsin	49.32%	2.5% loss	47.22%	.71% win

celebrity lifestyle. Most notably, the exit polls show that nationally and in all the states where the evangelical question was asked in both elections, the number of evangelical Christians was about the same or greater in 2016 than in 2004. And apart from the Carolinas, Trump outperformed Bush from twelve years earlier, sometimes substantially (table 10.2). While pollsters did not ask a moral values question in 2016 and there is no state-level data on the importance of the Supreme Court appointments question, these figures clearly show that evangelical Christians were not turned off by Trump's personal indiscretions or his onetime advocacy of liberal positions on social issues like abortion.

Of course, most of these states were not expected to be close. Trump won five of the eight listed in table 10.2 easily, and ultimately won all of them. However, given their importance, it is enlightening to take a closer look at the "deciding states" of Michigan, Pennsylvania, and Wisconsin. Notably, Bush outperformed Donald Trump in all three states in terms of percentage of the vote (table 10.3). However, Bush narrowly lost all three states to John Kerry while Trump won them, all by less than 1 percent. Significantly, if Hillary Clinton had won these three states, she would have won the presidency. While exit poll data on evangelicals is only available from Michigan for both 2004 and 2016 (table 10.2), it shows that more voters in this group went to the polls on Election Day in 2016 than in 2004 (by 3 percent), and substantially more of them supported Trump than had supported Bush twelve years earlier (by 10 percent). In such a close race, that increase could easily have made the difference.

Catholics, particularly white Catholics, were another group of voters where Donald Trump's positioning on the Supreme Court might have affected the outcome. Nationally, Trump significantly improved his performance among white Catholics compared to the three previous Republican nominees: Bush, John McCain, and Mitt Romney. And in Michigan, the only one of the three deciding states where exit pollsters identified voters by religion, Trump won 57 percent of the Catholic vote, and Catholics were 24 percent of all voters. In 2004 and 2008—when Catholics made up 29 and 26 percent of all Michigan voters, respectively—Bush and McCain won just 49 and 46 percent of that group, respectively. In 2012, Mitt Romney turned things around for Republicans in his native state as he won 55 percent of Catholics (25 percent of all voters). The exit polls from 2012 also clarify Romney's strength with white Catholics: he won 58 percent of white Catholics. According to the same exit poll, 23 percent of all voters were white Catholics, meaning that the vast majority of Catholics in Michigan that year were white. (Pew's Religious Landscape Study supports this figure, finding in 2014 that 85 percent of Michigan Catholics were white.)[57] While that more specific data isn't available for 2016, it is highly unlikely that the numbers changed dramatically in the space of four years. And again, Trump improved upon Romney's vote among all Michigan Catholic voters by 2 percent.

Still, it is not clear if the Court issue was as significant a factor as Trump concluded after his victory. As in 2004, some conservative groups highlighted the importance of the Court in the election because it helped advance their agenda. Consider, for example, National Rifle Association head Wayne LaPierre's video statement to NRA members and other gun owners shortly after the election. Looking straight at the camera, LaPierre boldly proclaimed: "the 5 million men and women of the National Rifle Association of America, along with the tens of millions of gun owners all over this country who followed your lead—achieved a truly extraordinary, historic, even heroic, accomplishment . . . you were the special forces that swung this election and sent Donald Trump and Mike Pence to the White House." He then explained the significance of the victory: "Soon, President Trump will nominate a constitutionally sound justice to replace Antonin Scalia on the Supreme Court. Make no mistake: that will be a generational victory for Second Amendment freedom—and you made it happen."[58]

LaPierre may have a point. Donald Trump's razor-thin victories in Michigan, Pennsylvania, and Wisconsin—states with deep traditions of hunting and gun ownership—may have been aided by his stance on gun rights, espe-cially given the possibility that *Heller* would be overturned or limited with a Clinton appointee to the Court. But of course, many factors can claimed as decisive in races that come down to so few votes.

Nevertheless, there is evidence from one of the deciding states (namely, Wisconsin) to suggest that the gun issue was a factor in Trump's success there. The Wisconsin Senate race featured a rematch between Republican incum-bent Ron Johnson and the former senator he beat six years earlier, Russ Fein-gold, and for much of the campaign season Feingold held a comfortable lead. However, as the campaign heated up, Johnson closed the gap—and one of the commercials that helped distinguish him from his Democratic opponent fo-cused on gun rights. Strikingly, in the August-released ad, Johnson did not challenge Feingold's record on gun rights by highlighting the former senator's votes on specific pieces of legislation while in the Senate. Rather, he noted that during his "eighteen-year Senate career he supported judges who voted to deny your individual right." Presumably, Johnson is referring to the *Heller* decision and Feingold's votes to confirm dissenting justices Ginsburg and Breyer, be-cause he adds: "one more liberal justice will flip the Court."[59]

In Pennsylvania, the gun-rights issue played a different role. There, in-cumbent Republican Pat Toomey attracted significant attention for his deci-sion to support gun control legislation requiring background checks follow-ing the late 2012 massacre at Sandy Hook Elementary School in Newtown, Connecticut. He also refused to endorse Donald Trump. The first decision cost him the NRA's endorsement, and both decisions threatened to cost him votes with his Republican base. As one report concluded, from the standpoint of gun-rights advocates the choice came down to picking "the lesser of two evils" in the Senate race: "Toomey, whom they see as a threat to the Sec-ond Amendment, and Democrat Katie McGinty, whom they see as a bigger threat." None other than Mike Bloomberg, the former New York City mayor and a staunch advocate of stricter gun control regulations, endorsed Toomey, which no doubt aided in his appeal to independents and more moderate vot-ers and allowed him to form a "slightly different" coalition than Trump. On Election Day, both won narrow victories in the Keystone State—Toomey by 1.3 percent and Trump by .77 percent. But according to at least one election analysis, "there can be little doubt that the surge in Republican turnout driven by Trump's candidacy made the difference for Toomey."[60]

★

In the third and final debate, Donald Trump began his answer to the Supreme Court question in the following terms: "The Supreme Court: It's What It's All

About." And after the election results were in, Trump consistently pointed to his promise to appoint conservative justices as one of the principal reasons for his victory. Exit polls showed that Trump was indeed correct in his conclusion that millions of voters cast their vote for him based on his determination to select conservative appointees for the federal judiciary, especially the Supreme Court. Of course, millions did the same for Hillary Clinton based on her promise to choose more progressive jurists for the high bench.

But those who viewed Supreme Court appointments as the single most important factor in determining their vote supported Trump in overwhelming numbers (table 10.1). Given the importance of the deciding states in Trump's victory, at the very least his positioning on the most salient judicial issues convinced enough social conservatives who may have been disturbed by his personal shortcomings and may have otherwise chosen not to vote at all.

But does the importance of the Court issue to Trump's victory lend support to the idea that his Court selections have more democratic legitimacy despite being numerical minority justices chosen by a minority president? There is merit to this claim, although it is difficult to assess how much because there are important limitations to it as well. First, as we've seen, the Court issue was just one of many Trump highlighted in his campaign, and he did not reference it as frequently as many commentators expected. He mentioned it at just some of his often rambling campaign rallies, in which he tended to discuss a slew of issues. At the same time, he discussed the second amendment more frequently and tried to wed it to the Court more generally. Moreover, surrogates like vice-presidential nominee Mike Pence devoted more attention to the Court issue, adding power to the legitimacy claim. But importantly, Schmidt writes, neither Trump nor Clinton led "the way . . . [in] using the Supreme Court as a campaign issue. The Court was a significant issue of the campaign, but it was not because the candidates sought to make it so."[61]

Second, Trump made much of his list of possible Supreme Court choices. But none of the three jurists he ultimately selected appeared on his first May 18 list of eleven. His second list of ten additional names—released on September 23, just three days before the first debate—included the following line: "This list is definitive and *I will choose only from it in picking future Justices of the United States Supreme Court*."[62] But, as noted earlier, only Neil Gorsuch made that updated list of twenty-one names. Brett Kavanaugh and Amy Coney Barrett would only appear on a Supreme Court list *after* the election.

Third, Trump's campaign was largely based on appealing to conservative voters and encouraging those who were previously apathetic to turn out and vote on Election Day. On that score, it succeeded overwhelmingly, particularly with less educated white voters. By focusing less on independent "swing voters," Trump was able to craft a conservative message that appealed to the base of the Republican Party. Indeed, even the casual voter likely understood the divergent approaches toward the Court of the two main candidates. At the same time, it is important to recall that Trump did not win the majority of the popular vote, capturing 45.93 percent. And as displayed in table 10.3, he won the three deciding states very narrowly. His tight path to an electoral college victory, therefore, should confer some legitimacy on his justices, but not enough to significantly close the democracy gap.

With the retirement of Anthony Kennedy—the swing justice—in July 2018 and the contentious confirmation of Brett Kavanaugh that fall, the Court would be on the ballot again in the midterm elections, the topic of chapter 11.

The "Kavanaugh Effect" and the 2018 Senate Elections

In a 2018 television ad, two young women appear on the screen to speak about their father, Kevin Cramer, the Republican candidate challenging Democratic Senator Heidi Heitkamp of North Dakota. After introducing themselves, Rachel and Annie stand up from their seats to reveal that Annie is pregnant. The dialogue continues:

RACHEL: We support our dad's strong commitment to life. Heidi Heitkamp disagrees. She even high-fived another senator after voting "yes" to allow late-term abortions.
ANNIE: She looked like she was celebrating.
ANNIE (rubbing her very pregnant stomach): Late-term abortion. Can you imagine?
RACHEL: That's why we're so proud. North Dakota can count on Dad to put life first.[1]

Later in the campaign, another ad about a pregnant woman appeared. In it, a middle-aged woman named Melanie looked directly into the camera and told her story: "I was nineteen, and I was pregnant. I wasn't married, and my family was very poor. I had to make a choice. My sister helped me choose life. She took me in, cared for me, was by my side when my baby was born. And cried with me when I let her go. My sister is Heidi Heitkamp, and I know she loves North Dakota as much as she loved my baby girl."[2]

When Heidi Heitkamp captured her Senate seat in 2012, she did so against very long odds, and as a result of a late surge. She won by less than 3,000 votes, just under 1 percent. Four years later, Donald Trump won North Dakota by nearly 36 percent. So, in an ideologically fractured America, it was always going to be difficult for a Democrat like Heitkamp to win reelection in a ruby-red state like North Dakota. This helps explain why she joined two other red-state Democrats—Joe Donnelly of Indiana and Joe Manchin of West Virginia—in support of Neil Gorsuch's confirmation in 2017.

But when it came time to vote on Brett Kavanaugh's nomination the following year, Manchin stood alone as the sole Democrat voting to confirm him for the High Court. Donnelly and Heitkamp voted "nay." In a video released via Twitter after she made her decision, Heitkamp explained why she planned to oppose Kavanaugh. To her, his performance before the Senate Judiciary Committee, following Christine Blasey Ford's testimony, raised questions about his "temperament, honesty, and impartiality." In a follow-up campaign ad, she was more direct: "First off, honestly, I don't think he told the truth. And even if he did, he showed himself to be too biased to be impartial." She then touted her support for Gorsuch, suggesting she would be willing to support other conservative nominees for the Court if reelected.[3]

Did Heitkamp's vote against Kavanaugh's confirmation lead to her defeat in the final Election Day tallies? After witnessing President Trump's second choice for the Court win confirmation by one of the narrowest margins in American history in early October, Republicans certainly warned of a coming conservative backlash—a "Kavanaugh effect"—once voters went to the polls. They reasoned that in reaction to the Democrats' treatment of Kavanaugh during the Senate Judiciary Committee hearings, conservative voters would punish the party's candidates a month later. In the 2018 Senate races in Indiana, Missouri, Montana, North Dakota, and West Virginia, a Democrat incumbent was up for reelection in a state Donald Trump won easily in 2016, by between 19 and 42 percent.[4] In two, Missouri and Montana, the incumbent senators—Claire McCaskill and Jon Tester—had opposed both Gorsuch and Kavanaugh. Two others, Indiana's Donnelly and North Dakota's Heitkamp, supported Gorsuch but not Kavanaugh. Only West Virginia's Manchin backed both. Of these five, only Tester and Manchin won reelection, which might suggest that there was a Kavanaugh effect—that the decision of three of these Democratic senators to oppose Kavanaugh hurt their reelection chances. Republican Senate majority leader Mitch McConnell certainly believed that the Kavanaugh hearings provided an "adrenaline shot" to the GOP's "core voters." As he explained, "we were worried about lack of intensity on our side, and I think the Kavanaugh fight certainly provided that. . . . It was extremely helpful."[5] And if that is right, it adds support to the argument that there is democratic legitimacy to be gained for the Court's current conservative majority on Election Day. If a candidate's positioning on Court vacancies and judicial issues aided his or her electoral victory, then I suggest there is a closer democratic connection between the results of the electoral process and an allied Court's potential doctrinal developments. However, as we'll see in the rest of this chapter, by exploring the Kavanaugh effect further I challenge the easy conclusion that votes on his nomination led to these defeats. This leads me to question the idea that the outcomes in these senatorial contests provide much democratic legitimacy to a Supreme Court otherwise subverted by the two shifts I've already described in parts I and II.

Talk of Kavanaugh's confirmation fight was a central feature of these campaigns. Moreover, President Donald Trump played up the importance of the Kavanaugh hearings on the campaign trail. For example, in one of his visits to Montana, he told the crowd: "it's an election of Kavanaugh, the caravan, law and order and common sense."[6] Trump traveled to Montana several times because he had a great desire to oust Jon Tester from the Senate. This was based on the Montana senator's role in successfully undermining the president's nomination of his former physician, Ronny Jackson, to be secretary of Veterans Affairs. Even before Tester announced he would oppose Kavanaugh, his Republican opponent had emphasized the Court as an issue. In a campaign ad attacking Tester's vote against Gorsuch, the Republican candidate, Matt Rosendale, challenged the senator's commitment to protecting the second amendment based entirely on his support for "Obama judges" like Sonia Sotomayor. In particular, Rosendale used a sentence from an opinion Sotomayor had joined, which read: "the right to possess a gun is clearly not a fundamental right."[7] That sentence, however, was from an unpublished opinion when Sotomayor was a judge on the second circuit court of appeals. It was also written in 2004, well before the 2008 Supreme Court *Heller* decision reached a different conclusion. In the Senate hearings considering her nomination to the high bench in 2009, she defended the line as a statement of long-established precedent at that time.[8] In addition to Rosendale's commercial, the NRA ran $400,000 worth of ads of its own, branding Tester as a member of the "anti-gun Left" based on his votes for Sotomayor and Elena Kagan, and against Trump nominee Neil Gorsuch.[9]

In Missouri, Republican challenger Josh Hawley also pursued an aggressive line of attack against incumbent Claire McCaskill for opposing "pro-Constitution judges." He argued that her and other liberal Democrats' votes against Gorsuch and Kavanaugh were designed to deny "the people's choice" by "overturning the results of the 2016 election." And early in their third and final debate, he sought to use the Senate Democrats' treatment of Kavanaugh to his advantage. In response to a question about the negativity of the campaign and McCaskill's charge that her challenger ignored Donald Trump's role in the coarsening of American politics in order to blame only Democrats, Hawley responded: "You look at what happened with the Brett Kavanaugh hearing. And yes, I'm afraid, senator, it was on one side. It was the Senate Democrats who launched a personal smear campaign against Brett Kavanaugh. It was the Senate Democrats who laid in wait to try and ruin him and his family, and by the way, destroy Dr. Ford in the process. It was the Senate Democrats who perpetrated that. And it was Hillary Clinton and Eric Holder who have encouraged, frankly, confrontation, if not violence."[10] In another ad, Hawley spread the blame to some in his party as well, criticizing Republicans for failing to "stand up" to Senate Democrats before vowing: "I will fight for the Supreme Court. It is the last line of defense for our values. It's worth the battle."[11]

Patrick Morrisey, the Republican candidate in West Virginia, pursued a similar line of attack based on judicially focused social issues against his Democratic opponent, incumbent Joe Manchin. He did so despite the fact that Manchin was the only Democrat to support both Gorsuch and Kavanaugh. For example, Morrisey condemned Manchin's record on gun rights based on his D rating from the NRA, and despite the senator's controversial target-shooting campaign ads in 2012 and 2018. (In 2012, the NRA endorsed Manchin in his Senate race, and he highlighted that support in an ad in which he loaded a gun and fired through a target. Notably, that target was environmental legislation known as the "Cap and Trade" bill, which was backed by fellow Democrat President Barack Obama.) Morrisey also criticized Manchin's support for funding for Planned Parenthood, the organization that—among many other things—manages clinics that provide abortion services. Nevertheless, the Republican challenger was unable to tag Manchin as a liberal, despite his countless attempts. As Morrisey admitted, Manchin's votes for Trump's two choices for the Court undermined his chances for victory.[12]

Like Heitkamp, Indiana's Joe Donnelly had supported Gorsuch before deciding to vote against Kavanaugh, noting similar concerns about the judge's "impartiality" and "judicial temperament."[13] His opponent was less aggressive than other GOP challengers in these five red states on the Court issue, however. While Republican Mike Braun mentioned Donnelly's Kavanaugh vote in both debates and ads, his campaign focused more on job creation and his ability as a businessman to bring a different perspective to Washington. As it did in other states, the NRA ran ads that focused on the Supreme Court, charging, "Joe Donnelly voted against your gun rights by voting against Brett Kavanaugh."[14] But on another hot-button social issue, Donnelly was a tougher target. Specifically, on abortion, he was pro-life. In turn, the abortion

TABLE 11.1. Importance of the Kavanaugh Vote, 2018 Percentages for Five States

State	Important	Voted for Democrat	Voted for Republican	Not Important	Voted for Democrat	Voted for Republican
Indiana	51	36	59	42	51	44
Missouri	49	43	55	46	52	47
Montana	47	29	68	51	62	34
North Dakota	42	36	64	54	56	44
West Virginia	40	51	43	56	52	46

issue garnered less attention in Indiana than in the other four races, making it a useful comparison to evaluate the Kavanaugh effect.

✶

Republicans captured three of these five Senate seats. Exit polls offer some evidence that opposition to Kavanaugh mattered in two of the three Democratic defeats, but it is unclear that a vote to confirm would have altered the Election Day results. To begin with, a majority of voters in only two of the five states under review here—Indiana and Missouri—said that the Kavanaugh vote was either "very important" or "somewhat important" to them. Notably, in both states, those voters supported the Republican by significant percentages, 59 percent in Indiana and 55 percent in Missouri (table 11.1). In the end, both Democrats lost by just under 6 percent of the vote.

However, it is essential to remember how McCaskill and Donnelly won in 2012. Specifically, both benefited greatly from highly controversial statements by their very conservative Republican opponents. In Missouri, Republican Congressman Todd Akin was so committed to the pro-life cause that in response to a question about allowing abortions in the case of rape, he answered: "*It seems to be, first of all, from what I understand from doctors, it's really rare. If it's a legitimate rape, the female body has ways to try to shut the whole thing down.*"[15] Many, including Republican presidential nominee Mitt Romney, denounced Akin's words. But despite calls for him to quit the race, he continued with his campaign. And while he had led in several early polls, support for him eroded after those comments. In the end, McCaskill won by more than 15 percentage points in a state Barack Obama lost by more than 9 percent. In Indiana, Joe Donnelly benefited from a similar statement made by his Republican opponent, Richard Mourdock. In the GOP primary, Mourdock, running as a Tea Party Republican, had trounced six-term senator Richard Lugar by more than 20 percentage points. And he had led in most general election polls in the matchup against Donnelly. But near the end of the campaign, he stumbled during a televised debate. Similar to Akin in Missouri, in response to a question about his opposition to abortion in the case of rape, Mourdock said: "I struggled with it myself for a long time, but I came to realize that life is that gift from God. And, I think, even when life begins in that horrible situation of rape, that is something that God intended to happen." Mourdock tried to limit the damage, suggesting that his words had been "twisted."[16] But the momentum was on Donnelly's side as Mourdock's poll numbers tumbled in the days following the debate. On Election Day, Donnelly captured the seat by nearly 6 percentage points. In the presidential race, after narrowly winning Indiana four years earlier, Obama lost the Hoosier State by more than 10 points.

In 2018, McCaskill's and Donnelly's Republican challengers, while quite conservative, were far more traditional candidates. And given the electoral fundamentals of both states (see tables 11.2, 11.3, and 11.4), Republicans were thought to have a very good chance to win both seats at the start of campaign season. Given the size of these Republican victories and the exit poll data, it's hard to make a case that a vote to confirm Kavanaugh would have altered the Election Day results. After all, McCaskill's vote against Gorsuch likely locked her into opposing Kavanaugh as well. In fact, a vote in support of the latter might have disenchanted liberal supporters in the state's urban centers. Of the 49 percent of respondents who thought the Kavanaugh vote was either "very important" or "important," 43 percent voted for McCaskill (table 11.1). That's more than the other three Democrats who opposed the nomination. Given his support of Gorsuch, Donnelly's opposition to Kavanaugh may have mattered more (table 11.1). But if it did, it's strange that Republican Mike Braun didn't emphasize it to a greater degree in the campaign.

Of course, exit polls are based on individuals who actually went to the polls. Therefore, it may be true, as Mitch McConnell suggests in the quote above, that the Kavanaugh hearings convinced conservatives who otherwise would not have voted to do so and to cast a ballot for the Republican candidate. If such a surge occurred, it would not be apparent in the exit poll data. Nevertheless, if we compare the makeup of the electorate of the 2016 and 2018 Senate races in these two states, the differences are not significant enough to alter the results. The 2018 Missouri electorate was actually more liberal and less conservative than it had been in 2016 (see table 11.4) when Republican Senator Roy Blunt defeated his Democratic challenger by less than 3 percentage points (and Donald Trump won the state by 18.5 percent).[17] In Indiana, the 2018 electorate was only slightly more conservative than it had been in 2016 when Republican Todd Young easily defeated former Democratic governor and senator Evan Bayh by nearly 10 percent (and Trump—with Indiana's

TABLE 11.2. Voter Ideology, Percentages for Indiana and Missouri (2016 vs. 2018)

State	Liberal	Voted for Democrat	Voted for Republican	Moderate	Voted for Democrat	Voted for Republican	Conservative	Voted for Democrat	Voted for Republican
Indiana—2018	20	86	8	40	59	37	40	10	88
Indiana—2016	22	80	14	40	48	45	38	15	81
Missouri—2018	23	90	9	38	60	37	39	8	91
Missouri—2016	20	86	10	38	60	36	42	14	83

TABLE 11.3. Views of Donald Trump as President, 2018 Percentages for Five States

State	Approve	Voted for Democrat	Voted for Republican	Disapprove	Voted for Democrat	Voted for Republican
Indiana	55	10	88	44	89	6
Missouri	53	8	90	46	92	7
Montana	51	9	88	48	95	3
North Dakota	61	12	88	38	94	6
West Virginia	63	28	69	35	92	4

TABLE 11.4. White Evangelical or Born-Again Christian Vote, 2018 Percentages for Five States

State	White Evangelical	Voted for Democrat	Voted for Republican	All Other Voters	Voted for Democrat	Voted for Republican
Indiana	41	23	72	59	59	38
Missouri	38	23	75	62	64	34
Montana	34	21	75	66	58	38
North Dakota	37	27	73	63	58	42
West Virginia	54	45	53	46	60	35

Mike Pence as the VP nominee—won by 19 percent). Indeed, even if the ideological makeup had been the same in 2018 as it had been in 2016, Joe Donnelly still wouldn't have won the race. That's in part due to the fact that in both states conservatives supported the Republican candidate by a greater margin—approximately 8 percent—than they had in 2016. The Kavanaugh confirmation battle might have helped boost that figure, but all else being equal Donnelly's path would still have been a difficult one. He would have won reelection only if significantly fewer conservatives went to the polls and/or a greater share of those voters supported him than had backed Bayh two years earlier.

In the other three states under review here—Montana, North Dakota, and West Virginia—a majority of voters said their Democratic senator's Kavanaugh vote was either a "minor factor" or not one at all (table 11.1). In North Dakota Heidi Heitkamp was a well-liked senator—even her opponent made this point in one of his ads[18]—but she never led in a single poll against Kevin Cramer after he captured the Republican nomination in a June primary. To many, she was the most vulnerable Democratic senator up for reelection in 2018. Indeed, in the last poll taken *before* she publicly stated her intention to vote against Kavanaugh, she trailed by twelve points. While she did raise large sums of money after that announcement, the race was likely already over. She lost by nearly 11 percentage points in a state Trump had won by more than 35. Given that Heitkamp trailed Cramer by this amount or more *before* she pledged to oppose to Kavanaugh, it's hard to make a case that that vote against confirmation mattered much on Election Day. In fact, it's possible these dire numbers freed her to oppose Kavanaugh, knowing it wouldn't matter anyway.

Montana's Tester and West Virginia's Manchin were the only two of these five Democrats to win reelection. In Montana, Tester underperformed with voters who thought the Kavanaugh vote was important in comparison to the other four Democrats (table 11.1). But he also outperformed those four with voters who didn't think it mattered much. Given this, there doesn't appear to have been much of a Kavanaugh effect in Montana.

En route to victory, Tester benefited from something else: his ability to denounce his opponent as a carpetbagger. Tester frequently compared his family's deep Montana roots to his Republican challenger's more recent arrival in "Big Sky Country." For example, in his closing statements in two debates, the senator stressed that he was a three-generation Montanan who farmed "the land [his] grandparents homesteaded" while his opponent was "a developer from Maryland, who made his millions there, came to Montana, bought a ranch, claims to be a rancher, but has no cows." Tester even nicknamed Rosendale "Maryland Matt."[19] Tester has always won his races by narrow margins. In 2006, it was by less than 1 percent. In 2012, the difference was 3.7 percent. In 2018, his margin of victory was essentially the same at 3.6 percent, despite Trump's popularity in the state (table 11.2) and his frequent visits there. And Tester did something in 2018 he had never done before—he captured more than 50 percent of the vote.

In West Virginia, a state Trump won by nearly 42 percent in 2016, Democratic incumbent Joe Manchin knew the electoral fundamentals (tables 11.2 and 11.3). And to help undercut potential Republican attacks, he supported both Gorsuch and Kavanaugh. Regarding his chances for reelection, the decision was a wise one. Given the Republican-friendly environment in West Virginia, a vote against either would likely have doomed his candidacy. Like Tester, Manchin also had an opponent originally from out of state. Although he was serving at the time as West Virginia's elected attorney general, Patrick Morrisey was originally from New Jersey. He had even run for Congress there. And during the campaign, as a means of distinguishing himself from the "Jersey boy," Senator Manchin emphasized his deep West Virginia roots and his longtime commitment to the state's voters: he had served as a state legislator, secretary of state, and governor before winning his senate seat in 2012. For his part, Morrisey tried to turn his out-of-state past to his favor, charging that Manchin was the candidate with "Jersey values." In an attempt to discount Manchin's votes to confirm President Trump's Supreme Court selections, he attacked Manchin for his support of Hillary Clinton. "If Hillary Clinton were president," Morrisey said, "we couldn't have Judge Gorsuch. We couldn't have Judge Kavanaugh. We would have abortion on demand because we'd have the most radical, pro-abortion president in history. The second amendment would be under vicious assault. . . . Those aren't West Virginia conservative values." He closed by saying that the pro-life, formerly NRA-endorsed Manchin "votes like a senator from New Jersey."[20] But it didn't work. In the end, despite Trump's popularity with West Virginians (table 11.2) and favorable Republican fundamentals such as the number of evangelical Christian voters (table 11.3), Manchin won reelection by just over 3 percent.

In sum, while the Kavanaugh confirmation was an element of the campaign conversation in these states, the evidence of a Kavanaugh effect is minimal. If the three defeated Democrats who voted against the nominee had instead backed him, it is unlikely that that support would have altered the results of the race. In fact, by moving to the right they might very well have turned off traditional Democratic voters in each of these states. In other words, with the likely exception of Manchin's win in West Virginia, the Kavanaugh vote—or the Kavanaugh effect—does not appear to have been decisive.

In the five other states where Democrats were seeking reelection that Trump won in 2016—Florida, Ohio, Michigan, Pennsylvania, and Wisconsin—there is also little evidence of a Kavanaugh effect. In four of these states, the Democratic senator sailed to a comfortable victory, and the exit pollsters didn't even ask a Kavanaugh-related question. In the increasingly red state of Ohio, Democratic incumbent Sherrod Brown took a populist approach to his opposition to Kavanaugh, noting: "After thoroughly reviewing his record. Meeting with him face-to-face, and listening to Ohioans, I am convinced Judge Kavanaugh would side with special interests over working people and threaten the rights of Ohioans." He added: "Working people need justices who will put their rights first, not justices who will side with insurance companies over cancer survivors, financial scammers over customers, or massive corporations over American workers."[21] In the one contest that was close, exit polls suggest that Republican Rick Scott won the Florida race by narrowly outperforming his opponent with voters who didn't think Senator Ben Nelson's opposition to the Kavanaugh confirmation was important and with those who did view it as important.

In Nevada, which Clinton narrowly won in 2016, Democrat Jacky Rosen ousted the Republican incumbent, Dean Heller. Notably, 57 percent of respondents said that Heller's vote to confirm Kavanaugh was "important," more than in any other state where the question was asked. However, those voters split evenly on the candidates, with 50 percent backing Heller and 46 percent in favor of Rosen. A majority of the 38 percent who said the vote was "not important" cast their ballot for Rosen, 51 to 46 percent. In other words, Heller's support for Kavanaugh does not appear to have been all that significant in a race that Rosen won by just over 5 percent.

One of the open seats, in Tennessee, is notable in showing the possibility that the Kavanaugh confirmation drove conservative voters to the polls. Republican Marsha Blackburn and Democrat Phil Bredesen sparred over Christine Blasey Ford's sexual assault allegations against Judge Kavanaugh. In a debate after the allegations became public but before the Senate Judiciary Committee held hearings on them, Blackburn said she would vote to confirm Kavanaugh no matter what Blasey Ford said in her testimony. Bredesen held back on taking a position on Kavanaugh's confirmation until he heard more from the alleged victim. After Blasey Ford's testimony and Kavanaugh's vehement denial before the Senate panel, Bredesen deliberated for a week before deciding to abandon his fellow Democrats and support President Trump's second choice for the Court. But according to the political scientist Joshua Stockley, that decision essentially came too late. "In the meantime, the partisan mood of the nation, including Tennessee, shifted against Democrats for their handling of the confirmation process. Blackburn used the issue to nationalize the race and to motivate her Republican base."[22] Exit polls showed

TABLE 11.5. Views on *Roe v. Wade*, 2018 Percentages for Five States

State	Overturn	Voted for Democrat	Voted for Republican	Keep as Is	Voted for Democrat	Voted for Republican
Indiana	32	13	85	61	59	36
Missouri	33	15	83	59	66	33
Montana	28	9	90	62	66	30
North Dakota	27	19	81	60	64	36
West Virginia	40	36	63	54	67	28

the difficulty of Bredesen's position: 55 percent of Tennessee respondents said they supported Kavanaugh's confirmation, while only 39 percent opposed it. And by winning 87 percent of those Tennesseans who supported Kavanaugh, Blackburn sailed to a comfortable victory.[23]

*

The exit polls reveal another, perhaps more surprising and significant piece of information about public opinion in the five states at the center of this discussion. As displayed in table 11.5, when asked about the Court's decision in *Roe v. Wade*, approximately 60 percent of respondents in four of these five states answered "keep as is."[24] About 30 percent of voters thought it should be overturned. In West Virginia, the figures were slightly less supportive of the decision, at 54 and 40 percent respectively. This clearly suggests that in these five very red states in 2018, there was not widespread support for a decision overturning *Roe*, which the Supreme Court ultimately did in *Dobbs* in 2022.

Some might interpret these data as a basis for concluding that these and other red states would not move to ban abortion after *Dobbs*. But that would be a misleading interpretation—one that overlooks the extent to which the most fervent pro-life voters are embedded in the Republican Party. In four of these five states, between 81 and 90 percent of voters who wished the Court to upend *Roe* voted for the Republican candidate. This was true even in Indiana, where both candidates espoused pro-life views.[25] Similarly, in West Virginia, 63 percent of anti-*Roe* voters backed the Republican, even though Senator Manchin is pro-life and supported both Gorsuch and Kavanaugh. In none of the five states did the GOP candidate come close to winning the clear majority of those voters who wanted to keep *Roe* "as is." This means that pro-life voters have essentially "captured" the Republican Party in these states, and no candidate who veers from that philosophy would stand much of a chance of winning a GOP primary (more on the "capture" concept in chapter 12).

Moreover, since Republicans control the governor's office and the state legislature by a substantial margin in all of these states, these figures suggest that they would act to outlaw abortions following a Court decision consti-tutionally discarding *Roe*. Indeed, three of these states acted before *Dobbs*. North Dakota was one of the early states to enact a "trigger law" that would automatically ban abortion after a decision constitutionally discarding *Roe*. Missouri passed a trigger law in 2019. West Virginia had a pre-*Roe* abortion ban on its books. And as expected, following *Dobbs*, Indiana moved to ban nearly all abortions.[26] Montana's state constitution protects abortion rights, but the state's Republican governor and Republican-controlled legislature nevertheless moved to limit the procedure in the state immediately after *Dobbs*. As of this writing, the state's courts are still considering this and ad-ditional legislation signed by the governor in early May 2023.[27]

✶

Of course, assessing the Kavanaugh effect is based on how Senate Democrats treated him during the confirmation hearings. Despite some anxious days for him and hopeful ones for the opposition, he was still confirmed. He is now a Supreme Court justice. We do not know—indeed cannot know—how the voters would have responded if the Senate had rejected Kavanaugh, tossed him to the side with the likes of Haynsworth, Carswell, and Bork. One might assume a failed confirmation vote would have had a greater impact on these races. But since three of the five Democrats lost anyway, any difference would have been at the margins. It is also important to mention that three of these five races took place in small states: Montana ranked 44th in population, North Dakota 47th, and West Virginia 39th. This fact highlights the unequal weight smaller red states have in our current politics, particularly when it comes to filling the Supreme Court with numerical minority justices and al-tering the Constitution (see chapters 2 and 13, respectively).

On the other hand, as with the 2016 presidential election, the presence of the Court issue in the campaigns of these triumphant Republican senators should not be disregarded from the standpoint of enhancing the democratic legitimacy of the High Court nominees they voted to confirm. Emphasizing judicial issues specifically and the Court generally en route to victory dis-plays in clear terms that a majority of voters in these specific states gener-ally supported a conservative doctrinal path, or at least did not consider it sufficiently problematic to vote for the Democratic candidate. But again, in conflict with the principles of majoritarianism, these states possess dispro-portionate power to elect senators who eventually help shape the Court. So, the extent to which these electoral results confer democratic legitimacy on the Court is undoubtedly minimal.

The Never-Ending Promise of a Conservative Court and the 2020 Presidential Election

In the emerging darkness of an early Minnesota night, President Donald J. Trump walked toward Air Force One for a flight back to Washington, DC. Having just finished one of his MAGA ("Make America Great Again") rallies amid the coronavirus pandemic, he stopped in front of a pack of reporters to say a few words and maybe take a few questions. Apparently, that moment was when the president first learned of the news rapidly spreading across the land. Justice Ruth Bader Ginsburg, the eighty-seven-year-old liberal icon popularly known simply as RBG, was dead. Trump appeared surprised by the news. With Elton John's "Tiny Dancer" playing in the background, he said she was "an amazing woman, whether you agreed or not . . . who led an amazing life." He added: "I am actually sad to hear that. I am sad to hear that."[1]

We found out a couple of days later that Trump only learned of Ginsburg's death after the rally because campaign aides feared that he would relay the news to the crowd if he was told earlier, and that the mostly maskless mass of red-hat-wearing devotees would cheer in celebration—like the Munchkins in the *Wizard of Oz*, who upon hearing of the demise of their evil enemy sang "Ding-dong, the witch is dead!"[2] That was the state of America's divide.

It was just weeks before Election Day, and some voters had already cast their ballots. How much would this news from the Court change the race for the White House? This chapter examines the impact of Ginsburg's death, the nomination and confirmation of Amy Coney Barrett, and the Court issue generally in the 2020 election campaign. I focus on the presidential campaign, but I also consider how these developments affected competitive Senate races. I examine how the Court's ideological makeup emerged as an issue in the campaign, and analyze exit polls and election results to assess its role in the final outcome and to make comparisons to the 2016 presidential contest.

Finally, I consider whether the importance of the Court issue in the 2020 race and other recent elections provides another kind of democratic legitimacy for an increasingly conservative Supreme Court, even though the Republican presidential candidate had only won the popular vote once from 1992 to 2020. As suggested earlier, if the Court issue was a dominant one in the presidential and/or Senate races, and if voters cast ballots based on that issue, then the Court might claim to represent a democratic choice. While there is validity to this claim of enhanced democratic legitimacy, the elections of 2016 and 2018 weren't referenda on the Court issue per se. And of course, voters did not vote directly on controversial judicial issues like abortion. In fact, at least on that one issue, the evidence suggests that if voters, even those in many red states, are untethered from primary politics, they will support consensus views inconsistent with the Court's rejection of abortion rights in *Dobbs*.

★

Perhaps the best way to analyze the Court issue in the 2020 presidential campaign is to divide the election cycle into two periods: before Ginsburg's death and after. Before she died, Republicans had been making the seemingly never-ending campaign promise of a conservative Court, and the central Court concern was the questionable ideological and institutional commitments of Chief Justice John Roberts. The COVID-19 pandemic changed many things in the United States in 2020, but it did not change a nearly annual occurrence in early summer when the Court typically releases its most controversial decisions: namely, an outpouring of conservatives' angst about the Supreme Court's ideological commitment to their cause. In 2020 specifically, conservatives complained about the voting behavior of the Republican-appointed chief justice on three cases: a 5–4 decision overturning state abortion regulations, a 6–3 ruling declaring that federal civil rights law protects LGBTQ employees from discrimination in the workplace, and another 5–4 decision rejecting President Trump's repeal of a Barack Obama order on Deferred Action for Childhood Arrivals (DACA).[3] In each case, Chief Justice Roberts had joined the Court's four liberals in the majority. In the LGBTQ-rights case, the Trump-appointed Neil Gorsuch joined the majority as well.

As these cases suggest, by the end of the 2019–20 term Roberts had secured his place as the swing justice, representing the ideological middle of the Court. This, of course, increased his power, allowing him to set the Court's ideological course. As the presidential campaign moved from the primary season to the pandemic-modified conventions, most expected that Roberts would maintain his position as the Court's ideological center for years to come, as long as the polls proved accurate and Democratic nominee Joe Biden won the presidency. Most expected that President Biden would fill the seats of the aging liberals—Ginsburg and the eighty-two-year-old Stephen Breyer—with ideologically similar nominees. They also expected the other four conservative justices to stay put, either because they were still quite young or because they would not voluntarily leave the bench so long as a liberal was in the White House. Finally, most expected that Roberts would not pursue a path of radical constitutional change, preferring instead a more gradual approach to the development of conservative doctrine that would better protect the institutional integrity of the Court. Ever since he became chief justice in 2005 Roberts had eschewed a steadfast commitment to Republican electoral promises on a host of judicial issues. While the Roberts Court was clearly a conservative one, it had not marched in lockstep with the GOP platform as conservatives had hoped and liberals had feared. Instead, it had trod its own doctrinal paths, clearly advancing conservatism in many areas but pursuing a more liberal direction in others. With Roberts at the center, the goal of a conservative Court hellbent on rewriting constitutional law appeared out of reach. But then Justice Ginsburg died.

✶

On Supreme Court vacancies, luck ran with Donald Trump. Not since Richard Nixon's first term nearly fifty years earlier had a president had the opportunity to fill more empty High Court seats so quickly. Nixon named four justices in two and a half years. President Trump selected three in his four years in office: Neil Gorsuch in 2017, Brett Kavanaugh in 2018, and Amy Coney Barrett in 2020. Significantly, two of the additions altered the ideological configuration of the Court, with Kavanaugh replacing Anthony Kennedy, the longtime swing justice, and Barrett succeeding Ginsburg, the second most liberal justice when she died.[4]

Before Ginsburg's death in mid-September, the president hadn't emphasized the Court issue on the campaign trail. Typically, at any given MAGA rally, he would brag about his judicial successes, promise more conservative selections and results if reelected, and denounce his opponent's agenda with a parade of horribles. For example, at a September 10 rally in Freeland, Michigan, Trump pledged: "We will appoint prosecutors, judges, and justices who believe in enforcing the law, not their own political agenda. [*cheers and applause*] . . . We will defend the dignity of work and the sanctity of life. [*cheers and applause*] We will uphold religious liberty, free speech, and the right to keep and bear arms. [*cheers and applause*] And you're lucky I'm here, because your Second Amendment would be gone if I wasn't. [*shouting*]."[5] In a speech a few days later, he warned his supporters about a Joe Biden presidency:

If he's elected, his radical supporters won't just be causing mayhem on the streets, they'll be running the Department of Justice, Department of Homeland Security, the Department of Education. And most importantly, they will put many judges on the United States Supreme Court. We can't have that. We'll have a totally different, totally different country; radical left judges. And that has to do with the Second Amendment. It has to do with right to life, it has to do with so many different things that will turn your world upside down. And they'll have one, two, three, or four, whoever's the next president. And hopefully, that's gonna be us. Not me, us. It's us. [*cheers and applause*][6]

After receiving his party's nomination for a second time in late August, Trump conjured the specter of a Biden victory: "If the Left gains power they will demolish the suburbs, confiscate your guns and appoint justices who will wipe away your Second Amendment and other constitutional freedoms."[7]

But at most rallies the president didn't discuss the Court in any detail—only with a line here and there. Gone were the references to appointing another Scalia. He had apparently already done that two times over, and his supporters expected him to do it again if given the chance. Unlike in 2016, there was no vacancy to dangle before the voters, so Trump emphasized other issues.

In early September, the president did update his list of possible Supreme Court picks, adding twenty more names. This list included a range of individuals, including three sitting Republican senators: Tom Cotton of Arkansas, Ted Cruz of Texas, and Josh Hawley of Missouri. The expanded list was likely designed to curry favor with their supporters and to suggest the possibility of an ostensibly unconventional choice as a nominee (even though all three attended elite undergraduate institutions and either Harvard or Yale Law School).[8] Their addition to Trump's list signaled a third thing as well. Seemingly everyone—themselves included—knew that they would not be chosen for the Court, but their inclusion sent a message to conservative voters. The names Cotton, Cruz, and Hawley certified that the other prospects on the list, unknown to most, must likewise be extraordinarily conservative.

Trump also used the opportunity to denounce Biden for not providing a list of his own nominees, and to reassert his commitments by asking if his opponent's nominees would:

- Protect life, or side with the abortion lobby?
- Protect religious liberty, or force nuns to pay for birth control?
- Protect the 2nd Amendment, or forcibly remove the rights of law-abiding people to defend themselves and their families?
- Protect law-abiding citizens and stand with police, or coddle criminals?

- Protect our borders, our communities, and America [*sic*] workers, or create new rights for illegal aliens?
- Protect taxpayers, or force people to buy products they do not want, like health insurance?
- Protect American entrepreneurs and individuals, or side with government regulators who spit out miles of red tape that strangles freedom, growth, and innovation?[9]

After Ginsburg's death, Trump altered course and started underscoring the Court's importance and the possibility that Democrats might undermine conservative gains if Biden captured the White House.

✳

The search for the third Trump justice was well underway even before Ginsburg died. The liberal justice's health struggles were well known, and she had been admitted to the hospital on three occasions in the last year. Liberals feared she would not make it to the end of the Trump presidency.

Of course, no one expected a vacancy to come so close to Election Day, giving the president and his allies in the Senate an opportunity to change the conversation of the campaign and to speak and act in ways that were in blatant contrast to 2016, when they refused to consider President Barack Obama's choice to fill the Scalia vacancy because—they asserted at the time—the nomination came in an election year. Trump was prepared to quickly fill Ginsburg's seat, refusing widespread calls—and reportedly RBG's own wishes—that he wait until after the election so the American people could choose who would appoint and approve the next justice. Indeed, the president announced his selection just eight days after the justice died.

Rumor had it that Trump had swiftly whittled his very long short list down to two: Barrett and Barbara Lagoa. Barrett was added to Trump's list in November 2017 and had apparently been a close second when the president chose Brett Kavanaugh to fill the Kennedy vacancy in July 2018. In 2020 she was a Trump-appointed court of appeals judge who had clerked for Scalia and spent many years on the faculty of Notre Dame Law School. Born and raised in the suburbs of New Orleans, she had a reputation as a deeply devoted Catholic committed to conservative positioning on the most hot-button social issues of the day. Lagoa was a new addition to Trump's list, added mere days before Ginsburg's death. But she had several electorally relevant assets. She was the first Hispanic woman to serve as a justice on the Supreme Court of Florida, a battleground state thought to be crucial to Trump's reelection chances. She was also the daughter of Cuban immigrants who fled the island after the Castro revolution. Florida officials pushed hard for her candidacy, suggesting her selection would clinch Florida for Trump (he won it anyway) and "might help the president in Hispanic-heavy Arizona and Nevada" (two states he eventually lost by narrow margins). Indeed, one news outlet reported that conservatives were deeply divided over whom Trump should choose, with one group making the electoral-based argument for Lagoa and the other insisting on "a can't-miss pick—someone who carries the lowest possible risk of becoming the next John Roberts or, worse, David Souter."[10] There was even talk of a meeting at Mar-a-Lago, Trump's Florida resort, to give Lagoa a chance to dazzle the president with her charm. But it was not to be. Trump's White House chief of staff, Mark Meadows, an advocate for Barrett, announced the meeting had been canceled. Trump would stay in Washington. News of the meeting's cancelation came the day after the president had met with Barrett for several hours.[11] A few days later he introduced her as the next justice of the Supreme Court. To top it off, he insisted that the introduction ceremony take place in the Rose Garden, where President Bill Clinton had introduced Ginsburg twenty-seven years earlier.[12] But the Barrett ceremony would be remembered for something else: held in the midst of the coronavirus pandemic, the gathering of the mostly maskless guests turned into a super-spreader event.

In truth, Lagoa didn't stand a chance. She didn't come close to measuring up on the anti-drift checklist outlined in chapter 7 (see table 7.2). In fact, she checked just two of the ten items (see table 12.1)—she was Catholic and younger than fifty-five. But both factors were less important than others and did not distinguish her from Barrett. Not only was Barrett Catholic; she had also graduated law school and taught for years at the most well-known Catholic university in America. At forty-eight, she was also more than four years younger than Lagoa. More significantly, and to the point, Lagoa had no connection to Washington, no connection to the Federalist Society, and no experience as a court of appeals judge or a clerk at the Court. To those movement conservatives on the precipice of producing an ideological dream Court, there were just "too many unknowns" to convince them that Lagoa was the right choice. Better to go with Barrett. She was a product of the conservative legal movement, and no one questioned her commitment to the Right's cause. Barrett could even be excused for lacking one of the items on the checklist: having worked in a Republican administration. She finished her clerkship with Justice Scalia near the end of the Clinton administration. And while she did stay in Washington to work at a DC law firm for a few years, she left for Notre Dame very early in the George W. Bush administration. Finally, the absence from her history of any connection to Harvard or Yale

TABLE 12.1. The 10-Point Anti-Drift Checklist, Amy Coney Barrett vs. Barbara Lagoa

Possible Nominee	Perceived Ideology	Administration Experience	Washington Experience	Court of Appeals Judge	Federalist Society	Harvard or Yale Law	Age (55 or younger)	DC Court of Appeals Judge	Supreme Court Clerk	Catholic	Total
Barrett	x		x	x	x		x		x	x	**7**
Lagoa							x			x	**2**

was a telling indication of the maturity of the conservative movement: recall that Notre Dame had emerged as an elite *conservative* law school. Few, if any, would question the credentials of a nominee who had both attended and taught there. Choosing someone with Ivy League credentials was no longer as important as it had been after the Hruska switch a half century earlier: the candidate pool for conservatives was now much deeper.

★

Even before President Trump settled on Amy Coney Barrett, Republicans were rejoicing about the possibility of changing the campaign's emphasis. Believing that the Kavanaugh confirmation hearings positively affected their showing in 2018 (chapter 11), they welcomed the chance to highlight the Court as a campaign issue. Indeed, just ten minutes after word of RBG's death was released, the campaign of Senator Joni Ernst of Iowa, facing a tough re-election race, "sent out Supreme Court themed calls for donations." Minutes later, the recently appointed Republican Kelly Loeffler of Georgia, also in a tight race, sent out a tweet to take political advantage of the new vacancy as well: "My prayers are with the Ginsburg family. Our country's future is at stake & @realDonaldTrump has every right to pick a new justice before the election. I look forward to supporting a strict constructionist who will protect the right to life & safeguard our conservative values."[13] Tennessee Senator Lamar Alexander explained his colleagues' eagerness: "the election can be about Trump or about COVID or about the Supreme Court. And I think, of those three, if it's about the Supreme Court, that traditionally has helped Republicans more." Alex Conant, a Republican strategist, agreed. "A couple of days ago, the biggest issue in this election was Donald Trump's handling of the pandemic. Now it's a battle over the Supreme Court." Sam Nunberg, a Trump 2016 campaign aide, highlighted the mobilization potential of the vacancy, suggesting the nomination of a third Trump justice "would increase 'turnout of disenchanted faith voters' and appeal to Catholics in crucial states."[14]

Senator John Cornyn of Texas gleefully envisioned Senate hearings for a third Trump nominee as "Kavanaugh on steroids."[15] But they weren't. Democrats understood there was little they could do to stop the GOP Senate majority from confirming Barrett. They understood that Republican senators, especially those who viewed Chief Justice Roberts as less ideologically reliable than they had once hoped, were determined to seize this chance to alter the composition of the Court, no matter the consequences. Their 2016 statements about the impropriety of confirming a nominee in an election year didn't matter to them now. Democrats countered not by vehemently attacking Barrett as they had done with Kavanaugh two years earlier, but by objecting to the selection and confirmation of a nominee so close to Election Day—the same position Republicans had asserted in 2016 and one that a majority of Americans endorsed in 2020.[16] With Democrats pushing that argument, Barrett was left fairly unscathed. Compared to the Kavanaugh battle, filled with allegations of sexual assault leveled at him, her confirmation hearings were a bore. And while the vote was close, the result was never in doubt. The Senate confirmed her 52–48. Only Republican Susan Collins, facing a fierce reelection fight in the blue state of Maine, crossed party lines to oppose confirmation.

Fresh off this victory, some Senate Republican candidates chose to run on a record of reconstituting the Court, making their support for Barrett a "centerpiece of their campaigns." For example, Senate majority leader Mitch McConnell "repeatedly trumpeted Justice Barrett and the other two Trump-nominated judges on the high court while not mentioning Mr. Biden's name once" when he campaigned for reelection one day in Kentucky.[17] Others thought Republicans "risk[ed] becoming victims of their own success" by simply celebrating these additions to the Court. As one news report speculated: "without the specter of a liberal court to motivate conservative voters anymore, they may find themselves without the issue that played a crucial role in Mr. Trump's unexpected victory four years ago and has fortified his political base throughout a tumultuous first term."[18] Playing up the GOP's judicial successes and essentially promising forthcoming conservative rulings on issues such as abortion would likely help mobilize Democrats. And according to one account, the Barrett nomination did "fire up [Democrats] against what they [saw] as Trump 'stealing' another court seat, as Democratic leader Chuck Schumer put it."[19]

Trump certainly understood this possibility and worked to counter it. Thus, while he fervently followed the wishes of those chanting "Fill that seat!" at his rallies, he didn't emphasize the Barrett nomination on the campaign trail after he made it. This is not to say that Trump was quiet about Barrett—he tweeted and answered questions about her, and his campaign issued numerous press releases about her qualities—but according to a search of presidential documents he didn't mention her name once at any of his rallies after choosing her for the high bench.[20] Instead, he suggested some uncertainty about how she would rule and turned to another possibility: that, if elected, Joe Biden and a Democratic Congress would seek to expand the size of the Court. Speaking at a rally in Johnstown, Pennsylvania on October 13, for example, Trump warned: "If they win, Democrats will pack the Supreme Court with radical left justices who will shred the 2nd amendment, empower violent mobs, and shield deadly criminals and terrorists." This tactic "confounded" some Republicans,[21] but Trump's strategy, which had worked so well in 2016, was to motivate his base—voters who didn't always show up on Election Day—with red meat rhetoric rather than to appeal to swing voters with a moderate tone. Staidly resting on his accomplishments wasn't likely to work in a race where polls showed him consistently trailing former vice president Biden.

✲

For most of the past generation, Democratic Senate candidates in battle-ground or traditionally Republican states have mostly played defense on the Court issue, occasionally warning of the impending horrors of a truly conservative Court. Few have dared to articulate a liberal constitutional vision. In fact, aside from occasional expressions of concern about the future of *Roe v. Wade* or Obamacare or the destructiveness of decisions like *Citizens United* or *Shelby County* to the progressive cause, most chose to speak about judicial issues only when necessary. This contrasts dramatically with their counterparts in the GOP. As has been described earlier, Republicans have in recent years consistently made Court-based appeals a cornerstone of their campaigns, promising to confirm conservatives committed to the constitutional decimation of long-standing liberal rulings. Some even brandished guns to highlight their support of the second amendment.

In 2020 there were some hints of a change. In the deep-red state of Alaska, for example, Al Gross, a physician, sought to use the Court issue to attack the Republican incumbent, Dan Sullivan. In one ad he appealed to Alaskans, a traditionally libertarian lot, with this: "Dan Sullivan's 100 percent opposed to a woman's right to choose. He'd let government force a pregnancy then deny the woman health care. Dr. Al Gross will keep government out of our personal lives."[22] In another, he criticized the attempt to install a new justice right before Election Day as an example of "Washington politicians" who were "politicizing" the Court. He ended with a statement and then a question for the incumbent: "Dan Sullivan, we both know it's only fair to let the voters cast their ballots in November before we decide. Will you vote to confirm a new Supreme Court justice before the next president is inaugurated?"[23] Sullivan's answer was clear. He did vote to confirm Amy Coney Barrett before Election Day. As the campaign neared its end, some polls suggested Gross was narrowing Sullivan's once wide lead. But the race wasn't that close, as the incumbent won by more than 12 percent. It's difficult therefore to take too much away from this result. On the one hand, it shows that Gross's efforts to use the Court issue to his advantage did not make enough of a difference in the reliably Republican state of Alaska. On the other hand, the fact that he sought to use the issue at all suggests that his campaign thought it might appeal to Alaskans. In this sense, it is an example of red-state Democratic Senate candidates using judicial issues in a new way.

Moreover, if we look to 2022 for a moment, in the race to permanently fill Alaska's sole House seat, left open after Republican Congressman Don Young died, Democratic candidate Mary Peltola employed Gross's tactics on abortion from two years earlier. In one ad, Peltola looked straight into the camera and made her pitch: "Choice is on the ballot. Our right to privacy is on the ballot. Alaskans can't stand by as the federal government creeps into our lives and our bodies. . . . I'm pro-choice and anti–federal overreach and I'll stand up for our right to privacy in D.C."[24] Of course, something significant had occurred in the two years between the two races. The Court had struck down *Roe* in *Dobbs*. That decision certainly made the end of access to abortion more likely. And by framing abortion as an individual right against governmental intrusion, Peltola employed the issue en route to defeating a cultural warrior of the first order: former Republican governor and 2008 vice-presidential nominee Sarah Palin.

Returning to 2020, presidential nominee Joe Biden also took a slightly more aggressive stance on the Court than had his Democratic predecessors, although his tone was certainly more tentative than progressives would have preferred. Specifically, Biden didn't speak to the traditional hot-button judicial issues such as abortion and marriage equality, and he rarely criticized the Court itself. Instead, he targeted the effort to push the Court to the right and focused mainly on the constitutionality of the Affordable Care Act (a.k.a. Obamacare). This press release for North Carolina illustrates Biden's standard line, which was also delivered in person: "Instead of focusing on expanding COVID-19 testing and contact tracing, [President Trump] is trying to get the U.S. Supreme Court to rip away access to health care and erase protections for more than 4 million North Carolinians with preexisting conditions."[25]

Biden also made a case for allowing the victor of the election to choose Ginsburg's replacement. When that failed, he complained that "Republicans jammed through her confirmation." Then, he put the attack on Obamacare and the Barrett confirmation together: "So now, through their craven abuse of political power, they have added to the court a Justice who criticized Chief Justice Roberts' previous decision to uphold the Affordable Care Act in the hopes that they can destroy the Affordable Care Act once and for all through the courts, no matter how many Americans they hurt in the process." He continued:

> So let's remember exactly what is at stake in this election. If you have diabetes, or asthma, or cancer, or even complications from COVID-19, you will lose the protections this law provides. Insurers will once more be able to jack up your premiums or deny you coverage. Women could again be charged more for their health care just because they're women. Children will no longer be

able to stay on their parents' health insurance until age 26. And on top of all that, overturning the ACA could mean that people have to pay to get a COVID-19 vaccine once it is available. That's right. The law that says insurers are required to cover recommended vaccines for free—that's the Affordable Care Act, too.[26]

Progressive talk of packing the Court also displayed a new level of confidence for Democrats, even though their party's nominee did not wish to entertain the idea of increasing the number of justices.[27] In fact, Trump and Republicans sought to use the issue against the former vice president more than Biden embraced it himself. With Biden ahead in the polls and election analysts predicting a Democratic majority in the Senate, Trump and his team highlighted the specter of Court-packing more than Barrett's appointment in hopes of rallying his base. For example, a radio ad from the runoff Senate election in Georgia, cut by the president's son, Donald J. Trump Jr., targeted the "radical Left's" agenda, which he said included "dismantling the Supreme Court." He continued: "They'll take away our second amendment rights and make it harder for law-abiding citizens to defend themselves in their own homes."[28] In other words, even though a conservative Court had been constructed, it was still necessary to come out to vote and elect Republicans to ensure that Democrats didn't demolish it by adding more justices.

In the first presidential debate, the moderator, Chris Wallace of Fox News, emphasized the potential for Court-packing if the Democrats gained control of the White House and Congress. The debate took place just three days after the president had nominated Barrett for the high bench vacancy, so Wallace understandably led with a Court-focused question. A tense exchange ensued. Biden stuck to his script, emphasizing the problematic timing of naming a replacement for Justice Ginsburg. But he did not criticize Barrett, even saying—a bit prematurely—"I'm not opposed to the justice, she seems like a very fine person." The issue for him was her position on Obamacare: "she thinks that the Affordable Care Act is not constitutional."[29]

The conversation then moved to the packing issue. But Biden didn't want to answer Wallace's question, calling it a distraction. Trump pushed hard for an answer. From there, the debate dissolved into a war of words rather than an exchange of ideas:

BIDEN: Whatever position I take on that, that'll become the issue. The issue is the American people should speak. You should go out and vote. You're voting now. Vote and let your Senators know how strongly you feel.
TRUMP: Are you going to pack the court?

BIDEN: Vote now.

TRUMP: Are you going to pack the court?

BIDEN: Make sure you, in fact, let people know, your Senators.

TRUMP: He doesn't want to answer the question.

BIDEN: I'm not going to answer the question.

TRUMP: Why wouldn't you answer that question? You want to put a lot of new Supreme Court Justices. Radical Left.

BIDEN: Will you shut up, man?

TRUMP: Listen, who is on your list, Joe? Who's on your list?

WALLACE: Gentlemen, I think we've ended this—

BIDEN: This is so un-presidential.

TRUMP: He's going to pack the court. He is not going to give a list.

WALLACE: We have ended the segment. We're going to move on to the second segment.

BIDEN: That was really a productive segment, wasn't it? Keep yapping, man.

TRUMP: The people understand, Joe.

BIDEN: They sure do.

Given the Court's decision in *Dobbs*, handed down less than two years later, it is somewhat surprising that candidates only briefly discussed *Roe* in the two debates, in the following exchange:

BIDEN: Let me finish. The point is that the President also is opposed to *Roe v. Wade*. That's on the ballot as well and the court, in the court, and so that's also at stake right now. And so the election is all—

TRUMP: You don't know what's on the ballot. Why is it on the ballot? Why is it on the ballot? It's not on the ballot.

BIDEN: It's on the ballot in the court.

TRUMP: I don't think so.

BIDEN: In the court.

TRUMP: There's nothing happening there.

BIDEN: Donald would you just be quiet for a minute.

TRUMP: You don't know her view on *Roe v. Wade*? You don't know her view.

WALLACE: Well, all right. All right. Let's talk. We've got a lot to unpack here, gentlemen. We've got a lot of time. On healthcare, and then we'll come back to *Roe v. Wade*.[30]

But they never did. Instead, the two main Court-related debate issues were Obamacare and the possibility of expanding the number of justices. *Roe* wasn't a part of the second and final debate, either.

On *Roe*, Trump actually downplayed his stance against abortion compared to four years earlier. For example, while he made his anti-abortion commitments clear, he never uttered the word *Roe* at any of his rallies.[31] And when asked about *Roe* near the campaign's end, he gave a very uncharacteristically evasive answer about his own views. Instead, he referred to his conversations with Barrett (and with Gorsuch and Kavanaugh) in a town hall meeting moderated by NBC's Savannah Guthrie:

TRUMP: Well, again, I'm not ruling on this. And *Roe v. Wade* is something that a lot of people would say, obviously, you're going to speak to somebody. Also two other great Justices, Justice Gorsuch, and Justice Kavanaugh . . . I never spoke to them about *Roe v. Wade*. . . . I think that perhaps it could get sent down to the states, and the states would decide. I also think perhaps nothing will happen. I have not talked to her about it. I think it would be inappropriate to talk to her about it. And some people would say, "You can talk to about it." I just think it would be inappropriate.

GUTHRIE: But what is your preference? Because agreed, that's not something you should talk to the judge about. But would you like to see *Roe versus Wade* overturned?

TRUMP: I would like to see a brilliant jurist, a brilliant person who has done this in great depth and has actually skirted [*sic*] this issue for a long time, make a decision. And that's why I chose her. I think that she's going to make a great decision. I did not tell her what decision to make. And I think it would be inappropriate to say right now, because I don't want to do anything to influence her. I want her to get approved, and then I want her to go by the law. And I know she's going to make a great decision for our country, along with the other two people I put there.

GUTHRIE: You're running as a pro-life Republican. Most pro-life Republicans would like to see *Roe v. Wade* overturned and abortion banned.

TRUMP: Many of them would. Perhaps most of them would. I am telling you, I don't want to do anything to influence anything right now. I don't want to go out tomorrow and say, "Oh, he's trying to give her a signal." Because I didn't speak to her about it. I've done the right thing in so doing. How she's going to rule, you're going to find out perhaps. Or you might not find out. It may never get there. It may never get there. We'll see what happens.[32]

When Trump did speak about abortion on the campaign trail, it was limited to a very specific procedure: "taxpayer-funded extreme late-term abortion." But even that talk diminished after he named Barrett to the high bench. For his part, Biden consistently expressed his support for *Roe*. But with regard to the Court, his emphasis was on protecting Obamacare.

✶

The election turned out to be much closer than many expected, with the president losing three states by less than 1 percent: Arizona (by .31 percent), Georgia (by .24 percent), and Wisconsin (by .63 percent). If Trump had won those three—a swing of just 43,000 votes out of the more than 155,512,210 cast for the two top candidates (.028 percent)—he would likely have recaptured the presidency, since the race would have ended with each candidate with 269 electoral votes. The tie would have thrown the race into the House of Representatives and, given the dictates of the process there, the House would certainly have awarded Trump the White House, even though Biden won the popular vote by 4.45 percent. In the Senate elections, the Democrats were able to wrest control of the Senate from the GOP, but by the narrowest of margins. Despite expectations that they would perform better, they captured just three seats to give them fifty. The incoming vice president, Kamala Harris, would wield the vote to break any ties. In the House, Democrats lost thirteen seats but maintained a slim majority.

✶

Given the new and different ways Americans voted during the COVID-19 pandemic, election analysts have cautioned against putting too much faith in exit polls.[33] With that caveat in mind, let's examine what those polls showed about the Court issue.

As described earlier (chapter 10), on the specific question of the importance of appointments to the Supreme Court Donald Trump had a sizeable advantage over his 2016 opponent among those voters who cared the most about appointments (table 12.2). But in 2020 that advantage was gone. Not only did far fewer respondents say the Court appointments were *the* most important factor determining their vote—down from 21 to 13 percent—but Trump no longer commanded a majority of those voters. He trailed Biden by 4 percent. In fact, he trailed Biden among all voters who cared at all about Supreme Court appointments.

On two judicial issues exit pollsters asked about, the numbers weren't good for Trump either. On the issue of what the Court should do with Obamacare, a clear majority (51 percent) wanted the justices to "keep it as is." Forty-four percent thought it should be overturned. Eighty percent of voters in the first group supported Biden; 78 percent in the latter group supported Trump.

TABLE 12.2. 2016 and 2020 Exit Poll: "In your vote, were Supreme Court appointments . . ."

Answer	Percent of 2016 Total	Percent of 2020 Total	Trump 2016	Clinton	Trump Advantage 2016	Trump 2020	Biden	Trump Advantage 2020
The most important factor	21	13	56	41	15	51	47	−4
An important factor	48	47	46	49	−3	45	54	−9
A minor factor	14	18	40	49	−9	48	51	−3
Not a factor at all	14	19	37	55	−18	49	49	0

TABLE 12.3. 2020 Presidential Exit Poll Question: "Abortion should be . . ."

State	Legal in all cases	Legal in most cases	Illegal in most cases	Illegal in all cases	Difference between Extreme Positions	Difference between Moderate Positions	Winning Margin
National	25%	26%	25%	17%	8% D	1% D	4.45% D
	80% D	68% D	72% R	81% R	1% R	4% R	
Georgia	22%	30%	28%	15%	7% D	2% D	0.24% D
	86% D	70% D	78% R	80% R	6% D	8% R	
Arizona	18%	35%	29%	11%	7% D	6% D	0.31% D
	93% D	65% D	80% R	76% R	17% D	15% R	
Wisconsin	22%	32%	27%	15%	7% D	5% D	0.63% D
	82% D	64% D	75% R	82% R	0%	11% R	
Pennsylvania	25%	30%	27%	13%	12% D	3% D	1.18% D
	85% D	67% D	83% R	85% R	0%	16% R	
Texas	18%	30%	31%	15%	3% D	1% R	5.57% R
	85% D	68% D	83% R	88% R	3% R	15% R	

On the issue of abortion, the numbers were closer. At the national level, there were more abortion rights than anti-abortion rights voters—in both the extreme (legal/illegal in all cases) and the moderate (legal/illegal in most cases) category (table 12.3)—but Trump was able to capture a slightly larger share of the latter group than Biden did of the former group. However, in four of the five battleground states with data on this issue, the story is quite different. In the four states Biden won narrowly, the abortion issue was clearly more advantageous for the Democrat than for the Republican, especially at the extreme. Not only were there more voters holding the extreme abortion rights position, but they were also more committed to Biden than extreme anti-abortion rights voters were to Trump. There were also more pro-abortion rights voters in the moderate categories, but here the anti-abortion rights group was far more committed to Trump than the former group was to Biden. Texas, which Trump won by 5.57 percent, shows the significance of a state with more anti-abortion rights fundamentals. There, even though there were slightly more pro-abortion rights voters (48 percent–46 percent), anti-abortion rights voters were much more committed to Trump than pro-abortion rights voters were to Biden, especially in the moderate category. So it's clear that in Texas abortion was a winning issue for Trump. But in the four more competitive battleground states, it wasn't.

Recall also that Donald Trump did particularly well with white evangelical Christians in 2016, despite concerns about his past positions and personal shortcomings. In 2020, those voters not only showed up to vote—increasing

TABLE 12.4. White Evangelical Christians, 2016 and 2020

State	Percent Total 2016	Percent Trump 2016	Percent Total 2020	Percent Trump 2020
National	26	80	28↑	76↓
Georgia	34	92	33↓	85↓
Michigan	27	81	26↓	73↓
Ohio	33	77	32↓	82↑

TABLE 12.5. Trump Vote in Three Battleground States, 2016 and 2020

State	Trump 2016	Margin–Result	Trump 2020	Margin–Result
Georgia	50.38%	5.09% win	49.23%	.23% loss
Michigan	47.25%	.77% win	47.77%	3.23% loss
Ohio	51.31%	8.07% win	53.18%	8.02% win

their turnout by 2 percent from 2016—they once again supported Trump by a wide margin at the national level, although slightly less than four years earlier (table 12.4). Responses in three battleground states with evangelical exit data, however, tell a more nuanced story. Trump won Georgia, Michigan, and Ohio in 2016, but he lost the first two four years later (table 12.5). The white evangelical vote may very well have played a role in those two defeats. Consider that in both Georgia and Michigan, fewer voters—1 percent in each state—identified themselves as white evangelical Christians in 2020 compared to 2016. And their support for Trump declined by 7 percent in Georgia and 8 percent in Michigan. Given the very close 2020 races in both states, if Trump had repeated his 2016 performance with these voters, he would have won them (all else being equal). In Ohio, he increased his numbers among white evangelical Christians and essentially matched his 2016 margin of victory.

Taken together, the data show that Donald Trump did not benefit from the Court issue in the same way that he had in 2016. As the Court moved to the right with the appointment of three Trump justices, the issue was less a driver of Republican turnout and more motivating for Democrats.[34]

✶

Turning to Senate races to see if the same conclusion holds, we have limited exit poll data on the abortion issue, and it is unfortunately not available for all the closely contested ones. Table 12.6 shows the states where the data are available, including some contests that were never in doubt. The data nevertheless allow us to explore four races that Republicans won and four that Democrats won. In examining these races, it's best to put them into three categories:

states with significant advantages on one side or the other and strong support for the extreme positions (Alabama and Colorado); states with a clear but less than overwhelming pro-abortion rights advantage (Arizona, Georgia, and Virginia); and states where voters were divided fairly evenly between the two sides (Iowa, Montana, and Texas).

In Alabama, it is easy to see why Republican Tommy Tuberville won election over the incumbent Democrat, Doug Jones. Voters opposed to legal abortions easily outnumbered voters who supported them. For this reason, it is not surprising that Tuberville and his allies ran ads highlighting Jones's opposition to Brett Kavanaugh and Amy Coney Barrett.[35] Notably, voters opposed to legal abortion were far more likely to back Tuberville than their counterparts were to back Jones. Indeed, a significant number of voters with moderate support for abortion rights backed Tuberville (33 percent). The data from Colorado tell a similar story, but one that was more advantageous for the pro-abortion rights Democrat, John Hickenlooper. In defeating GOP incumbent Cory Gardner, Hickenlooper benefited from both the overwhelming number of these voters and their support for his candidacy. While Gardner was able to attract more moderate abortion rights voters compared to Hickenlooper's success with anti-abortion moderates, it was insufficient to overcome the abortion rights advantages.

TABLE 12.6. 2020 Senate Exit Poll Question: "Abortion should be . . ."

State	Legal in all cases	Legal in most cases	Illegal in most cases	Illegal in all cases	Difference between Extreme Positions	Difference between Moderate Positions	Margin of Victory
Alabama	17%	25%	28%	24%	7% R	3% R	20.36% R
	n/a	67% D	87% R	92% R	n/a	20% R	
Arizona	18%	35%	29%	11%	7% D	6% D	2.35% D
	94% D	67% D	79% R	77% R	17% D	12% R	
Colorado	28%	36%	24%	8%	20% D	12% D	9.32% D
	88% D	62% D	83% R	78% R	10% D	?1% R	
Georgia	23%	30%	28%	16%	7% D	2% D	2% D
	84% D	67% D	79% R	77% R	7% D	12% R	1.23% D *
Iowa	21%	28%	29%	17%	4% D	1% R	6.59% R
	75% D	65% D	79% R	88% R	13% R	14% R	
Montana	15%	31%	31%	16%	1% R	0%	10.02% R
	89% D	69% D	84% R	n/a	n/a	15% R	
Texas	18%	30%	31%	15%	3% D	1% R	9.64% R
	80% D	64% D	83% R	88% R	8% R	19% R	
Virginia	25%	29%	26%	15%	10% D	3% D	12.08% D
	87% D	68% D	69% R	63% R	24% D	1% R	

*The first of these figures are from the general election.

The second group of states—Arizona, Georgia, and Virginia—had moderate abortion rights advantages as well, but not as significant as those in Colorado. Nevertheless, the sheer number of these voters and their willingness to support the abortion rights candidate clearly made a difference on Election Day. While the Virginia race was not close, Democrat Mark Kelly defeated incumbent Republican Martha McSally in Arizona by just 2.35 percentage points. Kelly benefited from the fact that extreme abortion rights voters not only outnumbered their ideological counterparts (18 percent to 11 percent), but were also more committed to him than their counterparts were to McSally (94 percent to 77 percent). In Georgia, two races—a regular one for a six-year term and a special one for a two-year term—were also very close. Indeed, both were only decided in early January 2021 runoff elections after no candidate secured the required majority the previous November. The data in table 12.6 represent the exit poll responses from the November regular election between the incumbent Republican David Perdue and the Democratic challenger Jon Ossoff, which Purdue won by 1.8 percent. The data show why the race was so close. While there were slightly more abortion rights voters, Purdue attracted a sizeable number of abortion rights moderates, undercutting Ossoff's advantage with extreme abortion rights voters. There is no data from the runoff elections, but both of those races were also very tight, reminiscent of the November Perdue-Ossoff race. In the runoffs, Ossoff beat Purdue by 1.23 percent in the regular election and Democratic challenger Raphael Warnock defeated Republican Kelly Loeffler by 2.08 percent in the special election.

Republicans won all three of the races in Iowa, Montana, and Texas, even though the Democrat candidates in Iowa and Montana at times led in the polls. In Texas, despite a slight abortion rights advantage, the data show that anti-abortion rights voters were more committed to the candidate who represented their interests than their counterparts were to Democratic challenger M. J. Hegar. As a result, Republican incumbent John Cornyn won handily. In Montana, Democrats thought they had a chance of winning in a state Trump had won by more than 20 percent in 2016 after they recruited the popular governor, Steve Bullock, as a candidate. In 2018 incumbent Jon Tester had beaten back a challenge from a well-financed Republican and, indeed, Bullock led in numerous polls in the leadup to Election Day. But the data on the abortion question show why he was unable to overcome the favorable Republican fundamentals in the state. Not only were there slightly more anti-abortion rights voters (47 percent to 46 percent), but they were also more enthusiastic about Republican Steve Daines than abortion rights voters were about Bullock. In answer to the exit poll question that limited responses to just "legal" or "illegal"—not shown in table 12.6—84 percent of voters opposed to legal abortion supported Daines, while 76 percent of voters who supported legal abortion backed Bullock. Quite simply, that division explains why Bullock lost to Daines by 10.02 percent.

The Iowa race is perhaps the most telling on the abortion question. As in Montana, Democrats were quite confident that their candidate, Theresa Greenfield, could defeat Republican incumbent Joni Ernst. And like Bullock in Montana, Greenfield led in several pre-election polls. The exit poll data also show that there were slightly more abortion rights voters (48 percent–46 percent). However, both groups of abortion-opposed voters—moderates and extremists—enthusiastically backed Ernst as compared to their ideological opposites' support for Greenfield. Why was Ernst able to do so well with these voters while also undercutting abortion rights support for Greenfield? The political scientist Douglas M. Brattebo helps explain in his analysis of Ernst's positioning during one of the debates: "Ernst reiterated her anti-abortion views, but in a blatant contradiction, also sought to reassure voters worried about her vote to confirm Justice Amy Coney Barrett to the Supreme Court, saying of the prospect of *Roe v. Wade* being overturned, 'I don't see that happening.' "[36] It was a strategy used by other Republicans in tough races, and, as we've seen, by the president as well.[37] We know now that Ernst's prediction was incorrect, but in 2020 a sufficient number of abortion rights voters supported her to ensure her reelection.

There are no exit poll data on the abortion issue for Maine, but this was perhaps the most important senate race for the Court issue in 2020. Running for reelection in a blue state during a presidential year, Susan Collins was thought to be one of the most vulnerable Republican incumbents. The Democrats had recruited a solid candidate, speaker of the Maine House Sara Gideon, and early polling suggested Collins was in deep trouble. One of the main criticisms of Collins, who supports abortion rights, was her decisive support of Brett Kavanaugh's nomination. Collins had given a lengthy speech on the floor of the Senate justifying her decision to support a nominee who most thought was chosen precisely to strike down *Roe*. But Collins didn't think the threat to *Roe* was as significant as her skeptics warned:

> There has also been considerable focus on the future of abortion rights based on the concern that Judge Kavanaugh would seek to overturn *Roe v. Wade*. Protecting this right is important to me. To my knowledge, Judge Kavanaugh is the first Supreme Court nominee to express the view that precedent is not merely a practice and tradition, but rooted in Article III of our Constitution

itself. He believes that precedent "is not just a judicial policy . . . it is constitutionally dictated to pay attention and pay heed to rules of precedent." In other
words, precedent isn't a goal or an aspiration; it is a constitutional tenet that
has to be followed except in the most extraordinary circumstances. . . . Noting that *Roe v. Wade* was decided 45 years ago, and reaffirmed 19 years later in
Planned Parenthood v. Casey, I asked Judge Kavanaugh whether the passage
of time is relevant to following precedent. He said decisions become part of
our legal framework with the passage of time and that honoring precedent is
essential to maintaining public confidence.[38]

Of course, Collins's expectations about Kavanaugh's commitment to precedent turned out to be incorrect. And when he joined the Court majority
in striking down *Roe* in *Dobbs*, Collins released a statement saying that the
justice had provided "misleading" answers on *Roe* to gain her support.[39]

But in 2020, *Roe* was still in place and Ginsburg's death afforded Collins a
chance to make amends to those Mainers who disagreed with her Kavanaugh
vote. Indeed, she was the only Republican to vote against the confirmation of
Amy Coney Barrett. Her reasoning was straightforward: "In fairness to the
American people, who will either be re-electing the president or selecting a
new one, the decision on a lifetime appointment to the Supreme Court should
be made by the President who is elected on November 3rd." She added: "It's
a matter of principle, it's a matter of fairness. In a democracy, we should play
by the same rules and the fact is that there has not been a confirmation of a
Supreme Court justice in a presidential election year since 1932."[40]

Her support for Gorsuch and Kavanaugh and then her opposition to Barrett allowed Collins to advance her message that she was truly an independent voice in the Senate. And Maine voters endorsed that idea by reelecting
her by a comfortable margin of 8.6 percent. Her victory was especially pain-
ful for Democrats since Joe Biden won the state by 9.07 percent. Soon after
the election, Democrat Senate leader Chuck Schumer of New York said that
RBG's death was one of the two reasons the Democrats didn't retake the Senate after the November election (and needed to win the two Georgia runoffs
in January to do so). "Ginsburg's death let Collins reshape the debate about
filling Supreme Court vacancies. . . . [She] appealed to Democrats, independents and undecideds by opposing filling her seat until voters picked the next
president."[41] With two Georgia runoff victories, the Democrats did take control of the Senate, but the narrow majority meant that one Democrat—most
often either Joe Manchin of West Virginia or Kyrsten Sinema of Arizona—
could scuttle or reshape a great deal of legislation.

★

Returning now to the core question: does this data suggest that Trump and GOP senate candidates' emphasis on the Court issue in the 2016, 2018, and 2020 elections heighten the Court's democratic legitimacy?

Among other things, Donald Trump distinguished himself from both the 2016 Republican primary field and past presidential candidates by providing a list of possible Supreme Court picks. That first list came with a cautionary statement (chapter 10): "The following list of potential Supreme Court justices is representative of the kind of constitutional principles I value and, as president, I plan to use this list as a guide to nominate our next United States Supreme Court justices."[42] Despite that caution, on at least one occasion on the campaign trail he said he would to select from that initial list of eleven, although none of the three justices he chose were on it.[43] He promised more with his second list in late September 2016. Then, Trump said that list would be "definitive."[44] But it wasn't. As noted earlier, only his first choice—Neil Gorsuch—was on that list. The Trump White House even bragged that the president had chosen Gorsuch from the list at the time of his nomination, releasing a statement titled "Doing What He Said He Would: President Trump's Transparent, Principled and Consistent Process for Choosing a Supreme Court Nominee." It led with the following: "TRANSPARENT: President Trump provided an initial list of eleven possible candidates to the American people to replace Justice Antonin Scalia as far back as May, 2016. In September, the President added ten more names, providing a final list of twenty-one candidates. President Trump promised 'this list is definitive and I will choose only from it in picking future Justices of the United States Supreme Court.'"[45]

Should it matter that President Trump clearly broke his pledge with the selections of Kavanaugh and Barrett? While some might argue that it shouldn't since those two were ideologically akin to others on the list, a closer look assigns more significance to the broken promise. According to one study, Gorsuch was one of the most conservative of the twenty-one on Trump's late September list. Two of the twenty-one were considered to be "moderately conservative," including one who was said to be the runner-up to Gorsuch. But the additions of Kavanaugh and Barrett (and three others) in November 2017 pushed the overall profile of the list to the right. Indeed, when they were being considered for the Kennedy vacancy, both were thought to be more conservative than Justice Gorsuch had been during his short time on the Court.[46] The addition and ultimate selection of Kavanaugh also contradicted Trump's anti-Washington, anti-establishment messaging during the 2016 campaign. Kavanaugh was the definition of a Washington insider. In fact, all three of his choices were easily members of the supreme elite (chapter 7). Thus, at the very least, Trump's abandonment of the twenty others on his pre-election list in favor of Kavanaugh and Barrett drains away some of the democratic legitimacy the Court might have gained from a victorious president who pledged to name only individuals from a specific, "definitive" list before the election and, furthermore, ran on an anti-establishment, anti-Washington message.

✳

Donald Trump certainly deserves credit for outlining his judicial agenda. While the president didn't always highlight it on the campaign trail, any voter paying attention knew the differences between the two candidates on the Court issue in 2016 and 2020. This was not always the case in past elections, as Republicans were less explicit than Trump about their judicial commitments and Democrats generally minimized the Court issue.

In fact, in his widely discussed 2004 book *What's the Matter with Kansas? How Conservatives Won the Heart of America*, Thomas Frank—a public historian from the Left—complained about Republicans using culture war issues to attract voters but never delivering on their campaign promises. As he wrote: "Abortion is never halted. Affirmative action is never abolished. The culture industry is never forced to clean up its act."[47] Indeed, a number of scholars—myself included—argued that the Rehnquist Court's limited conservatism actually benefited the Republican Party the most by advancing its ideological interests without going so far in that direction as to tear GOP alliances asunder.[48] By this reading of the political scene, the Rehnquist Court and the early Roberts Court had been nearly perfect fits for the Grand Old Party. For example, as an indication of the cautiousness of at least some Republicans at the turn of the century, George W. Bush never uttered the word *Roe* in his entire presidency. For him, it is truly a word unspoken. During his attempt to save the Miers nomination, he did publicly refer to himself as a "pro-life president" (a first), but he still refused the opportunity to state a clear stance on the decision itself.[49] Of course, this does not mean that the president didn't speak on the issue of abortion. He certainly did. However, he preferred to speak in generalities, and about more popular restrictions on the procedure, such as bans on partial-birth abortions. Bush surely chose that path because he understood that a majority of Americans opposed overturning the *Roe* decision (66 percent according to a 2006 poll). In avoiding a specific stance, the president could speak to his anti-abortion voters with "culture of life" phrases but not pay the price of a rigid anti-*Roe* stance with potential voters who supported abortion rights.

But Donald Trump was much different. He had no difficulty discussing the end of *Roe*. For example, in the final debate of the 2016 presidential campaign, he promised to appoint "pro-life justices on the Court," and predicted that those additions would mean a decision disrupting *Roe* would "happen automatically." He then described late-term abortions in graphic language—"you can take the baby and rip the baby out of the womb." To emphasize the point, he repeated the line. His running mate was even more direct about his desire for an end to *Roe*. In 2016, Mike Pence said: "I want to live to see the day that we put the sanctity of life back at the center of American law and we send *Roe v. Wade* to the ash heap of history."[50] Trump and Pence's more direct language about *Roe* is partly based on the two men's style. But it is also based on strategy. Trump won the presidency by rallying his base to the polls, even more so than Bush had done in 2004. Indeed, Trump seemed almost unconcerned with trying to appeal to swing voters. And he certainly didn't carefully choose his words in hopes of easing any concerns about his candidacy. As president, Trump continued to unabashedly advance the anti-abortion cause. For example, he was the first president to attend the annual March for Life, held on the anniversary of the *Roe* decision. Other Republican presidents had spoken to the group—but by phone. Literally phoning it in wasn't sufficient for Trump. He explained why: "We're here for a very simple reason: to defend the right of every child, born and unborn, to fulfill their God-given potential. . . . Unborn children have never had a stronger defender in the White House. . . . And to uphold our founding documents, we have confirmed 187 federal judges who apply the Constitution as written, including two phenomenal Supreme Court Justices: Neil Gorsuch and Brett Kavanaugh."[51] Hillary Clinton certainly had the opportunity to highlight the possibility of a conservative Court if Trump was elected, but she mainly focused on a different strategy—one that emphasized the shortcomings of her opponent and the historic nature of her campaign. Likewise, Joe Biden employed a very targeted approach when discussing Trump's appointments to the Court. He certainly could have been more aggressive in challenging the judicial path Trump was trailblazing with them—but he chose not to be.

I argue that Trump's emphasis on the Court issue, particularly in 2016, should confer some democratic legitimacy on the Court. But then again, the added legitimacy must be considered minimal given that he didn't win the popular vote in either of his races, losing to Clinton 48.02 percent to 45.93 percent (more than 2.8 million votes) and to Biden 51.26 percent to 46.8 percent (more than 7 million votes). Moreover, his more evasive 2020 answers, particularly on the abortion issue, should be considered as well. There is even some indication that Trump's messaging was less about advancing the conservative cause than about reviving up his base to turn out on Election Day. Specifically, after the Court struck down *Roe* Trump reportedly both took credit—although he also noted "God Struck Down *Roe*"—and worried that the result would undermine Republicans at the polls.[52] In other words, he was not acting like past presidents who had succeeded in reshaping the Court—presidents who had articulated a constitutional vision, trounced their electoral opponents, and then celebrated the resulting Court successes as an endorsement of their principles. Finally, the Democratic candidates in both 2016 and 2020 didn't really press the matter, largely conceding the judicial field to their opponent. If they had put up a more aggressive defense and were defeated while doing so, there would be more power in the claim to enhanced democratic legitimacy for the Court's conservative path.

✳

Looking beyond the candidates' rhetoric, do exit polls tell us anything more about how voters might view later decisions of the Court? Again, the data available are most complete on the abortion issue. In delving into the 2020 exit poll data, let's consider the four answers to the abortion question—see tables 12.3 and 12.6—in relation to the Court's abortion rulings in *Roe*, *Casey*, and *Dobbs*. While *Roe* did not endorse the idea that "abortion should be *legal* in *all* cases," it did allow for that possibility. Although no state sanctioned it, it is reasonable to suggest that those most supportive of *Roe* would select that answer if asked. Next is the *Casey* decision of 1992, which allowed states to restrict access to abortion before the point of viability as long as a state's laws didn't pose an "undue burden" on the right to choose. That decision most closely aligns with the exit poll answer: "abortion should be *legal* in *most* cases." Next consider the *Dobbs* decision, which allows states to ban abortion entirely. *Dobbs* obviously corresponds with the exit poll answer that "abortion should be *illegal* in *all* cases." The fourth answer—"abortion should be *illegal* in *most* cases"—is the trickiest to correlate with a particular Supreme Court ruling. It's very likely that many of the voters who chose this response had the traditional exceptions in mind: namely, that abortion should be illegal except in cases of rape, incest, or to save the life of the mother. But there are other possibilities. For example, some voters who chose this response may have been thinking in terms like Chief Justice Roberts in his concurring opinion in *Dobbs*. Roberts didn't think the Court should overturn *Roe*, but he did vote to uphold the Mississippi law that banned abortions after fifteen weeks. Perhaps some of the voters who selected this answer wanted to limit *Roe* further than *Casey* had but not to the extent that *Dobbs* ultimately did.

With these linkages in mind, the national figures show that very few voters—just 17 percent—supported the position the Court ultimately endorsed in *Dobbs*. Of course, the Court did not ban all abortions across the nation with its decision, but it did allow for that possibility. And the five justices in the majority knew that many states had trigger laws in place that would outlaw and criminalize abortion once they announced their opinion. They were not deciding *Dobbs* in a vacuum. Even in the very red state of Alabama (table 12.6), the Senate election exit polls show that less than a quarter of voters supported the position that became law—given the state's trigger law—once *Dobbs* was handed down. In Texas, perhaps the state most aggressively seeking to prevent women from obtaining abortions in the leadup to *Dobbs*, that figure was just 15 percent. Three percent *more* voters supported the extreme position possible with *Roe* (tables 12.3 and 12.6). And soon after *Dobbs*, the Texas Supreme Court allowed a 1925 law still on the books to go back into effect, even though the law had been unenforceable for nearly fifty years and was passed at a time when non-white men and women were essentially excluded from the political process and white women had only recently secured the right to vote.

Not surprisingly, in the battleground states that decided the presidential election and control of the Senate the numbers are even starker. In Arizona, just 11 percent of voters supported the position possible after *Dobbs*. In Pennsylvania, it was 13 percent; in Georgia and Wisconsin, 15 percent. In all four states, between 18 and 25 percent of exit poll respondents supported the other extreme—that abortion should be legal in all cases. And in all four of them, more voters supported the more moderate abortion rights position than supported the moderate anti-abortion position. Nevertheless, as in Texas, the Republican attorney general in one of these states, Arizona, sought to enforce a pre-*Roe* ban on abortion. The law, which allows anyone who aids a woman to obtain an abortion to be sentenced to two to five years in prison, first passed in 1864—that is, nearly a half century before Arizona became a state.[53]

With so little popular support for the idea, why do we have so many states banning abortions and electing presidents and senators committed to appointing justices who are hostile to abortion rights? In short, the Republican party has been "captured" by pro-life forces. I use this term differently than the political scientist Paul Frymer, who introduced the concept of "electoral capture" in his book *Uneasy Alliances: Race and Party Competition in America*. Writing in the late 1990s, Frymer argued that the two major parties mainly vied for the support of white swing voters. In turn, African American and LGBTQ voters had been effectively "captured" by the Democratic Party. On the other side, evangelical Christians were a "captured minority" of the GOP.[54]

But now, the table has turned for the Republican Party. The exit poll data from above suggest that anti-abortion forces have effectively captured the party—not the other way around. Swing voters are no longer the targets for appeal. Rather, revving up the base for outsized turnout is the key to victory, particularly in battleground states. Therefore, to win the 2016 Republican presidential nomination, the leading candidates committed to the extreme anti-abortion position and advocated overturning *Roe*. Again, just a decade earlier, George W. Bush pursued a far tamer "culture of life" approach. One of the early leaders in the 2008 race for the Republican presidential nomination—Rudy Giuliani—had long been an advocate of reproductive rights.[55] In his 1994 challenge to the legendary liberal senator from Massachusetts, Ted Kennedy, Mitt Romney—the 2012 GOP presidential nominee—expressed support for *Roe* and said he "believe(d) abortion should be safe and legal in this country."[56]

The move to the right on the abortion issue has also happened in Republican primary races for US Senate seats, even in battleground states. This GOP commitment to the anti-abortion cause combined with Donald Trump's luck with high bench vacancies—aided and abetted by the Republican Senate's stonewalling of Merrick Garland—led to the construction of a Court that constitutionally discarded *Roe* in *Dobbs*. It may look like the Court is still following the election returns, and in a very limited sense that is true. But this Court is the result of a polarized political process—a process far different from the one that built the Court that overturned *Plessy* in *Brown*, perhaps the most famous example the majority justices provided for overturning precedent in *Dobbs*.

Soon after the Court discarded *Roe*, voters in one red state were given a chance to vote on abortion rights. And they very clearly sided with the abortion rights position. In Thomas Frank's Kansas, which Trump won by more than 20 percent in 2016 and just under 15 percent in 2020, voters soundly rejected a call to amend the state's constitution to allow the state legislature to strictly curtail or even ban abortion. Republicans control the legislature with a supermajority and had intentionally chosen an early August primary election in hopes that turnout would be both low and conservative. After all, registered Republicans outnumber Democrats nearly two to one there. And unaffiliated voters, the second largest group in the state, would have no other reason to vote. Nevertheless, Kansans came out in droves, stunning political observers by defeating the referendum 59 percent to 41 percent. An analysis after that vote suggested that if provided the same opportunity—to vote directly on the issue—voters in forty of the fifty states would do the same.[57]

If correct, this shows just how important the rules of the game are to the result. An open vote for all to participate in—no matter the partisan affiliation of the voter—is much different from a vote confined to a single party primary in which candidates vie for the most committed—and often the most ideological—voters.

Confronting Detours and Dead Ends:
Liberal Resistance and Frustration in the
Age of Conservative Dominance on the Court

13

How a Numerical Minority Rules the Law
and Prevents Progressive Political Change

In February 1937 political cartoonists were fascinated by the ages of the Supreme Court justices, and a book by the Washington journalists Drew Pearson and Robert S. Allen, *The Nine Old Men*, had been on the *New York Times* bestseller list for weeks. The book's tales of the justices' behavior so alarmed one senator that he called for a congressional investigation into their alleged activities. Cartoonists piled on, depicting the justices as decrepit and near death. One cartoon put the justices, ancient and exhausted, on the football gridiron, where the president stars as the "ingenious quarterback." But a vigorous President Franklin D. Roosevelt has left the huddle with the justices to plead for help from the referee (i.e., Congress), telling him "Those fellows don't know it, but they're through." He demands "six substitutes."

Roosevelt employed this attention—almost fascination—with the justices' ages to try to convince Congress to add six more to the Court. But in truth, the central argument of the Court-packing plan was less about the justices' biological ages and more about the age of their ideas and their hostility to the New Deal. After all, one of the New Dealers' heroes was Louis Brandeis, who at eighty was the oldest justice, and another, Oliver Wendell Holmes, had retired from the bench seven years earlier at the age of ninety. Imbued with the spirit of legal realism, New Dealers charged that the Court-packing plan was necessary so that the president could appoint men who could keep up with the times—to ensure that legal interpretation was consistent with social realities.[1] Frustrating their efforts were justices like the much-hated James McReynolds, the Court's second-longest-serving member, who had vowed in Roosevelt's first term to never leave the high bench "as long as that crippled son-of-a-bitch is in the White House."[2] Such an attitude helped FDR become the first president since James Monroe—more than a century before—to

serve a full first term without an opportunity to alter the Court's composition.[3] Moreover, in that first term, the Court had constitutionally shredded
his first New Deal, voiding legislation designed to return the nation to economic prosperity. In early 1937, fresh off a historic electoral landslide, FDR
feared the justices would do likewise and undercut his second New Deal—a
new batch of laws aimed at economic and social reform.

February 5, 2016, was the seventy-ninth anniversary of Roosevelt's introduction of the Court-packing plan. The Court, unchanged since Elena Kagan became a member six years earlier, was not much younger than the one
President Roosevelt had assailed with his plan. At seventy, the average age of
the justices was just two years younger than that of their anti–New Deal predecessors. But perhaps more importantly, the members of the 2016 Court had
served noticeably *longer* than those of the mid-1930s—18.3 years on average
compared to 14.7 years for those of nearly eight decades earlier. The reason
was simple. More recent presidents had selected nominees at a younger age
and, once confirmed, those justices were staying longer.

Yet, newspapers—either online or in print—did not run a flurry of car-
toons mocking the justices as disconnected and decrepit, and no books
about the elderly and anachronistic men and women of the Court appeared
on the *New York Times* bestseller list. Instead, that week, *Notorious RBG*—a
book *celebrating* the Court's oldest member—appeared on that list for the
eighth time. And there was little talk during the 2016 presidential primaries
of Court-packing as necessary to constrain the Court. With four justices near
or older than eighty, the belief was that the next president would have a
chance to alter the Court based on the wishes of the democratic electorate. As
things turned out, Donald Trump filled those empty seats—a minority president chose three nominees destined for status as numerical minority justices
and determined to strictly adhere to movement conservativism. So, in 2024
progressives are talking about packing the Court, knowing that more conservative decisions uprooting liberal doctrine are to come and due to the extremely limited possibilities to strike back.[4] This chapter examines why those
possibilities are so limited.

Age and longevity on the Court have reshaped its place in American democracy; in short, they have widened the Court's democracy gap. With the
justices serving far longer than ever before, opportunities to alter its makeup
through presidential elections—by voting for specific candidates to secure
desirable Court appointments—are blocked, and those who want to reform
the Court are diverted down long detours, waiting for justices to die or retire. Under the circumstances, the amendment process is one of the few routes
for change if a long-entrenched conservative Court constructs constitutional

doctrine that defies the will of the majority. While Article V of the Constitution allows for two amendment avenues, to date only one has been used. In the twenty-seven times the Constitution has been altered, Congress has passed an amendment by a two-thirds vote and then three-fourths of the states have ratified it. The alternative path, amendment through a constitutional convention, has never been used. But, as I discuss below, that may soon change.

The amendment process is designed to protect a numerical minority against even a substantial majority, but in today's America it effectively allows for what I call "minuscule rule," empowering just a tiny fraction of Americans to thwart constitutional change. And it does so in a way that heavily favors those on the right of the nation's ideological dividing line. As this chapter shows, progressives should be wary of the amendment path, for it is essentially a constitutional dead end for them.

*

Are the justices America's popes? I don't ask this question to joke about the number of Catholics on the Court or about how nominees are chosen only from the "judicial monastery." I make the comparison because of the justices' lifetime tenure and increasing longevity. And I argue that this combination of tenure and longevity has troubling implications for the Court's place in American democracy.

Some might imagine that justices have always kept their seats on the high bench for a long time, but it's actually a relatively new phenomenon. It's difficult to pinpoint precisely when the trend began, but the confirmation of Richard Nixon's last justice, William Rehnquist, is perhaps the best place to start. Rehnquist and six of the next eight justices of the divided government era are among twenty-five (out of 115) of the longest-serving members of the Court, ever. Furthermore, three of those seven died while still on the high bench, obviously planning to stay even longer. And one, Clarence Thomas, isn't done yet.

Up until the divided government era, the average tenure for a justice was about sixteen and a half years. Today, those who leave after less than two decades are the exception.[5] In fact, there's only been one—David Souter—who did so in the last twenty-five years, and he served nearly nineteen years. In addition, more are staying until death. More than fifty years elapsed between Robert Jackson's death in 1954 and Rehnquist's in 2005.[6] After Jackson died while still on the Court—at just sixty-two years old—nineteen justices retired to a life off the high bench.[7] Counting Rehnquist, three of the last seven justices to leave the Court died while still on the bench after having served an average of thirty years, and at an advanced age. Three of the four who retired—John

Paul Stevens, Anthony Kennedy, and Stephen Breyer—did so at the ages of ninety, eighty-two, and nearly eighty-four, respectively, and after serving more than thirty years on average. Two of the three who died—William Rehnquist and Ruth Bader Ginsburg—suffered through serious bouts of cancer. The third—Antonin Scalia—was clearly an ill man, so much so that his personal doctor said there was no need for an autopsy after his body was discovered. His family agreed.[8] Presidents shouldn't have to wait for justices to die to name a replacement. They're not supposed to be popes.[9]

It was not uncommon during the first seven decades of the twentieth century (see chapter 9) for a justice to receive consideration for political office. But today, that is no longer the case. There's been no serious recent discussion of a justice leaving to assume another position in the political world. The Court is unquestionably the last stop for those chosen for membership; justices leave either to retire from public office entirely, or feet first. Even not-so-subtle hints to aging justices from like-minded presidents typically don't work as they once did. Recall that Lyndon Johnson engineered a vacancy for Thurgood Marshall (chapter 6). He created another vacancy by convincing JFK-appointed Arthur Goldberg to step down to become US Ambassador to the United Nations. Compare those examples to President Obama's feeble attempt to convince Ruth Bader Ginsburg to retire in 2013. According to reports, Obama invited the eighty-year-old, two-time pancreatic cancer survivor to the White House for a private lunch. "Treading cautiously, he did not directly bring up the subject of retirement . . . [but he did] raise the looming 2014 midterm elections and how Democrats might lose control of the Senate. Implicit in that conversation was the concern motivating his lunch invitation—the possibility that if the Senate flipped, he would lose a chance to appoint a younger, liberal judge who could hold on to the seat for decades." Ginsburg, however, was unmoved, saying later, "I think one should stay as long as she can do the job." Around the same time, she expressed optimism about the future. "There will be a president after this one, and I'm hopeful that that president will be a fine president."[10] She clearly thought staying on the Court was worth the gamble. To her critics on the Left, she seemed more concerned about her personal legacy than about the principles she espoused during her career.[11]

Liberals understandably agonized over Ginsburg's health and advanced age during the 2020 presidential campaign, hoping she would live until after the election. The journalist Margaret Talbot joked in a late 2019 New Yorker article, "surely, no American has more atheists and agnostics praying for her good health than Ginsburg does."[12] During the COVID-19 pandemic, yard signs appeared in the Adams Morgan neighborhood of Washington, DC: "RBG works less than 5 miles from here. If you won't wear a mask to protect your friends and family, do it to protect RBG."[13]

Is this an indication of a healthy democracy? Should supporters of one political party wake up every day hoping that an eighty-seven-year-old woman with serious health issues is still alive? Fellow justices swear that those who stay until an advanced age haven't lost a step in their capacity to do the work.[14] While some find that difficult to believe, it's really beside the point. My argument is that presidents and senators—as the elected representatives responsible for naming and confirming justices—should have the opportunity to do so regularly. That's been the case for most of American history.

But increasingly, presidents have been denied the opportunity to alter the Court as frequently as they did in the past. Since its membership was set at nine in 1869 there have been seven presidential terms in which no new justice has been added to the Court. Three of those terms have occurred in the last twenty-five years.[15] As I noted in chapter 1, it's quite possible today, in 2024, that there will not be another Court vacancy for a decade. Assume that Justice Thomas serves until 2034, as he once promised he would,[16] and assume that none of the younger justices die or retire before him. That would mean an approximate twelve-year gap between the confirmation of Ketanji Brown Jackson and the appointment of the next justice. If Joe Biden (or Donald Trump) does not serve a second term, a new president elected in 2024 and re-elected in 2028 would not have a chance to shape the Court at all. In the more than 230 years of the presidency, only four presidents—three elected and one unelected—have not had the opportunity to name a Supreme Court justice. The three elected were William Henry Harrison, who died after thirty-one days in office; Zachary Taylor, who died after sixteen months in office; and Jimmy Carter, who was defeated after one term. In addition, following the assassination of Abraham Lincoln, an opposition Congress prevented the unelected Andrew Johnson from filling two vacancies (chapter 3).

A Court unchanged for twelve years will also be unprecedented. Under the definition used here, there have been 109 so-called natural Courts—i.e., "a period during which the membership of the Court remains stable"—over the course of American history.[17] Many of these are quite short. The average is a little more than two. But they've grown longer in recent years. There have only been ten natural Courts of five years or longer in nearly 225 years. But four of those have come in the last fifty years, including three of the longest five (table 13.1). In addition, the more recent natural Courts have had nine justices, whereas the earlier ones had seven. In other words, even

TABLE 13.1. Ten Longest Natural Courts

Natural Court	Begin Date	End Date	Elapsed Time—Days	Elapsed Time—Months	Elapsed Time—Years
Marshall 6*	2/3/1812	9/1/1823	4228	138	11.58
Rehnquist 6	8/3/1994	9/29/2005	4075	133	11.16
Roberts 4	8/7/2010	4/10/2017	2438	80	6.67
Waite 6	4/3/1882	1/18/1888	2116	69	5.79
Burger 4	12/19/1975	9/25/1981	2107	69	5.77
Hughes 3	3/14/1932	8/19/1937	1984	65	5.43
Chase 1**	12/15/1864	3/14/1870	1915	62	5.24
Taney 8	8/10/1846	10/10/1851	1887	62	5.17
Marshall 9*	1/11/1830	1/14/1835	1829	60	5.01
Burger 5	9/25/1981	9/26/1986	1827	60	5.00

Source: Epstein, Segal, Spaeth, and Walker (2021, 411–21) list the dates of all natural courts.

*Marshall 6 and 9 had seven justices.

**There were two deaths on Chase 1 natural court (on May 30, 1865, and July 5, 1867). But given the Senate's refusal to allow President Andrew Johnson to fill any seats (chapter 3) and under the definition of a "natural court" used here, Chase 1 lasted until the arrival of the next new justice in mid-March 1870. Chase 1 also began with ten justices.

when change was nearly 30 percent more likely because there were more justices who might die or retire, there was less of it. (Significantly, this figure does not account for the tremendous change in life expectancy over this period.)

Turnover of the justices was a centerpiece of Robert Dahl's argument about the Court's harmonious place in American democracy: "Over the whole history of the Court, on the average one new justice has been appointed every twenty-two months. Thus a president can expect to appoint about two new justices during one term of office; and if this were not enough to tip the balance on a normally divided court, he is almost certain to succeed in two terms. . . . The fact is, then, that the policy views dominant on the Court are never for long out of line with the policy views dominant among the lawmaking majorities of the United States."[18]

At the time of his writing, in 1957, a president could indeed expect a regular rate of turnover on the Court. For example, during the thirty-six years of the New Deal era, there was a vacancy every 1.71 years on average (even though there were none in FDR's first term).[19] But with justices staying longer (figure 13.1), vacancies are far rarer today.[20] During the twenty-four years of the polarization period, there has been a vacancy every three years, even with the four between 2016 and 2022.[21]

And this trend does not promise to end, especially since wealthy Americans are living longer and presidents are appointing justices at a younger age.[22] In 1835, when Chief Justice John Marshall died, his tenure on the Court had stretched over thirty-four years. For the *next 140 years*, only one other justice served longer, and that by a mere 114 days.[23] But if the justices of today stay on their current course, Marshall's mark will become commonplace. Assuming all stay on the Court until their eighty-fifth birthday—a few months older than the mean age of the last five justices to depart—they will have served thirty-three years *on average* (figure 13.1).

This tenure is especially striking given that five of the nine currently on the Court are numerical minority justices—three of them appointed by a minority president. Finally, as noted in chapter 1, Justice Thomas's stated reason for serving a very long time is revenge, to pay back those who opposed him through the years: "The liberals made my life miserable for 43 years, and I'm going to make their lives miserable for 43 years."[24] While the wounds of the confirmation process were undoubtedly still fresh when Thomas uttered those words, they should nevertheless terrify any good Democrat; but, much more importantly, they should scare the daylights out of any good democrat, with a *small* d. Enabling change is central to democracy. It can't survive if opportunities for adjustment are foreclosed. In a democracy, the people are supposed to rule—but consider that more than 40 percent of America's population was born after Thomas ascended to the Court in 1991. If he stays as long as promised, that figure will rise to approximately 60 percent by the time he departs. That might be acceptable if he were the only justice determined to serve well into old age, but clearly he's not.

✶

Of course, amending the Constitution provides an alternative to altering the Court's decisions. But that path is essentially a dead end for progressives.

Imagine the following. All of the United States is scheduled to vote on a proposal, and residents in all but one of the fifty states are able to do so. The

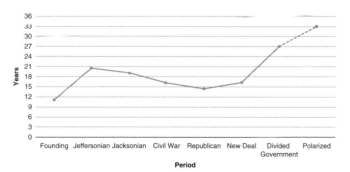

FIGURE 13.1. Average Length of a Justice's Tenure, by Period

results are overwhelming. All the people in forty-nine states support the proposal. No one opposes it. It is a moment of unity and renewal for the nation. But for some reason, Californians cannot vote. They vote the very next day, and once again, support for the proposal is enormous. More than 80 percent of Californians vote in favor it. But stunningly, the proposal doesn't pass. It falls short by a whisker. How can this be in a nation that has been on the forefront of democracy for more than two centuries? How can an idea with the backing of more than 95 percent of the nation not become the law of the land? In reality, this hypothetical is quite similar to the constitutional amendment process in the United States.

I'll return to this scenario later, but first consider why the opportunity to amend the Constitution is important for understanding the legitimacy of the Supreme Court today. In defending his brand of constitutional interpretation, Justice Antonin Scalia often argued that the practice of originalism would allow democracy to flourish. For example, he didn't believe the original meaning of the Constitution conferred on women the right to obtain an abortion, but if state legislators wanted to pass such legislation there was no constitutional provision to prevent them from doing so. To win that right for women, he asserted, abortion rights activists should have to use the channels of democracy, not simply convince five unelected "wise men" in robes to interpret the Constitution creatively, as in *Roe*. That argument is clear enough. The founders "knew there would be a need for change," Scalia said, "and that's why they had an amendment provision."[25]

It is quite rare to amend the Constitution, and it's occurred very infrequently over the last 237 years. Ten of the twenty-seven amendments, moreover, were passed at one time, with the Bill of Rights in 1791. Three others—the 13th, 14th, and 15th—were ratified only after a civil war and muscular tactics by northern victors in southern states. Two amendments—the 18th and the 21st—deal with the same issue, prohibition, and cancel each other out. And several, like the 20th, 25th, and 27th, are quite technical, and more easily attracted bipartisan support. In fact, the last of those three, which requires an intervening House election before pay raises can take effect for all members of Congress, is the only amendment ratified in the last five decades, and it took more than two centuries for that to happen.

Scalia understood the difficulty of the amendment process. In fact, when asked if there were any flaws in the Constitution, he pointed to that process:

> The one provision that I would amend is the amendment provision. And that was not originally a flaw. But the country has changed so much. With the divergence in size between California and Rhode Island—I figured it out once,

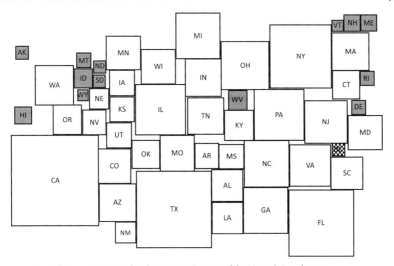

FIGURE 13.2. Thirteen Least Populated States, 4.4 Percent of the Nation's Population

I think if you picked the smallest number necessary for a majority in the least populous states, something like less than 2 percent of the population can prevent a constitutional amendment. But other than that, some things have not worked out the way the framers anticipated. But that's been the fault of the courts, not the fault of the draftsmen.[26]

Scalia's calculations were accurate. He arrived at 2 percent by cutting the total population of the thirteen least populated states in half, since he was focusing on a bare majority necessary to prevent ratification. Recently, the population of those thirteen states was 14,339,485. Half of that amount is approximately 7.2 million—2.2 percent of the nation's total population. (As we see in figure 13.2, which is a Demers cartogram where each state is scaled to population size, the thirteen shaded states are quite small compared to the rest of the nation.) Scalia adds that this "flaw" was not present at the time of the founding, and this too is accurate. At that time the four least populated states needed to prevent an amendment made up about 9.7 percent of the nation's entire population; a bare majority of this "blocking bloc" of states was about 4.8 percent. That's more than double the 2.2 percent it would take today.

Now, let's return to our California hypothetical. As by far the most populous state in the land today, California's nearly 40 million residents make up 12.1 percent of the nation's total population. The thirteen smallest states can easily fit within California (figure 13.3). In fact, they add up to just 36 percent of its population.

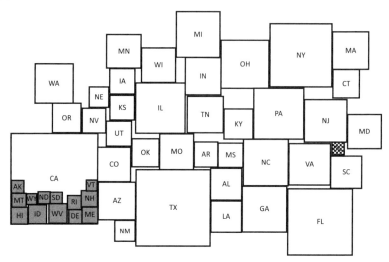

FIGURE 13.3. Thirteen Least Populated States Compared to California, 36 Percent of California's Population

If just 19 percent of all California residents opposed the proposal in our hypothetical, that would still be more than the 2.2 percent in Scalia's calculations ($12.1 \times .19 = 2.3$). In other words, a bare majority of the population in the thirteen smallest states is equal to less than 20 percent of California's population. In fact, a bare majority in the smallest blocking bloc of states is significantly less than the entire population of a single California county: with more than 10 million people, Los Angeles is the state's—and the nation's—most populous county. Of course, the residents of just one of the nation's more than 3,000 counties cannot block a constitutional amendment. But far fewer people than LA County's 10 million, dispersed across the thirteen smallest states, can certainly do so.

Some might object to Scalia's 2 percent figure, since not all the small states are similar in ideological outlook and therefore are unlikely to unite in opposition to a constitutional amendment.[27] While most are red, some (like Rhode Island and Vermont) are quite blue. So perhaps it's better to specify and total the populations of the thirteen smallest red and blue states. I'll use the states Donald Trump won in 2016 as the red states and those Hillary Clinton won as the blue states.[28] The combined population of the blocking bloc of states Trump won equals 7.5 percent of the population. Using Scalia's formula, it would still only require about 3.7 percent of the population to stall an amendment, which is less than the nonpartisan figure of 4.8 percent at the founding. The number for blue states is slightly higher than the nonpartisan founding figure: the thirteen smallest blue states account for 13.3 percent of the population; half of that number is 5.7. Combined, neither the thirteen smallest red states nor the thirteen smallest blue states equal the size of California. They represent 63 and 93 percent of that state's population, respectively.

While the size difference between the thirteen smallest red states and the thirteen smallest blue states is fairly insignificant, things diverge dramatically if we examine the thirteen *most* Republican and the thirteen *most* Democratic states. While Donald Trump did win twelve of the thirteen smallest red states by more than 10 percent and won the thirteenth (Iowa) by nearly that amount, consider what happens if only the reddest of the red states are used in our analysis (figure 13.4). Trump won thirteen states by more than 20 percent. The closest of these was Montana, which he won by 20.2 percent. His largest margin of victory came in neighboring Wyoming, where he won by 46.3 percent of the vote. Together, these thirteen deep-red states made up 10.6 percent of the nation's population in 2018. Using Scalia's formula again, that means that approximately 5 percent of the nation's population, located in states with very like-minded Republican voters, could block a proposed amendment.

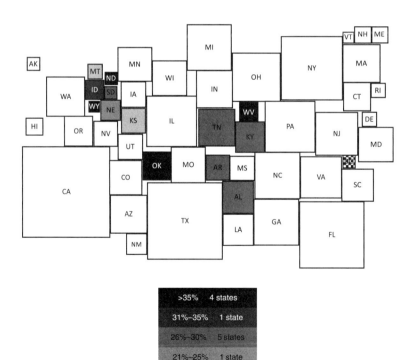

>35%	4 states
31%–35%	1 state
26%–30%	5 states
21%–25%	1 state
16%–20%	2 states
11%–15%	0 states

FIGURE 13.4. Thirteen Reddest States, 10.6 Percent of the Nation's Population

>35%	0 states
30%–35%	2 states
25%–29%	3 states
21%–25%	1 state
16%–20%	3 states
11%–15%	4 states

FIGURE 13.5. Thirteen Bluest States, 34.7 Percent of the Nation's Population

Turning to the bluest states, even though Hillary Clinton won the popular vote by 2.8 million, she didn't come close to winning thirteen states by more than 20 percent. She did, however, capture thirteen states by more than 10 percent of the vote. Her widest margin of victory in those states was in Hawaii at 32.2 percent; her narrowest was in Oregon at 11 percent. Added together, the population of these bluest states is 34.7 percent of the entire nation (figure 13.5). Half of that percentage equals 17.4 percent, and that's what it would take to reach a bare majority in the thirteen most Democratic states. While still low, it is more than three times the 5 percent figure for the thirteen most Republican states and nearly four times the nonpartisan figure at the time of the founding.

But in fact, the best number to use is dramatically lower than any of these figures. Population really isn't the best measure since it has no connection to the democratic process by which voters elect members of state legislatures. And in all but one case these legislatures have been responsible for considering past constitutional amendments.[29] So, the better questions are: (1) How many state legislators does it take to block a constitutional amendment? and (2) How many voters supported those legislators in their most recent election? There are 7,386 state legislators nationwide. Since only one house of a legislature is needed to stall a constitutional amendment in a particular state—and all states have two, except for unicameral Nebraska—we just need to know the numbers of the smaller of the two bodies to arrive at the number of state legislators necessary to block a constitutional amendment. In the forty-nine states with a bicameral legislature, the Senate side has the fewest members. Assuming all members of a state senate vote, the minimum number in the thirteen smallest states is just 222 (or 3 percent of all state legislators).

When we keep this process in mind, it makes more sense to focus on the vote totals for state legislators in their most recent election rather than state population totals. That's because population totals count everyone, including those—like anyone under eighteen years of age—who cannot vote. Using vote totals instead, the number of voters who supported those 222 state senators in their most recent election is shockingly small. Approximately 1.55 million voters cast their ballot for those senators; that's *less than one-half of 1 percent* of the US population, or about *1 percent* of all voters in the 2020 presidential election. That's all it would take to elect the minimum number of state legislators necessary to thwart a constitutional amendment in a nation of 331 million. This isn't minority rule. It's minuscule rule.

If it takes so few state legislators to successfully block a constitutional amendment, then it follows that it's extraordinarily difficult to *pass* an amendment. Surprisingly, that's not exactly true. As an example, take the extraordinarily popular 26th amendment, which lowered the voting age from twenty-one to eighteen. Congress passed it in late March 1971, and three-fourths of the states had ratified it just over three months later, on July 1, 1971. Of course, this rapid ratification took place amid the Vietnam War, when the average age of an American soldier was nineteen.

Amendments like the 26th aside, it should be far more difficult to ratify an amendment on a controversial substantive issue such as abortion or marriage equality.[30] Some legal scholars, like the University of Chicago law professor Eric Posner, have criticized just that difficulty. Posner goes so far as to suggest that the "U.S. Constitution is impossible to amend," underscoring that it "may as well be written in stone." Unlike Scalia, Posner believes that this is an area where "the founders blundered." Criticisms of the difficulty of the amendment process are not new. The political scientist Darren Patrick Guerra notes that they date at least as far back as the progressive era in the early part of the twentieth century. The political scientist Donald Lutz even produced a model to prove "the U.S. Constitution is the most difficult to amend of any constitution currently existing in the world today." The rigid-ity of Article V, in fact, is often said to be a reason for the "judicial expansion of the Constitution"[31]—in other words, the charge that the Court "legislates" from the bench. Given his distaste for such Court action, this may explain why Scalia thought the amendment article should itself be amended.

Posner's take on the amendment process was part of a book review of then former—now late—Supreme Court Justice John Paul Stevens's *Six Amend-ments: How and Why We Should Change the Constitution*. As the book's title suggests, Stevens—who was statistically the most liberal justice for nearly two decades (from 1991 until his retirement in 2010)—outlines six areas where he believes the Constitution needs to be fixed "to avoid future crises before they occur."[32] Posner agrees with Stevens's desire for a constitutional "retooling." His critique focuses on the process. He simply doesn't think Article V affords the opportunity for such change. "In most countries," he writes, "we could seriously consider the changes to the Constitution that Stevens proposes—or, for that matter, a different set of amendments from the Tea Party. But in our country, we can't. Any proposal to amend the Constitution is idle because it's effectively impossible." To bolster his case Posner refers to Scalia's 2 percent figure and quotes the late justice's view on Article V: "it ought to be hard, but not that hard."[33]

In one sense, Posner and Scalia are spot on. It is far easier to block a pro-posed amendment to the Constitution than it was at the time of the founding. But Posner and Scalia both miss a fundamental aspect of the process because they only examine one side of the coin: the *ease of preventing* the adoption of an amendment. Counterintuitively, however, not only is it far easier today to block a constitutional amendment than it was in 1787; it is also far easier to *ratify* one. To explain, I will first consider changes in population figures from the founding era until today, as I did with my analysis of blocking an amendment; then I will consider the number of state legislators necessary to ratify an amendment and the number of votes they won in their most recent election.

At the time of the founding, the ten smallest states—three-fourths of the thirteen original states—made up 56.7 percent of the nation's population, a clear majority.[34] Today (figure 13.6), the thirty-eight smallest states—three-fourths of the current fifty—make up just 40 percent of the population, well short of a majority.[35] So in terms of percentage of the population, it's easier today than in 1787 to ratify an amendment—not more difficult, as Posner and Scalia suggest. It is another avenue for minority rule, since voters in states with a distinct minority of the nation's population can shape constitutional rule for all of America. Put another way, a majority of the states have a minority of the

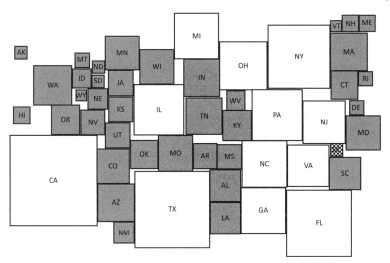

FIGURE 13.6. Thirty-Eight Least Populated States, 40 Percent of the Nation's Population

population. To take this to a more fine-grained level of analysis, at the barest minimum, the support of 2,725 state legislators—744 state senators and 1,981 state representatives—would be sufficient to pass a constitutional amendment in the legislatures of the thirty-eight smallest states. Approximately 30 million voters supported those legislators in their most recent election (slightly less than 15 million in the state senate races and slightly less than 15 million in the state house races). That's about 19 percent of the total number of voters in the 2020 presidential election, and 9 percent of the nation's 2020 population.[36] And those percentages don't even account for the fact that many of those voters likely voted in both the state senate and state house races. In other words, the 30 million figure double-counts many voters.

If we look at the states in partisan terms, it becomes clear that the path for a proposed amendment that advances conservative interests is far smoother than that of one that advances progressive interests, and that in this sense the amendment process is lopsided. In other words, Posner errs in writing that six Tea Party–sponsored amendments would face the same level of difficulty as Stevens's progressive measures. In part, this is simply because there are more conservative red states than liberal blue ones. For example, in 2016, even though Hillary Clinton won the popular vote by more than 2 percentage points, she still won only twenty of the fifty states.

Furthermore, in terms of population, a "ratifying alliance" of the thirty-eight reddest states comprises 66 percent of the nation as a whole (figures 13.7 and 13.8).[37] So, using Scalia's bare majority argument, if two-thirds of both

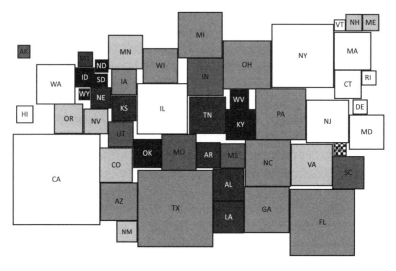

FIGURE 13.7. Thirty-Eight Reddest States, 66 Percent of the Nation's Population

houses of Congress passed an amendment, it would be possible for just one-third of the nation's population—33.2 percent, specifically—to ratify it. To be sure, this is still an unlikely scenario, since the 38th reddest state in 2016 was Oregon, which was still quite blue. Clinton beat Trump there by just under 11 percent of the vote. Nevertheless, ratification of a conservative amendment is within reach, since Clinton won six of the eight blue states necessary to reach a thirty-eight-state ratifying alliance by 5.3 percent or less. And she won four of them by less than 3 percent. Moreover, after the 2019 elections, Republicans controlled both houses of the legislature in all the states Donald Trump won (plus Minnesota's Senate).[38]

Of course, it would be difficult for a highly partisan constitutional proposal to gain the support of two-thirds of both houses of Congress—the first step in the only amendment process used in American history. At the height of their power in 2015, Republicans controlled 56.8 percent of the seats in the House of Representatives and 54 percent in the Senate. That's significant, but still quite far from the necessary 66.7 percent. But there is another option for the thirty-eight reddest states. The Constitution allows for an alternative path to alteration: namely, a constitutional convention. According to Article V, if two-thirds of the states (thirty-four) agree to call a convention, then Congress "shall" convene one. No vote in Congress is required. Rather, the amendments that emerge from that national convention would become part of the nation's ruling document if three-fourths of the states (thirty-eight) ratify them, either by a vote of state legislatures or in ratifying conventions. This path effectively bypasses Congress, and three-fourths of the states can radically alter the Constitution, which means that the reddest states could succeed by this alternative path.

In contrast, it's far more difficult—verging on impossible—for the bluest states to ratify an amendment advancing progressive interests or to approve measures emanating from a constitutional convention. That's because the thirty-eight bluest states make up a whopping 90 percent of the nation's

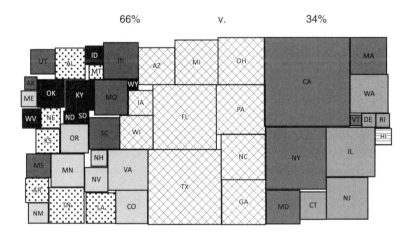

FIGURE 13.8. Thirty-Eight Reddest States vs. Twelve Bluest States

population (figures 13.9 and 13.10). And the reddest of these "blue" states was Montana, which Trump won by more than 20 percent in 2016. Again, since Clinton only won twenty states, nearly as many Trump states—eighteen, specifically—would have to join a liberal alliance to ratify an amendment or request a convention. In today's polarized America, that's all but impossible. So, when Hillary Clinton vowed to pursue the constitutional amendment route if her effort to convince a Supreme Court majority to overturn *Citizens United* was unsuccessful (chapter 10), she should have known she was offering an empty promise, since it was highly unlikely Republicans would join forces with her.

Unfortunately for progressives, it is indeed correct to conclude that the Constitution, to borrow Posner's words, "may as well be written in stone." Meanwhile, conservatives are seeking to use their constitutional amendment advantage. A group on the Right called Convention of States Action has been leading this effort, hoping a constitutional convention would lead to amendments severely restricting the power of the federal government. Rick

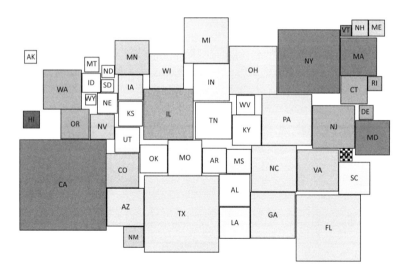

>30% D	1 state
20%–29% D	5 states
10%–19% D	7 states
0%–9% D	7 states
.1%–10.99% R	10 states
11%–20% R	8 states

FIGURE 13.9. Thirty-Eight Bluest States, 90 Percent of the Nation's Population

90%   v.   10%

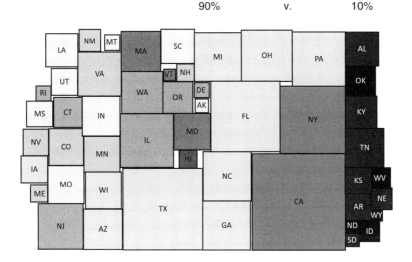

>30% D	1 state
20%–29% D	5 states
10%–19% D	7 states
0%–9% D	7 states
.1%–10.99% R	10 states
11%–20% R	8 states
21%–30% R	7 states
>30% R	5 states

FIGURE 13.10. Thirty-Eight Bluest States vs. Twelve Reddest States

Santorum, the former Pennsylvania senator who recently joined forces with the group, admits that "we may not even be in an absolute majority when it comes to the people who agree with us."[39] Nevertheless, they are seeking to exploit this imbalance.

This constitutional "flaw" or "blunder" developed relatively quickly after the Constitution was ratified due to the nature of the nation's expansion. At the time of the founding, the states were fairly evenly split, at least with regard to one of the fundamental issues dividing the new nation: the institution of slavery. There were five southern states—located below the Mason-Dixon Line—with enslaved populations greater than 25 percent. The total population—both enslaved and not—of those five states was 49.0 percent of the nation. There were seven northern states with mostly "free" populations, although New York and New Jersey would not abolish slavery until just before and just after the turn of the century, respectively.[40] The population of those seven states was 49.4 percent of the nation's total. In between—both literally and figuratively—was Delaware, with an enslaved population of just over 15 percent and a population comprising 1.6 percent of the entire nation's populace. While the three-fifths clause of the Constitution reduced the population of enslaving states for the purposes of representation, the five southern states could nevertheless effectively block a constitutional amendment or an attempt to call a convention.

But as the nation added new states to the original thirteen, far more often than not they were quite small and had not yet developed significant populations. And while a few of those additions have blossomed into some of the nation's largest—including California—most of the "newest" states remain sparsely populated. Specifically, of the thirteen states that entered the union most recently—all but two well over a century ago—seven remain among the smallest thirteen. None are among the most populated twelve states.[41] The combination of political polarization with these state demographics has created a lopsided constitutional amendment process, with a thumb on the scale for the nation's most conservative states. In the past, this mattered less because there was far less ideological cohesion in the parties around certain constitutional concerns. Today, however, the parties are divided largely along these lines, and few politicians are willing to cross the dividing line into bipartisanship.

The founders believed that there ought to be a way to alter the nation's ruling document, if a supermajority of voters were so inclined. But the process they put into place is now out of alignment, making it all but impossible for one side in particular to amend the Constitution. Such a flaw is deeply problematic for a democratic nation. Providing avenues for change is essential in a democracy. One that doesn't allow enough change, or heavily favors one side over another, may very well cease to be a democracy at all.

14

Reducing the Democracy Gap at the
Coalface of Constitutional Politics

A system of government that makes the People subordinate to a committee of nine
unelected lawyers does not deserve to be called a democracy.
ASSOCIATE JUSTICE ANTONIN SCALIA, dissenting in *Obergefell v. Hodges*
June 25, 2015[1]

Deep underground, immersed in darkness and dust, miners who struck rock
at the coalface—where the core of the work is done—were at the center of
a constitutional crisis in the 1930s. In case after case, and for many years,
the Supreme Court had rejected government efforts to regulate an industry
with a long history of doing things its own way—of mistreating miners and
scorning workplace democracy. Then, in the midst of the 1936 presidential
election, the justices sided once again with the mine owners, crushing New
Deal hopes for a new judicial day. But soon thereafter, things would change.
The Court, pushed by politics and then transformed through appointment,
finally relented, crafting the necessary constitutional doctrine to buttress a
powerful federal government committed to progressive reform, including
unprecedented protections for miners.[2]

This history of the Court in the 1930s is highly relevant for today's progressives. Arguably, it suggests the best way forward for them. Historically,
Supreme Courts have not marched quickly forward to advance the principles
of whatever political regime put the justices in place, but have taken more circuitous routes. Even with the best attempts to find the "right" nominees to articulate the regime's principles, we should not expect otherwise. The elected
representatives at the heart of a political regime work to forge the institutional
mission of the Court, but they do not determine the precise content of its decisions. The justices are not bots built to function as programmed. There is
not a clear line, for example, from the election of Republican presidents and
Senates committed to choosing and confirming conservative justices to the
constitutional repudiation of *Roe v. Wade*, notwithstanding what politicians
tell voters on the campaign trail. The justices decide on their own terms and
in their own time.[3] We can try to predict what will happen and when, but we

should expect to be mistaken. For at the coalface of constitutional lawmaking, the justices decide.

For the Supreme Court of today, judicial autonomy is even more pronounced. Past Supreme Courts were independent, but they nevertheless worked in concert with a larger political regime. The Court of today is different; indeed, the way it has been constructed makes it truly unprecedented in American history. Not only is it untethered to a dominant political regime like the ones Robert Dahl and Robert McCloskey observed sixty years ago; it is also misaligned with consensus views on some of the most pressing issues of the day. Masquerading as judicial independence, judicial isolation reigns.

Without the linkages that moored past Courts to a dominant political regime, we might have expected this Court to be cautious. The five numerical minority justices that form the conservative majority today understand that they were narrowly chosen, and could accordingly have pursued a more moderate path. But largely they have not. Eschewing judicial modesty, they have acted as though they have a democratically endorsed mandate to rewrite the law. Most strikingly, in *Dobbs*, they delivered a decision that eliminated the fundamental right for women to end a pre-viability pregnancy despite widespread approval of *Roe* and its status as established law for nearly a half century. Indeed, the result in *Dobbs* was in conflict with the conclusions of fifteen of the twenty-three justices who had an opportunity to consider the right to choose since 1973—nine Republican appointees and six Democratic appointees.[4] Yet in *Dobbs*, the five numerical minority justices took the nation down a different path.

In that decision, those justices could have sided with the more modest but still very conservative position advanced by Chief Justice John Roberts in his concurring opinion, one that upheld the Mississippi statute but retained a more limited right to choose as the law of the land. But they did not. Keen to the reality that politics change after a transformative decision like *Dobbs*, they could have written into the nation's legal code that laws banning or strictly restricting abortion that were passed before *Roe* could not take effect until a legislature spoke again, even if in the end the legislature simply passed that same exact law once again. But they did not. The numerical minority justices could have extended that idea, breaking new ground, by disallowing "trigger laws" so that a state debate about abortion could freely take place—unencumbered by earlier legislative action—in the altered space of a post-*Dobbs* world, especially since such laws were by definition unconstitutional when they were enacted. Aside from allowing for a lucid democratic process and discussion over a deeply divisive issue, this would have afforded women, healthcare providers, and abortion clinics in red states time to understand the consequences of *Dobbs*. But they did not.

Liberals fear that *Dobbs* is just the start. With the gate now swung open, the five numerical minority justices, at times (but not always) aided by the indisputably conservative chief justice, will unleash a judicial avalanche that will bury any progressive rulings still in place. And indeed, after *Dobbs*, affirmative action was next on the doctrinal chopping block.[5] With the long-detested *Roe* and *Bakke* discarded, this conservative core will likely seek to further protect gun rights, further advance business interests, further restrict voting rights, further allow states to criminally prosecute anyone aiding a woman seeking an abortion (including nurses and doctors), and further restrict LGBTQ rights by endorsing religious-based refusals of service and by reconsidering the decision that constitutionally sanctioned same-sex marriage.[6] If Justice Clarence Thomas has his way, it may even reconsider constitutional bans against the criminalization of consensual same-sex intimacy (*Lawrence v. Texas*) and the sale of contraceptives (*Griswold v. Connecticut*).[7]

Many liberals, and others, fear these doctrinal possibilities—that these justices will do what they want, when they want. In turn, progressive forces have begun to formulate and organize their next moves to try to tame or even reclaim the Court. Some law school professors have contributed their share of desperate, idiosyncratic—and eventually politically doomed—proposals.[8] Some other imaginative reforms to tame or redirect a runaway Court have been considered in the past but rejected because they ultimately rely on the justices to comply with a rule that could easily be circumvented: For example, requiring the justices to agree unanimously before overturning a federal statue. Or requiring congressional action unlikely to happen in polarized times, perhaps by allowing Congress to pass again a law declared unconstitutional by the Court by a two-thirds or three-fourths vote. A constitutional amendment to alter the Court or its powers would of course be best. But as we saw in chapter 13, that process is stacked against progressives today.

In this chapter, I consider two other proposals that have received widespread attention: packing the Court, and limiting justices' tenure on the high bench. I end by discussing another possibility—using the combination of the numerical minority status of this Court's majority, together with its dramatic and disruptive decision-making, to rally voters to the polls. If the past is indicative, failure in the Supreme Court may very well provide progressives with opportunities to reshape the political landscape. This certainly happened in the 1930s. Such success may take longer to achieve, but it will restore the power of majoritarianism. This power existed, as Dahl and McCloskey observed, for much of the nation's history and allowed the Court to work as an ally of American democracy, and with all but unquestioned legitimacy. With all these reforms, I consider the extent to which they might reduce the democracy gap and restore at least some of the Court's democratic legitimacy.

*

Court-packing is a fairly simple idea that has been used several times in the past and proposed even more often, typically when the Court makes an unpopular decision and elected lawmakers respond by seeking to alter its ideological equilibrium.

The phrase usually conjures thoughts of the 1930s and President Franklin D. Roosevelt's much-maligned plan to add six new justices to undercut the power of the conservative justices on the Court who had judicially devastated his first New Deal (chapter 13). Some continue to argue that his plan threatened democracy,[9] even though the group most responsible for torpedoing it were senators seeking to protect white supremacy and one-party rule in the South.[10] Moreover, it is difficult to argue that the plan was a threat to democracy when the Court was the institution resisting the will of the voters, represented by the Democratic Party's overwhelming victories in 1932 and 1936, which included two presidential landslides and the capture of approximately 80 percent of House and Senate seats.

It is highly unlikely the Court would have remained at nine had it continued to resist these forces of democracy. In this sense, some have learned the wrong lesson from 1937. The Court-packing plan didn't fail because Americans were ferociously committed to a Court of nine. The Court's composition was not a politically sacrosanct issue. The plan failed because the Court—and most especially Justice Owen Roberts—acceded to the realities of a dominant, democratically elected political regime and altered its doctrinal course. Democracy prevailed.

In today's polarized America, however, we have no comparable dominant regime. And a Court-packing proposal passed by a Democratic Congress and signed by a Democratic president could soon be countered with another passed by a Republican Congress and signed by a Republican president. In reaction to the *Brown* decision, some southern congressmen proposed to dramatically alter the Court in hopes of weakening it. What about a Court multiple times larger than nine? Is that where we would be headed if the size of the Court were increased now? Probably not. But Court-packing seems too blunt a tool for the task at hand. More importantly, it is unlikely to work in the long run. And it certainly wouldn't solve the problem of contentiousness in the confirmation process, or the approval of more numerical minority justices. It wouldn't alter a justice's tenure on the bench. It wouldn't diminish the power of the supreme elite, although it would obviously allow more of that group to serve. Indeed, it could very well end up weakening the Court's authority rather than restoring some of its democratic legitimacy.

*

As we know, the justices don their black robes for much longer than they once did. And unlike other areas of politics, where it's possible to challenge an incumbent every two or four or six years, unless they die (or are impeached and removed) the justices alone decide when to depart, when to step aside. This creates a host of problems for altering the Court organically and instilling it with democratically induced change on a regular basis (chapter 13). This is why, in the current nomination game, nominees have to be of a certain (relatively young) age, despite the Constitution's silence on the matter. Our current confirmation politics encourage relatively young nominees, with the knowledge that they will serve for a very long time untouched by voters—that is, by the voices and forces of democracy.

In making these youthful selections appointing presidents and confirming Senates are not attempting to advance a democratic cause; rather, they hope to isolate these justices and their decision-making from democracy. The idea is not to provide the Court with this sort of independence for a noble purpose. It is to safeguard the Court out of fear that the American people might seek to disrupt its doctrinal work by electing presidents and senators who would appoint and approve justices who veer from the nominator's preferred course of constitutional law.

The elimination of lifetime tenure would go a long way to addressing these concerns. The most attractive proposal would be to provide a justice with an eighteen-year term, meaning that there would be a formalized vacancy every two years—a president who serves a full four-year term would have the opportunity to select two new justices. Additional measures would need to be taken to ensure Senate cooperation, but those are technicalities that can be addressed at a later date. Such a nomination system would widen the range of possible selections. Potential nominees who are now discarded because they are older than sixty would have a chance to serve on the high bench once again. And, to recall, many of America's most renowned justices joined the Court around or after that age (and at a time when life expectancy was much lower). Aging justices would no longer need to hold on until the election of an ideologically friendly president, as both Justices Antonin Scalia and Ruth Bader Ginsburg sought to do. Retirements would become a matter of routine rather than strategy. Voters would know with much greater clarity what their presidential vote would mean for the Court in the next four years. The supreme elite would still hold sway, but like Court-packing, this term limit would give presidents additional opportunities to choose from outside the judicial monastery. Contentiousness in the Senate might be reduced as well with such a routinized system. Knowing that another nomination would come before them in two years and again two years after that, senators would have less incentive to vote on purely ideological grounds every time, although that is by no means a certainty. Such a system should work to depoliticize the Court and, most importantly, to allow democratically sanctioned change to occur after each election, not just when a justice dies or retires. Of course, instituting such a reform would not be easy. There are some who believe it can be accomplished legislatively.[11] That's essential, because a constitutional amendment to remove life tenure from the justices would certainly stall in the states (chapter 13).

✶

From the brokenness of defeat in the mid-twentieth century, conservatives eventually emerged strong and defiant, working to appeal to voters with judicial-based themes in hopes of convincing enough of them to support their plan to reshape the Court and rewrite the legal doctrine they detested. Success was at times fleeting and at other times enduring. Despite GOP dominance over the selection process since 1969—appointing (and confirming) a vast majority of the justices since that year—conservative Republican candidates time and again were the ones voicing complaints about the nation's highest tribunal on the campaign trail.

Today, it appears that the change they long desired has finally arrived, as a Court of six conservatives follows a decidedly rightward path. Apparently, conservatives chose right by broadening their appeal across the land—taking advantage of a constitutional arrangement that dramatically favors small states and those who live there. It took more than fifty years and incredible strokes of luck, but they have prevailed. Liberal complaints have been whipped away in the wind. The Court is now theirs.

This brief summary of the constitutional politics of the last half century provides a basis for the final proposal I consider here. It requires no congressional action and no constitutional amendment. It does, however, require a great deal of organizing and mobilizing effort. In short, the progressives of today may be forced to do the same as the conservatives of the past two generations, given that they can no longer rely on the courts for relief. Indeed, for too long progressives have gone to court, and relied on the Supreme Court, to pursue change. To quote the political scientist Gerald Rosenberg, courts were "like fly-paper" for progressive reformers who "succumb[ed] to the 'lure of litigation.'"[12] By pursuing this litigation liberalism, they lost sight of the demands of a constitutional structure, which requires broad-based politics and demands that parties strive to win in densely populated states and sparsely populated ones, too. To win, progressives will need to labor at the grassroots, to focus on convincing voters "on the doorsteps," as they say in Britain, rather than convincing five attorneys with elite law degrees sitting high above the rest in a courtroom adorned with red velvet drapes in the white marble palace atop Capitol Hill.

As Republicans have done since the days of Nixon, and as Roosevelt's Democrats did in the 1930s and 1940s, progressives should use Americans' discontent with the Court to advance their cause, broadening their appeal in states where they struggle to win today. This will be difficult, and those most impacted by negative court decisions will surely suffer. But in order for the Court to be imbued with democracy, the people must play their part. Doing otherwise will likely be shortsighted and counterproductive. The potential of this strategy is not only electoral but also doctrinal: some of the justices may have second thoughts about pursuing a full-throated ideological agenda if political winds turn against them. This certainly happened in the 1930s with Justice Roberts's "switch in time that saved nine." And the evidence suggests it occurred again in certain areas of the law in the late 1960s and 1970s. As several have observed, "the justices read the newspapers too." They are cloistered, but they may still be affected by events outside their hallowed chambers.

It may be too much to expect a political approach to solve the problems of the Supreme Court's democracy gap, especially after I have spent much of this book discussing how the justices are increasingly isolated from the political branches. However, the impact of the *Dobbs* decision on the 2022 midterm elections gave us some indication of how this might play out, as Democrats turned a promised "red tide" into a ripple by highlighting the abortion issue. Even the former president, Donald Trump, thought *Dobbs* undermined the GOP at the polls.[13]

Political regimes do not last forever. It may be, as the legal scholar Jack Balkin argues, that America is currently experiencing a period of "constitutional rot," and will soon move into a new "cycle of constitutional time."[14] And progressives' efforts to fight judicial doctrine they despise may aid in the formation of the next political regime, one more sympathetic to their doctrinal desires.

To end where I began: this book is not intended as a critique of the conservative ideology that dominates the Court today. It is instead a critique of the way the Court was won and the way that five numerical minority justices have used their power. This final proposal is designed to restore the Court's connection to American democracy—to reduce the Court's democracy gap in hopes of enhancing its legitimacy in the eyes of the American people.[15] In doing so, the Court might restore its standing across the land at a time when we may need it most.[16]

Notes

Chapter One

1. Antonin Scalia quoted in Murphy 2014, 232.

2. Roe v. Wade, 410 U.S. 113 (1973); Dobbs v. Jackson Women's Health Organization, 597 U.S. ___ (2022).

3. According to a mid-January 2022 Marquette Law School poll, 73 percent of respondents did not think the Court should overturn *Roe*; 28 percent thought it should. Charles Franklin, "New Marquette Law School Poll National Survey Finds Approval of the Supreme Court at New Lows, with Strong Partisan Difference over Abortion and Gun Rights," Marquette University Law School Poll, July 22, 2022, https://law.marquette.edu/poll/2022/07/20/mlspsc09-court-press -release/.

4. After the *Dobbs* decision, another Marquette Law School poll found that 61 percent of respondents thought the Court was motivated "mainly by politics," compared to 39 percent who thought it was motivated "mainly by law." Franklin, "New Marquette Law School Poll National Survey."

5. Dahl 1957, 279–95; McCloskey 1960, 224.

6. Importantly, I use the phrase "democratic legitimacy" rather than "judicial legitimacy" when discussing how the current Court is historically distinct from past Courts. I do so because I argue—like Dahl and McCloskey—that the historical source of the Court's legitimacy lies mainly in its connections with the democratically elected branches of government. I argue that the current Court's legitimacy crisis does not stem wholly from popular disagreement with a judicial decision like *Dobbs*. Rather, the legitimacy crisis is the result of developments in the appointment and confirmation processes that make the Court less representative of the majority's will than in the past. Additionally, I do not argue that the Court is less democratically legitimate because its members are unelected. Obviously, the justices have been unelected since the Court's creation. On judicial legitimacy, see Gibson and Caldeira 2009 and Gibson 2022.

7. In their work, Paul Collins and Lori Ringhand argue that confirmation hearings for Supreme Court nominees have traditionally worked to enhance democracy by introducing future justices to the people. But this function can only be fulfilled if the nominees answer the senators' questions. And in their most recent work, they show that the Trump justices were the least forthcoming nominees in approximately forty years. Collins and Ringhand 2013 and Ringhand and Collins 2018, 2021.

8. But according to Christopher Schmidt (2018), still not to the extent we might have expected.

9. Neil A. Lewis, "2 Years After His Bruising Hearing, Justice Thomas Can Rarely Be Heard," *New York Times*, November 27, 1993.

10. Even if President Joe Biden were reelected in 2024, he would be the first president since James Madison—when there were just seven justices—to serve full two full terms and make only one appointment to the high bench. And his successor would need to serve six years before there would be a vacancy.

11. Jimmy Carter, who served as president from 1977 to 1981.

12. McCloskey 1960, 225.

Chapter Two

1. Before the ratification of the 17th amendment in 1913, senators were chosen by state legislatures, and therefore there is no way to tabulate whether any of the justices confirmed before that date were "numerical minority justices."

2. For ideological scores of the justices, see Martin and Quinn n.d.

3. I count all the votes collected by all the senators who supported and opposed a nominee in their most recent election. For senators who were appointed due to a vacancy, I count the votes of their predecessors.

4. Some might argue that this formulation places too great an emphasis on the heavily populated state of California. But even if all of the Golden State's nearly fifteen and a half million votes for its two Democratic senators were excluded from the equation, both Neil Gorsuch and Brett Kavanaugh would still easily fit the definition of a "numerical minority justice." Moreover, since one California senator opposed his nomination and one supported it, Clarence Thomas would also still fit the definition of a numerical minority justice. Only Samuel Alito and Amy Coney Barrett would lose that distinction if the votes of California were entirely excluded. Alternatively, if one of the state's senators had hypothetically supported both Alito and Barrett, both would be numerical minority justices. Moreover, at the time of the confirmation votes of these five justices there was not a significant partisan imbalance in the representation of the ten most populated states. For example, at the time of the confirmation votes on Gorsuch and Kavanaugh, eleven Democrats and nine Republicans represented the ten most populated states. For the Barrett vote, each party held ten of those twenty seats. In 2016 Donald Trump won seven of these states; in 2020 he won just four. However, the three that flipped—Georgia, Michigan, and Pennsylvania—were decided by very narrow margins in both elections.

5. Throughout the book, I use "George Bush" in reference to the 41st president, George Herbert Walker Bush. I refer to the 43rd president as "George W. Bush."

6. On the Thomas confirmation, see Comiskey 2004 and Mayer and Abramson 1994.

7. Then Vice President George Bush defeated Massachusetts Governor Michael Dukakis by winning forty states and 53.4 percent of the popular vote (a 7.72 percent margin).

8. Bush won reelection in 2004 over Massachusetts Senator John Kerry by winning thirty-one states and 50.3 percent of the popular vote (a 2.46 percent margin).

9. Neil A. Lewis, "2 Years After His Bruising Hearing, Justice Thomas Can Rarely Be Heard," *New York Times*, November 27, 1993.

10. Students for Fair Admissions, Inc. v. President & Fellows of Harvard College and Students for Fair Admissions, Inc. v. University of North Carolina, ___ U.S. ___ (2023).

11. Thomas, concurring opinion in *Dobbs*, 3. Dobbs v. Jackson Women's Health Organization, 597 U.S. ___ (2022).

12. See Levinson 2006.

13. Some might suggest that complaints about the disproportionate power of smaller states are akin to a disgruntled NBA basketball coach complaining about the outcome of a game in the final days of 1979. Please allow me to explain. On December 16, 1979, before a sellout crowd in the famed Madison Square Garden, the Boston Celtics defeated the New York Knicks in a very close game. But from the perspective of the beginning of that year, there was something odd about the result. Indeed, the *Boston Globe* headline seemed to tell the tale: "Celtics Steal One from Knicks, 99–96." While the Celtics had scored one more field goal than the Knicks, Boston had made two fewer foul shots. If the game had been played six months earlier, this combination would have resulted in a tie, since field goals were worth two points and foul shots one point. A tie would have led to overtime, and the Knicks would have had another opportunity to win the game. But there was no overtime on this night. The Celtics won, and the Knicks's coach did not complain. What gives? Well, at the start of the 1979–1980 season, the NBA changed the rules, instituting a three-point line. And in this game, only the Celtics' star rookie, Larry Bird, made any shots from behind that line. In fact, Bird made 3 three-point shots, and the Celtics left New York with smiles on their faces, despite scoring one fewer basket. Is this an appropriate analogy for the structure of American politics? Republicans would likely argue that it is. Teams should understand the rules of the game and construct their rosters and their strategy accordingly. Democrats would likely argue otherwise. After all, why should the votes in one state be worth more than those in another? In basketball, there's a reason for the difference. A player takes a foul shot from the *free* throw line—a.k.a. the "charity stripe"—when the opposing team is forbidden from defending, and is awarded just one point for a made shot. A three-point shot must be taken from behind a line far away from the hoop with the defensive team allowed to contest the attempt. All other shots are worth two points (i.e., those taken from within the three-point line and with the other team playing defense). But there's no comparable difference of difficulty when it comes to winning states in an election.

14. Reynolds v. Sims, 377 U.S. 533 (1964).

15. The three were: Bill Nelson of Florida, and Tim Kaine and Mark Warner of Virginia.

16. See generally Bickel 1986.

17. Bickel 1986, 16–22.

18. Although McCloskey died in 1969, Sanford Levinson gave new life to *The American Supreme Court* by adding chapters for a second edition in 1994. The original text was unchanged (although the book pagination has changed). Now in its sixth edition, it has been required reading in countless undergraduate law courses over the years. McCloskey 1960, 225 (6th edition, ed. Sanford Levinson, 2016).

19. Brown v. Board of Education of Topeka, Kan., 347 U.S. 483 (1954), supplemented *sub nom*; Brown v. Board of Education of Topeka, Kan., 349 U.S. 294 (1955).

20. Dahl 1957, 279, 295.

21. On realignment theory, see generally Burnham 1970; Key 1955; and Sundquist 1983.

22. Dahl 1957, 293. See also Whittington 2019, 287–88.

23. Dahl 1957, 285.

24. Casper 1976, 51–52; see also Adamany 1973; Funston 1975; Gates 1992; Lasser 1985.

25. McCloskey 1960, 224.

26. McCloskey, 224.

27. Shapiro 1978, 194.

28. Shapiro 1991, 145–46. In reaching these conclusions, scholars advancing these lines of argument typically depended on realignment theory and the reliability of the appointment process to explain the representative connection between the Court and the voting public (as Dahl did), or have argued (as Shapiro did), that the political branches aren't that democratic anyway, so it's appropriate for the courts "to act when the legislatures won't." In support of the first of these arguments, scholars have pointed out that the Court rarely invalidates major congressional statutes; that it often supports the government's position when the United States is a party in a case; and that court-curbing proposals introduced in response to controversial decisions seldom succeed in Congress. In support of the second, Shapiro, for example, considers congressional and presidential politics. Regarding the former, he writes: "[T]here is no reason to believe that the self-preservation demands of Congress are likely to correspond to the demands of the majority, or that each social interest is likely to receive that degree of attention which its numerical strength in the population might warrant." And to the latter, he notes that the presidency "can hardly be understood in simplistic majoritarian terms" (Shapiro 1966, 21, 22). On the connection between the Court and the American public, see, for example, Segal and Spaeth 1993, 332. They write: "The displacement of the liberal Warren Court with increasingly conservative Burger and Rehnquist Courts did not result because of congruence with public sentiment. It resulted because Nixon, Reagan, and Bush populated the judiciary with persons in their own ideological image." See also Rosen 2006, Freidman 2009, Gibson and Caldeira 2009, and Clark 2011. On the undemocratic nature of the political branches, see Shapiro 1964, 240–41; Shapiro 1966, 17–21, 32; see also Levinson 2006.

29. Dahl 1957, 291.

30. See, e.g., Ackerman 1991; Dworkin 1996; Ely 1980.

31. Dahl 1957, 283.

32. Dahl, 283, emphasis added.

33. Dahl, 293.

34. This was so because, as he concluded, "the Court is almost powerless to affect the course of national policy. In the absence of substantial agreement within the alliance, an attempt by the Court to make national policy is likely to lead to disaster, as the *Dred Scott* decision and the early New Deal cases demonstrate. . . . Thus, the Court is least effective against a current lawmaking majority—and evidently least inclined to act. It is most effective when it sets the bounds of policy for officials, agencies, state governments or even regions, a task that has come to occupy a very large part of the Court's business" (Dahl, 293–94).

35. Dahl, 293–94 In the 1990s, another group of scholars revisited this question of the connection between the democratically elected branches of government and the courts. This exploration effectively began with the 1993 publication of Mark Graber's seminal article, "The Nonmajoritarian Difficulty: Legislative Deference to the Judiciary." There Graber argued that instead of presenting a counter-majoritarian problem, judicial review is more likely to present a "nonmajoritarian difficulty"—that is, "when the real controversy is between different [minority] members of the dominant national coalition, or 'the clashing majority difficulty' when the real controversy is between lawmaking majorities of different governing institutions." Judicial activity in these times, then, cannot be adequately explained by exploring the counter-majoritarian difficulty, since there is usually no clear majority on many of the most controversial issues of the day. As Graber explains: "all exercises of the judicial power do not have the same relationship to democratic values. Realistic theories of the judicial function, thus, must examine the

extent to which particular instances of judicial review actually promote or retard deliberate policy-making, majoritarianism, and political accountability. In some instances, judicial review is clearly inconsistent with ordinary understandings of democratic majoritarianism" (Graber 1993, 37, 72). Following Graber, numerous scholars added to the regime politics or "political regimes" analysis, providing examples of how politics and law interact to make policy on a variety of matters. While most have been empirically based, showing how politics works to construct law, democratic linkages are often apparent. For example, in my own work on the Nixon administration, I argue that Nixon not only successfully used the powers of the presidency to shape the Court doctrinally, but also used the Court issue as a means of attracting votes at the ballot box (see generally McMahon 2011). While not a focus of that work, the majoritarianism link between successes in electoral politics and doctrinal shifts in the nation's highest tribunal is clear. Nevertheless, following Graber, regime politics scholars have been less interested in the need to "prove" the legitimacy of the Court's action, as Dahl set out to do. But see Whittington 2019, 306–14.

36. See note 24 above.

37. Indeed, Dahl writes, "the main objective of presidential leadership is to build a stable and dominant aggregation of minorities with a high probability of winning the presidency and one or both houses of Congress" (Dahl 1957, 294).

38. McCloskey 1960, 225.

Chapter Three

1. McMahon 2004, chapter 4.

2. Quoted in Dalin 2017, 46.

3. I borrow the phrase "electoral connection" from Mayhew 1974.

4. This does not account for the Senate's ability to restrict presidential choice preemptively through the tradition of "senatorial courtesy." While not a formal rule, this custom held that a senator from the home state of a nominee could object to the selection of an individual the senator deemed unacceptable. In turn, a president aware of a potential objection might make a different choice. The political scientist Henry Abraham (1999, 19) notes that the practice "at least partially account[ed] for [the] rejection of several nominations to the Supreme Court."

5. Elsewhere, I define a contested confirmation as one in which at least 20 percent of the voting senators oppose the nomination (McMahon 2007 and 2016). However, both of those works focus only on nominations made after 1900. Given the contentiousness of the confirmation process during the nineteenth century, and the fact that a few of the votes in the twentieth century barely surpassed the 20 percent figure, I have raised the contentiousness bar to 25 percent or more in this analysis to better reflect the nature of opposition during the nearly two centuries of Supreme Court nominations under consideration here.

6. I do not count certain nominations. Specifically, I exclude the following nominations a president sent to the Senate: (1) if the Senate did not act on a nomination, but did confirm the same nominee with little opposition when the same president re-nominated him again soon thereafter (i.e., Pierce Butler and the second John M. Harlan); and (2) if a president withdrew a nomination to fill an associate position in order to appoint the same nominee to chief justice (i.e., John Roberts). I do include the nomination of Homer Thornberry, and I do so based on the thinking that while the Senate could deny Associate Justice Abe Fortas's elevation to chief, he would still stay on the Court if that nomination failed. Therefore, in rejecting Fortas's move to

the center chair, the Senate effectively denied Thornberry a seat on the high bench. I also count the nomination of Douglas Ginsburg because while President Ronald Reagan never officially sent it to the Senate, he had every intention of doing so when he announced his choice. Additionally, I treat voice votes for Senate confirmation as unanimous votes. While it is clear that some voice votes did not mean that all voting senators supported a particular nominee, I am focusing on nominations that attracted significant opposition (more than 25 percent of voting senators). It seems reasonable to conclude that those confirmed by voice vote did not attract this level of opposition. Moreover, since there is no historical record of the level of opposition for these votes, my only options were to exclude them entirely or to treat them as unanimous. Given the number of voice votes over the period under consideration, the first option was hardly an option at all. Therefore, I chose the admittedly problematic second option. Finally, when the Senate did not have a floor vote on a nomination, I reasoned that the number of senators in opposition was at least equal to the number necessary to block the nomination. Before the filibuster, that represented a majority of 51 percent. After the filibuster became part of Senate rules in 1917, it represented 34 percent and then—after 1975—41 percent of senators in opposition. Those percentages are represented in figures 3.1 and 3.2. However, to display all votes with the same percentage of senators opposed in a year when there was more than one, I altered the percentages slightly.

7. There were also two instances where the Senate confirmed a nominee who then declined to serve on the Court.

8. I define a narrow win as one in which the victor captured less than 50 percent of the popular vote in a two-candidate contest and won by less than a 5 percent margin.

9. McCloskey 1960, 225.

10. I consider the Jacksonian period to have begun in 1824, four years prior to Andrew Jackson's election to the presidency, because that was the first presidential election in which the popular vote mattered. Additionally, Jackson captured the largest share of the popular vote in that election with 41.36 percent. John Quincy Adams won just 30.92 percent of that vote. While Jackson also won a plurality of electoral votes, he did not have a majority of them. That sent the race to the House of Representatives, which elected Adams president.

11. The appointees of the president at the end of the period also struggled to win confirmation.

12. Although as I note below, one—William Smith—declined to serve.

13. Nettels 1925, 225–26; see also Braver 2020, 2762–68, and Crowe 2012, chapter 3.

14. Abraham 1999, 76–77.

15. Dred Scott v. Sandford, 60 U.S. (19 How.) 393 (1857), superseded by U.S. Const. amend. XIV.

16. Abraham 1999, 93.

17. The Senate also confirmed Roscoe Conkling in 1882, but he declined to serve. However, the vote of 39–12 (23.53 percent opposing) does meet the necessary level of 25 percent of senators in opposition to be defined as contentious.

18. Dalin 2017, 50.

19. Norris quoted in Hendel 1951, 79.

20. Exactly 25 percent of voting senators opposed Sherman Minton's confirmation. A number of factors—including the comparatively low number of senators voting—make that vote—48 to 16—unusual. Indeed, ten senators announced their support for him but were absent for the vote (McMahon 2007, 940).

21. Gallup Poll # 1968-0764, "Supreme Court/Religion/Middle East," Question 9, USGAL-LUP.764.Q09, Gallup Organization (Roper Center for Public Opinion Research, Cornell University, 1968), Dataset, DOI: 10.25940/ROPER-31087744.

22. FDR also elevated Harlan Fiske Stone from associate to chief.

23. "Senators vs. the Court," *New York Times*, July 13, 1968, 26.

24. See generally Baker 1983; Kalman 1990; McMahon 2011.

25. Buchanan 2014, 278. The justices' vote was much more complicated in *Jacobs v. New York* than Buchanan describes. Jacobs v. New York, 388 U.S. 431 (1967).

26. While Segal and Cover did not generate a rating for Thornberry because the filibuster of Fortas meant there would be no vacancy for him to fill, Burger's score of .115 was the most conservative of all the nominees since 1937, the year their ratings begin.

27. Douglas did not serve the full term, retiring on November 12, 1975, shortly after its beginning in early October. He had suffered a debilitating stroke nearly a year earlier but stayed on the Court despite serious limitations.

28. Indeed, LBJ sought to convince senators that by effectively replacing Warren with Thornberry, the Court would be more moderate (Kalman 2017, 137–38).

29. The ideological scores in this chapter are from Martin and Quinn's 2017–2018 analysis. Year-to-year updates typically result in minor changes. For example, in Martin and Quinn's most recent (2021–2022) analysis, the 1975–1976 scores for Douglas and Rehnquist are −7.929 and 4.474, respectively. See Martin and Quinn n.d.

30. From 2014 to 2016, swing justice Anthony Kennedy's ideological rating veered into the negative side of the ideological divide. He returned to the conservative fold in 2017 and remained there until his retirement a year later.

31. McMahon 2018a, 355–56.

32. The Senate also rejected two nominees appointed by President Grant in 1873 and 1874. But as noted above, the Senate's treatment of Grant's nominees was unusually hostile for an electorally dominant president.

Chapter Four

1. "Rather's Familiar Quotations," *The Atlantic*, March 2005, https://www.theatlantic.com /magazine/archive/2005/03/rathers-familiar-quotations/303736/.

2. Hubert Humphrey's 13 in 1968; George McGovern's 1 in 1972; Jimmy Carter's 23 in 1976 and 6 in 1980; Walter Mondale's 1 in 1984; and Michael Dukakis's 10 in 1988. The Democrats also won the District of Columbia in each of these six presidential races.

3. See the Martin-Quinn scores, for example.

4. For example, a late August/early September 2000 Gallup poll showed 62 percent of respondents approved of "the way the Supreme Court is handling its job," while 29 percent disapproved. This was the last time Gallup asked this question in the divided government era. When Gallup asked the question in a poll conducted from September 1 to September 16, 2022, the Court's approval had fallen to 40 percent, and 58 percent disapproved. Data available at https:// news.gallup.com/poll/4732/supreme-court.aspx.

5. I do not include the nomination of Homer Thornberry nor the elevation of William Rehnquist to chief here. I exclude these because with the filibuster of Fortas, there was no vacancy for Thornberry to fill, since Fortas was still an associate justice. Similarly, even if the Senate rejected Rehnquist's move to the center chair, he would have remained on the Court. In other words, I include only those appointments that potentially added a new member to the Court.

6. For two of the vacancies—those of Abe Fortas in 1969 and Lewis Powell in 1987—two nominees failed before a third was confirmed.

7. See Massaro 1990. On Fortas, see also Kalman 1990. On Carswell, see also McMahon 2011. On Bork, see also Bronner 1989.

8. Massaro 1990, 15–17.

9. According to Martin-Quinn scores.

10. I use these first three time periods because presumably senators and the appointing president would best be able to estimate a nominee's potential ideology as a justice during the time closest to the confirmation vote.

11. Ideology scores in table 4.1 are from Martin and Quinn's 2017–2018 analysis. See note 29 in chapter 3 regarding slight year-to-year changes.

12. These scores estimate the perceived ideology and qualifications of nominees based on analysis of editorials from six major newspapers at the time of their appointment. For ideology—the focus here—a score of 0 is the most conservative and 1 is the most liberal. Scalia had a more conservative rating—based on Segal-Cover scores—than Rehnquist (both for his appointment as associate and his elevation to chief). Burger, Blackmun, and Scalia had more conservative ratings than Thomas.

13. Evans and Novak 1971, 159.

14. McMahon 2011, chapter 6. It is also important to note that the Segal-Cover scores were not very good predictors of the eventual ideological voting records of the Nixon justices. For example, while Burger and Blackmun had the same exact Segal-Cover score (table 4.1), they did not vote like "Minnesota Twins" soon after they both assumed their seats on the high bench (figure 4.1).

15. Massaro 1990, 86.

16. Massaro (1990, 133) adds that this does not mean Carswell was destined for defeat: "Carswell's conservative ideology made confirmation more difficult but not impossible."

17. Frank 1991.

18. Specifically, 39.5 percent of Republican senators voted against Haynsworth's confirmation, making up 30.9 percent of the opposition. In Carswell's case, 31.7 percent of GOP senators opposed him, which was 25.5 percent of those voting against confirmation. Thus, party disunity was a factor in both defeats. If Republican senators had united in support of their president's choice—and Democratic senators did not vote differently—both Haynsworth and Carswell would have easily won confirmation (McMahon 2007, 922–24; see also McMahon 2011, chapter 6).

19. McMahon 2011, 123, 129.

20. Kennedy quoted in Bronner 1989, 98.

21. Forty Senate Republicans supported Bork.

22. After the 1982 elections, the southern delegation was split in two, each party with eleven seats.

23. Black and Black 2002, 83.

24. In 1971, of the thirty Democrats voting in support of Rehnquist's nomination, twenty represented either the South or a southern border state. Of those twenty-three Democrats voting against confirmation, only one was from the South and another from a border state. Fifteen years later, the southern Democrats also supported Rehnquist's elevation to chief, although with Republicans in the majority Democratic support was not required. Of the sixteen Democrats supporting his elevation, ten represented a southern state and two a border state. Only two southerners opposed Rehnquist's second confirmation. However, as noted below, successful opposition to Rehnquist's elevation would not have altered the ideological dynamics of the Court, since he would have remained as an associate justice.

25. For an explanation of the significance of biracial coalitions for southern Democratic candidates in the 1986 Senate elections, see McMahon 2007, 927–28.

26. Smith 1993; Robert H. Bork, "Civil Rights—A Challenge," *The New Republic*, August 31, 1963, 21–24.

27. Steven V. Roberts, "White House Says Bork Lacks Votes for Confirmation," *New York Times*, September 26, 1987, A32.

28. The two Senate Democrats who supported confirmation were Ernest "Fritz" Hollings of South Carolina and David Boren of the border state of Oklahoma.

29. Segal-Cover score. Only Antonin Scalia matched that rating for the justices appointed from 1937 to 2010.

30. His Segal-Cover score was .365.

31. Savage 1992, 5; quoted in Massaro 1990, 196.

32. See, for example, Bork 1990 and 1996.

33. Kevin Cope and Joshua Fischman, "It's Hard to Find a Federal Judge More Conservative than Brett Kavanaugh," *Washington Post*, September 5, 2018, https://www.washingtonpost.com/news/monkey-cage/wp/2018/09/05/its-hard-to-find-a-federal-judge-more-conservative-than-brett-kavanaugh/?noredirect=on&utm_term=.e2997c7c5507.

34. Savage 1992, 5.

35. Richard Nixon, "Remarks Announcing Judge Warren Earl Burger to be Chief Justice of the United States," May 21, 1969, American Presidency Project, https://www.presidency.ucsb.edu.

36. McMahon 2011, 88–89, 114.

37. According to Martin-Quinn scores.

38. O'Brien 1991, 103–26, 103.

39. Ford quoted in O'Brien, 104.

40. O'Brien, 109, 112.

41. Buchanan quoted in O'Brien, 121.

42. According to Martin-Quinn scores.

43. McMahon 2011, 130–31.

44. Believing Powell to be an "elitist" who did not display "any deep feelings for little people," Democratic Senator Fred Harris of Oklahoma opposed him. Perhaps notably, Harris had announced he was not seeking reelection in 1972. Fred P. Graham, "Senate Confirms Powell by 89 to 1 for Black's Seat," *New York Times*, December 7, 1971.

45. McMahon 2011, 149–50.

46. As California governor, Reagan had signed even stronger pro-choice legislation.

47. On the internal disputes between social conservatives and the Reagan White House on the possibility of an O'Connor appointment, see Flowers 2019, chapter 3.

48. All quotes appear in Witt 1986, 7.

49. Author interview with Reagan pollster Richard Wirthlin, July 2006.

50. Savage 1992, 5.

51. Fred P. Graham, "Burger and Blackmun: Opinions Similar," *New York Times*, April 15, 1970.

52. On Burger's maneuvering on *Roe*, see Woodward and Armstrong (1979) 1981, 199–202.

53. According to Martin-Quinn scores.

54. Steve A. Matthews to Special Project Committee, May 23, 1986, 7–8, Peter Wallison Files, Reagan Presidential Library, https://www.reaganlibrary.gov/public/digitallibrary/smof/counsel/wallison/oa14287/40-592-70155996-oa14287-013-2017.pdf.

55. Quoted in Maltz 2003, 141–42.

56. Quoted in Linda Greenhouse, "Reagan Nominates Anthony Kennedy to the Court," *New York Times*, November 12, 1987.

57. Fineman quoted in Gitenstein 1992, 330.

58. Maureen Dowd, "Dole Wary That Abortion May Color Court Selection," *New York Times*, July 23, 1990.

59. Yalof 1999, 191–92.

60. Richard L. Berke, "Senators Divided on Asking Souter His Abortion View," *New York Times*, July 25, 1990.

61. Morgan 2006, 55. Of course, Republican President Dwight D. Eisenhower appointed Brennan to the Court.

62. Toobin 2012, 122.

63. Lyndon B. Johnson's selection of Thurgood Marshall in 1967 and Bill Clinton's choice of Ruth Bader Ginsburg in 1993.

64. Yalof 1999, 200–201.

65. Yalof, 203–5.

66. McMahon 2011, 7–8.

67. McMahon 2011, chapter 7.

68. "Nixon's Not So Supreme Court," *Time*, October 25, 1971.

69. McMahon 2011, 162.

70. Just three of the forty-one Republicans voting opposed Rehnquist's confirmation. The result—despite a Democratic majority in the Senate—was a contested but fairly comfortable victory for President Nixon's sixth High Court nominee. Republicans may have fallen into line with the Rehnquist vote because of Nixon's willingness to challenge incumbent members of his own party in the 1970 midterm elections and because of the upcoming presidential campaign season.

71. Of the thirty Democrats voting in support, twenty represented either the South or a southern border state. Of those twenty-three Democrats voting against confirmation, only one was from the South and another from a border state.

72. Richard Nixon, telephone conversation with Attorney General John Mitchell, October 21, 1971, Richard Nixon Presidential Library, Yorba Linda, CA.

73. With two Republicans absent, even if all voting Democrats joined the two dissenting Republicans, the vote would have produced a tie, with Vice President George Herbert Walker Bush undoubtedly casting the deciding vote in favor of confirmation.

74. Abraham 1999, 292.

75. From the 2021–2022 Martin-Quinn analysis.

76. According to Wallace Johnson, a Nixon Justice Department attorney who aided with both Rehnquist confirmations, Rehnquist and the team assembled by the Reagan White House "did not prepare any defense nor anticipate any issues arising over the significance of being the Chief as opposed to an Associate." Rather, they believed Senate liberals would oppose Rehnquist based on his ideology; email message from Johnson to author, June 8, 2013.

77. Benno C. Schmidt Jr., "The Rehnquist Court: A Watershed," *New York Times*, June 22, 1986.

78. "Valid Doubts About Justice Rehnquist," *New York Times*, September 11, 1986. See also Yarbrough 2000, chapter 1.

79. Of the sixteen Democrats supporting confirmation, ten represented a southern state and two represented a border state. Only two southerners, both Tennessee Democrats, opposed Rehnquist's second confirmation.

80. Rehnquist did move noticeably to the center after he became chief. During his tenure

as associate justice, his Martin-Quinn average was a 4.18; as chief, it dipped all the way down to 1.98.

81. The word "Bork" even made it into the dictionary. Merriam-Webster's defines it as follows: "to attack or defeat (a nominee or candidate for public office) unfairly through an organized campaign of harsh public criticism or vilification"—https://www.merriam-webster.com/dictionary/bork. For a fuller definition, see Safire 2008, 74–75.

82. The "Saturday Night Massacre" stemmed from President Richard Nixon's desire to fire special prosecutor Archibald Cox in the midst of the Watergate scandal. Attorney General Elliot Richardson refused to follow the president's order to dismiss Cox and resigned immediately. Nixon then ordered the next in line, Deputy Attorney General William Ruckelshaus, to fire Cox. Like Richardson, Ruckelshaus refused and resigned immediately. As Solicitor General, Bork was the third highest ranking official in the Justice Department. With Richardson and Ruckelshaus gone, Nixon asked him to carry out the deed. Bork agreed and fired Cox. It all happened on the evening of Saturday, October 20, 1973.

83. Yalof 1999, 153.

84. Quoted in Biskupic 2009, 106.

85. *The Italian Americans*, "Breaking Through," clip from episode 4, "The American Dream," written and directed by John Maggio, aired February 24, 2015, on PBS, https://www.pbs.org/video/italian-americans-breaking-through/.

86. Segal-Cover scores begin in 1937.

87. Quoted in Mayer and Abramson 1994, 20. Thomas's perceived ideological score of .160 was higher (i.e., more liberal) than those of Rehnquist, Scalia, Bork, and Ginsburg, but from the conservative perspective it represented a significant improvement over the preceding two Republican nominees (Kennedy and Souter). Indeed, the political scientist Michael Comiskey concludes that Thomas was "lightly qualified, politically extreme, and temperamentally injudicious" (2004, 132); see also Maureen Dowd, "Bush's 'Best Man,'" *New York Times,* July 2, 1991.

88. If not for the late sexual harassment revelations from Anita Hill, the 52–48 Democratic majority Senate would have confirmed Thomas by a slightly more comfortable margin. Three Democrats—Richard Bryan and Harry Reid of Nevada, and Joe Lieberman of Connecticut—joined the opposition after hearing of Anita Hill's accusations. Richard L. Berke, "The Thomas Nomination: Senators Who Switched Tell of Political Torment," *New York Times*, October 15, 1991.

89. For instance, according to Jane Mayer and Jill Abramson, both Georgia's Wyche Fowler and North Carolina's Terry Stanford supported Thomas because they expected that their support would aid their reelection campaigns (1994, 206). In addition, L. Marvin Overby and his colleagues display, using a logistical regression model, that moderate Democratic senators from states with high African American populations had a greater likelihood of voting for Thomas, especially if they were facing reelection in 1992 (Overby et al. 1992).

90. Indeed, despite their commitment to a conservative Court, Ronald Reagan and George Bush made three appointments—O'Connor, Kennedy, and Souter—that, according to Segal-Cover scores, were the most moderate Republican nominees since Eisenhower's selection of Potter Stewart in 1959. Moreover, both Clinton nominees were the two most moderate appointed by a Democratic president since President Harry Truman's choices, Harold Burton and Tom Clark—Segal-Cover scores .280 and .500, respectively—in the 1940s.

91. Tushnet 2005, 9–11; see also Keck 2007.

92. Morgan 2006, 51, 55, emphasis added. His six issues are: civil rights, speech, establishment clause, unenumerated fundamental rights, criminal procedure, and federalism.

93. Segal and Spaeth 2002, 217, emphasis added.

94. As noted above, there were also no vacancies during the one-term presidency of Jimmy Carter.

95. FDR also elevated Harlan Fiske Stone—who had been appointed by a Republican president—from associate to chief. Including Stone, he made nine appointments to the Court, but one—James Byrnes—served only one year.

96. Arthur Goldberg resigned to become US ambassador to the United Nations.

97. Based on Quinn-Martin scores, the four most conservative justices at the end of the 1960–61 term were: Clark (.797), Whittaker (1.278), Frankfurter (1.763), and Harlan (1.907). The first three would retire by the end of LBJ's presidency. Segal and Spaeth (2002, 219–20) do make this same point about the ideological significance of departures.

98. The four most conservative justices at the end of the 1980–81 term were: Stewart (.669), Powell (.829), Burger (1.419), and Rehnquist (4.336). The first three would retire by the end of Reagan's presidency.

99. On abortion, see, for example, Keck and McMahon 2016.

100. See, for example, McMahon 2004 and 2011.

101. Rehnquist survived a contested confirmation twice; his 1986 elevation to chief occurred during GOP control of the Senate. See also note 6 above.

102. McMahon 2007.

103. McCloskey 1960, 225, 224.

Chapter Five

1. Green 2017.

2. Dahl 1957, 283.

3. See, however, Graber 1993.

4. Officially, the sixth version of the Rehnquist Court went unchanged for eleven years and two months (August 3, 1994–September 29, 2005). The earlier Court—the sixth version of the Marshall Court—was in place for eleven years and seven months (February 3, 1812–September 1, 1823). Epstein et al. 2021, 411–21.

5. On super-precedent, see Gerhardt 2006.

6. Greenburg 2007, 241–42. The elder Bush also considered his choice of Souter a mistake (Kaplan 2018, 55).

7. Greenburg 2007, 265.

8. Jim Yardley, "Bush Choices for Court Seen as Moderates," *New York Times*, July 9, 2000; Editorial, "A Republican Full House," *New York Times*, December 2, 1999.

9. See Sunstein 2005 for a discussion of these divisions within conservative judicial thought.

10. To be sure, Republican thought on a more ideologically conservative Court was not united. After Miers's forced withdrawal, Republican Congressman Tom Davis of Virginia, considered one of the party's sharpest electoral strategists, warned of a "sea change in suburban voting patterns" if an unflinching conservative Court discarded *Roe*. "If *Roe v. Wade* is overturned," Davis speculated, "you're going to have a lot of very nervous suburban candidates out there. . . . It's easy to say you're for a culture of life, but the answer is what do you do about it at that point." The Republican pollster Linda DiVall saw less of a suburban backlash on the horizon than Davis did, but still thought an anti-*Roe* decision would put the GOP further on the

defensive in suburban areas. Quoted in Dan Balz, "Rep. Davis Warns of Backlash if *Roe v. Wade* Is Overturned," *Washington Post*, November 17, 2005.

11. See, for example, *Frontline* interviews with leading Republican strategists, retrieved by author in October 2008 at: http://www.pbs.org/wgbh/pages/frontline/shows/architect/rove/2004.html.

12. Ceaser and Busch 2005; Toobin 2007, 264–65.

13. Quoted in Greenburg 2007, 213.

14. Bush 2010.

15. Elisabeth Bumiller, "Pillow-Talk Call for a Woman to Fill O'Connor Seat," *New York Times*, July 18, 2005; Bush 2010, 99.

16. Greenburg 2007, 247–48. Harriet Miers was among the White House lawyers who supported Alito (Greenburg 2007, 247).

17. Greenburg 2007, 245. In his 2010 memoir, Bush notes that he wanted a diverse pool of candidates for the Supreme Court from the start of his presidency, telling then White House counsel Alberto Gonzales that the "list should include women, minorities, and people with no previous experience on the bench" (Bush 2010, 97).

18. George W. Bush, "Nomination of Harriet Miers to the Supreme Court," October 3, 2005, American Presidency Project, https://www.presidency.ucsb.edu.

19. Quoted in Greenburg 2007, 264.

20. Greenburg, 265–66.

21. Quoted in Greenburg, 256; see also Toobin 2007, 283.

22. Jeffrey Toobin, "Full Court Press," *New Yorker*, April 17, 2017. On the Federalist Society, see also Hollis-Brusky 2015 and Teles 2008.

23. William Kristol, "Disappointed, Depressed and Demoralized: A Reaction to the Harriet Miers Nomination," *Weekly Standard*, October 3, 2005.

24. Toobin 2007, 292–93.

25. At the same time, the Segal-Cover perceived qualifications scores highlight the concerns about Miers in comparison to Roberts and Alito. For these three, the perceived qualifications scores—ranging from 0 (least qualified) to 1 (most qualified)—were: Roberts (.970), Miers (.360), and Alito (.810).

26. Quoted in Toobin 2007, 293.

27. The tendency of conservatives to shift to the left as been termed the "Greenhouse Effect." I discuss it in detail in chapter 7. Greenburg defines it as "the temptation a justice faces to drift left to appeal to the press, and to veteran *New York Times* Supreme Court reporter Linda Greenhouse in particular" (Greenburg 2007, 161). See also Baum and Devins 2010 and Devins and Baum 2019.

28. In particular, his administration's response to Hurricane Katrina in late August was considered woefully inadequate, and the War in Iraq was producing an alarming rise in violence and American causalities. Driven by these events, his approval rating dipped below 40 percent. Added to this increasingly problematic climate, Miers consistently performed poorly in practice hearings and in individual meetings with senators (more on that in chapter 7).

29. Greenburg 2007, 282–84; Toobin 2007, 294–97.

30. Toobin 2007, 297.

31. Quoted in Lara Jakes Jordan, "Specter Warns Bush on Picks for Top Court," *Pittsburgh Post-Gazette*, November 4, 2004.

32. Toobin 2007, 266.

33. Ideology scores in table 5.1 are from Martin and Quinn's 2021–2022 analysis.

34. Hollis-Brusky 2015, 155; Greenburg 2007, 187–93.

35. Bush 2010, 98.

36. For more on the Roberts/Kavanaugh relationship before both joined the Court, see Calmes 2021, 11.

37. The four occasions are as follows: Fortas and Thornberry in 1968; Burger and Haynsworth in 1969 (while Nixon did not appoint Haynsworth until August 18, 1969, when senators confirmed Burger on June 9, 1969, they did so with the knowledge that the president would soon make another appointment to fill the Fortas seat. Fortas resigned on May 14, 1969); Powell and Rehnquist in 1971; and Rehnquist and Scalia in 1986. It's important to note that in 1968 and 1986, there was effectively only one vacancy, since Fortas and Rehnquist would stay on the Court if denied elevation. And that's what happened when the Senate effectively filibustered Fortas's attempted move to chief, thereby precluding consideration of the Thornberry nomination. Nevertheless, by selecting an associate for chief, the appointing president named two jurists, both of whom the Senate would have to confirm.

38. McMahon 2007, 938.

39. His Segal-Cover score was also higher (i.e., more liberal) than Rehnquist's when he was appointed in both 1971 and 1986. Finally, the average Martin-Quinn score for Rehnquist's last five years was 1.4214, while the average for Roberts's first five years was the ever so slightly more liberal 1.4116.

40. Charles Schumer, "Judging by Ideology," *New York Times*, June 26, 2001.

41. "Confirmation Hearing on the Nomination of John G. Roberts, Jr. to be Chief Justice of the United States," *Committee on the Judiciary, United States Senate*, September 12–15, 2005, 378–79, https://www.govinfo.gov/content/pkg/GPO-CHRG-ROBERTS/pdf/GPO-CHRG-ROBERTS.pdf.

42. Toobin 2007, 298.

43. Scherer 2005, 11–27, 26–27.

44. Sheryl Gay Stolberg and David D. Kirkpatrick, "Top Democrat Says He'll Vote No on Roberts," *New York Times*, September 21, 2005.

45. McMahon 2007.

46. David D. Kirkpatrick, "Kerry Gets Cool Response to Call to Filibuster Alito," *New York Times*, January 27, 2006.

47. Chafee had already made clear his distaste for George W. Bush by writing in the president's father's name when he cast his ballot in 2004. In 2010, Chafee won the Rhode Island governorship as an independent before joining the Democratic Party in 2013. He briefly sought his new party's 2016 presidential nomination. In 2019, he left the Democrats for the Libertarian Party. In 2020, he unsuccessfully sought that party's presidential nomination. So, clearly Chafee's views were inconsistent with the 2005 Republican majority in the Senate.

48. "Remarks on the Nomination of Amy Coney Barrett to Be a United States Supreme Court Associate Justice," September 26, 2020, American Presidency Project, https://www.presidency .ucsb.edu.

49. Garner 2018, 3.

50. Jimmy Carter was the only Democrat to serve as president during this period, and there was no Supreme Court vacancy during his four years in the White House.

51. Erickson quoted in Alan Rappeport and Charlie Savage, "Donald Trump Releases List of Possible Supreme Court Picks," *New York Times*, May 18, 2016.

52. Emphasis added. The September 23, 2016, Trump statement including the updated list is available at https://www.breitbart.com/politics/2016/09/23/donald-trump-expands-supreme -court-justice-list-includes-mike-lee/, accessed April 23, 2019.

53. Devins and Baum 2019.

54. Alicia Parlapiano and Karen Yourish, "Where Would Neil Gorsuch Fit on the Supreme Court?," *New York Times*, January 31, 2017. See also Epstein, Martin, and Quinn 2016a and 2016b.

55. Gorsuch 2006, 4–5, 170.

56. Kaplan 2018, 46.

57. To be sure, the elimination of the filibuster began with the November 2013 decision of Democratic Senate majority leader Harry Reid to remove the 60-vote rule on all judicial nominations, except those for the Supreme Court.

58. In his first four terms on the high bench, he has averaged a Martin-Quinn score of just under 1 (.982). In his last full term, Scalia's score was a 1.62.

59. Kaplan 2018, 52.

60. The other "extreme conservative" was Republican Senator Mike Lee of Utah. As the most conservative member of the Senate, they predicted that if selected he would be "to the right of even Thomas." Epstein, Martin, and Quinn 2018, 7. Available at: https://static1.squarespace .com/static/60188505fb790b33c3d33a61/t/6050e26214e1e364335b4a3d/1615913570955/Replacing JusticeKennedy.pdf.

61. Christine Blasey Ford, "Kavanaugh Hearing: Transcript," *Washington Post*, September 27, 2018, https://www.washingtonpost.com/news/national/wp/2018/09/27/kavanaugh-hearing -transcript/.

62. https://insider.foxnews.com/2018/09/27/chris-wallace-christine-blasey-ford-testimony -rachel-mitchell-disaster-republicans.

63. "Kavanaugh Hearing: Transcript," *Washington Post*, September 27, 2018, https://www .washingtonpost.com/news/national/wp/2018/09/27/kavanaugh-hearing-transcript/.

64. Yalof 1999, 164.

65. Hill's allegations also altered the final confirmation vote for Thomas, see note 88 in chapter 4.

66. Murkowski ultimately agreed to pair her "no" vote with the "yes" vote of another Republican who was absent to attend his daughter's wedding. As a result, the final vote was 50 to 48.

67. Ginsburg's figures were 23 percent and 11 percent—Epstein, Martin, and Quinn 2020, 8.

68. Nicholas Fandos, "Senate Confirms Barrett, Delivering for Trump and Reshaping the Court," *New York Times*, October 26, 2020.

69. Toobin 2012, 125.

70. Specifically, thirty-one senators, all Republicans, opposed Sotomayor (31.3 percent of the vote). Thirty-seven senators—thirty-six Republicans and Democrat Ben Nelson of the red state of Nebraska—opposed Kagan (meaning GOP opposition was 36 percent of the vote). Only Republicans opposed Fuller and Lamar. Twenty Republicans opposed Fuller (31.9 percent) in a July 20, 1888, vote. And twenty-eight Republicans opposed Lamar (46.7 percent) in a January 16, 1888, vote.

71. Toobin 2012, 127; Biskupic 2014, 97.

72. D'Amato would nevertheless lose the race to Chuck Schumer.

73. Toobin 2012, 127; Biskupic 2014, 160.

74. Biskupic 2014, 166.

75. Milbank quoted in Biskupic, 169.

76. Toobin 2012, 127; Biskupic 2014, 160.

77. David Axelrod, "A Surprising Request from Justice Scalia," CNN, March 9, 2016, https://www.cnn.com/2016/02/14/opinions/david-axelrod-surprise-request-from-justice-scalia/index.html.

78. Peter Baker, "Kagan Nomination Leaves Longing on the Left," *New York Times*, May 10, 2010.

79. Adam Liptak, "Court Under Roberts Is Most Conservative in Decades," *New York Times*, July 24, 2010; see also Landes and Posner 2009 and Epstein, Landes, and Posner 2013.

80. Toobin 2012, 221.

81. Toobin, 226.

82. Ben Nelson of Nebraska.

83. Epstein, Martin, and Quinn 2018, 7. Available at: https://static1.squarespace.com/static/60188505fb790b33c3d33a61/t/6050e26214e1e364335b4a3d/1615913570955/ReplacingJusticeKennedy.pdf.

84. However, Richard Mourdock, Lugar's successful Republican challenger, would lose the general election to Democrat Joe Donnelly. Many commentators attributed Donnelly's win in otherwise Republican Indiana to Mourdock's comments about rape late in the campaign. In response to a question about abortion during a late October debate, he said: "even when life begins in that horrible situation of rape, that it is something that God intended to happen." Quoted in Jonathan Wiesman, "Rape Comment Draws Attention in Indiana," *New York Times*, October 24, 2010.

85. Gail Russell Chaddock, "Retiring Senators: Why Are So Many Calling It Quits?," *Christian Science Monitor*, February 22, 2010; Olympia J. Snowe, "Why I'm Leaving the Senate," *Washington Post*, March 1, 2012.

86. The other Republicans were: Susan Collins of Maine and Lindsay Graham of South Carolina. Obama lost South Carolina. He also lost Nebraska, the home state of the sole Democrat—Ben Nelson—who opposed Kagan.

87. See, for example, Cable News Network (CNN), CNN/ORC Poll: 2016 Presidential Election/ Primary and Caucus Process/ Donald Trump and Hillary Clinton Comparisons/ Transgender Protection and Gay Rights, Question 70, USORC.050616.R36, Opinion Research Corporation, (Roper Center for Public Opinion Research, Cornell University, 2016), Dataset, DOI: 10.25940/ROPER-31095604.

88. Levitsky and Ziblatt 2018, 145–46.

89. Forty-three senators were opposed; the remaining twelve were absent.

90. On the specifics of the Fortas vote, see Massaro 1990, 25–31.

91. Or was Warren's decision to retire reached after he concluded that Nixon would likely win the White House, the real attempt at theft? Surely no one accused the chief justice, the leader of the Court's drive to expand American democracy by protecting civil rights and individual liberties, of undermining it. Rather, the decision was viewed as a deft political move. Some senators did call on LBJ to allow the victor of the presidential election in November to fill the seat. But no one expected him to listen. For its part, the *New York Times* editorial board likened these Senate obstructionists to those who had once funded "Impeach Earl Warren" billboards on roadways across America. "The words do not come out that way but the tune comes through. . . . President Johnson has not the right to appoint another liberal to replace Chief Justice Warren." "Senators vs. the Court," *New York Times*, July 13, 1968.

92. McMahon 2011, 34; Buchanan 2014, 276.

93. This is evident in the lives of nominees the Senate rejected during the New Deal and divided government eras, who undoubtedly wondered if it was worth it at all. Most notoriously,

after his defeat, G. Harrold Carswell left his Court of Appeals judgeship to run for the Senate in Florida, only to be routed in the GOP primary. The most stinging line in his opponent campaign: "In these trying times, this country needs excellence in the Senate—not more mediocrity" (McMahon 2011, 142). A few years later, after returning to private practice, he was arrested for simple battery (i.e., unwanted touching) and for making an "unnatural and lascivious" advance on an undercover vice squad officer he met in a shopping mall men's room and then drove to a secluded wooded area. After the arrest, he was hospitalized for "nervous exhaustion and depression." He was hospitalized again a few years after that when a man Carswell had invited back to his hotel room repeatedly hit him on the head "with a sharp, heavy object." ("Carswell Indicted on Vice Charge," *News-Press* [Fort Myers], July 1, 1976, 3; "Carswell Attacked in Atlanta Hotel Room," *Tallahassee Democrat*, September 12, 1979, 7.) Robert Bork left the appellate bench as well after his failed bid for the Court. He became a best-selling author of books that celebrated his conservatism, but tinged with an anger about what might have been. Only Clement Haynsworth stayed on the Court of Appeals, earning a reputation as a very fine judge who had been treated very unfairly by the US Senate. "Several senators sent him private communications saying their criticism of his judicial philosophy and ethics were not directed at him personally . . . but this was of little help." As he recalled, "I was the one whose head was being pounded." And those questions about his ethics always remained (Brett Barnes, "Rejected Nixon Appointee Clement Haynsworth Dies," *Washington Post*, November 23, 1989). See also Frank 1991. For his part, by the end of the confirmation process Justice Abe Fortas was a diminished man, no longer praised in Washington in superlative terms. Less than a year later, he was forced to resign from the Court under threat of impeachment or indictment. It was the result of a plan hatched by the Nixon White House and carried out by Justice Department officials, including Attorney General John Mitchell—and Assistant Attorney General William Rehnquist (Jenkins 2012, 91–93; see also Kalman 1990, 317–78; Kalman 2017). After his resignation, Fortas remained in DC, returning to private practice and even appearing before his former High Court colleagues on occasion. But if LBJ had not sought to elevate him to chief justice in the summer of 1968, he most likely would have been sitting next to those on the bench, not standing in front of them.

94. According to one report, Garland was most worried "that he would be dragged through the mud, and he was very thankful that never happened to him and his family" (Hulse 2019, 158).

95. In the case of Fortas, this majority was bipartisan.

96. Kalman 2017, 194; see also Jenkins 2012, 91–93.

97. Dean 2001, 11; McMahon 2011, 113–14.

98. Amelia Thomson-DeVeaux and Rachael Dottle, "If Justice Kennedy Retires, His Replacement Could Undermine His Legacy," *FiveThirtyEight*, April 16, 2018; Epstein, Martin, Segal, and Westerland 2007, 303–25. Updated data available at: https://epstein.usc.edu/jcs.

99. See also Steven Mazie, "The Supreme Court Justices Do Not Seem to Be Getting Along," *The Atlantic*, January 16, 2023, https://www.theatlantic.com/ideas/archive/2023/01/supreme-court-justices-public-conflict/672494/.

100. McCloskey 1960, 225.

Chapter Six

1. See chapter 9.

2. The recently retired Stephen Breyer also attended the public honors Lowell High School in San Francisco.

3. For what it's worth, the 2024–2025 *U.S. News* rankings for the two schools are 27 and 56, respectively.

4. Centre Law School ceased operations in 1912. Centre College still exists as a small liberal arts college. In 1956, Saint Paul Law School merged with Minneapolis-Minnesota College of Law to become William Mitchell College of Law. In 2015, William Mitchell College of Law merged with Hamline University School of Law to become Mitchell Hamline School of Law.

5. Kalman 2017, 137; William Rehnquist, "Letter to the Editor: A Reply to Two Editorials on the Carswell Nomination," *Washington Post*, February 14, 1970.

6. Kalman 2017, 237; Congressional Record, March 16, 1970, 7487.

7. Kalman 2017, 237.

8. This figure includes Lewis Powell and Ruth Bader Ginsburg. Powell graduated from Washington and Lee School of Law and then earned a Master of Laws (LLM) degree at Harvard Law. Ginsburg attended Harvard Law for her first two years, then transferred to Columbia for her third year.

9. Here, I include only those nominees of the twentieth and twenty-first centuries the Senate confirmed. I also do not count associate justices elevated directly to chief: namely, Harlan Fiske Stone in 1941, and William Rehnquist in 1986. I do include Charles Evans Hughes twice because he left the Court for fourteen years before returning as chief, in which case he was filling a vacancy, not moving chairs. If the Senate had failed to confirm him, he would not have been a member of the Court. Stone and Rehnquist would have kept their associate positions in such a scenario.

10. Warren Burger attended the University of Minnesota, Minneapolis.

11. Charles Whittaker attended what is now the University of Missouri-Kansas City School of Law.

12. Chetty et al. 2017.

13. Markovits 2019, 134, 17.

14. They include information on all nominees, but my focus here is only on those who served on the Court. They add: "The families of some of the nominees, especially in the earlier years of the nation, experienced major upward or downward shifts in their economic status. In such cases, we code the nominees according to that status that best describes the largest segment of their childhood." Epstein, Walker, Staudt, Hendrickson, and Roberts 2022.

15. Harrison 1987, 217, 193.

16. It is interesting to note that these two switches in the socioeconomic backgrounds of a majority of the justices were nearly or totally complete *before* the reconstructive presidencies of Abraham Lincoln and Franklin D. Roosevelt. Given their conflict with the Court, it would not be surprising for either Lincoln or Roosevelt to push the Court in a new direction, as both did. But at least on these terms, change was underfoot before their presidencies. In the second case, the nature of the Senate may have played a role, as five of the seven justices appointed after the entire Senate had been elected by popular vote came from families from the least wealthy three classes.

17. To be sure, questions about their qualifications were likely due more to their race and ethnicity. As noted earlier, Thomas is Black, and Sotomayor is of Puerto Rican descent. See Stephen L. Carter, "What Thurgood Marshall Taught Me," *New York Times Magazine*, July 14, 2021.

18. Both of Jackson's parents started as public school teachers but moved up the educational administrative ladder. Her father, Johnny Brown, earned his JD and eventually became the top attorney for the Dade County School Board. Her mother, Ellery Brown, became the principal at Miami's New World School of the Arts, a magnet public high school.

19. "The American Middle Class Is Losing Ground," Pew Research Center, December 9, 2015, https://www.pewsocialtrends.org/2015/12/09/the-american-middle-class-is-losing-ground/.

20. Joan Biskupic, "An Exclusive Club: Harvard, Yale and Former Clerks Dominate Supreme Court," CNN, October 8, 2018, https://www.cnn.com/2018/10/08/politics/supreme-court-elite -harvard-yale-clerks/index.html.

21. Roberts replaced Rehnquist after his death; Kavanaugh replaced Kennedy after his retirement; Jackson replaced Breyer after his retirement.

22. See also Yalof 1999 and Epstein, Knight, and Martin 2003.

23. William Howard Taft (William McKinley), Fred Vinson (Harry Truman), and Thurgood Marshall (Lyndon B. Johnson).

24. Although in two cases (Taft and Marshall) the decision to leave the Court of Appeals was seemingly based on a presidential promise to appoint the judge to the Supreme Court at a later date.

25. Frankfurter 1957, 795, emphasis added.

26. Blaustein and Mersky 1978.

27. As I write in my book *Nixon's Court*, "four factors most affect[ed] Nixon's two 1971 selections: First, his definition of an acceptable 'conservative' was wide and he didn't inquire deeply—or demand an extensive examination—about the ideological purity of his possible nominees. Put another way, appearance seemed to matter more than a clear commitment to conservative ideals. Second, his political focus was not exclusively southern, but rather was consistent with his desire to build a broad-based national coalition that included the South. Third, he was largely unconcerned about the confirmation climate for his candidates until the very end of the selection process. Fourth, criticisms—mainly from the left—of his tendency to select politically symbolic 'legal lightweights' in hopes of expanding his electoral coalition dominated his thinking in the final moments of the process" (McMahon 2011, 148).

28. Epstein, Knight, and Martin 2003, 914.

29. Rehnquist added: "The combination of inadequate pay and a drawn-out and uncertain confirmation process is a handicap to judicial recruitment across the board, but it most significantly restricts the universe of lawyers in private practice who are willing to be nominated for a federal judgeship." "Chief Justice's 2001 Year-End Report on the Federal Judiciary," News Media, Supreme Court of the United States, January 1, 2002, https://www.supremecourt.gov/publicinfo /year-end/2001year-endreport.aspx.

30. US Senate Justice Committee Questionnaire for Jackson's Supreme Court nomination, https://www.judiciary.senate.gov/imo/media/doc/Jackson%20Public%20SJQ.pdf. The Office of the Federal Public Defender and the US sentencing commission are part of the judicial branch, meaning Justice Jackson never worked outside of the federal judiciary in her many years in government.

31. The exceptions are: Clarence Thomas's short stint as a young attorney in Saint Louis; Elena Kagan's four years at the University of Chicago Law School; Neil Gorsuch's decade-plus on the 10th Court of Appeals in Denver, Colorado; and Amy Coney Barrett's decade and a half at Notre Dame Law School.

32. Even during a confirmation process, nominees typically face a Senate whose ranks include a majority of attorneys.

33. See also Shemtob 2011–2012.

34. On Gorsuch's religion, see Daniel Burke, "What Is Neil Gorsuch's Religion? It's Complicated," CNN Politics, March 22, 2017, https://www.cnn.com/2017/03/18/politics/neil-gorsuch

-religion/. Ketanji Brown Jackson is the other Protestant currently on the Court. She identifies as a nondenominational Protestant.

35. Brandeis and Cardozo for the entirety of the latter's tenure (1932–1938), and Brandeis and Frankfurter for approximately three weeks in 1939.

36. O'Connor and Souter identified as Episcopalian, Rehnquist as Lutheran, and Stevens as simply "Protestant."

37. Yalof 1999, 201.

38. Thomas 2008, 6.

39. De Hart 2018, 305.

40. The other six twentieth-century justices who were over 60 at the time of their nomination were: Horace Lurton (65), George Sutherland (60), James Byrnes (62), Warren Burger (61), Harry Blackmun (61), and Lewis Powell (64). I do not include the sitting associate justices who were elevated to chief at an age past 60. As noted above, no one confirmed by the Senate in the twenty-first century was older than 55, although two failed nominees were: Harriet Miers (60) and Merrick Garland (63).

41. Comiskey 2004, 91.

42. Blaustein and Mersky 1978.

43. See, for example, Nelson 2013 and Epstein, Walker et al. 2022.

44. In addition to the background characteristics I've already discussed, there are a few others that are worth mentioning. I raise them mainly because they define significant swaths of the nation's population today. But as I also note, they described more sitting justices in the past than justices on the Court today.

> Immigration: In a nation whose population is more than 13 percent foreign-born, none of the justices are immigrants. Two are children of at least one immigrant parent. Samuel Alito's father arrived from Italy as an infant. Sonia Sotomayor's parents came to New York City from the US territory of Puerto Rico as young adults. There have only been a half dozen foreign-born justices. George Washington appointed three of those six. The most distinguished of the other three was Felix Frankfurter, who was appointed by FDR in 1939 and served until 1962.

> Military: According the US Department of Veterans Affairs (VA), there were approximately 20.4 million US veterans in 2016, which was less than 10 percent of the nation's adult population. Service in the military was far more common in the past for both the nation as a whole and for those who served on its highest court. About a third of all justices served in one of the military branches. The most notable military veteran who became a justice was undoubtedly Oliver Wendell Holmes, "who served the Union in the Civil War as part of the fabled Twentieth Massachusetts Infantry Regiment. He was wounded three separate times at three separate battles." While at Princeton, Justice Alito was enrolled in ROTC. He also served in the Army Reserves. Alito was on active duty for training for three months. None of the others have been in the military. And none of the justices have served during wartime or on the field of battle. Kristen Bialik, "The Changing Face of America's Veteran Population," Pew Research Center, November 10, 2017, https://www.pewresearch.org/fact-tank/2017/11/10/the-changing-face-of-americas-veteran-population, https://www.theatlantic.com/national/archive/2012/08/none-of-the-supreme-court-justices-has-battle-experience/260973/.

45. Marshall was the last justice of the New Deal period.

46. Thomas 2008, chapter 1.

47. As Joan Biskupic (2014, 22) writes, "in 1957, when the Sotomayors moved into Bronxdale Houses, a low-rent city-run housing project . . . the 'projects' did not have the stigma they gained in the 1960s. . . . Many of the first residents, including the Sotomayors, had come from small, decrepit tenements. Their new homes evoked a sense of prosperity."

48. Thomas and Sotomayor also represent the ideological extremes of the current Court. Thomas has been easily the most conservative justice since he joined the high bench. In recent years, Sotomayor's voting record has been the most liberal.

49. Ginni Thomas, "Justice Clarence Thomas Opens Up on Life, Faith, and His Interracial Marriage," *The Daily Signal*, January 7, 2018, https://www.dailysignal.com/2018/01/07/justice -clarence-thomas-opens-life-faith-interracial-marriage/.

50. In addition to Columbia, the Ivies are Brown, Cornell, Dartmouth, Harvard, Penn, Princeton, and Yale.

51. The other Ivy is Dartmouth. The two Canadian schools are McGill and the University of Toronto.

52. Gladwell 2008, 82–83.

53. Malcolm Gladwell, "Getting In," *The New Yorker*, October 2, 2005.

54. Philip Elman quoted in Kluger 1975, 593–94.

55. Black quoted in Tushnet 1994, 142.

56. Alsop and Catledge 1938, 301; *Time* quoted in Ball 1996, 93; David Lawrence of the *Chicago Tribune* quoted in Leuchtenburg 1995, 186.

57. Newman 1997, 237.

58. Harrison 1987, 296.

59. See Davis 1978 and McMahon 2004, chapter 4.

60. Feldman 2010, 59; Ball 1996, 103; Newman 1997, 225.

61. Van der Veer Hamilton 1972, 5–9, 20.

62. Newman 1997, 8.

63. He had objected to the punishment they gave his sister.

64. Newman 1997, 16–20.

65. Feldman 2010, 54.

66. Feldman 2010, 55; Newman 1997, 30, 32.

67. Dunne 1977, 99.

68. Chambers v. Florida, 309 U.S. 227 (1940); King 2012, 53–54.

69. Feldman 2010, 72–73.

70. Newman 1997, 155–56.

71. Suitts 2005.

72. Paris and McMahon 2015, 78.

73. Van der Veer Hamilton 1972, 304; transcript for PBS documentary, *The Supreme Court* available at: https://www.thirteen.org/wnet/supremecourt/about/pop_transcript3.html. Notably, Black is buried in Arlington National Cemetery in Virginia.

74. Kluger 1975, 210.

75. King 2012, 5, 2–3.

76. Williams 1998, 130–42, 140.

77. King 2012, 17–18.

78. Williams 1998, 138–39.

79. Williams, 142.

80. Williams, 63.

81. Williams, 315; Kalman 2017, 32.

82. "Retirement of Justice Marshall," C-Span, video recording and transcript, June 28, 1991, https://www.c-span.org/video/?18624-1/retirement-justice-marshall.

83. "Texan, 39, Chosen: Civil Rights Advocate Has Been in Justice Agency 6 Years," *New York Times*, March 1, 1967. For a detailed discussion of the president's maneuvering to secure the vacancy for Marshall, see Kalman 2017, chapter 3.

84. Kalman 2017, 91.

85. Williams 1998, 329–30.

86. Kalman 2017, 93.

87. A public ceremony at the Court, with the president in attendance, took place the following day—Williams 1998, 338.

Chapter Seven

1. Yarbrough 2008, vii. Blackmun does add: "But that comes to everybody unless he is a person of great arrogant confidence in himself, I think," *The Justice Harry A. Blackmun Oral History Project*, July 6, 1994–December 15, 1995, 11, https://memory.loc.gov/diglib/blackmun-public /page.html?FOLDERID=D0901&SERIESID=D09.

2. Although see the discussion of Ruth Bader Ginsburg in chapter 8. Harlan was also different given that he only spent fourteen months on the Court of Appeals compared to Blackmun's more than ten years there.

3. I don't include Rehnquist's elevation to chief among the first group because he did not become a "new" justice—he just switched seats. I do include it in the second group because it required Senate confirmation.

4. McMahon 2011, 159.

5. I discuss in detail the decision to select Rehnquist in McMahon 2011, chapter 7.

6. The three main alternatives Nixon considered. Specifically, another southerner (with Powell), a woman, and a Catholic.

7. More specifically, the political scientists Neal Devins and Lawrence Baum define the phenomenon as "the pattern in which some Supreme Court Justices have drifted away from the conservatism of their early votes and opinions towards the stated preferences of cultural elites, including left-leaning journalists and the 'liberal legal establishment that dominates at elite law schools'" (Baum and Devins 2010, 1518). See also note 27 in chapter 5.

8. McMahon 2011, 156.

9. Greenhouse 2005, 48.

10. Nixon would later refer to Carswell as "a bad egg" (McMahon 2011, 129).

11. Yalof 1999, 153.

12. In order of appointment, the four members of his administration were: Stanley Reed as solicitor general, William O. Douglas as chair of the Securities and Exchange Commission, Frank Murphy as attorney general, and Robert Jackson as attorney general. Hugo Black and James Byrnes were US senators. Harlan Fiske Stone was an associate justice before FDR elevated him to chief. Before that, he had been President Calvin Coolidge's attorney general. Wiley Rutledge was a judge on the DC Circuit Court.

13. In actuality, General Hugh Johnson referred to Frankfurter in 1935 as "the most influential single individual in the United States" (Schlesinger 1960, 390).

14. John Marshall Harlan.

15. As noted earlier, Scalia was the first Italian American to become a justice. Douglas Ginsburg's Judaism does not appear to have been a significant factor in his selection (Dalin 2017, 283).

16. Avery and McLaughlin 2013, 27.

17. Linda Greenhouse, "Court Nominee for Supreme Court Admits He Used Marijuana and Regrets It," *New York Times*, November 6, 1987.

18. Dalin 2017, 254.

19. According to an analysis of the oral arguments of the 2004–5 term, Scalia elicited by far the most laughs of any justice, winning in a "landslide" (Wexler 2005, 59).

20. Greenburg 2007, 89–90.

21. Luttig clerked for then Judge Scalia at the DC Court of Appeals.

22. Greenburg 2007, 90–91.

23. Keck and McMahon 2016, 54.

24. Bork also went to Chicago for his BA. Ginsburg attended the Ivy League Cornell for her undergraduate degree.

25. Quoted in McMahon 2011, 163.

26. In addition to emphasizing a high-quality education, as we will see below, another rationale for choosing nominees with connections to these to schools developed over the course of successive Republican administrations: experience in ideological battles raging more fiercely on elite college campuses.

27. This score made Thomas, at least according to Segal and Cover, the most "liberal" of the Republican justices considered a conservative success. But many thought he was just as conservative as Scalia—see note 87 in chapter 4.

28. Avery and McLaughlin 2013, 135.

29. I identify being a judge on the DC Court of Appeals as an additional factor given its importance in the selection of Republican nominees. While circuit court judges were favored over all others, serving on the DC Court was a clear bonus for potential nominees.

30. President Richard Nixon first appointed Garth to the federal district court and then to the third court of appeals.

31. On Gorsuch's religion, see Daniel Burke, "What Is Neil Gorsuch's Religion? It's Complicated," CNN Politics, March 22, 2017, https://www.cnn.com/2017/03/18/politics/neil-gorsuch -religion/.

32. Thomas 2008, 30, 42.

33. There was a similar shared religious background for Democratic nominees. Five of the last seven Democratic nominees were Jewish: Fortas to chief, Ginsburg, Breyer, Kagan, and Garland. Sotomayor is Catholic Jackson identifies as a nondenominational Protestant.

34. Opus Dei is a secretive arm of the Catholic Church known for its conservative positions.

35. Although before becoming a Protestant, Miers was a Catholic. For his part, Bork converted to Catholicism in 2003.

36. Specifically, 50.3 years.

37. Specifically, 54.5 years.

38. Specifically, 51.3 years.

39. Specifically, 56.0 years.

40. Bush 2010, 101.

41. Hollis-Brusky and Wilson 2020, 44.

42. Rehnquist, whom Reagan appointed as chief in 1986, also attended Stanford Law. But he

was first appointed as an associate justice by Nixon in 1971. Ruth Bader Ginsburg attended Harvard Law for two years before transferring to Columbia Law to finish her degree.

43. The publication dates are from Amazon.com. There may have been similar books by conservative activists released during this time, but if so, my search did not turn them up.

44. Meese, "A Constitutional Crisis," in Sutherland 2005, 12.

45. Michael Isikoff, "The Truth Behind the Pillars," *Newsweek*, December 24, 2000.

46. Schmidt 2018.

47. "A Republican Full House," *New York Times*, December 2, 1999; Elisabeth Bumiller, "Bush Vows to Seek Conservative Judges," *New York Times*, March 29, 2002.

48. Bush, October 4, 2005, press conference, https://georgewbush-whitehouse.archives.gov /news/releases/2005/10/20051004-1.html. He made the same point in his memoir: "I was looking for someone who shared my judicial philosophy, *and whose values wouldn't change over time*" (Bush 2010, 96, 98, emphasis added).

49. Bush 2010, 100.

50. Bush, 100.

51. Bush, 101; Jeanne Cummings, "Point Man for Miers Juggles Allegiances," *Wall Street Journal*, October 26, 2005; Jeffrey Toobin, "Full Court Press," *New Yorker*, April 17, 2017. See also Peter Baker and Amy Goldstein, "Nomination Was Plagued By Missteps From the Start," *Washington Post*, October 28, 2005.

52. Bush 2010, 101.

53. Bush, 101.

54. Using the same logic, all conservative thinkers would come from red states. But just a few sentences earlier, she praised the work of Antonin Scalia, born and raised in very blue New York. Coulter herself was born in New York and raised in Connecticut.

55. Robert Bork interview with Madeleine Brand, NPR's *Day to Day*, October 11, 2005, https://www.npr.org/templates/story/story.php?storyId=4954108.

56. Coulter, "This Is What 'Advice and Consent' Means," Anncoulter.com, October 5, 2005, https://anncoulter.com/2005/10/05/this-is-what-advice-and-consent-means/; reprinted in Coulter 2013, 252-54.

57. David D. Kirkpatrick, "Senators in G.O.P. Voice New Doubt on Court Choice," *New York Times*, October 26, 2005.

58. "Bork Calls Miers Nomination a 'Disaster,'" Robert Bork interview with Tucker Carlson, MSNBC, October 7, 2005, https://www.nbcnews.com/id/wbna9623345.

59. Interview with author, May 2003. Toobin 2007, 268-69.

60. Mike Allen and Charles Lane, "President to Oppose Race-Based Admissions," *Washington Post*, January 15, 2003. See also Amy Goldstein and Dana Milbank, "Bush Joins Admissions Case Fight," *Washington Post*, January 16, 2003.

61. Gonzales 2016, 75-77.

62. Greenburg 2007, 188, 225-26, 246-47; Toobin 2007, 267-70.

63. A passage from Alexander Hamilton's *Federalist Paper #76* didn't help the Bush team undercut this concern. For Hamilton, the "advise and consent" clause empowered the Senate to make the president "both ashamed and afraid to bring forward, for the most distinguished or lucrative stations, candidates who had no other merit than that of coming from the same State to which he particularly belonged, or of being in some way or other personally allied to him, or of possessing the necessary insignificance and pliancy to render them the obsequious instruments of pleasure" (quoted in Hendrik Hertzberg, "Quagmiers," *The New Yorker*, October 9, 2005).

64. Robert H. Bork, "Slouching Towards Miers," *Wall Street Journal*, October 19, 2005.

65. George Will, "Can This Nomination Be Justified?," *Washington Post*, October 5, 2005.

66. Bush, "Interview with Matt Lauer of NBC's 'Today' Show in Covington, Louisiana," October 11, 2005, American Presidency Project, https://www.presidency.ucsb.edu.

67. See Bork-Carlson interview, note 58 above.

68. Elisabeth Bumiller, "Longtime Advisor: Never Sat as Judge—Many Social Views Remain Unclear," *New York Times*, October 5, 2005.

69. Elisabeth Bumiller, "Bush Works to Reassure G.O.P. Over Nominee for Supreme Court," *New York Times*, October 9, 2005.

70. Peter Baker and Amy Goldstein, "Nomination Was Plagued by Missteps from the Start," *Washington Post*, October 28, 2005.

71. Of course, Ronald Reagan chose to withdraw the Douglas Ginsburg nomination in 1987—he wasn't forced to do so. See chapter 4.

72. Quoted in Massaro 1990, 118–19.

73. Lincoln Chafee of Rhode Island was the exception. For more on Chafee, see note 46 in chapter 5.

Chapter Eight

1. Michael Kranish, "Michelle Childs, a Potential Supreme Court Pick, Recalls Being 'Devastated' at Father's Gunshot Death," *Washington Post*, February 12, 2022. The gunshot wounds were reported to have been self-inflicted.

2. Christina Wilkie, "GOP Sen. Lindsey Graham Predicts That Supreme Court Prospect J. Michelle Childs Would Win More than 10 Republican Votes," CNBC.com, February 14, 2022.

3. Amber Phillips, "What to Know About Ketanji Brown Jackson, Biden's Pick for the Supreme Court," *Washington Post*, February 25, 2022.

4. As noted earlier, there were no court vacancies during Jimmy Carter's one term in office.

5. Sotomayor received 59 votes from Democrats since Senator Ted Kennedy of Massachusetts, battling cancer at the time, did not vote. Seven Republicans supported her confirmation as well.

6. "Remarks by the President and Solicitor General Elena Kagan at the Nomination of Solicitor General Elena Kagan to the Supreme Court," May 10, 2010, https://obamawhitehouse.archives.gov/the-press-office/remarks-president-and-solicitor-general-elena-kagan-nomination-solicitor-general-el.

7. Obama 2020, 389–90.

8. Peter Baker and Jeff Zeleny, "Obama Picks Kagan, Scholar but Not Judge, for Court Seat," *New York Times*, May 10, 2010.

9. As noted earlier, Ruth Bader Ginsburg completed two years at Harvard Law before transferring to Columbia to complete her law degree.

10. With the Segal-Cover score of .160 for conservatives in mind (see chapter 7), I define a liberal firebrand as a nominee with a score greater than .84 (i.e., .160 away from the most liberal score possible). Sotomayor was the closest with a .78. There is no Segal-Cover score for Jackson. On her ideology, see Epstein, Martin, and Quinn, "Replacing Justice Breyer," January 24, 2022. They concluded that all of Biden's potential nominees, including Jackson, were "ideologically fairly close to Breyer and Kagan." In fact, Jackson was perceived as slightly *more*

NOTES TO PAGES 153–159

conservative than the justice she replaced. The piece is available at https://static1.squarespace
.com/static/60188505fb790b33c3d33a61/t/61f1855081fb31470cda3c37/1643218256396/Replacing
JusticeBreyer.pdf.

11. Only with the strong urging of Columbia Law School's Gerald Gunther was she hired to
clerk for federal Judge Edmund L. Palmieri in the southern district of New York.

12. William J. Clinton, "Background Briefing by Senior Administration Officials," June 14,
1993, American Presidency Project, https://www.presidency.ucsb.edu.

13. Consider, for example, that in his 750-plus-page memoir covering his pre–White House
life and his first term, President Obama devoted approximately five pages to the historic Sotomayor nomination. He gave the Kagan selection even less attention—just two sentences (Obama
2020, 387–91, 566). In his nearly thousand-page tome, Clinton spends even less time on his two
nominees for the Court. The Ginsburg choice garnered slightly more than a page; the Breyer
selection slightly less (Clinton 2005, 424–525, 592).

14. Ginsburg 2016, 40.

15. Abraham 1999, 318.

16. McMahon 2004, 130. Despite their differences, Cuomo voiced deep Italian delight when
President Reagan selected Scalia for the Court in 1986, exclaiming "Finalmente!"—an Italian
word that roughly to translates to "it's about time." He added: "My first reaction was a visceral
burst of pride. It showed the upward mobility of Italian-Americans. It's a magnificent moment.
July 4 is coming up. I just visited Ellis Island where my immigrant mother landed. Now we have
a Supreme Court justice who says, 'My friends call me Nino.'" Cuomo continued, "My second
reaction also was positive. Here's a bright, thoughtful lawyer, a professor of law, with reverence
for the law, picked for the highest court, a man eminently qualified." Ben Wattenberg, "An Italian-
American on the Court—Finalmente!," *Orlando Sentinel*, June 26, 1986.

17. Toobin 2007, 72; Stephanopoulos 1999, 172.

18. Stephanopoulos 1999, 173–74.

19. Toobin 2007, 72.

20. Yalof 1999, 199; Toobin 2007, 70.

21. Hirshman 2015, 206.

22. De Hart 2018, 305.

23. Hirshman 2015, 205.

24. Carmon and Knizhnik 2015, 85.

25. Ginsburg 1992, 1185. Note: The date of the publication is correct, even though the lecture
took place on March 9, 1993. The law review must have been behind in its publication schedule.

26. Carmon and Knizhnik 2015, 85.

27. De Hart 2018, 310.

28. Carmon and Knizhnik 2015, 86; De Hart 2018, 309–10.

29. Stephanopoulos 1999, 173.

30. "Supreme Court Justice Scalia Sits Down with Chris Wallace on Fox News Sunday," Fox
News, July 29, 2012, https://video.foxnews.com/v/1760716797001#sp=show-clips.

31. Hulse 2019, chapter 6.

32. Center for American Progress, "New Poll Shows Americans Overwhelmingly Support
a Hearing and a Vote on Merrick Garland's Nominations," May 9, 2016. However, see Eugene
Kiely, "SCOTUS Nomination: What Polls Say," FactCheck.org, March 19, 2016, https://www.fact
check.org/2016/03/scotus-nomination-what-polls-say/.

33. Hulse 2019, chapters 5 and 7.

34. Joan Biskupic, "Why Merrick Garland Should Keep Hoping," CNN Politics, October 23, 2016, https://www.cnn.com/2016/10/23/politics/hillary-clinton-merrick-garland-supreme-court.

35. "Presidential Debate at the University of Nevada in Las Vegas," October 19, 2016, American Presidency Project, https://www.presidency.ucsb.edu.

36. "Presidential Debate," October 19, 2016.

37. "If I have the opportunity to make any Supreme Court appointments I'm going to look broadly and widely for people who represent the diversity of our country, who bring some common-sense, real-world experience." J. D. Durkin, "Did Clinton Just Suggest She Would Fill Empty SCOTUS Seat with Someone Other Than Merrick Garland?," *Mediaite*, September 15, 2016, https://www.mediaite.com/tv/did-clinton-just-suggest-she-would-fill-empty-scotus-seat-with-someone-other-than-merrick-garland/.

38. Hulse 2019, 157–58.

39. At the time of Sotomayor's confirmation vote in 2009, the Democrats held 60 seats. A year later, when Kagan won confirmation, their total had shrunk by one to 59 seats. In 1993 and 1994, when Ginsburg and Breyer were confirmed, the Democratic majority stood at 56 to the Republican minority of 44.

Chapter Nine

1. "Justice Thomas Loves the RV Lifestyle," RVBusiness, June 14, 2004, https://rvbusiness.com/justice-thomas-loves-the-rv-lifestyle/, emphasis added; see also "Justice Clarence Thomas—RV Enthusiast," The World, August 6, 2009, https://www.pri.org/stories/2009-08-06/justice-clarence-thomas-rv-enthusiast.

2. "The Joseph Story Distinguished Lecture with Justice Clarence Thomas," Heritage Foundation, YouTube video, October 23, 2015, https://www.youtube.com/watch?v=Md9lxQeBuwA.

3. "Justice Clarence Thomas: Personal Reflections on the Court, His Jurisprudence, and His Education," Conversations with Bill Kristol, YouTube video, October 22, 2016, https://www.youtube.com/watch?v=Q3rZknW5gAk.

4. District of Columbia v. Heller, 554 U.S. 570 (2008).

5. Biskupic 2009, 19, 21–22.

6. "Supreme Court Justice Kagan on Pro Bono Service," C-Span, October 24, 2018, https://www.c-span.org/video/?453535-1/supreme-court-justice-discusses-pro-bono-service; "Supreme Court and Constitutional Law," C-Span, March 17, 2014, https://www.c-span.org/video/?318317-1/conversation-sc-justice-kagan.

7. Obama quoting Kagan, "Remarks on the Nomination of Solicitor General Elena Kagan to be a Supreme Court Associate Justice," May 10, 2010, https://obamawhitehouse.archives.gov/the-press-office/remarks-president-and-solicitor-general-elena-kagan-nomination-solicitor-general-el.

8. Segal and Spaeth 2002; Epstein and Knight 1998.

9. The first two figures exclude William Rehnquist's elevation to chief in 1986.

10. *Confirmation Hearing on the Nomination of Samuel A. Alito, Jr. to be an Associate Justice of the Supreme Court of the United States*, Committee on the Judiciary, United States Senate, January 9–13, 2006, 55, https://www.judiciary.senate.gov/imo/media/doc/GPO-CHRG-ALITO.pdf.

11. "Remarks on the Nomination of Amy Coney Barrett to be a United States Supreme Court Associate Justice," September 26, 2020, American Presidency Project, https://www.presidency.ucsb.edu.

12. "Trump Announces Brett Kavanaugh as Supreme Court Nominee: Full Video and Transcript," *New York Times*, July 9, 2018, https://www.nytimes.com/2018/07/09/us/politics/trump-supreme-court-announcement-transcript.html.

13. She rose to become a circuit court judge in Montgomery County, Maryland.

14. "Kavanaugh Hearing: Transcript," *Washington Post*, September 27, 2018, https://www.washingtonpost.com/news/national/wp/2018/09/27/kavanaugh-hearing-transcript/; Eliza Relman, "Trump Keeps Repeating a False Claim About Kavanaugh's Academic Past at Yale," *Business Insider*, October 2, 2018.

15. Daniel Markovits writes in *The Meritocracy Trap*: "Yale [Law School] admits 8 percent of applicants (making the admissions competition four times as intense today as it was at mid-century). The median admitted student received an A average in college and scored above the 99th percentile on the Law School Admission Test (LSAT)" (Markovits 2019, 7).

16. There's no evidence Kavanaugh tried to correct the record on either count.

17. "Confirmation Hearing on the Nomination of Hon. Brett M. Kavanaugh to be an Associate Justice of the Supreme Court of the United States," Committee on the Judiciary, United States Senate, Part 1 of 2, September 4, 5, 6, 7, and 27, 2018. 109–10. Of course, most of those born before *Brown* or *Bolling v. Sharpe*—both decided on May 17, 1954—would have graduated high school by 1972 at the latest, when the future justice was just seven years old. Brown v. Board of Education of Topeka, Shawnee Cty., Kan., 347 U.S. 483 (1954); Bolling v. Sharpe, 347 U.S. 497 (1954).

18. Obergefell v. Hodges, 576 U.S. 644 (2015), first emphasis in original, second one added.

19. See, for example, Leiter 2015.

20. Frankfurter 1957, 795–96.

21. When asked to comment on this and a similar Holmes quote—"a page of history is worth a volume of logic"—Scalia did not hide his skepticism. "If you're talking about applying the Constitution to events [or] phenomena that didn't occur at the time [of the founding]. If you're talking about establishing a realistic law that can be followed by the lower courts, the only tool you have is logic. . . . Logic is essential to a genuine system of laws. If you're not bound by logic, you just have random decisions. . . . It is reason and logic that provides order and justice, fairness." "A Conversation with Antonin Scalia, hosted by Calvin Massey," *Legally Speaking*, University of California Television, YouTube video, September 2010, question begins at approximately 1:14:20, https://www.youtube.com/watch?v=KvttIukZEtM.

22. Scalia-Massey interview, quote at approximately 45:00.

23. Marshall dissenting, U.S. v. Kras, 409 U.S. 434 (1973), 460.

24. Stephen L. Carter, "What Thurgood Marshall Taught Me," *New York Times Magazine*, July 14, 2021.

25. Rodell 1955, 120.

26. Robin 2019.

27. Joan Biskupic's lecture at the University of California, Irvine School of Law, September 14, 2016, https://www.law.uci.edu/news/videos/biskupic-guestspeaker-2016sept14.html.

28. Biskupic 2014, 211.

29. Schuette v. Coalition to Defend Affirmative Action, 572 U.S. 291 (2014), 45–46 (slip opinion).

30. Maltz 2006, 199.

31. Maltz, 209.

32. Segal and Spaeth 2002, 86.

33. Epstein and Knight 1998.

34. Hall 2018, 15.

35. Although the strategic model emphasizes rationality over other characteristics.

36. Democratic presidents have chosen from their own version of the "supreme elite," but they have done so with more attention to the idea that personal experiences matter. For example, when President Barack Obama was deciding on his first nominee for the Supreme Court, one of the factors tilting the scale in favor of Sonia Sotomayor was her continuing connection to her community, which (as she writes in her memoir, *My Beloved World*) helped transform her from a Puerto Rican kid living in the "projects" in the Bronx to a justice of the Supreme Court of the United States. Sotomayor had biography on her side, but the president wanted to make sure it would matter. In turn, when Obama called her to inform her of his intention to nominate her to the Court, he asked her to make two promises: "First, you have to remain the person you are. And second, to stay connected to your community" (quoted in Toobin 2012, 138). Knowing Sotomayor's background and her determination, as she put it during her introduction ceremony, "to strive to never forget the real-world consequences of [her] decisions" apparently helped convince the president of the rightness of his choice ("Transcript of Obama-Sotomayor Announcement," May 26, 2009, https://www.cnn.com/2009/POLITICS/05/26/obama.sotomayor.transcript/index.html). In a similar vein, as noted earlier, Obama spoke of Elena Kagan's judicial empathy. Aside from being conditioned to decide in a more liberal manner, such sentiments suggest a commitment to staying the ideological course.

37. Jim Lindgren, "Elena Kagan: I Love the Federalist Society! I Love the Federalist Society!," *The Volokh Conspiracy*, May 10, 2010, http://volokh.com/2010/05/10/elena-kagan-i-love-the-federalist-society-i-love-the-federalist-society/; Devins and Baum 2019, 138–39.

38. Mario Cuomo is one example. Then Senate majority leader George Mitchell is another.

39. Devins and Baum 2019, 10–11, 12.

40. Today such relationships would undoubtedly raise concerns about judicial independence.

41. Dahl 1957, 284–85.

42. To help combat such perceptions, Roosevelt elevated the Republican-appointed Harlan F. Stone to chief; Truman appointed Harold Burton, a former Republican senator from Ohio.

43. And the president concurred with the justice's decision.

44. David McCullough adds that Truman's comment about Clark, "like others of his observations to [author Merle] Miller, was more harsh than he meant or he indicated at the time"—McCullough 1992, 901; Youngstown Sheet & Tube Company v. Sawyer, 343 U.S. 579 (1952).

45. McMahon 2004, 19, 11.

46. Shapiro 1978, 194, 193.

47. McCloskey 1960, 17.

48. Dahl 1957, 294.

49. Jackson 1955; see also "A Conversation with Antonin Scalia" at 3:30, https://www.youtube.com/watch?v=KvttIukZEtM.

50. Douglas 1974, 329.

51. FDR did elevate the Republican-appointed Stone. But that appointment did not add a Republican to the Court.

52. Gunther 1994, 563.

53. The other was Judge John J. Parker, the onetime Hoover nominee the Senate rejected in 1930. While Stone held Hand in high regard, he dismissed him for being "obviously too old" (Ferren 2004, 212–13).

54. Ferren 2004, 213.

55. Although see Gunther (1994, 562) on Douglas's story.

56. Gunther 1994, 568.

57. Quoted in Ferren 2004, 221.

58. Here are some examples: Jimmy Byrnes left the Court at the start of the Second World War to serve as "Assistant to the President" and later served as Secretary of State and then Governor of South Carolina. Roosevelt seriously considered William O. Douglas for the vice presidency in 1944 and an attempt was made to draft him as the Democratic presidential nominee in 1948. FDR considered Robert H. Jackson for the vice presidency in 1944 as well, and Jackson took a leave from the Court to lead the prosecution team at Nuremburg. Although Earl Warren was not the choice of a Democratic president, out of President Dwight D. Eisenhower's five selections he was the most similar to them. He had been the governor of California and the Republican vice presidential nominee in 1948, and he was expected to be named solicitor general until fate intervened with the unexpected death of Chief Justice Fred Vinson. Also, as chief justice, Warren headed up the commission to investigate the assassination of President John F. Kennedy, using the Court's credibility to help resolve a tragic question facing the nation. Arthur Goldberg left the Court to serve as US ambassador to the United Nations, and later ran unsuccessfully for governor of New York. Abe Fortas continued to serve as a close advisor to President Lyndon Johnson after he became a justice.

59. George 2008, 1337–40. See also Friedman 1983 and Crowe 2012.

60. This excludes the elevation of Edward White to chief and the second nomination of Charles Evans Hughes. Before their initial nominations, both were politicians. White was a US senator from Louisiana, although before that he was a justice on the Pelican State's Supreme Court. Hughes was the governor of New York. The Senate-rejected nominee of the Republican era, John J. Parker, was also a court of appeals judge (4th circuit).

61. On Thomas, see Neil A. Lewis, "The Thomas Nomination; Judiciary Panel Deadlocks, 7-7, on Thomas Nomination to Court," *New York Times*, September 28, 1991. On Kagan, see, Nina Totenberg, "Should Kagan's Lack of Judicial Experience Matter?," *National Public Radio*, May 12, 2010, https://www.npr.org/2010/05/12/126764692/should-kagans-lack-of-judicial-experience-matter.

62. Kaplan 2018, 43.

63. "Kavanaugh Hearing: Transcript," *Washington Post*, September 27, 2018, https://www.washingtonpost.com/news/national/wp/2018/09/27/kavanaugh-hearing-transcript/.

64. The only sitting Republican-appointed justice with experience on Capitol Hill is Clarence Thomas. The only other one named after Nixon's election was John Paul Stevens, who worked briefly in Congress in the 1950s. One of the three Democratic appointees—Kagan—has very limited experience on the Hill. The recently retired Stephen Breyer had far more extensive experience there.

65. Obama voted against Roberts and Alito. Biden voted against Thomas, Roberts, and Alito. For Clarence Thomas's nomination, Biden, as Senate Judiciary chair, was at the center of the storm. In 2019, in the days after he announced his campaign for the presidency, he felt the need to apologize for some of his actions during the committee's hearings. But his apology wasn't to Thomas. It was to Anita Hill. Biden didn't apologize directly to Hill but said: "I'm sorry for the way she got treated. . . . Look at what I said and didn't say; I don't think I treated her badly." He added: "As the committee chairman, I take responsibility that she did not get treated well. I take responsibility for that" (quoted in Chris Mills Rodrigo, "Timeline: A History of the Joe Biden–Anita Hill Controversy," *The Hill*, May 4, 2019). President Obama also said he regretted one of his actions as a senator. Specifically, in 2006, he took part in a disastrous filibuster of the Alito

nomination, saying that he thought the judge "was somebody who is contrary to core American values, not just liberal values" (Obama quoted in Jeff Zeleny, "Obama Joins Filibuster Bid against Alito," *Chicago Tribune*, January 30, 2006). Ten years later, the Obama White House said the president believed his participation in the filibuster was a mistake (Jordan Fabian, "White House: Obama 'Regrets' His Filibuster of Supreme Court Nominee," *The Hill*, February 17, 2016). (As a senator, Vice President Biden supported the filibuster as well.) Notably, the White House released the statement a few days after Justice Scalia's death and as the president was preparing to appoint a replacement who would require confirmation by a Republican-controlled Senate. Obama was straightforward with regard to why he joined the filibuster: "There are times where folks are in the Senate and they're thinking . . . is this going to cause me problems in a primary? Is this going to cause me problems with supporters of mine? And so people take strategic decisions" (Barack Obama, "The President's Press Conference in Rancho Mirage, California," February 16, 2016, American Presidency Project, https://www.presidency.ucsb.edu).Whatever the explanation and whatever one thinks of Anita Hill's charges against Thomas or Alito's values, it shouldn't surprise any of us if they harbor some contempt for the Senate (and possibly for Presidents Obama and Biden as well). In contrast to Obama and Biden, the last two Democrats to serve as senators before ascending to the presidency and the vice presidency—John F. Kennedy and Lyndon B. Johnson—voted to confirm all the nominees appointed to the Court during their time in the Senate, including five appointed by Republican Dwight D. Eisenhower.

66. Here I include Rehnquist's elevation from associate to chief in 1986. As noted earlier, the one exception—Elena Kagan—had been nominated to the DC court of appeals but was not confirmed due to Senate delay and an expiring Clinton presidency.

67. Bork served as the acting attorney general after the "Saturday Night Massacre," making him the only divided government nominee to serve in a cabinet-level post.

68. Nixon named Blackmun after the defeat of Haynsworth and Carswell. The latter did serve in the Justice Department and as a federal judge (first at the district court and then the court of appeals). But all three appointments were outside of Washington.

69. Thomas 2008, 192.

70. As a result, Chief Justice Roberts is the only one of the five who spent more time in the executive than in the judicial branch before appointment to the Supreme Court.

71. Devins and Baum 2019, 40.

72. On the significance of this relationship for the Republican Party, see Peretti 2020.

73. Under the definition from above, Kagan is the only one who would fit the description of an administration person. See note 101 below.

74. Devins and Baum 2019, 132–33.

75. Devins and Baum, 133; Hollis Brusky 2015, 21. Calabresi makes an important point, although he is hardly an unbiased observer. With regard to audience, it's essential to ask if the conservative justices are so eager for adulation that they will be guided by the approval of members of the Federalist Society. One would assume they are not. For example, given his notable conservative lapses, has the Federalist Society really "checked" Chief Justice Roberts? Given his unparalleled conservatism ever since he joined the Court, has it ever needed to check Justice Thomas? Is it possible that justices like Scalia and Thomas lead the thinking of members of the Federalist Society rather than pandering to please them? At the very least, wouldn't the relationship between a justice and a group like the Federalist Society be more reciprocal—and more an intellectual exchange of ideas—rather than a thumbs-up or down? For example, Scalia and Thomas strongly disagreed about how extensively the ideas of originalism should be incorporated into

Supreme Court doctrine. Scalia thought originalism's implementation should be more limited than does Thomas. Some in the Federalist Society undoubtedly prefer Scalia's approach; others are more convinced by Thomas's more radical way. Seemingly both pleased the Federalist Society crowd despite this intellectual quarrel. In other words, members of the Federalist Society will tolerate—even celebrate—a range of conservatism. Nevertheless, there are limits.

76. Devins and Baum 2019, 151.

77. Devins and Baum, 133.

78. "A Conversation with Associate Justice Clarence Thomas," https://mediasite.video.ufl .edu/Mediasite/Play/89374250b14749a9958da667a4cd571a; see also Adam Liptak, "A Well-Traveled Path from Ivy League to Supreme Court," *New York Times*, September 6, 2010.

79. Baum 2014, 338; see also Adam Liptak, "A Sign of Court's Polarization: Choice of Clerks," *New York Times*, September 6, 2010.

80. Ginni Thomas, "Justice Clarence Thomas Opens Up on Life, Faith, and His Interracial Marriage," *The Daily Signal*, January 7, 2018 https://www.dailysignal.com/2018/01/07/justice-clarence -thomas-opens-life-faith-interracial-marriage/.

81. "Justice Thomas Opens Up."

82. Bork 2002, 196, 217, 221.

83. Scalia dissent, Romer v. Evans, 517 U.S., 620, 636; Devins and Baum 2019, 51.

84. Devins and Baum 2019, 151.

85. "Justice Thomas Opens Up."

86. Thomas, quoted in *Created Equal: Clarence Thomas in His Own Words*, written and directed by Michael Pack, aired May 18, 2020, on PBS, https://www.amazon.com/Created-Equal -Clarence-Thomas-Words/dp/B08HFYY3FL.

87. Although see Joshua Kaplan, Justin Elliott, and Alex Mierjeski, "Clarence Thomas and the Billionaire," *ProPublica*, April 6, 2023, https://www.propublica.org/article/clarence-thomas -scotus-undisclosed-luxury-travel-gifts-crow; and Brett Murphy and Alex Mierjeski, "Clarence Thomas' 38 Vacations: The Other Billionaires Who Have Treated the Supreme Court Justice to Luxury Travel," *ProPublica*, August 10, 2023, https://www.propublica.org/article/clarence-thomas -other-billionaires-sokol-huizenga-novelly-supreme-court. See also Jo Becker and Julie Tate, "Clarence Thomas's $267,230 R.V. and the Friend Who Financed It," *New York Times*, August 5, 2023.

88. See Fjelstul 2014. A comprehensive 2021 RV industry study reported the following demographics for owners of "motorcoaches" (the type of vehicle Thomas owns): "40% are between ages 18–54 and 66% are ages 55+. 46% are female and 53% are male. 42% are retired and 74% live with no children in the home. Among those who are in the workforce, 58% of Class A owners make over $65,000." Available at https://www.rvia.org/news-insights/go-rving-rv-owner -demographic-profile-class-motorhomes. However, overall RV demographics changed dramatically in recent years, driven in part by lifestyle changes and more remote work opportunities during and after the pandemic. As Jeff Clemishaw writes, "the cliché stereotype of retired, snow-birding RVers is long over." Buyers are getting younger and more racially diverse. Clemishaw, "Industry Report Reveals RV Demographics Are Changing," *RV Travel*, November 12, 2022, https://www.rvtravel.com/industry-report-reveals-rv-demographics-changing-1078b/.

89. "A Conversation with Associate Justice Clarence Thomas," https://mediasite.video.ufl.edu /Mediasite/Play/89374250b14749a9958da667a4cd571a; see also Adam Liptak, "A Well-Traveled Path from Ivy League to Supreme Court," *New York Times*, September 6, 2010.

90. Recently, Democrats have clearly been tagged with the elitist label.

91. Markovits 2019, 61–62.

92. Hollis-Brusky and Wilson 2020, 43–46.

93. Keith E. Whittington, "The Judicial Review of Congress Database, 1789–2022," July 2022, https://scholar.princeton.edu/kewhitt/judicial-review-congress-database. See also Whittington 2019.

94. Hirschl 2004, 12. Laura Kalman (2017) discusses the clear "cronyism" behind LBJ's choices of Abe Fortas and Homer Thornberry for the Court.

95. Schmidhauser 1959, 10.

96. Five of the eight justices appointed in this century were raised in upper-middle-class homes. Alito, Sotomayor, and Jackson are the exceptions (although see note 18 in chapter 6 regarding Jackson). Only Alito, Kagan, and Jackson attended public high schools. However, Kagan went to an elite honors high school in Manhattan. Barrett is the only one not to attend an Ivy at the undergraduate level.

97. Barrett attended Notre Dame Law School.

98. See table 9.3 for the clerkships of the Republican-appointed justices. Of the Democratic appointees, Kagan clerked for Judge Abner Mikva of the US Court of Appeals for the DC Circuit and then for Thurgood Marshall. Sotomayor is the only justice appointed in the polarized period who did not clerk for an appeals court judge or a Supreme Court justice. As noted earlier, she instead worked as assistant district attorney in the New York County District attorney's office under the legendary Robert Morgenthau.

99. Four of the eight justices appointed in the polarized period worked in the solicitor general's office. Kagan's experience—as solicitor general—came at the end of her pre-Court career.

100. See table 9.3. Sotomayor is the exception. After a short time at a DC law firm, Kagan became a professor at the University of Chicago before moving on to Harvard. Between stints at Harvard (the second primarily as dean of the law school), she spent four years in the Clinton administration—first as associate White House counsel and then as deputy assistant to the president for domestic policy—and one year as Barack Obama's solicitor general. During the Carter presidency, Alito was an assistant US attorney in the District of New Jersey.

101. Barrett, Jackson, and Sotomayor are the exceptions; none of them worked in the federal executive branch. However, Jackson was nominated by President Barack Obama in 2009 to serve on the US sentencing commission, which is part of the federal judiciary. In Kavanaugh's case, the Ken Starr–led investigation of the Clintons meant that he didn't need to wait for a Republican administration.

102. See table 9.3. As explained earlier, President Clinton named Kagan to the DC court of appeals, but his term expired before the Senate acted on her nomination.

103. See table 9.3. Barrett is the exception. Barrett might have been appointed at an earlier age, but the Democrat Barack Obama controlled the presidency from 2009 to 2017. She was appointed to the court of appeals in Donald Trump's first year as president, when she was forty-five. Jackson was thirty-eight when Obama appointed her to the US sentencing commission. She had just turned forty-two when he appointed her to the federal district court. She was fifty when Joe Biden elevated her to the DC Court of Appeals. Sotomayor was thirty-seven years old when George Bush appointed her district court judge. President Clinton nominated her to the court of appeals on her forty-third birthday.

104. Of those who served in both the federal executive branch and the federal judiciary before appointment to the high court, Roberts in the only one to have served longer in the former post. Again, this is because of the Senate's inaction on his first nomination to the court of appeals. But as noted above, even while working as a private lawyer in Washington, he argued often before the Supreme Court.

105. Posner 2008, 306.

106. McCloskey 1960, 223.

107. Former Agriculture Secretary and Congressman Dan Glickman has made a similar point: "What's needed on the court are qualified individuals whose personal experiences vary from those of their colleagues." He points to *Citizens United* as an example of why the Court should be more diverse with regard to background. *Citizens United* "was an extremely long opinion that was full of legalese and short on practical understanding of the impact of unlimited money on political campaigns. I can't help but think that if more of the justices had more direct experience in politics they may have thought twice about couching their ruling in purely legal scholarship and had more sense about the real life impact of their decision." Valerie Strauss, "The 'Cloistered' Harvard-Yale Monopoly on the Supreme Court," *Washington Post*, July 10, 2018.

Chapter Ten

1. "Roosevelt Accused of 'Slurring' Court," *New York Times*, October 27, 1932; Byrnes 1958, 65. It is also interesting to note that during the Roosevelt administration's battle with the Supreme Court over the validity of the New Deal, the four most conservative justices (Willis Van Devanter, James C. McReynolds, George Sutherland, and Pierce Butler) were labeled the "Four Horsemen" of the Old Order.

2. La Follette had issued sharp attacks against the Court's decisions on child labor and the use of labor injunctions, and his party's platform called for a constitutional amendment allowing for Congress to override judicial decisions and for the nonpartisan election of judges.

3. "Text of President Hoover's Address Before a Great Throng at Indianapolis," *New York Times*, October 29, 1932; Byrnes 1958, 65.

4. Engel 2011, 186, 189.

5. Pew Research Center, "Public's Views of Supreme Court Turned More Negative Before News of Breyer's Retirement," February 2, 2022, https://www.pewresearch.org/politics/2022/02/02/publics-views-of-supreme-court-turned-more-negative-before-news-of-breyers-retirement/.

6. Charles Franklin, "New Marquette Law School Poll National Survey Finds Approval of the Supreme Court at New Lows, with Strong Partisan Difference over Abortion and Gun Rights," July 22, 2022, https://www.marquette.edu/news-center/2022/new-marquette-law-poll-national-survey-finds-approval-of-supreme-court-at-new-lows.php.

7. Schmidt 2018, 416; see also Stephenson 1999.

8. Schechter v. United States, 295 U.S. 495 (1935).

9. Leuchtenburg 1999, 2111.

10. See, generally, Leuchtenburg 1999.

11. See, for example, Burns 1956, Conkin 1967, Davis 1993, Lasser 1988, McKenna 2002, and Nelson 1988.

12. United States v. Carolene Products, 304 U.S. 144 (1938).

13. In the South, he promised the president would outlast his critics and successfully appoint "a Southern strict constructionist" (Kalman 2017, 249–50; McMahon 2011, 137).

14. Goodridge v. Dept. of Public Health, 798 N.E. 2d 941 (Mass. 2003); Lawrence v. Texas, 539 U.S. 558 (2003); Stenberg v. Carhart, 530 U.S. 914 (2000); Elk Grove Unified School District v. Newdow, 542 U.S. 1 (2004); Gratz v. Bollinger, 539 U.S. 244 (2003); and Gutter v. Bollinger, 539 U.S. 306 (2003). For a fuller discussion of the "moral values" in the 2004 election, see McMahon 2005.

15. Jeffrey Toobin, "Ashcroft's Ascent: How Far Will the Attorney General Go?," *New Yorker*, April 15, 2002, 63. Although variation in exit poll wording makes it difficult to tell whether evangelical Christians made up a greater share of the electorate in 2004 than in 2000, the political scientist John Green's polling showed that President Bush increased his share of the evangelical vote by 5 percent in 2004, from 71 percent to 76 percent (Green cited in Laurie Goodstein and William Yardley, "Bush Benefits from Efforts to Build a Coalition of the Faithful," *New York Times*, November, 5 2004; see also John C. Green, "The American Religious Landscape and Political Attitudes: A Baseline for 2004," https://assets.pewresearch.org/wp-content/uploads/sites/11/2007/10/green-full.pdf).

16. Thomas B. Edsall, "Exit Poll Data Inconclusive on Increase in Evangelical Voters," *Washington Post*, November 8, 2004.

17. Moreover, the two Kerry states (Michigan and Oregon) were the only ones where the same-sex ban did not pass by more than 20 percent of the vote.

18. Martin and Quinn n.d.; see also Epstein, Landes, and Posner 2013.

19. Schmidt 2018.

20. Schmidt.

21. Lesley Stahl, "Justice Scalia on the Record," *60 Minutes*, April 27, 2008, transcript available at www.cbsnews.com/news/justice-scalia-on-the-record/2/.

22. Notably, Sotomayor joined Ginsburg and Breyer in dissent in the 2010 gun-rights case of McDonald v. City of Chicago, 561 U.S. 742 (2010). Kagan did join the Court in 2010, but after that case had already been decided.

23. Trump continued with the following words: "Now the Justices are going to do things that are so important, and we have such great Justices, you saw my list of 11 that have been vetted and respected. (APPLAUSE). And have gotten great. And they a little bit equate—but if you don't do the right thing, either you're not going to have a Second Amendment or you're not going to have much of it left. And you're not going to be able to protect yourself, which you need, which you need. You know, when the bad guys burst into your house, they're not looking about into Second Amendments, and, do I have the right to do this? OK, the bad guys aren't going to be giving up their weapons. But the good people will say, 'oh, well, that's the law.' No, no, not going to happen, we can't let it happen. We can't let that happen. (APPLAUSE)." American Presidency Project, https://www.presidency.ucsb.edu.

24. Scalia, Citizens United v. Federal Election Commission, 558 U.S. 310 (2010).

25. Donald Trump did critique the campaign finance system in more general terms, especially during the Republican primaries.

26. Scalia, Planned Parenthood of Southeastern Pennsylvania v. Casey, 505 U.S. 833 (1992).

27. See Keck and McMahon 2016.

28. Scalia, Obergefell v. Hodges, 576 U.S. 644 (2015).

29. Joshua Gillin, "Hillary Clinton Says Donald Trump 'Wants to Undo Marriage Equality,'" *PolitiFact*, November 3, 2016, www.politifact.com/truth-o-meter/statements/2016/nov/03/hillary-clinton/hillary-clinton-says-donald-trump-wants-undo-marri/.

30. This issue attracted some attention after Trump's selection of Indiana Governor Mike Pence as his vice presidential nominee given his state's passage of the Religious Freedom Restoration Act in 2015. After widespread protests, the law was later amended.

31. Robert Barnes, "Affordable Care Act Survives Supreme Court Challenge," *Washington Post*, June 25, 2015.

32. Scalia, King v. Burwell, 576 U.S. 473 (2015).

33. "Republican Candidates Debate in Greenville, South Carolina," February 13, 2016, American Presidency Project, https://www.presidency.ucsb.edu.

34. "Republican Candidates Debate in Greenville, South Carolina."

35. Emily Crockett, "Donald Trump Stood Up for Planned Parenthood at the Republican Debate," *Vox*, February 13, 2016, https://www.vox.com/2016/2/13/10988338/donald-trump-planned-parenthood-gop-debate.

36. Ted Cruz, "The Right Stuff," *National Review*, July 20, 2005, www.nationalreview.com/article/214989/right-stuff-ted-cruz.

37. "Republican Candidates Debate in Greenville, South Carolina."

38. Trump quoted in Alan Rappeport and Charlie Savage, "Donald Trump Releases List of Possible Supreme Court Picks," *New York Times*, May 18, 2016.

39. Joshua Gillin, "Hillary Clinton Says Donald Trump 'Wants to Undo Marriage Equality,'" *PolitiFact*, November 3, 2016, www.politifact.com/truth-o-meter/statements/2016/nov/03/hillary-clinton/hillary-clinton-says-donald-trump-wants-undo-marri/. Gillin misidentifies this tweet as in response to the *Obergefell* decision, announced the day after *King v. Burwell*. Roberts dissented in *Obergefell*, and Trump tweeted a few hours before the announcement of *Obergefell*.

40. This does not include Oklahoma, which is traditionally considered a border state. Trump lost that state to Cruz as well.

41. "Democratic Candidates Debate in Flint, Michigan, March 6, 2016," American Presidency Project, https://www.presidency.ucsb.edu.

42. "Presidential Debate at the University of Nevada in Las Vegas, October 19, 2016," American Presidency Project, https://www.presidency.ucsb.edu; Tommy Christopher, "Bernie Sanders Won't Make Gun Control a Litmus Test for Supreme Court Nominees," *Mediaite*, March 24, 2016, www.mediaite.com/tv/bernie-sanders-wont-make-gun-control-a-litmus-test-for-supreme-court-nominees/.

43. Donald J. Trump, "Address Accepting the Presidential Nomination at the Republican National Convention in Cleveland, Ohio," July 21, 2016, American Presidency Project, https://www.presidency.ucsb.edu.

44. Hillary Clinton, "Address Accepting the Presidential Nomination at the Democratic National Convention in Philadelphia, Pennsylvania," July 28, 2016, American Presidency Project, https://www.presidency.ucsb.edu. On the Republican effort to control election law, see Peretti 2020.

45. Immediately after the video's release, some speculated that Trump would abandon his run and turn the race over to vice presidential candidate Mike Pence. At that point, the Clinton campaign preemptively sought to highlight Pence's staunchly conservative pro-life positions.

46. Hillary Clinton, "Remarks at the University of New Hampshire in Durham," September 28, 2016, American Presidency Project, https://www.presidency.ucsb.edu. See also Gillin, "Hillary Clinton Says Donald Trump 'Wants to Undo Marriage Equality.'"

47. "Presidential Debate at the Washington University in St. Louis, Missouri," October 9, 2016, American Presidency Project, https://www.presidency.ucsb.edu.

48. "Presidential Debate at the Washington University."

49. "Presidential Debate at the University of Nevada in Las Vegas."

50. Joan Biskupic, "Justice Ruth Bader Ginsburg Calls Trump a 'Faker,' He Says She Should Resign," CNN Politics, July 13, 2016, https://www.cnn.com/2016/07/12/politics/justice-ruth-bader-ginsburg-donald-trump-faker/.

51. "Presidential Debate at the University of Nevada in Las Vegas."

52. "Presidential Debate at the University of Nevada in Las Vegas." On Clinton and Obama, see Keck and McMahon 2016 and McMahon 2009.

53. Reena Flores and Major Garrett, "Donald Trump Expands List of Possible Supreme Court Picks," CBS News, September 23, 2016, https://www.cbsnews.com/news/donald-trump -expands-list-of-possible-supreme-court-picks/.

54. Trump, "Rally in Ashburn Virginia," YouTube video, August 2, 2016, quote around 38:30, https://www.youtube.com/watch?v=nzgxdzFSvGs.

55. Trump, "Remarks at a Rally at the University of North Carolina in Wilmington," August 9, 2016, American Presidency Project, https://www.presidency.ucsb.edu.

56. To be sure, some speculated that if Hillary Clinton won the 2016 race, the Republican majority in the Senate might move to confirm Merrick Garland during a lame duck session, given his age and more moderate ideology. By doing so, they would prevent Clinton from replacing Scalia with a younger and more liberal justice.

57. Pew Research Center, "U.S. Public Becoming Less Religious," November 3, 2015, https:// www.pewresearch.org/religion/religious-landscape-study/.

58. Wayne LaPierre, "Our Time Is Now," November 2016, transcript available at www.nratv .com/series/wayne-lapierre/episode/wayne-lapierre-season-1-episode-11-our-time-is-now.

59. Ron Johnson, "Protecting the 2nd Amendment," YouTube video, 0:30, August 9, 2016, https://www.youtube.com/watch?v=oka8exyPph4; see also Jonathan Anderson, "Testing Ron Johnson Claim on Russ Feingold, Judges and Second Amendment," *PolitiFact*, October 19, 2016, www.politifact.com/wisconsin/statements/2016/oct/19/ron-johnson/testing-ron-johnson -claim-russ-feingold-judges-and/. Feingold also voted against the confirmation of Samuel Alito and supported John Roberts. Both justices joined Scalia's majority opinion in *Heller* (District of Columbia v. Heller, 554 U.S. 570 [2008]).

60. Eric Garcia, "Pennsylvania Senate Race Could Come Down to Guns," *Roll Call*, August 29, 2016, www.rollcall.com/news/politics/toomey-might-be-lesser-of-two-evils-for-gun-owners; Yost, Redman, and Thompson 2017, 24.

61. Schmidt 2018, 444.

62. Adam Liptak, "Trump's Supreme Court List: Ivy League? Out. The Heartland? In," *New York Times*, November 14, 2016, emphasis added.

Chapter Eleven

1. Kevin Cramer for Senate, "Respecting Life," YouTube video, September 4, 2018, https:// www.youtube.com/watch?v=k7lRqmdAgeQ.

2. Heidi for North Dakota, "Melanie," YouTube video, November 13, 2018, 0:32, https://www .youtube.com/watch?v=h7yLYb5gM0o.

3. Tal Axelrod, "Heitkamp Releases Ad Explaining Kavanaugh No Vote," *The Hill*, October 4, 2018, https://thehill.com/homenews/senate/410030-heitkamp-releases-ad-explaining-kava naugh-no-vote; Heidi for North Dakota, "For Our Country," YouTube video, November 13, 2018, 0:32, https://www.youtube.com/watch?v=WN9wjvFAgxY.

4. Democrats were also up for reelection in five other states Trump won by smaller margins, some by very narrow margins. In four of these states—Michigan, Ohio, Pennsylvania, and Wisconsin—the Democratic incumbent won reelection by a comfortable margin. In Florida, Democrat Ben Nelson lost in a squeaker.

5. Christal Hayes and William Cummings, "Democratic Senators Lost in Battleground States After Voting Against Kavanaugh," *USA Today*, November 7, 2018, https://www.usatoday.com /story/news/politics/elections/2018/11/07/kavanaugh-effect-midterm-elections/1915457002/. The political scientist Walter Clark Wilson adds: "Support for the appointment of conservative, anti-abortion justices has been oft-cited as the main issue that explains what otherwise appears to be hypocritical support for President Trump by evangelicals, and many on the conservative side sought to match Kavanaugh's fierce indignation in his Senate testimony in order to mobilize conservative Christians in their campaigns. While it is difficult to say the extent to which the issue impacted election outcomes, the success of Republican Senate candidates in states with major evangelical populations, such as Missouri, Tennessee, North Dakota, and Florida, suggests that the issue may have been an effective mobilizer for the GOP" (Wilson 2019, 303).

6. Trump quoted in Emily Cochrane, " 'That's My Kind of Guy,' Trump Says of Republican Lawmaker Who Body-Slammed a Reporter," *New York Times*, October 19, 2018.

7. Matt Rosendale, "2nd Amendment," YouTube video, September 4, 2018, https://www.you tube.com/watch?v=Ac9HRqTTAeY.

8. NRA, "Defend Freedom. Defeat Two-Faced Tester!," YouTube video, September 6, 2018, https://www.youtube.com/watch?v=AuqwhCm_MZs.

9. Matthew Brown, "Montana Senate Candidates Clash over Kavanaugh Nomination," Associated Press, YouTube video, September 20, 2018, https://www.youtube.com/watch?v=Auq whCm_MZs.

10. "Campaign 2018: Missouri Senate Debate," C-Span, October 25, 2018, https://www.c-span .org/video/?453648-1/missouri-senate-debate&start=282.

11. Josh Hawley, "McCaskill Voting No on Kavanaugh Is 'Typical,' " YouTube video, October 5, 2018, https://www.youtube.com/watch?v=vPLaAyGv_3M; Josh Hawley, "Circus," YouTube video, October 3, 2018, https://www.youtube.com/watch?v=zjhe0xOG6pQ.

12. Matthew Umstead, "Morrisey: Manchin's Kavanaugh Vote Will Hamper Re-election Bid," Herald-Mail Media, October 8, 2018, https://www.heraldmailmedia.com/news/tri_state/west _virginia/morrisey-manchin-s-kavanaugh-vote-will-hamper-re-election-bid/article_b856108c -cb4e-11e8-9602-f363561ef869.html.

13. "Campaign 2018: Indiana Senate Debate," C-Span, October 8, 2018, https://www.c-span .org/video/?452487-1/indiana-senate-debate&start=451.

14. NRA, "D.C. Joe Has Got to Go," YouTube video, October 25, 2018, https://www.youtube .com/watch?v=4M0YlGUgeCQ.

15. Lori Moore, "Rep. Todd Akin: The Statement and the Reaction," *New York Times*, August 20, 2012, https://www.nytimes.com/2012/08/21/us/politics/rep-todd-akin-legitimate-rape -statement-and-reaction.html?mtrref=undefined.

16. Catalina Camia, "GOP's Mourdock Says Rape, Abortion Comments 'Twisted,' " *USA Today*, October 24, 2012, https://www.usatoday.com/story/news/politics/2012/10/24/mourdock -rape-god-intended-indiana-senate/1653745/.

17. In that race, the NRA highlighted the Supreme Court as well, but in a far less dramatic fashion than it had done two years later. See, for example, All Political Ads, "Hillary Clinton & Jason Kander Agree on Every Major Issue," YouTube video, September 28, 2016, https://www .youtube.com/watch?v=c1wn_b2pNg4.

18. Kevin Cramer for Senate, "Veterans Roundtable," YouTube video, August 2, 2018, https:// www.youtube.com/watch?v=HOrEx8IRMf4.

19. "Campaign 2018: Montana Senate Debate," C-Span, September 29, 2018, https://www
.c-span.org/video/?452053-1/montana-senate-debate&start=3177; KRTV News, "Montana's U.S.
Senate Candidates Debate," YouTube video, October 14, 2018, https://www.youtube.com/watch
?time_continue=3250&v=C182vB2ucKw; Phil Drake, "When Will Senate Candidates Face Off?
It's Debatable," *Great Falls Tribune*, June 11, 2018.

20. "Campaign 2018: West Virginia Senate Debate," C-Span, November 1, 2018, https://
www.c-span.org/video/?453317-1/west-virginia-senate-debate&start=3139.

21. Brown quoted in Slaven, Blumberg, and Binning 2019, 238.

22. Stockley 2019, 270.

23. 2018 Tennessee exit poll available at CNN.com, https://www.cnn.com/election/2018/exit
-polls/tennessee/senate.

24. One unknown is how respondents interpreted the response "keep as is," especially since
recent Supreme Court decisions, while not overturning *Roe*, have enabled states to place substantial burdens on abortion access.

25. The abortion issue is so politically charged that terms are controversial as well. I generally use the terms "pro-life" (for those who oppose abortion rights) and "pro-choice" (for those
who support them). I do so because individuals who hold these competing positions typically
use them to describe themselves. In chapter 12, I use "pro" and "anti" abortion rights.

26. Arika Herron, "Indiana Adopts Near-Total Abortion Ban as Governor Signs SB 1 into
Law," *Indianapolis Star*, August 5, 2022, https://www.indystar.com/story/news/politics/2022/08/05
/indiana-abortion-law-passed-final-vote-to-come/65391000007/.

27. Caroline Kitchener, Kevin Schaul, N. Kirkpatrick, Daniela Santamariña, and Lauren Tier-
ney, "Abortion Is Now Banned or Under Threat in These States," *Washington Post*, June 24, 2022,
https://www.washingtonpost.com/politics/2022/06/24/abortion-state-laws-criminalization-roe/;
Jared Gans, "Montana Governor Signs Multiple Anti-Abortion Measures," *The Hill*, May 4, 2023,
https://thehill.com/homenews/state-watch/3987727-montana-governor-signs-multiple-anti
-abortion-measures/.

Chapter Twelve

1. C-Span, "President Trump on Death of Ruth Bader Ginsburg," YouTube video, September 18, 2020, https://www.youtube.com/watch?v=knlJWu815C0.

2. After all, one leading right-wing provocateur had depicted Ginsburg as "a witch, an evil-
doer, a monster," quoted in the documentary *RBG*, directed by Julie Cohen and Betsy West,
2018, 1:38, https://www.amazon.com/RBG-Ruth-Bader-Ginsburg/dp/B07CT9Q5C6/ref=sr_1_1
?crid=2XUCPXG0W49BJ&keywords=rbg+movie&qid=1684531048&sprefix=RBG+movie%2
Caps%2C320&sr=8-1.

3. June Medical Services v. Russo, 591 U.S. ___ (2020), Bostick v. Clayton County,
590 U.S. ___ (2020), and Department of Homeland Security et al. v. Regents of the University
of California, 590 U.S. ___ (2020).

4. On the significance of Barrett replacing Ginsburg, see also Greenhouse 2021.

5. Trump, "Remarks at 'Make America Great Again Rally' in Freeland, Michigan," September 10, 2020, American Presidency Project, https://www.presidency.ucsb.edu.

6. Trump, "Remarks at 'Make America Great Again Rally' in Mosinee, Wisconsin," September 17, 2020, American Presidency Project, https://www.presidency.ucsb.edu.

7. Trump, "Address Accepting the Republican Presidential Nomination," August 27, 2020, American Presidency Project, https://www.presidency.ucsb.edu.

8. Cotton received both his BA and his JD from Harvard. Cruz attended Princeton for his undergraduate degree and then Harvard Law. Hawley earned his BA at Stanford and his JD at Yale Law.

9. Trump Press Release, "President Releases List of Prospective Supreme Court Nominees, Biden Must Do the Same," September 9, 2020, https://trumpwhitehouse.archives.gov/briefings-statements/remarks-president-trump-judicial-appointments/.

10. Alex Isenstadt and Marc Caputo, "Trump-World Clashes over Barrett vs. Lagoa," *Politico*, September 22, 2020. On the perceived ideology of the two, see also Epstein, Martin, and Quinn 2020.

11. Jonathan Swan and Alayna Treene, "Meadows: Trump Will Not Meet with Lagoa in Florida," *Axios*, September 22, 2022.

12. Ariane de Vogue, Kaitlan Collings, and Kevin Liptak, "How Trump Picked Amy Coney Barrett over Barbara Lagoa for the Supreme Court," *CNN.com*, September 26, 2020.

13. Andrew Naughtie, "'Only a Ghoul Would Tweet Something Like This': Republican Senators Under Fire for Online Responses to Ruth Bader Ginsburg's Death," *The Independent*, September 19, 2020.

14. Peter Baker, "With Nothing Else Working, Trump Races to Make a New Supreme Court Justice the Issue," *New York Times*, September 22, 2020.

15. Jonathan Martin and Maggie Haberman, "Why the Supreme Court Fight Is a Tightrope for Trump in November," *New York Times*, September 26, 2020.

16. Reid J. Epstein, "How Barrett and the Court Fight Are Influencing Swing Voters," *New York Times*, September 28, 2020.

17. Maggie Haberman, Alexander Burns, and Jonathan Martin, "As Election Day Arrives, Trump Shifts Between Combativeness and Grievance," *New York Times*, November 2, 2020.

18. Jeremy W. Peters, "'Fat and Happy' with a Conservative Court, Are Republicans Losing a Winning Issue?," *New York Times*, October 27, 2020.

19. Lisa Mascaro, Zeke Miller, and Mary Clare Jalonick, "GOP Senators See Political, Principle Gain in Court Fight," *Washington Post*, September 23, 2020.

20. Based on a word search at the American Presidency Project, https://www.presidency.ucsb.edu.

21. Excerpts from President Donald J. Trump's Remarks at Tonight's Make America Great Again Rally in Johnstown, Pennsylvania, October 13, 2020, American Presidency Project, https://www.presidency.ucsb.edu; Maggie Haberman, Alexander Burns, and Jonathan Martin, "As Election Day Arrives, Trump Shifts Between Combativeness and Grievance," *New York Times*, November 2, 2020.

22. Dr. Al Gross, "Hiding," YouTube video, October 9, 2020, https://www.youtube.com/watch?v=TrxdjfuNtPI.

23. Dr. Al Gross, "SCOTUS / Dr. Al Gross for U.S. Senate," YouTube video, September 19, 2020, https://www.youtube.com/watch?v=X5ewrV2Tv3A.

24. Mary Peltola for Congress, "Right to Privacy," YouTube video, October 14, 2022, https://www.youtube.com/watch?v=qUlZwC6o5qY.

25. Biden, "Statement by Vice President Joe Biden on President Trump's Visit to North Carolina," September 2, 2020, American Presidency Project, https://www.presidency.ucsb.edu.

26. Biden, "Remarks by Vice President Joe Biden in Wilmington, Delaware," October 28, 2020, American Presidency Project, https://www.presidency.ucsb.edu.

27. See, for example, Carl Hulse, "Progressives Begin New Push to Elevate Supreme Court as a Campaign Issue," *New York Times*, July 1, 2020.

28. Audio available at https://dcs.megaphone.fm/AXIOS9653473909.mp3?key=c83159a9c630400749007c7e612ce081.

29. "Presidential Debate in Cleveland, Ohio," September 29, 2020, American Presidency Project, https://www.presidency.ucsb.edu.

30. "Presidential Debate in Cleveland, Ohio," September 29, 2020, American Presidency Project, https://www.presidency.ucsb.edu.

31. Based on a word search at the American Presidency Project website: https://www.presidency.ucsb.edu.

32. Trump, "Remarks in a Town Hall Meeting with Savannah Guthrie of NBC News at the Perez Art Museum in Miami, Florida," October 15, 2020, American Presidency Project, https://www.presidency.ucsb.edu.

33. See, for example, Robert Griffin, "Don't Trust the Exit Polls. This Explains Why," *Washington Post*, November 10, 2020.

34. See also Tagliarina 2022.

35. Lansford 2022, 219.

36. Brattebo 2022, 254.

37. Kendall Karson, "On Campaign Trail, Vulnerable GOP Senators Play Down a More Conservative Supreme Court," *ABCNews.com*, October 6, 2020.

38. "Read Susan Collins's Speech Declaring Support for Kavanaugh," *New York Times*, October 5, 2018.

39. Karl Hulse, "Kavanaugh Gave Private Assurances. Collins Says He 'Misled' Her," *New York Times*, June 24, 2022.

40. Emily Cochrane, "After Susan Collins Again Says She Won't Back Judge Barrett, Trump Lashes Out," *New York Times*, October 16, 2020.

41. Glen Johnson and Alayna Treene, "Scoop: Schumer's Regrets," *Politico*, November 30, 2020. Schumer also blamed the fact that Cal Cunningham "couldn't keep his zipper up." North Carolina's Cunningham was leading in the polls against incumbent Republican Senator Thom Tillis when an extramarital scandal broke. He ended up losing to Tillis by 1.75 percent.

42. Alan Rappeport and Charlie Savage, "Donald Trump Releases List of Possible Supreme Court Picks," *New York Times*, May 18, 2016.

43. Trump, "Rally in Ashburn Virginia, August 2, 2016," YouTube video, October 26, 2017, quote around 39:30, https://www.youtube.com/watch?v=nzgxdzFSvGs.

44. Adam Liptak, "Trump's Supreme Court List: Ivy League? Out. The Heartland? In," *New York Times*, November 14, 2016.

45. Trump Press Release, "Doing What He Said He Would: President Trump's Transparent, Principled and Consistent Process for Choosing a Supreme Court Nominee," January 31, 2021, American Presidency Project, https://www.presidency.ucsb.edu.

46. Epstein, Martin, and Quinn 2018.

47. Frank 2004, 6–7.

48. Indeed, serious people began making serious arguments questioning whether Republican presidents were actually interested in the end of *Roe*. Tom Keck and I discuss some of these arguments in Keck and McMahon 2016, 36–37.

49. Based on a word search at the American Presidency Project, https://www.presidency.ucsb.edu.

50. Hannah Levintova, "Pence Tells Evangelicals He'll Help Trump Restrict Abortion Rights," *Mother Jones*, September 10, 2016.

51. "Remarks by President Trump at the 47th Annual March for Life," January 24, 2020, American Presidency Project, https://www.presidency.ucsb.edu.

52. Josh Dawsey, "Trump Publicly Praises Roe's Repeal—But Privately Frets About Impact," *Washington Post*, June 24, 2022; Nikki McCann Ramirez and Asawin Suebsaeng, "In Private, Trump 'Keeps Shitting All Over' the End of *Roe v. Wade*," *Rolling Stone*, June 24, 2022.

53. Eliza Fawcett, "Arizona Justice Reinstates Strict Abortion Ban from 1864," *New York Times*, September 22, 2022.

54. Frymer 1999.

55. Although see Kevin J. McMahon and Thomas M. Keck, "Rudy of Two Minds on Abortion," *Hartford Courant*, October 11, 2007.

56. "Massachusetts Senatorial Debate," C-SPAN, October 25, 1994, https://www.c-span.org/video/?61101-1/massachusetts-senatorial-debate.

57. Nate Cohn, "Kansas Result Suggests 4 out of 5 States Would Back Abortion Rights in Similar Vote," *New York Times*, August 4, 2022.

Chapter Thirteen

1. There were problems with the argument, however. In truth, much of the Court had only recently been constructed, the product of the long domination of the presidency by Republicans. Three of the justices were confirmed less than seven years before FDR released his plan. And two of the three longest-serving members—seemingly the most behind the times—were the only two Democratic appointees, including Brandeis.

2. Leuchtenburg 1995, 121.

3. He was also one of only two elected presidents since the popular vote began to matter in 1824 who served a full term without a Supreme Court vacancy. There were also no vacancies in Woodrow Wilson's second term (1917–21). Before the popular vote mattered, there were no vacancies in James Madison's second term (1813–17) and James Monroe's first (1817–21).

4. See, for example, Feldman 2021.

5. For a discussion of the politics surrounding the retirement of Supreme Court justices, see Ward 2003.

6. The Court did witness seven deaths from 1938 to 1954 (Cardozo, 1938; Butler, 1939; Stone, 1946; Murphy, 1949; Rutledge, 1949; Vinson, 1953; and Jackson, 1954). However, all had served relatively short terms—between 6 and 21 years—and were comparatively young—between 55 and 73—when they died.

7. Although two (Black and Harlan) were very close to death and two others (Frankfurter and Douglas) had recently suffered a stroke. Several others cited health concerns and a desire to limit their workload.

8. Souter, Stevens, and Kennedy retired in 2009, 2010, and 2018 respectively. Rehnquist (age 80), Scalia (79), and Ginsburg (87) died in 2005, 2016, and 2020, respectively. Despite dying suddenly, there was no autopsy completed after Scalia's body was discovered.

9. Of course, Pope Benedict XVI stepped down from the papacy in 2013, the first pontiff to do so in six centuries.

10. Adam Liptak, "Court Is 'One of Most Activist,' Ginsburg Says, Vowing to Stay," *New York Times*, August 24, 2013.

11. See, for example, Darragh Roche, "Ruth Bader Ginsburg's 'Cult of Personality' Doomed *Roe v. Wade*—Experts," *Newsweek*, May 4, 2022.

12. Margaret Talbot, "Is the Supreme Court's Fate in Elena Kagan's Hands?," *The New Yorker*, November 18, 2019.

13. Rosa Cartagena, "These New 'Wear a Mask' Signs Invoke RBG, and They're Awesome," *Washingtonian*, July 16, 2020.

14. For example, Antonin Scalia said he saw no evidence of decline in any of the individuals he served with on the Court, "A Conversation with Antonin Scalia, hosted by Calvin Massey," Legally Speaking, University of California Television, YouTube video, September 2010, at 9:40, https://www.youtube.com/watch?v=KvttIukZEtM.

15. The seven terms are as follows: Wilson 2 (March 4, 1917–March 3, 1921); Coolidge 2 (March 4, 1925–March 3, 1929); FDR 1 (March 4, 1913–January 20, 1937); Carter (January 20, 1977–January 20, 1981); Clinton 2 (January 20, 1997–January 20, 2001); W. Bush 1 (January 20, 2001–January 20, 2005); and Obama 2 (January 20, 2013–January 20, 2017). Of course, there was a vacancy in Obama 2, but the Republican Senate successfully prevented him from naming a new justice. Moreover, Harlan F. Stone began his Supreme Court service two days before President Calvin Coolidge took the oath of office for a second time (after winning election in his own right). Previously, Coolidge was completing Warren Harding's first term. Harding named four justices. Before 1869, there were three presidential terms without the addition of a new justice: Madison 2 (March 4, 1813–March 3, 1817); Monroe 1 (March 4, 1817–March 3, 1821); and Lincoln/Johnson (March 4, 1865–March 3, 1869). As explained in the main text above, the lack of new justices during the Lincoln/Johnson term was the result of Lincoln's assassination and congressional manipulation. There were two vacancies unfilled during these years. President Johnson tried unsuccessfully to fill one.

16. Neil A. Lewis, "2 Years After His Bruising Hearing, Justice Thomas Can Rarely Be Heard," *New York Times*, November 27, 1993.

17. While there are several ways to determine "natural courts," in the seventh edition of *The Supreme Court Compendium* Lee Epstein, Jeffrey A. Segal, Harold Spaeth, and Thomas G. Walker define them as beginning "when a new justice takes the oath of office and continu[ing] until the next new justice takes the oath" (Epstein, Segal, Spaeth, and Walker 2021, 421). This definition results in fewer natural courts because it does not count those with long vacancies.

18. Dahl 1957, 284–85.

19. There were twenty-one justices appointed in those thirty-six years (excluded Stone's elevation to chief). 36/21=1.71.

20. Here's another way to consider the same phenomenon: In the forty-four years from when Jimmy Carter took the oath of office until Donald Trump's final day in the White House, there have been seven presidencies spanning over eleven terms. During that time, there were thirteen vacancies on the Court to fill; that's approximately one every three years and three months. In the forty-four years before that (1933–1977), there were also seven presidencies. But during those eleven terms, there were twenty-six vacancies—exactly double the number from the recent period, one every year and nine months. Let's take it back even farther. In the forty-four years before that (1889–1932), there were nine presidencies, and once again, twenty-six vacancies in those eleven terms.

21. There have been eight justices appointed so far in those twenty-four years. 24/8=3.

22. "Higher income was associated with longer life at all income levels. Men in the bottom 1% of the income distribution at the age of 40 years had an expected age of death of 72.7 years.

Men in the top 1% of the income distribution had an expected age of death of 87.3 years, 14.6 years (95% CI, 14.4–14.8 years) higher than those in the bottom 1%. Women in the bottom 1% of the income distribution at the age of 40 years had an expected age of death of 78.8 years. Women in the top 1% had an expected age of death of 88.9 years, which is 10.1 years (95% CI, 9.9–10.3 years) higher than life expectancy for women in the bottom 1%." Chetty et al. 2016, 1750–66, https://www.ncbi.nlm.nih.gov/pmc/articles/PMC4866586/. The 2021 salaries for associate justices and the chief justice were $268,300 and $280,500, respectively. Assuming no other income and individual status, this salary would put the justices near the top 5 percent of wage earners. Many of the justices have earned higher salaries prior to becoming a justice, or earned additional money by publishing a book while on the Court. Recently, Justice Thomas has been criticized for the number of gifts he has received from a billionaire friend—see Joshua Kaplan, Justin Elliott, and Alex Mierjeski, "Clarence Thomas and the Billionaire," *ProPublica*, April 6, 2023, https://www.propublica.org/article/clarence-thomas-scotus-undisclosed-luxury-travel-gifts-crow. See also Brett Murphy and Alex Mierjeski, "Clarence Thomas' 38 Vacations: The Other Billionaires Who Have Treated the Supreme Court Justice to Luxury Travel," *ProPublica*, August 10, 2023, https://www.propublica.org/article/clarence-thomas-other-billionaires-sokol-huizenga-novelly-su preme-court; Jo Becker and Julie Tate, "Clarence Thomas's $267,230 R.V. and the Friend Who Financed It," *New York Times,* August 5, 2023.

23. Justice Stephen Johnson Field (May 20, 1863–December 1, 1897). Unlike Marshall, Field retired from the high bench, and lived for another sixteen months.

24. Quoted in Devins and Baum 2019, 133; original source, Lewis, "2 Years After His Bruising Hearing."

25. "Uncommon Knowledge with Justice Antonin Scalia," interview with Peter Robinson, YouTube video, October 30, 2012, around 20:00, https://www.youtube.com/watch?v=DaoLMW5AF4Y.

26. Jennifer Senior, "In Conversation: Antonin Scalia," *New York Magazine*, October 4, 2013.

27. Mike Rappaport, "Scalia and Ginsburg on Constitutional Amendments," *Law & Liberty*, April 22, 2014, https://www.lawliberty.org/2014/04/22/scalia-and-ginsburg-on-constitutional-amendments/.

28. I use the 2016—instead of the 2020—election results because they provide a clearer portrait of the implications of political polarization in our constitutional structure. Most notably, in 2016, Donald Trump captured the presidency (despite losing the popular vote) and did so by winning 30 of the 50 states (several by very narrow margins).

29. The 21st amendment, which repealed the 18th (prohibition), is the only amendment to be ratified via state conventions.

30. But see Guerra 2013, chapter 6.

31. Guerra 2013, 152; Levinson 2006, 21 ; Lutz 2006.

32. Stevens 2014, 13.

33. Eric Posner, "The U.S. Constitution Is Impossible to Amend," *Slate*, May 5, 2014, https://slate.com/news-and-politics/2014/05/amending-the-constitution-is-much-too-hard-blame-the-founders.html.

34. Using Scalia's formula, a bare majority in those states made up 28.3 percent of the total.

35. A bare majority in those states would be half of that, 20.1 percent.

36. This analysis was conducted using state legislative election results from 2018 to 2022. It is important to note given that I use races with the lowest vote totals that two of the thirty-eight

states—Hawaii and Louisiana—cancel some state legislative races in which a candidate runs unopposed, thereby resulting in zero total votes. Florida cancels uncontested elections as well.

37. 2018 population figures.

38. This does not include Nebraska, since its unicameral legislature is nonpartisan. Emily Badger, Quoctrung Bui, and Adam Pearce, "Republicans Dominate State Politics. But Democrats Made a Dent This Year," *New York Times*, November 10, 2018, https://www.nytimes.com/interactive/2018/11/10/upshot/republicans-dominate-state-politics-but-democrats-made-a-dent.html?mtrref=www.nytimes.com.

39. Grace Panetta and Brent D. Griffiths, "Republicans' Next Big Play Is to 'Scare the Hell Out of Washington' by Rewriting the Constitution. And They're Willing to Play the Long Game to Win," *Insider*, July 31, 2022.

40. New York and New Jersey—which abolished slavery in 1799 and 1804, respectively—had the largest enslaved populations of these seven states, with just over 6 percent each. The other five states had enslaved populations ranging from 0 (Massachusetts) to 1.38 percent (Rhode Island).

41. Washington is the most populated at 13.

Chapter Fourteen

1. Obergefell v. Hodges, 576 U.S. 644 (2015).

2. Cases include Carter v. Carter Coal Company, 298 U.S. 238 (1936), and National Labor Relations Board v. Jones & Laughlin Steel Corporation, 301 U.S. 1 (1937).

3. McMahon 2004, 19, 219; see also Keck and McMahon 2016, 37.

4. If the newly confirmed Justice Ketanji Brown Jackson is added to that list, the figure would likely rise to sixteen.

5. Students for Fair Admissions, Inc. v. President & Fellows of Harvard College and Students for Fair Admissions, Inc. v. University of North Carolina, ___ U.S. ___ (2023).

6. *Obergefell v. Hodges.*

7. Thomas wrote in *Dobbs*: "In future cases, we should reconsider all of this Court's substantive due process precedents, including *Griswold*, *Lawrence*, and *Obergefell*. Because any substantive due process decision is 'demonstrably erroneous,' we have a duty to 'correct the error' established in those precedents." Dobbs v. Jackson Women's Health Organization, 597 U.S. ___ (2022).

8. See the bipartisan report Presidential Commission on the Supreme Court 2021 for a discussion of several such proposals. See also Epps and Sitaraman 2021.

9. Levitsky and Ziblatt 2018.

10. McMahon 2004, 79–86.

11. See Presidential Commission on the Supreme Court 2021, chapter 3, part IV, for a discussion of Congress's power to limit the terms of Supreme Court justices by statute.

12. Rosenberg 1991, 2008, 427.

13. Jared Gans, "Trump Says 'Abortion Issue' Responsible for GOP Underperforming Expectations in Midterms," *The Hill*, January 1, 2023.

14. Balkin 2020.

15. This may take the form of a popular constitutionalism Mark Tushnet develops in *Taking Back the Constitution*, in which he suggests a "progressive alternative [that] combines a reinvigorated system of public participation in democratic self-government with commitments to the thicker and more social-democratic government that characterized the New Deal/Great Society order at its height" (Tushnet 2020, x).

16. According to Jeffrey M. Jones of Gallup, "Americans' confidence in the court has dropped sharply over the past year and reached a new low in Gallup's nearly 50-year trend. Twenty-five percent of US adults say they have 'a great deal' or 'quite a lot' of confidence in the US Supreme Court, down from 36% a year ago and five percentage points lower than the previous low recorded in 2014." Jones, "Confidence in U.S. Supreme Court Sinks to New Low," *Gallup.com*, June 23, 2022.

References

Abraham, Henry J. 1999. *Justices, Presidents, and Senators: A History of the U.S. Supreme Court Appointments from Washington to Clinton.* New York: Rowman & Littlefield.

Ackerman, Bruce A. 1991. *We the People*, Vol. 1, *Foundations.* Cambridge, MA: Harvard University Press.

Adamany, David. 1973. "Legitimacy, Realigning Elections and the Supreme Court." *Wisconsin Law Review* 3: 790–846.

Alsop, Joseph, and Turner Catledge. 1938. *The 168 Days.* Garden City, NY: Doubleday, Doran.

Avery, Michael, and Danielle McLaughlin. 2013. *The Federalist Society: How Conservatives Took the Law Back from Liberals.* Nashville, TN: Vanderbilt University Press.

Baker, Liva. 1983. *Miranda: Crime, Law and Politics.* New York: Atheneum.

Balkin, Jack M. 2020. *The Cycles of Constitutional Time.* New York: Oxford University Press.

Ball, Howard. 1996. *Hugo L. Black: Cold Steel Warrior.* New York: Oxford University Press.

Baum, Lawrence, and Neal Devins. 2010. "Why the Supreme Court Cares About Elites, Not the American People." *Georgetown Law Journal* 98: 1515–81.

Beth, Richard, and Betsy Palmer. 2011. "Supreme Court Nominations: Senate Floor Procedure and Practice, 1789–2011." *Congressional Research Service*, March 11.

Bickel, Alexander M. 1986. *The Least Dangerous Branch: The Supreme Court at the Bar of Politics.* 2nd edition. New York: Bobbs-Merrill.

Biskupic, Joan. 2005. *Sandra Day O'Connor: How the First Woman on the Supreme Court Became Its Most Influential Justice.* New York: Ecco/Harper Collins.

———. 2009. *American Original: The Life and Constitution of Supreme Court Justice Antonin Scalia.* New York: Sarah Crichton Books.

———. 2014. *Breaking In: The Rise of Sonia Sotomayor and the Politics of Justice.* New York: Sarah Crichton Books.

———. 2019. *The Chief: The Life and Turbulent Times of Chief Justice John Roberts.* New York: Basic Books.

Black, Earl, and Merle Black. 1987. *Politics and Society in the South.* Cambridge, MA: Harvard University Press.

———. 2002. *The Rise of Southern Republicans.* Cambridge, MA: Harvard University Press.

Blaustein, Albert P., and Roy M. Mersky. 1978. *The First One Hundred Justices: Statistical Studies on the Supreme Court of the United States.* Hamden, CT: Shoe String Press, Archon Books.

Bork, Robert H. 1990. *The Tempting of America: The Political Seduction of the Law.* New York: Free Press.

———. 1996. *Slouching Toward Gomorrah: Modern Liberalism and American Decline.* New York: Reagan Books.

———. 2002. "Adversary Jurisprudence." In *The Survival of Culture: Permanent Values in a Virtual Age*, ed. Hilton Kramer and Roger Kimball. Chicago: Ivan R. Dee.

Brattebo, Douglas M. 2022. "Iowa U.S. Senate Campaign: Confirmation of Party Realignment in the Hawkeye State." In *The Roads to Congress 2020: Campaigning in the Era of Trump and COVID-19*, ed. Sean D. Foreman, Marcia L. Godwin, and Walter Clark Wilson, 245–64. New York: Palgrave Macmillan.

Braver, Joshua. 2020. "Court-Packing: An American Tradition?" *Boston College Law Review* 61, no. 8 (November): 2747–2808.

Bronner, Ethan. 1989. *Battle for Justice: How the Bork Nomination Shook America.* New York: W. W. Norton.

Buchanan, Patrick J. 2014. *The Greatest Comeback: How Richard Nixon Rose from Defeat to Create the New Majority.* New York: Crown Forum.

Burnham, Walter Dean. 1970. *Critical Elections and the Mainsprings of American Politics.* New York: W. W. Norton.

Burns, James McGregor. 1956. *Roosevelt: The Lion and the Fox 1882–1940.* New York: Harcourt Brace Jovanovich.

Busch, Andrew E. 2007. *The Constitution on the Campaign Trail: The Surprising Political Career of America's Founding Document.* Lanham, MD: Rowman & Littlefield.

Bush, George W. 2010. *Decision Points.* New York: Crown.

Byrnes, James F. 1958. *All in One Lifetime.* New York: Harper & Brothers.

Calmes, Jackie. 2021. *Dissent: The Radicalization of the Republican Party and Its Capture of the Court.* New York: Twelve.

Carmon, Irin, and Shana Knizhnik. 2015. *Notorious RBG: The Life and Times of Ruth Bader Ginsburg.* New York: Day Street Books.

Carter, Stephen L. 1995. *The Confirmation Mess: Cleaning Up the Federal Appointments Process.* New York: Basic Books.

Casper, Jonathan. 1976. "The Supreme Court and National Policy Making." *American Political Science Review* 70: 50–63.

Ceaser, James, and Andrew Busch. 2005. *Red Over Blue: The 2004 Elections and American Politics.* New York: Rowman & Littlefield, 2005.

Chemerinsky, Erwin. 2014. *The Case Against the Supreme Court.* New York: Viking.

Chetty, Raj, John N. Friedman, Emmanuel Saez, Nicholas Turner, and Danny Yagan. 2017. "Mobility Report Cards: The Role of Colleges in Intergenerational Mobility." National Bureau of Economic Research, working paper 23618, July. https://doi.org/10.3386/w23618.

Chetty, Raj, Michael Stepner, Sarah Abraham, Shelby Lin, Benjamin Schuderi, Nicholas Turner, Augustin Bergeron, and David Cutler. 2016. "The Association Between Income and Life Expectancy in the United States, 2001–2014." *JAMA* 315, no. 16 (April 26): 1750–66.

Clark, Tom S. 2011. *The Limits of Judicial Independence.* New York: Cambridge University Press.

Clayton, Cornell W., and Howard Gillman, eds. 1999. *Supreme Court Decision-Making: New Institutionalist Approaches.* Chicago: University of Chicago Press.

Clayton, Cornell W., and David May. 1999. "A Political Regimes Approach to the Analysis of Legal Decisions." *Polity* 32 (Winter): 233–52.

Clayton, Cornell W., and J. Mitchell Pickerill. 2004. "Guess What Happened on the Way to Revolution? Precursors to the Supreme Court's Federalism Revolution." *Publius: The Journal of Federalism* 34, no. 3 (Summer): 85–114.

Clinton, William Jefferson. 2005. *My Life*. New York: Vintage Books.

Collins, Paul M., Jr., and Matthew Eshbaugh-Soha. 2019. *The President and the Supreme Court: Going Public on Judicial Decisions from Washington to Trump*. New York: Cambridge University Press.

Collins, Paul M., Jr., and Lori A. Ringhand. 2013. *Supreme Court Confirmation Hearings and Constitutional Change*. New York: Cambridge University Press.

Comiskey, Michael. 2004. *Seeking Justices: The Judging of Supreme Court Nominees*. Lawrence: University Press of Kansas.

Conkin, Paul. 1967. *The New Deal*. New York: Crowell.

Coulter, Ann. 2013. *Never Trust a Liberal Over 3, Especially a Republican*. Washington, DC: Regnery Publishing, Inc.

Crowe, Justin. 2012. *Building the Judiciary: Law, Courts, and the Politics of Institutional Development*. Princeton, NJ: Princeton University Press.

Crowe, Justin, and Christopher F. Karpowitz. 2007. "Where Have You Gone, Sherman Minton? The Decline of the Short-Term Supreme Court Justice." *Perspectives on Politics* 5, no. 3 (September): 425–45.

Cruz, Ted. 2020. *One Vote Away: How a Single Supreme Court Seat Can Change History*. Washington, DC: Regnery Publishing.

Dahl, Robert A. 1957. "Decision-Making in a Democracy: The Supreme Court as a National Policy-Maker." *Journal of Public Law* 6: 279–95.

Dalin, David G. 2017. *Jewish Justices of the Supreme Court: From Brandeis to Kagan*. Waltham, MA: Brandeis University Press.

Davis, Kenneth S. 1993. *FDR, Into the Storm 1937–1940: A History*. New York: Random House.

Davis, Steve. 1978. "The South as 'the Nation's No. 1 Economic Problem': The NEC Report of 1938." *Georgia Historical Society* 62, no. 2 (Summer): 119–32.

Dean, John W. 2001. *The Rehnquist Choice: The Untold Story of the Nixon Appointment that Redefined the Supreme Court*. New York: Free Press.

Decker, John F. 1992. *Revolution to the Right: Criminal Procedure Jurisprudence During the Burger-Rehnquist Court Era*. New York: Garland.

De Hart, Jane Sherron. 2018. *Ruth Bader Ginsburg: A Life*. New York: Vintage Books.

Devins, Neal, and Lawrence Baum. 2019. *The Company They Keep: How Partisan Divisions Came to the Court*. New York: Oxford University Press.

Douglas, William O. 1974. *Go East, Young Man: The Early Years: The Autobiography of William O. Douglas*. New York: Random House.

Dunne, Gerald T. 1977. *Hugo Black and the Judicial Revolution*. New York: Simon and Schuster.

Dworkin, Ronald. 1996. *Freedom's Law: The Moral Reading of the American Constitution*. New York: Oxford University Press.

Ely, John Hart. 1980. *Democracy and Distrust: A Theory of Judicial Review*. Cambridge, MA: Harvard University Press.

Engel, Stephen M. 2011. *American Politicians Confront the Court: Opposition Politics and Changing Responses to Judicial Power*. New York: Cambridge University Press.

Epps, Daniel, and Ganesh Sitaraman. 2021. "The Future of Supreme Court Reform." *Harvard Law Review Forum* 134:398–414.

Epstein, Lee, and Jack Knight. 1998. *The Choices Justices Make.* Washington, DC: Congressional Quarterly Press.

Epstein, Lee, Jack Knight, and Andrew D. Martin. 2003. "The Norm of Prior Judicial Experience and Its Consequences for Career Diversity on the U.S. Supreme Court." *California Law Review* 91, no. 4 (July): 903–66.

Epstein, Lee, William M. Landes, and Richard A. Posner. 2013. *The Behavior of Federal Judges: A Theoretical and Empirical Study of Rational Choice.* Cambridge, MA: Harvard University Press.

Epstein, Lee, Andrew D. Martin, and Kevin Quinn. 2016a. "Possible Presidents and Their Possible Justices." September 15. https://static1.squarespace.com/static/60188505fb790b33c3d33a61/t/6050e3f9b980b95b1ca7097b/1615913977303/PossibleNominees.pdf.

———. 2016b. "President-Elect Trump and His Possible Justices." December 15. https://static1.squarespace.com/static/60188505fb790b33c3d33a61/t/6050e3c5c886fd052d958d09/1615913926044/PossibleTrumpJustices.pdf.

———. 2018. "Replacing Justice Kennedy." https://static1.squarespace.com/static/60188505fb790b33c3d33a61/t/6050e26214e1e364335b4a3d/1615913570955/ReplacingJusticeKennedy.pdf.

———. 2020. "Replacing Justice Ginsburg." Report, September 21. https://static1.squarespace.com/static/60188505fb790b33c3d33a61/t/60447dcccc3c7b44bb68c2b7/1615101388838/ReplacingJusticeGinsburg.pdf.

———. 2022. "Replacing Justice Breyer." Report, January 24. https://static1.squarespace.com/static/60188505fb790b33c3d33a61/t/61f1855081fb31470cda3c37/1643218256396/ReplacingJusticeBreyer.pdf.

Epstein, Lee, Andrew Martin, Jeffrey Segal, and Chad Westerland. 2007. "The Judicial Common Space." *Journal of Law, Economics, and Organization* 23: 303–25.

Epstein, Lee, and Jeffrey A. Segal. 2005. *Advice and Consent: The Politics of Judicial Appointments.* New York: Oxford University Press.

Epstein, Lee, Jeffrey A. Segal, Harold J. Spaeth, and Thomas G. Walker. 2021. *The Supreme Court Compendium: Data, Decisions, and Developments.* 7th ed. Washington, DC: Congressional Quarterly.

Epstein, Lee, Thomas G. Walker, Nancy Staudt, Scott Hendrickson, and Jason Roberts. 2022. "The U.S. Supreme Court Justices Database." Last updated October 28. Accessed January 30, 2023. https://epstein.usc.edu/justicesdata.

Evans, Rowland, Jr., and Robert D. Novak. 1971. *Nixon in the White House: The Frustration of Power.* New York: Random House.

Feldman, Noah. 2010. *Scorpions: The Battles and Triumphs of FDR's Great Supreme Court Justices.* New York: Twelve.

Feldman, Stephen M. 2021. *Pack the Court! A Defense of Supreme Court Expansion.* Philadelphia, PA: Temple University Press.

Ferren, John M. 2004. *Salt of the Earth, Conscience of the Court: The Story of Justice Wiley Rutledge.* Chapel Hill: University of North Carolina Press.

Fjelstul, Jill. 2014. "RV Association Members' Profile: A Demographic Segmentation and Lifestyle Exploration." *Journal of Tourism Insights* 5, no. 1 (July).

Flowers, Prudence. 2019. *The Right-to-Life Movement, the Reagan Administration, and the Politics of Abortion.* Cham, Switzerland: Palgrave Pivot.

Frank, John P. 1991. *Clement Haynsworth, the Senate, and the Supreme Court.* Charlottesville: University Press of Virginia.

Frank, T. 2004. *What's the Matter with Kansas? How Conservatives Won the Heart of America.* New York: Metropolitan Books/Henry Holt.

Frankfurter, Felix. 1957. "The Supreme Court in the Mirror of Justices." *University of Pennsylvania Law Review* 105, no. 6 (April): 781–96.

Friedman, Barry. 2009. *The Will of the People: How Public Opinion Has Influenced the Supreme Court and Shaped the Meaning of the Constitution.* New York: Farrar, Straus and Giroux.

Friedman, Richard D. 1983. "The Transformation in the Senate Response to Supreme Court Nominations: From Reconstruction to the Taft Administration and Beyond." *Cardozo Law Review* 5: 1–95.

Frymer, Paul. 1999. *Uneasy Alliances: Race and Party Competition in America.* Princeton, NJ: Princeton University Press.

Funston, Richard. 1975. "The Supreme Court and Critical Elections." *American Political Science Review* 69: 795–811.

Garner, Brian A. 2018. *Nino and Me: My Unusual Friendship with Justice Antonin Scalia.* New York: Threshold Editions.

Gates, John B. 1992. *The Supreme Court and Partisan Realignment: A Macro- and Microlevel Perspective.* Boulder, CO: Westview Press.

George, Tracey E. 2008. "From Judge to Justice: Social Background Theory and the Supreme Court." *North Carolina Law Review* 86: 1333–68.

Gerhardt, Michael J. 2006. "Super Precedent." *Minnesota Law Review* 90: 1204–31.

Gibson, James L. 2022. "Losing Legitimacy: The Challenges of the Dobbs Ruling to Conventional Legitimacy Theory." Social Science Research Network, September 1. https://ssrn.com/abstract=4206986 or http://dx.doi.org/10.2139/ssrn.4206986.

Gibson, James L., and Gregory A. Caldeira. 2009. *Citizens, Courts, and Confirmations: Positivity Theory and the Judgments of the American People.* Princeton, NJ: Princeton University Press.

Gillman, Howard. 2002. "How Political Parties Can Use the Courts to Advance Their Agendas: Federal Courts in the United States, 1875–1891." *American Political Science Review* 96: 511–24.

———. 2004. "Martin Shapiro and the New Institutionalism in Judicial Behavior Studies." *Annual Review of Political Science* 7: 363–82.

———. 2006. "Party Politics and Constitutional Change: The Political Origins of Liberal Judicial Activism." In *The Supreme Court and American Political Development,* ed. Ronald Kahn and Ken I. Kersch. Lawrence: University Press of Kansas.

Gillman, Howard, and Cornell Clayton, eds. 1999. *The Supreme Court in American Politics: New Institutionalist Interpretations.* Lawrence: University Press of Kansas.

Ginsburg, Ruth Bader. "Speaking in a Judicial Voice." *NYU Law Review* 67 (December): 1185.

Ginsburg, Ruth Bader, with Mary Hartnett and Wendy W. Williams. 2016. *My Words.* New York: Simon & Schuster.

Gitenstein, Mark. 1992. *Matters of Principle: An Insider's Account of America's Rejection of Robert Bork's Nomination to the Supreme Court.* New York: Simon & Schuster.

Gladwell, Malcolm. 2008. *Outliers: The Story of Success.* Boston: Little Brown.

Goldman, Sheldon. 1997. *Picking Federal Judges: Lower Court Selection from Roosevelt Through Reagan*. New Haven, CT: Yale University Press.

———. 2006. "The Politics of Appointing Catholics to the Federal Courts." *University of St. Thomas Law Review* 4: 193–220.

Gonzales, Alberto R. 2016. *True Faith and Allegiance: A Story of Service and Sacrifice in War and Peace*. Nashville, TN: Thomas Nelson.

Gorsuch, Neil M. 2006. *The Future of Assisted Suicide and Euthanasia*. Princeton, NJ: Princeton University Press.

Graber, Mark A. 1993. "The Nonmajoritarian Difficulty: Legislative Deference to the Judiciary." *Studies in American Political Development* 7 (Spring): 35–73.

———. 2005. "Constructing Judicial Review." *American Review of Political Science* 8: 425–51.

Green, Joshua. 2017. *Devil's Bargain: Steve Bannon, Donald Trump, and the Storming of the Presidency*. New York: Penguin Press.

Greenburg, J. C. 2007. *Supreme Conflict: The Inside Story of the Struggle for Control of the United States Supreme Court*. New York: Penguin Press.

Greenhouse, Linda. 2005. *Becoming Justice Blackmun: Harry Blackmun's Supreme Court*. New York: Times Books.

———. 2021. *Justice on the Brink: The Death of Ruth Bader Ginsburg, the Rise of Amy Coney Barrett, and Twelve Months That Transformed the Supreme Court*. New York: Random House.

Guerra, Darren Patrick. 2013. *Perfecting the Constitution: The Case for the Article V Amendment Process*. Blue Ridge Summit, PA: Lexington Books.

Gunther, Gerald. 1994. *Learned Hand: The Man and the Judge*. Cambridge, MA: Harvard University Press.

Hall, Matthew E. K. 2018. *What Justices Want: Goals and Personality on the U.S. Supreme Court*. New York: Cambridge University Press.

Harrison, Robert. 1984. "The Breakup of the Roosevelt Supreme Court: A Contribution of History and Biography." *Law and History Review* 2: 165–221.

———. "The Breakup of the Roosevelt Court: The Contribution of History and Biography." Ph.D. diss., Columbia University, 1987.

Hendel, Samuel. 1951. *Charles Evans Hughes and the Supreme Court*. New York: King's Crown Press.

Hirschl, Ran. 2004. *Towards Juristocracy: The Origins and Consequences of the New Constitutionalism*. Cambridge, MA: Harvard University Press.

Hirshman, Linda. 2015. *Sisters in Law: How Sandra Day O'Connor and Ruth Bader Ginsburg Went to the Supreme Court and Changed the World*. New York: Harper Collins.

Hollis-Brusky, Amanda. 2015. *Ideas with Consequences: The Federalist Society and the Conservative Counterrevolution*. New York: Oxford University Press.

Hollis-Brusky, Amanda, and Joshua C. Wilson. 2020. *Separate But Faithful: The Christian Right's Radical Struggle to Transform Law and Legal Culture*. New York: Oxford University Press.

Hulse, Carl. 2019. *Confirmation Bias: Inside Washington's War Over the Supreme Court, from Scalia's Death to Justice Kavanaugh*. New York: Harper Collins.

Jackson, Robert H. 1955. *The Supreme Court in the American System*. Cambridge, MA: Harvard University Press.

Jefferson, Renee Knake, and Hannah Brenner Johnson. 2020. *Shortlisted: Women in the Shadows of the Supreme Court*. New York: New York University Press.

Jenkins, John A. 2012. *The Partisan: The Life of William Rehnquist.* New York: Public Affairs.

Kahn, Ronald, and Ken I. Kersch, eds. 2006. *The Supreme Court and American Political Development.* Lawrence: University Press of Kansas.

Kalman, Laura. 1990. *Abe Fortas: A Biography.* New Haven, CT: Yale University Press.

———. 2017. *The Long Reach of the Sixties: LBJ, Nixon, and the Making of the Contemporary Supreme Court.* New York: Oxford University Press.

Kaplan, David A. 2018. *The Most Dangerous Branch: Inside the Supreme Court's Assault on the Constitution.* New York: Crown Publishing.

Keck, Thomas M. 2004. *The Most Activist Supreme Court in History: The Road to Modern Judicial Conservatism.* Chicago: University of Chicago Press.

———. 2007. "Party Politics or Judicial Independence? The Regime Politics Literature Hits the Law Schools." *Law & Social Inquiry* 32, no. 3: 511–44.

———. 2014. *Judicial Politics in Polarized Times.* Chicago: University of Chicago Press.

Keck, Thomas M., and Kevin J. McMahon. 2016. "Why *Roe* Still Stands: Abortion Law, the Supreme Court, and the Republican Regime." *Studies in Law, Politics, and Society* 70: 33–83.

Key, V. O., Jr. 1955. "A Theory of Critical Elections." *Journal of Politics* 17, no. 1: 3–18.

King, Gilbert. 2012. *Devil in the Grove: Thurgood Marshall, the Groveland Boys, and the Dawn of a New America.* New York: Harper Collins.

Kluger, Richard. 1975. *Simple Justice: The History of* Brown v. Board of Education *and Black America's Struggle for Equality.* New York: Vintage Books.

Kramer, Larry D. 2004. *The People Themselves: Popular Constitutionalism and Judicial Review.* New York: Oxford University Press.

Landes, William M. and Richard A. Posner. 2009. "Rational Judicial Behavior: A Statistical Study." *Journal of Legal Analysis* 1, no. 2 (Summer): 775–831.

Lansford, Tom. 2022. "Alabama U.S. Senate Race: A Referendum on the Trump Presidency." In *The Roads to Congress 2020: Campaigning in the Era of Trump and COVID-19*, ed. Sean D. Foreman, Marcia L. Godwin, and Walter Clark Wilson, 209–26. New York: Palgrave Macmillan.

Lasser, William. 1985. "The Supreme Court in Periods of Critical Realignment." *Journal of Politics* 47: 1174–87.

———. 1988. *The Limits of Judicial Power.* Chapel Hill: University of North Carolina Press.

Leiter, Brian. 2015. "Constitutional Law, Moral Judgment, and the Supreme Court as Super-Legislature." *Hastings Law Journal* 66: 1601–16.

Leuchtenburg, William E. 1995. *The Supreme Court Reborn: The Constitutional Revolution in the Age of Roosevelt.* New York: Oxford University Press.

———. 1999. "When the People Spoke, What Did They Say? The Election of 1936 and the Ackerman Thesis." *Yale Law Journal* 108: 2077–2114.

Levin, Mark. 2005. *Men in Black: How the Supreme Court Is Destroying America.* Washington, DC: Regnery Publishing.

Levinson, Sanford. 2006. *Our Undemocratic Constitution: Where the Constitution Goes Wrong (And How We the People Can Correct It).* New York: Oxford University Press.

Levitsky, Steven, and Daniel Ziblatt. 2018. *How Democracies Die.* New York: Crown Publishing.

Lovell, George I. 2003. *Legislative Deferrals: Statutory Ambiguity, Judicial Power, and American Democracy.* New York: Cambridge University Press.

Lutz, Donald. 2006. *Principles of Constitutional Design.* New York: Cambridge University Press.

Maltese, John Anthony. 1995. *The Selling of Supreme Court Nominees.* Baltimore, MD: Johns Hopkins University Press.

Maltz, Earl M. 2006. "Biography Is Destiny: The Case of Justice Peter V. Daniel." *Brooklyn Law Review* 71, no. 1: 199–209.

Markovits, Daniel. 2019. *The Meritocracy Trap: How America's Foundational Myth Feeds Inequality, Dismantles the Middle Class, and Devours the Elite*. New York: Penguin Press.

Martin, Andrew D., and Kevin M. Quinn. n.d. "Martin-Quinn Scores." Accessed May 10, 2023. https://mqscores.lsa.umich.edu/index.php.

Mason, Robert. 2004. *Richard Nixon and the Quest for a New Majority*. Chapel Hill: University of North Carolina Press.

Massaro, John. 1990. *Supremely Political: The Role of Ideology and Presidential Management in Unsuccessful Supreme Court Nominations*. Albany: State University of New York Press.

Mayer, Jane, and Jill Abramson. 1994. *Strange Justice: The Selling of Clarence Thomas*. Boston: Houghton Mifflin.

Mayhew, David. 1974. *Congress: The Electoral Connection*. New Haven, CT: Yale University Press.

McCloskey, Robert. 1960. *The American Supreme Court*. Chicago: University of Chicago Press. (Sanford Levinson ed., 6th ed. 2016).

McCullough, David. 1992. *Truman*. New York: Simon & Schuster.

McKenna, Marian C. 2002. *Franklin Roosevelt and the Great Constitutional War: The Court-Packing Crisis of 1937*. New York: Fordham University Press.

McMahon, Kevin J. 2004. *Reconsidering Roosevelt on Race: How the Presidency Paved the Road to Brown*. Chicago: University of Chicago Press.

———. 2005. "A 'Moral Values Election'? The Culture War, the Supreme Court, and a Divided America." In *Winning the White House, 2004: Region by Region, Vote by Vote*, ed. Kevin J. McMahon, David M. Rankin, Donald W. Beachler, and John Kenneth White, 23–46. New York: Palgrave Macmillan.

———. 2007. "Presidents, Political Regimes, and Contentious Supreme Court Nominations: A Historical Institutional Model." *Law & Social Inquiry* 32, no. 4 (Fall): 919–54.

———. 2008. "Explaining the Selection and Rejection of Harriet Miers: George W. Bush, Political Symbolism, and the Highpoint of Conservatism." *American Review of Politics* 29 (Fall): 253–70.

———. 2009. "Searching for the Social Issue." In *Winning the White House, 2008*, ed. Kevin J. McMahon, David M. Rankin, Donald W. Beachler, and John Kenneth White, 59–78. New York: Palgrave Macmillan.

———. 2011. *Nixon's Court: His Challenge to Judicial Liberalism and Its Political Consequences*. Chicago: University of Chicago Press.

———. 2016. "Confirming Chiefs: Ideology, Opportunity, and the Court's Center Chair." In *The Chief Justice: Appointment and Influence*, ed. David J. Danelski and Artemus Ward, 120–44. Ann Arbor: University of Michigan Press.

———. 2018a. "Will the Court Still 'Seldom Stray Very Far'? Regime Politics in a Polarized America." *Chicago-Kent Law Review* 93, no. 2: 343–71.

———. 2018b. "'The Supreme Court: It's What It's All About' . . . Or Was It? Analyzing the Court Issue in the 2016 Presidential Election." In *Conventional Wisdom, Parties, and Broken Barriers in the 2016 Election*, ed. Jennifer C. Lucas, Christopher J. Galdieri, and Tauna S. Sisco, 41–60. Blue Ridge Summit, PA: Lexington Books.

Moore, Roy. *So Help Me God: The Ten Commandments, Judicial Tyranny, and the Battle for Religious Freedom*. Nashville, TN: Broadman and Holman Publishing.

Morgan, Richard E. 2006. "The Failure of the Rehnquist Court." *Claremont Review of Books* 4, no. 6 (Spring): 51–55.

Murphy, Bruce Allen. 2014. *Scalia: The Court of One*. New York: Simon & Schuster.

Nelson, Garrison. 2013. *Pathways to the US Supreme Court: From the Arena to the Monastery*. New York: Palgrave Macmillan.

Nelson, Michael. 1988. "The President and the Court: Reinterpreting the Court-Packing Episode of 1937." *Political Science Quarterly* 103 (Summer): 267–93.

Nemacheck, Christine L. 2007. *Strategic Selection: Presidential Nomination of Supreme Court Justices from Herbert Hoover to George W. Bush*. Charlottesville: University of Virginia Press.

Nettels, Curtis. 1925. "The Mississippi Valley and the Federal Judiciary, 1807–1837." *Mississippi Valley Historical Review* 12, no. 2 (September): 202–26.

Newman, Roger K. 1997. *Hugo Black: A Biography*. Second edition. New York: Fordham University Press.

Noonan, John T., Jr. 1981. "The Catholic Justices of the United States Supreme Court." *Catholic Historical Review* 67, no. 3 (July): 369–85.

Obama, Barack. 2020. *A Promised Land*. New York: Crown Publishing.

O'Brien, David M. 1991. "The Politics of Professionalism: President Gerald R. Ford's Appointment of Justice John Paul Stevens." *Presidential Studies Quarterly* 21, no. 1 (Winter): 103–26.

Overby, L. Marvin, Beth M. Henschen, Michael H. Walsh, and Julie Strauss. 1992. "Courting Constituents? An Analysis of the Senate Confirmation Vote on Justice Clarence Thomas." *American Political Science Review* 86: 997–1003.

Paris, Michael, and Kevin J. McMahon. 2015. "Absolutism and Democracy: Justice Hugo L. Black's Free Speech Jurisprudence." In *Judging Free Speech: First Amendment Jurisprudence of US Supreme Court Justices*, ed. Helen Knowles and Steven Lichtman, 75–97. New York: Palgrave.

Peretti, Terri. 1999. *In Defense of a Political Court*. Princeton, NJ: Princeton University Press.

———. 2007. "Where Have All the Politicians Gone? Recruiting for the Modern Supreme Court." *Judicature* 91: 112–22.

———. 2020. *Partisan Supremacy: How the GOP Enlisted Courts to Rig America's Election Rules*. Lawrence: University Press of Kansas.

Perry, Barbara A. 1989. "The Life and Death of the 'Catholic Seat' on the United States Supreme Court." *Journal of Law & Politics* 6: 55–92.

———. 1991. *A "Representative" Supreme Court? The Impact of Race, Religion, and Gender on Appointments*. New York: Greenwood Press.

Pickerill, J. Mitchell, and Cornell W. Clayton. 2004. "The Rehnquist Court and the Political Dynamics of Federalism." *Perspectives on Politics* 2 (June): 233–48.

Posner, Richard A. 2008. *How Judges Think*. Cambridge, MA: Harvard University Press.

Presidential Commission on the Supreme Court of the United States. 2021. *Final Report*. December. https://www.whitehouse.gov/wp-content/uploads/2021/12/SCOTUS-Report-Final.pdf.

Ringhand, Lori A., and Paul M. Collins Jr. 2018. "Neil Gorsuch and the Ginsburg Rules." *Chicago-Kent Law Review* 92, no. 3: 475–504.

———. 2021. "Improving the Senate Judiciary Committee's Role in the Confirmation of Supreme Court Justices." *British Journal of American Legal Studies* 10, no. 3: 364–78.

Robertson, Pat. *Courting Disaster: How the Supreme Court Is Usurping the Power of Congress and the People*. Nashville, TN: Thomas Nelson Publishers.

Robin, Corey. 2019. *The Enigma of Clarence Thomas*. New York: Metropolitan Books.

Rodell, Fred. 1955. *Nine Men: A Political History of the Supreme Court from 1790–1955*. New York: Random House.

Rosen, Jeffrey. 2006. *The Most Democratic Branch: How the Courts Serve America*. New York: Oxford University Press.

Rosenberg, Gerald N. 1991. *The Hollow Hope: Can Courts Bring About Social Change?* Chicago: University of Chicago Press.

Safire, William. 2008. *Safire's Political Dictionary*. New York: Oxford University Press.

Savage, David. 1992. *Turning Right: The Making of the Rehnquist Supreme Court*. New York: John Wiley & Sons.

Schally, Phyllis. 2004. *The Supremacists: The Tyranny of Judges and How to Stop It*. Dallas, TX: Spence Publishing Company.

Scherer, Nancy. 2005. *Scoring Points: Politicians, Activists, and the Lower Federal Court Appointment Process*. Stanford, CA: Stanford University Press.

Schlesinger, Arthur M., Jr. *The Politics of Upheaval*. Boston: Houghton Mifflin Company, 1960.

Schmidhauser, John R. 1959. "The Justices of the Supreme Court: A Collective Portrait." *Midwest Journal of Political Science* 3, no. 1 (February): 1–57.

Schmidt, Christopher W. 2014. "The Challenge of Supreme Court Biography: The Case of Chief Justice Rehnquist." *Constitutional Commentary* 29: 271–91.

———. 2018. "The Forgotten Issue: The Supreme Court and the 2016 Presidential Campaign." *Chicago-Kent Law Review* 93, no. 2: 411–52.

Segal, Jeffrey A. 1987. "Senate Confirmation of Supreme Court Justices: Partisan and Institutional Politics." *Journal of Politics* 49: 998–1015.

Segal, Jeffrey A., and Albert D. Cover. 1989. "Ideological Values and the Votes of U.S. Supreme Court Justices." *American Political Science Review* 83 (June): 557–65.

Segal, Jeffrey A., and Harold J. Spaeth. 1993. *The Supreme Court and the Attitudinal Model*. New York: Cambridge University Press.

———. 2002. *The Supreme Court and the Attitudinal Model Revisited*. New York: Cambridge University Press.

Shapiro, Ilya. 2020. *Supreme Disorder: Judicial Nominations and the Politics of America's Highest Court*. Washington, DC: Regnery Gateway.

Shapiro, Martin M. 1964. *Law and Politics in the Supreme Court*. Glencoe, IL: The Free Press of Glencoe.

———. 1966. *Freedom of Speech: The Supreme Court and Judicial Review*. Englewood Cliffs, NJ: Prentice-Hall.

———. 1978. "The Supreme Court: From Warren to Burger." In *The New American Political System*, ed. Anthony King. Washington, DC: American Enterprise Institute, 179–211.

———. 1991. "Chief Justice Rehnquist and the Future of the Supreme Court." In *An Essential Safeguard: Essays on the United States Supreme Court and Its Justices*, ed. D. Grier Stephenson, 145–64. Westport, CT: Greenwood Publishing.

Shemtob, Zachary Baron. 2011–12. "The Catholic and Jewish Court: Explaining the Absence of Protestants on the Nation's Highest Judicial Body." *Journal of Law and Religion* 27, no. 2: 368–69.

Silverstein, Mark. 1994. *Judicious Choices: The New Politics of Supreme Court Confirmations*. New York: Norton.

Skowronek, Stephen. 1993. *The Politics Presidents Make: Leadership from John Adams to George Bush*. Cambridge, MA: Harvard University Press.

Slaven, Michael D., Melanie J. Blumberg, and William C. Binning. 2019. "A Senate Trifecta: Ohio, Pennsylvania, and West Virginia." In *The Roads to Congress 2018: American Elections in the Trump Era*, ed. Sean D. Foreman, Marcia L. Godwin, and Walter Clark Wilson, 233–57. New York: Palgrave Macmillan.

Smith, J. Clay, Jr. 1993. "Bloody Crossroads: African Americans and the Bork Nomination: A Bibliographic Essay." *Harvard BlackLetter Law Journal* 10: 133–47.

Sotomayor, Sonia. 2013. *My Beloved World*. New York: Alfred A. Knopf.

Stephanopoulos, George. 1999. *All Too Human: A Political Education*. Boston: Little, Brown.

Stephenson, Donald Grier, Jr., ed. 1991. *An Essential Safeguard: Essays on the United States Supreme Court and Its Justices*. Westport, CT: Greenwood Publishing.

———. 1999. *Campaigns and the Courts: The U.S. Supreme Court in Presidential Elections*. New York: Columbia University Press.

Stevens, John Paul. 2014. *Six Amendments: How and Why We Should Change the Constitution*. Boston: Little, Brown.

Stockley, Joshua. 2019. "Tennessee Senate Race: Call It What You Want, but Tennessee Is a Red Wall to the South." In *The Roads to Congress 2018: American Elections in the Trump Era*, ed. Sean D. Foreman, Marcia L. Godwin, and Walter Clark Wilson, 259–77. New York: Palgrave Macmillan.

Suitts, Steve. 2005. *Hugo Black of Alabama: How His Roots and Early Career Shaped the Great Champion of the Constitution*. Montgomery, AL: NewSouth Books.

Sundquist, James. 1983. *Dynamics of the Party System: Alignment and Realignment of Political Parties in the United States*. Washington, DC: Brookings Institution Press.

Sunstein, Cass R. 2005. *Radicals in Robes: Why Extreme Right-Wing Courts Are Wrong for America*. New York: Basic Books.

Sutherland, Mark I., ed. 2005. *Judicial Tyranny: The New Kings of America?* St. Louis, MO: Amerisearch, Inc.

Tagliarina, Daniel. 2022. "Judicial Nominations and Trump's Complicated Relationship with the Courts." In *The 2020 Presidential Election: Key Issues and Regional Dynamics*, ed. Luke Perry, 93–112. New York: Palgrave Macmillan.

Teles, Steven M. 2008. *The Rise of the Conservative Legal Movement: The Battle for Control of the Law*. Princeton, NJ: Princeton University Press.

Thomas, Clarence. 2008. *My Grandfather's Son: A Memoir*. New York: Harper Perennial.

Toobin, Jeffrey. 2007. *The Nine: Inside the Secret World of the Supreme Court*. New York: Doubleday.

———. 2012. *The Oath: The Obama White House and the Supreme Court*. New York: Doubleday.

Tushnet, Mark. 1994. *Making Civil Rights Law: Thurgood Marshall and the Supreme Court, 1936–1961*. New York: Oxford University Press.

———. 2005. *A Court Divided: The Rehnquist Court and the Future of Constitutional Law*. New York: Norton.

———. 2006. "The Supreme Court and the National Political Order: Collaboration and Confrontation." In *The Supreme Court and American Political Development*, ed. Ronald Kahn and Ken I. Kersch, 117–37. Lawrence: University Press of Kansas.

———. 2020. *Taking Back the Constitution: Activist Judges and the Next Age of American Law*. New Haven, CT: Yale University Press.

Van der Veer Hamilton, Virginia. 1972. *Hugo Black: The Alabama Years*. Baton Rouge: Louisiana State University Press.

Ward, Artemus. 2001. "The Nominations Presidents Make: Appointing Justices to the U.S. Supreme Court." *Congress and the Presidency* 28: 63–84.

———. 2003. *Deciding to Leave: The Politics of Retirement from the United States Supreme Court.* Albany: State University of New York Press.

Ward, Artemus, and David L. Weiden. 2007. *Sorcerers' Apprentices: 100 Years of Law Clerks at the United States Supreme Court.* New York: New York University Press.

Wexler, Jay D. 2005. "The Laugh Track." *Green Bag,* 2nd ser., 9, no. 1 (Autumn): 59–61.

Whittington, Keith. 2005. "'Interpose Your Friendly Hand': Political Supports for the Exercise of Judicial Review by the United States Supreme Court." *American Political Science Review* 99, no. 4: 583–96.

———. 2007a. *Political Foundations of Judicial Supremacy: The Presidency, the Supreme Court, and Constitutional Leadership in U.S. History.* Princeton, NJ: Princeton University Press.

———. 2007b. "Presidents, Senates, and Failed Supreme Court Nominations." *The Supreme Court Review* 2006: 401–38.

———. 2019. *Repugnant Laws: Judicial Review of Acts of Congress from the Founding to the Present.* Lawrence: University Press of Kansas.

Williams, Juan. 1998. *Thurgood Marshall: American Revolutionary.* New York: Three Rivers Press.

Wilson, Walter Clark. 2019. "Lessons Learned from the 2018 Election." In *The Roads to Congress 2018: American Elections in the Trump Era,* ed. Sean D. Foreman, Marcia L. Godwin, and Walter Clark Wilson, 299–311. New York: Palgrave Macmillan.

Witt, Elder. 1986. *A Different Justice: Reagan and the Supreme Court.* Washington, DC: Congressional Quarterly.

Woodward, Bob, and Scott Armstrong. (1979) 1981. *The Brethren: Inside the Supreme Court.* New York: Avon Books.

Yalof, David Alistair. 1999. *Pursuit of Justices: Presidential Politics and the Selection of Supreme Court Nominees.* Chicago: University of Chicago Press.

Yarbrough, Tinsley E. 2008. *Harry A. Blackmun.* New York: Oxford University Press.

Yost, Berwood, Jackie Redman, and Scottie Thompson. 2017. "The 2016 Pennsylvania Presidential and U.S. Senate Elections: Breaking Pennsylvania's Electoral Habits." *Commonwealth* 19, no. 2: 3–26.

Index